AN INTRODUCTION
TO THE
EMBRYOLOGY OF ANGIOSPERMS

McGRAW-HILL PUBLICATIONS IN
THE BOTANICAL SCIENCES

Edmund W. Sinnott, *Consulting Editor*

There are also the related series of McGraw-Hill Publications in the Zoological Sciences, of which E. J. Boell is Consulting Editor, and in the Agricultural Sciences, of which R. A. Brink is Consulting Editor.

AN INTRODUCTION

TO THE

EMBRYOLOGY

OF ANGIOSPERMS

BY

P. MAHESHWARI

Professor of Botany, University of Delhi
Delhi, India

McGRAW-HILL BOOK COMPANY, INC.

NEW YORK   TORONTO   LONDON

1950

AN INTRODUCTION TO THE EMBRYOLOGY OF ANGIOSPERMS

VII

39620

PREFACE

In these days of intense activity, when hundreds of papers are being published in every field of botany in a steadily increasing number of periodicals and in a multitude of languages, no apology is needed for an attempt to summarize the existing state of our knowledge in any branch of the subject and to point out the future possibilities in it. Since the publication of Coulter and Chamberlain's "Morphology of Angiosperms" in 1903, no comprehensive account of this aspect of botany has appeared in the English language.

The original impetus for writing this work resulted from a course of lectures which I gave on the subject in 1930 when I was teaching at the Agra College. Several colleagues and pupils then suggested that I should produce a book on the embryology of angiosperms. This suggestion was repeated by Professor G. Tischler of the University of Kiel, whom I visited in 1936. Teaching and administrative duties and other difficulties made it impossible for me to carry on this work in India at the speed I should have liked. Soon after the war was over in 1945, therefore, I took the manuscript to the United States in order to revise it and put it in shape for publication.

In a strict sense, embryology is confined to a study of the embryo, but most botanists also include under it the events which lead on to fertilization. I am in agreement with this wider comprehension of the subject and have therefore included in this volume not only an account of the embryo and endosperm, but also an account of the development of the male and female gametophytes and fertilization. To emphasize the recent trends of research in the subject, two chapters of a general nature have been added, one dealing with embryology in relation to taxonomy, and the other with experimental embryology. In the former, an attempt has been made to indicate the possibilities of the embryological method in the solution of problems of systematic botany. In the latter, emphasis has been placed on the contacts between embryology, cytology, genetics, and plant physiology.

v

In compiling my materials I must acknowledge the immense help which I received from the writings of the late Professor K. Schnarf, whom I came to know rather intimately during my stay in Vienna in 1936. Without the existence of his books, entitled "Embryologie der Angiospermen" (1929), "Vergleichende Embryologie der Angiospermen" (1931), and "Vergleichende Zytologie des Geschlechtsapparates des Kormophyten" (1941), my task would have been appreciably greater. Mention must also be made of the numerous and very valuable publications of Professor E. C. R. Souèges (Paris), Professor K. V. O. Dahlgren (Uppsala), Dr. J. Mauritzon (Motala), Dr. F. Fagerlind (Stockholm), Dr. Å. Gustafsson (Svalöf), and Dr. H. Stenar (Södertalje), upon which I drew rather freely. Professor Dahlgren, Dr. Gustafsson, and Dr. Stenar also favored me with their advice and criticisms whenever I applied to them for help. In addition, a host of teachers and students in the United States gave me every possible encouragement in the work. To record my gratitude to all of them in any complete fashion would fill several pages. I therefore content myself with naming a few who took special interest in the project. To Professors R. H. Wetmore and I. W. Bailey I am heavily indebted for the free use of their facilities and their assistance in other ways during my several months' stay at Harvard. Professor A. F. Blakeslee and Mary E. Sanders, Smith College, Northampton; Professor E. W. Sinnott, Yale University; Professors A. J. Eames and L. W. Sharp, Cornell University; Drs. D. C. Cooper, R. A. Brink, and C. L. Huskins, University of Wisconsin; Dr. Th. Just, University of Notre Dame, now at the Field Museum of Natural History, Chicago; Professor J. T. Buchholz, University of Illinois; Professor A. S. Foster, Professor G. L. Stebbins, Mrs. M. S. Cave, Drs. L. Constance, Katherine Esau, and C. M. Rick, all of the University of California; Professor G. M. Smith, Stanford University; Dr. D. A. Johansen, Pomona, and Professor A. W. Haupt, University of California at Los Angeles, gave me the benefit of their suggestions and criticisms. Last but not least, my colleagues and pupils, Dr. B. M. Johri, Reayat Kahn, S. Narayanaswami, and J. S. Agrawal gave me their fullest cooperation in the preparation of the bibliography and revision of the proofs.

Only a few of the illustrations are original, most of them having been borrowed from the works of other authors. Considerable care has been exercised, however, in their selection not only that the text may be made as clear as possible but also that the student may acquire some familiarity with the names and contributions of the better known embryologists, both past and present. While most of the copying and redrawing was done by me personally, I am glad to acknowledge the very able assistance I received from a few friends. Figures 36, 68, 92, and 214 were drawn by Mrs. J. A. Adams of Poughkeepsie, N. Y., daughter of my former teacher, the late Dr. Winfield Dudgeon of Allahabad; Miss C. Pratt, Harvard University, drew Figures 24, 41, 59, 65, 74, 89, 104, 118, 121, and 167; Dr. B. G. L. Swamy, Bangalore, drew Figures 19, 145, 149, 150, 153, and 163; Mrs. M. S. Cave, University of California, drew Figure 14; Miss C. G. Nast, Wayne University, drew Figure 111; and my former research assistant, Ashraful Haque, University of Dacca, drew Figures 21, 43, 47, 54, 60, 61, 82, 85, 91, 147, 148, 152, 154, 157, 158, 159, 161, 162, 164, 165, 170, 172, 173, 175, 191, and 216. To all these I wish to tender my most grateful thanks for the willingness with which they cooperated with me.

A word about the citation of literature. No attempt has been made to give a complete list of all that has been published on angiosperm embryology, as this would make the volume too cumbersome, but it is hoped that the references which have been cited will facilitate the task of the student who wishes to acquire fuller information.

In a work of this nature it is unavoidable that there should be some errors of judgment and also oversights and omissions. I should appreciate the suggestions and criticisms of those who use the book.

P. Maheshwari

University of Delhi, India
July, 1950

CONTENTS

CHAPTER 1

HISTORICAL SKETCH

In tracing the history of a branch of natural science it is customary to go back to the days of Aristotle. The greater part of his technical writings is unfortunately lost to us, but it seems fairly certain that he did not recognize the presence of sex in plants. He believed instead that the male and female principles were so blended that they generated of their own accord and the offspring arose from the superfluous food in the plant.

Aristotle bequeathed his library and collections to his favorite pupil Theophrastus. In his "Enquiry into Plants," written in the third century B.C., the latter referred to the pollination of the date palm, presumably on the basis of the account of Herodotus, who had traveled in the East in the fifth century B.C. The Arabs and Assyrians, Herodotus found, used to have a special ceremony at a certain time of the year, in which a man climbed up a male tree, brought down the inflorescence, and handed it over to the high priest, who touched the female inflorescences with it, in order to ensure a good supply of dates.

Approximately three hundred years after Theophrastus, Pliny wrote an encyclopedia of natural history in which he mentioned the male palm with its erect leaves as having somewhat of a military bearing, while the females with their softer foliage and feminine ways bent toward it, to save themselves as it were from the curse of virginity or widowhood. However, Pliny did not make any observations of his own. His writings and ideas were based on other people's reports and on the literature on the subject that existed in those days.

After this the problem of sexuality in plants seems to have been laid aside and forgotten for hundreds of years. Indeed, many scientists of the fifteenth and sixteenth centuries totally denied the occurrence of sex in plants and regarded even the mention of it as inappropriate and obscene. Some thought the stamens to be excretory organs and the pollen to be a waste product.

1

It was only with the invention of the microscope that actual observation of the sexual cells took the place of conjectures. Leeuwenhoek (1677)[1] discovered the sperms of some animals but mistook them at first for "Wild animalcules" arising in the seminal fluid by some sort of putrefaction.

In his "Anatomy of Plants," Grew (1682) made the first explicit mention of the stamens as the male organs of the flower. He thought that the pollen grains, by merely falling upon the stigma, transmitted to the ovary a "vivifick effluvium" which prepared it for the production of the fruit.

Rudolph Jakob Camerarius (1694), Director of the Botanical Garden at Tübingen, approached the matter more scientifically. He observed that in a female mulberry tree, which was growing without any male plants in the vicinity, the fruits contained only abortive seeds. Inspired by this discovery he next took some female plants of *Mercurialis annua* and kept them in pots completely isolated from the influence of male plants. Here too, he found that, although the plants grew well, not one of the fruits contained a fertile seed. This encouraged him to make further observations, which he summarized in a famous treatise called "De sexu plantarum." He carefully described the flower, anthers, pollen, and ovules. On removing the male flowers (*globuli*) of *Ricinus* before the anthers had shed and preventing the growth of the younger ones, he never obtained any perfect seed but only empty fruits which withered and fell to the ground. A similar lack of seed formation was noted in *Zea mays* when the stigmas had been removed from the young ear. In conclusion he said: "In the plant kingdom, the production of seed, which is the most perfect gift of nature and the general means of maintenance of the species, does not take place unless the anthers have previously prepared the young plant contained in the ovary." To the anthers, in his opinion, was to be attributed, therefore, the role of the male sexual organs just as the ovary with its style was considered the female sexual organ.

We thus see that although Camerarius was not clear about the exact manner in which the pollen functioned, he nevertheless made a notable contribution to our knowledge by showing that some kind

---

[1] Dates in parentheses refer to works listed in the bibliography at the end of each chapter.

of interaction between the stamens and carpels is necessary for the production of seed-bearing fruits.

About sixty-five years later, Joseph Gottlieb Kölreuter (1761), physician and professor of natural history at Wurtemberg, published four parts of a treatise dealing with his experiments on sex in plants. He fully confirmed the work of Camerarius and gave a detailed account of the importance of insects in flower pollination. He also produced hybrids in *Nicotiana*, *Dianthus*, *Matthiola*, and *Hyoscyamus* and showed that if the stigma of a plant received its own pollen and that of another species at the same time, ordinarily the former alone was effective. This, he said, was the reason why hybrids were so rare in nature, although they could be produced artificially.

FIG. 1. Giovanni Battista Amici. (*Photograph obtained through the courtesy of Dr. E. Battaglia.*)

Discovery of the Pollen Tube. After the role of the pollen began to be understood, the next step was to determine the exact manner in which it influenced the ovule. Accident supplied the starting point of some important discoveries. An Italian mathematician and astronomer named Giovanni Battista Amici (1824), who was also a good microscope maker, found that the stigma of *Portulaca oleracea* was covered with hairs which contained some granules or particles inside them. Curiosity prompted him to ascertain whether they moved in the same way as the granules he had seen in the cells of *Chara*. It pleased him to find that they did. While repeating the observation, he accidentally saw a pollen grain attached to the hair he had under observation. Suddenly the pollen grain split open and sent out a kind of tube or "gut" which grew along the side of the hair and entered the tissues of the stigma. For three hours he kept it under observation and watched the cytoplasmic granules circulate inside it, but eventually he lost sight of them and could not say whether they returned to the grain, entered the stigma, or dissolved away in some manner.

Amici's discovery stimulated the young French botanist Brongniart (1827) to examine a large number of pollinated pistils with a view to understanding the interaction between the pollen and the stigma and the introduction of the fertilizing substance into the ovule. He found the formation of the pollen tubes (he called them "spermatic tubules") to be a very frequent occurrence but persuaded himself to believe that, after penetrating the stigma, the tubes burst and discharged their granular contents, which he likened to the spermatozoids of animals and considered to be the active part of the pollen. He thought he saw these "spermatic granules" vibrating down the whole length of the style and entering the placenta and ovule, and he drew a series of figures to illustrate the whole process. In appreciation of this work, Brongniart was awarded a prize by the Paris Academy of Sciences and recommended for admission to the Academy.

Amici (1830) applied himself once again to the problem, studying *Portulaca oleracea, Hibiscus syriacus,* and other plants, and wrote a letter to Mirbel in which he put the following question: "Is the prolific humor passed out into the interstices of the transmitting tissue of the style, as Brongniart has seen and drawn it, to be transported afterwards to the ovule, or is it that the pollen tubes elongate bit by bit and finally come in contact with the ovules, one tube for each ovule?" His observations completely ruled out the first alternative, and he definitely concluded in favor of the second.

About the same time, Robert Brown (1831, 1833) saw pollen grains on the stigmas and pollen tubes in the ovaries of certain orchids and asclepiads but was uncertain as to whether the tubes were always connected with the pollen grains. He thought instead that, at least in some cases, the tubes arose within the style itself, although possibly they were stimulated to develop in consequence of the pollination of the stigma.[2]

Schleiden's Theory of the Origin of the Embryo. Meanwhile other workers also became interested in the problem, and in 1837 Schleiden published some very detailed observations on the origin

---

[2] It now seems that Brown was at times confusing pollen tubes with the elongated cells of the transmitting tissue in the style.

and development of the ovule. He confirmed Amici's statement that the pollen tubes make their way from the stigma to the ovule, entering the latter through the micropyle. His lively imagination carried him too far, however, for he asserted that the extremity of the pollen tube pushes the membrane of the embryo sac before it and directly becomes the embryonal vesicle, which then undergoes a number of divisions to produce the embryo. The cotyledons were said to arise laterally, while the original apical point remained more or less free and formed the plumule. To him the embryo sac was, therefore, a sort of nidus or incubator within which the end of the pollen tube was nourished to give rise to the new plantlet. If this were really the case, there would of course be no sexuality in plants. Nevertheless, with the influence he commanded and the sharp tongue with which he denounced all opponents, Schleiden found a number of warm supporters. One of them, Schacht, sponsored this absurd idea with special enthusiasm.

Fig. 2. Matthias Jakob Schleiden. (*Photograph obtained through the courtesy of Prof. W. Troll.*)

Amici boldly opposed the views of Schleiden. In a meeting of the Italian naturalists, held at Padua in 1842, he tried to prove that the embryo did not arise from the tip of the pollen tube but from a portion of the ovule which was already in existence and was fertilized by the fluid in the tube.

Schleiden (1845) gave a most spirited reply to this and said that after his careful and thorough investigation of 1837 it was ridiculous on the part of novices in the field to raise such meaningless objections. He described some fresh observations on *Cucurbita* and offered to demonstrate the utter falsity of Amici's observations and the complete truth of his own to anyone who visited him.

Discovery of the True Relation between the Pollen Tube and the Embryo. In spite of Schleiden's criticism, Amici continued further work on the subject. In 1847 he produced decisive evidence (Fig. 3) to show that in *Orchis* (which he found to be specially suited for such studies), a body, the germinal vesicle, was already present inside the embryo sac *before* the arrival of the pollen tube, and that it was this vesicle which gave rise to the embryo, stimulated no doubt by the presence of the pollen tube.

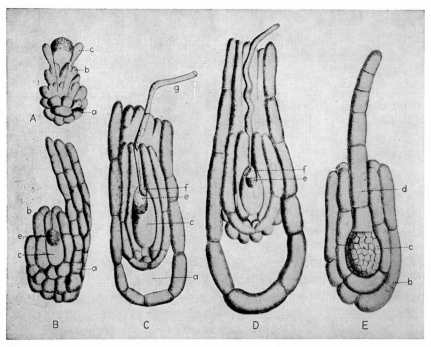

FIG. 3. Development of ovule and embryo in *Orchis*. Note pollen tube in *C* and *D* and suspensor haustorium in *E*. (*After Amici, 1847*.)

Support for Amici's views now came forward from other quarters. In a famous document, entitled "Die Entstehung des Embryo der Phanerogamen," consisting of 89 quarto pages and 14 copper plates with no fewer than 429 figures, Wilhelm Hofmeister (1849) published his observations on 38 species belonging to 19 genera and showed that in every case the embryo originated from a preexisting cell in the embryo sac and not from the pollen tube. He described his observations in such a clear and dignified manner that they immediately carried conviction and were soon confirmed by other workers from

England, France, and Germany. In less than two years after the publication of this memoir and in spite of his lack of a proper university training, the University of Rostock conferred upon Hofmeister the degree of Doctor of Philosophy *honoris causa*, thereby giving formal recognition to his high position as a scientific investigator. A few of Hofmeister's illustrations of the embryo sac and the relation between the pollen tube and the egg are presented in Fig. 5.

Fig. 4. Wilhelm Hofmeister.

Schleiden and Schacht continued to hold their previous opinion. Schacht brought out a large monograph in 1850, with 26 plates and a considerable number of drawings. These were beautifully executed, but in every case he mistook the egg cell for the tip of the pollen tube (Fig. 6). In conclusion he said: "The tendency towards error is so inherent in human nature that the work of one's head, like that of his hand, is never perfect, and consequently I do not hold mine to be free from error and misconception, but I have tried to minimize these as much as possible. . . . In chief matter, *i.e.*, the origin of the embryo from the pollen tube, no one can convince me that there has been any mistake or misconception. . . . My preparations are so conclusive on this point that I can confidently look forward to answering any criticisms that may be directed against it." The Imperial Institute of the Netherlands at Amsterdam accepted Schacht's essay and awarded him a prize for its production.

However, the evidence against Schleiden and Schacht soon became so overwhelming that eventually both of them had to retract their opinions, and in 1856 Radlkofer published a comprehensive review of the question accepting Hofmeister's conclusions *in toto*. Schleiden soon gave up all botanical work and settled down in Dresden as a private teacher of history and philosophy.

In this connection it is interesting to recall the words of the famous anatomist Hugo von Mohl, who, in 1863, at the time of Amici's death, wrote as follows: "Now that we know Schleiden's doctrine to have been an illusion, it is instructive, although sad, to look back to

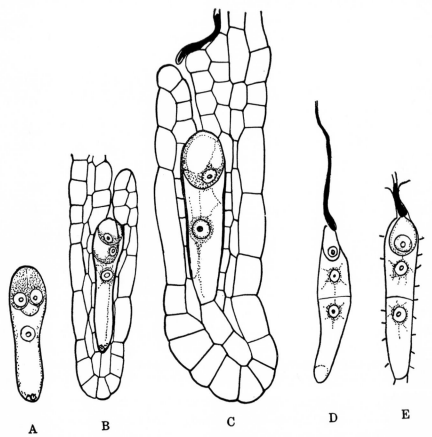

A   B   C   D   E

FIG. 5.   Ovules and embryo sacs of *Monotropa hypopitys*, before and after fertilization.   *A,B*, embryo sacs at time of fertilization.   *C*, same, showing pollen tube about to enter micropyle.   *D,E*, Fertilized embryo sacs, showing early stages in formation of endosperm.   (*After Hofmeister, 1849.*)

the past and see how readily the false was accepted for the true; how some, renouncing all observation of their own, dressed up the phantom in theoretical principles; how others, with microscope in hand, but blinded by their preconceptions, believed that they saw what they could not have seen and sought to establish the correctness of Schleiden's notions with the aid of hundreds of figures which had anything but truth to recommend them; and how an academy by rewarding such work gave fresh proof of the well-known experience that prize-essays are little adapted to contribute to the solution of a doubtful question in science."

Discovery of Sexual Fusion in Lower Plants. During this interval greater progress was being made with lower plants and animals. Thuret, in 1854, showed that in *Fucus* the eggs must be activated by sperms before they can germinate to give rise to new plants, and

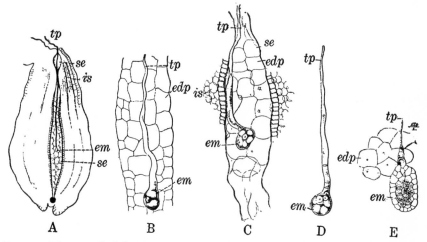

Fig. 6. The so-called development of embryo from pollen tube in *Martynia lutea* (*tp* = pollen tube; *em* = embryo; *edp* = endosperm; *is* = integument; *se* = embryo sac). *A*, l.s. ovule. *B–D*, stages in development of "pollen-tube embryo." *E*, older embryo, together with a few of the surrounding endosperm cells. (*After Schacht, 1850.*)

later he also obtained hybrids by associating the ova and sperms of different forms. In 1855 Pringsheim observed spermatozoids in the little horns (antheridia) of *Vaucheria* and showed that no further development occurs unless the spermatozoids enter the ovum. The decisive observation was made in 1856 in *Oedogonium*, where he saw the moving spermatozoid come in contact with the egg and force its way inside the latter. On the basis of these and similar discoveries in lower animals, the German zoologist Oscar Hertwig (1875) made a general statement that the essential feature of fertilization is the union of two nuclei, one furnished by the male parent and the other by the female.

In the phanerogams, where sex was supposed to be more apparent than in cryptogams, the actual demonstration did not come until a few years later, no doubt because of the technical difficulties in making any direct observations on the embryo sac, which is surrounded by the opaque tissues of the nucellus and the integuments.

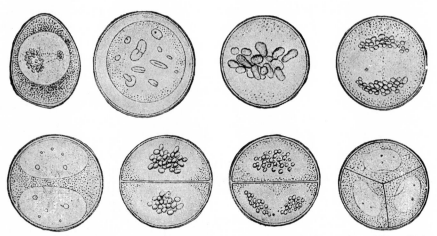

Fig. 7. Stages in formation of microspore tetrads in *Tradescantia*. (*After Hofmeister, 1848; reproduced from Sharp, 1943.*)

Discovery of the Nature and Development of Male and Female Gametophytes. Among early students of the development of pollen, Hofmeister (1848) presented some surprisingly good illustrations of

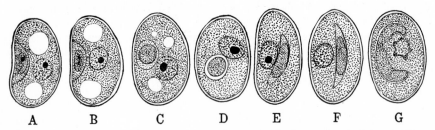

A   B   C   D   E   F   G

Fig. 8. Development of male gametophyte of *Tradescantia virginica*. (*After Elfving, 1879.*)

the process of tetrad formation (Fig. 7), and Reichenbach, Hartig and several other workers noted the presence of two nuclei in whole mounts of the mature pollen grains of several angiosperms. Strasburger (1877) and his pupil Elfving (1879) extended these observations to cover several families and demonstrated the widespread occurrence of the binucleate condition in pollen grains (Fig. 8).

They further found that one of these nuclei originally lies in a small cell cut off at the periphery of the pollen grain but later becomes free by a dissolution of the partition wall. Elfving also germinated pollen grains in artificial media, and when this was unsuccessful, he made preparations of pollen tubes from dissected styles. Here he was able to find the three nuclei which we now know to be the two male gametes and the tube or vegetative nucleus.

Fig. 9. Edward Strasburger. (*Photograph obtained through the courtesy of Prof. A. W. Haupt.*)

Unfortunately both Strasburger and Elfving made the mistake of interpreting the smaller cell in the pollen grain as vegetative or prothallial and the larger as generative. They further thought that all the nuclei in the pollen tube dissolved and disappeared before fertilization. These mistakes were, however, rectified by Strasburger in a subsequent paper (1884), which will be referred to later.

For our knowledge of the organization of the embryo sac we are indebted in the first instance to the works of Hofmeister (1847–1861). Working wholly with cleared preparations and freehand sections, he succeeded in identifying the two groups of cells at the opposite poles of the embryo sac. Those lying at the micropylar end were designated as the "germinal" or "embryonal" vesicles, all capable of giving rise to embryos and therefore to be regarded as homologous with the corpuscula (archegonia) of the gymnosperms. The cells at the chalazal end were considered to be prothallial, and the embryo sac itself was interpreted as homologous with the megaspore or female gametophyte of the heterosporous pteridophytes and the gymnosperms.

Although Hofmeister's work was important, he failed to distinguish clearly between the synergids and the egg and regarded all three of them as having the same function. Further, he was unable to trace the mode of origin of the embryo sac, the general opinion in those days being that it arose by the simple enlargement of a cell of the nucellus.

Further knowledge of the development and organization of the embryo sac became available as the result of a concentrated attack on the problem made by several botanists during the years 1877 to 1881. To be named specially in this connection are Warming,

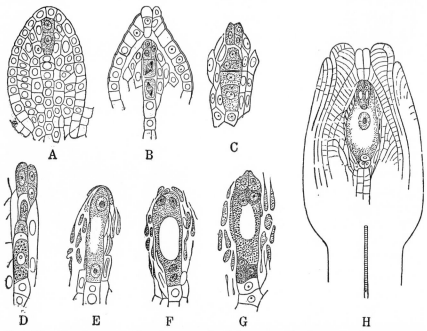

Fig. 10.   Development of embryo sac in *Polygonum divaricatum*.   *A*, megaspore mother cell separated from nucellar epidermis by primary wall cell.   *B*, dyad cells in division.   *C*, tetrad of megaspores with wall cells above.   *D*, functioning megaspore.   *E–G*, embryo sacs, showing two, four, and eight nuclei.   *H*, l.s. ovule, showing mature embryo sac.   (*After Strasburger, 1879.*)

Vesque, Strasburger, Fischer, Ward, Jönsson, Treub and Mellink, and Guignard.   Strasburger (1879) demonstrated that at first one of the nucellar cells becomes differentiated as the megaspore mother cell (Fig. 10*A*) and goes through two divisions to give rise to a row of four cells (Fig. 10*B,C*).   Of these, the three micropylar cells soon degenerate and the chalazal alone enlarges and functions (Fig. 10*D*). The nucleus of this cell (the functioning megaspore) divides thrice to give rise to two groups of four nuclei, one at the micropylar end and the other at the chalazal end of the cell (Fig. 10*E–G*).   From the former arise the egg apparatus (consisting of an egg cell and two synergids) and the upper polar nucleus; from the latter, the three antipodal cells and the lower polar nucleus. The polar nuclei were observed to fuse in the center to form a secondary nucleus, which

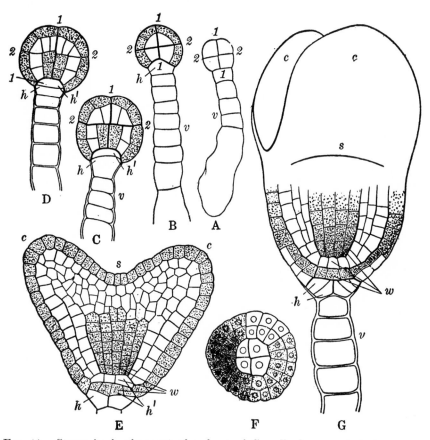

FIG. 11. Stages in development of embryo of *Capsella bursa-pastoris* (v = suspensor; h-h' = hypophysis; c-c = cotyledons; s = stem tip; w = radicle; the shaded portions represent the dermatogen and plerome). (*After Hanstein, 1870; reproduced from Sachs, 1874.*)

gave rise to the endosperm (Fig. 10H). The synergids were regarded as modified structures assisting in the process of fertilization.

Treub and Mellink (1880) confirmed these observations but also noted certain exceptions. In a few plants they found that the megaspore mother cell divides into only two daughter cells, of which either the upper (as in *Agraphis patula*) or the lower (as in *Narcissus*

tazetta) can give rise to the embryo sac.   In *Lilium* and *Tulipa* the
formation of daughter cells was found to be entirely omitted so that
the embryo sac arises directly from the megaspore mother cell.

The Embryo.   Hanstein (1870) was the first to follow the sequence
of early cell divisions in the development of the embryo.   He gave a
detailed description of the embryogeny in *Capsella* and *Alisma*

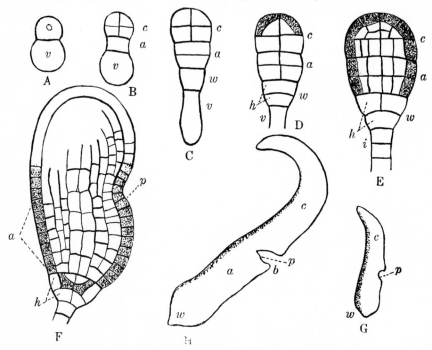

F『ɢ. 12.   Stages in development of embryo of *Alisma plantago* (*v* = suspensor;
h = hypophysis; *w* = radicle; *p* = plumule; *c* = cotyledon; *b* = first leaf; the
ₛhaded portions represent the dermatogen).   (*After Hanstein, 1870; reproduced
rom Sachs, 1874.*)

(Figs. 11, 12).   Famintzin confirmed these observations in 1879, and
in the same year Treub described the embryos of several orchids
with their remarkable suspensor haustoria.   Two years later Guignard (1881) gave a full account of the extremely massive suspensors
of the Leguminosae.

At about this time, detailed investigations were also made on the
peculiar phenomenon of polyembryony.   Long ago Leeuwenhoek
(1719) had noted the occurrence of more than one embryo in certain

orange seeds, and other instances of a similar nature were listed by Alexander Braun (1859). In no case, however, had the origin of the abnormality been satisfactorily studied from the developmental point of view. Strasburger, in 1878, demonstrated for the first time that in *Funkia* (= *Hosta*) *ovata, Coelebogyne* (= *Alchornea*) *ilicifolia, Nothoscordum fragrans*, and *Citrus aurantium*, the nucellar cells lying close to the apex of the embryo sac become richly protoplasmic and divide to form small groups of cells which project into the cavity of the embryo sac and grow into embryos (Fig. 13). Subsequent work

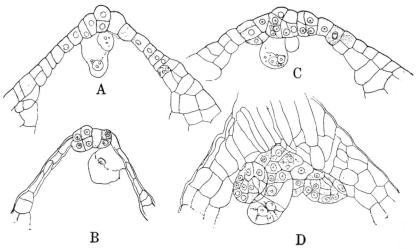

FIG. 13. Development of adventive embryos in *Funkia* (= *Hosta*)*ovata. A*, upper part of nucellus and embryo sac. *B,C*, enlargement and division of some of the nucellar cells. *D*, more advanced stage, showing young zygotic embryo and several nucellar embryos. (*After Strasburger, 1878*.)

by others revealed further possibilities, such as an origin of embryos from the cells of the integument, or from those of the suspensor, or from components of the embryo sac other than the egg. In *Allium odorum*, Tretjakow (1895) and Hegelmaier (1897) showed that even antipodal cells could give rise to embryos.

Discovery of Syngamy. These were all notable advances, but the most important of all was Strasburger's (1884) discovery of the actual process of syngamy, or the fusion of the male and female gametes. In a memorable paper, entitled "Neue Untersuchungen über den Befruchtungsvorgang bei den Phanerogamen," he corrected some of the mistakes he had made in 1877 on the organization of the male gametophyte. He now confessed that, owing to its similarity both in position and origin with the prothallial cells of gymnosperms, the small lenticular cell in the angiosperm pollen grain had been formerly misinterpreted by him as being the "vegetative" cell. Also, in the earlier studies in his laboratory (which had been based on whole mounts stained with iodine green) the nuclei in the pollen grains were often quite indistinguishable and had therefore been supposed to have degenerated. His improved technique (such as staining with picrocarmine and the cutting of the larger pollen grains into thin sections), devised after 1877, had shown that

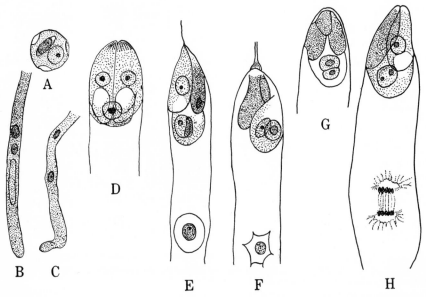

FIG. 14. Fertilization in *Monotropa hypopitys*. *A*, pollen grain stained in iodine green and acetic acid to show vegetative and generative nucleus. *B,C*, tips of pollen tubes showing the two male nuclei; in *B* the vegetative nucleus is also visible. *D*, upper part of embryo sac, showing egg apparatus. *E–G*, stages in union of male and female nuclei. *H*, syngamy completed; primary endosperm nucleus dividing. (*After Strasburger, 1884.*)

this was really not the case. It was now clear that the first division of the microspore gives rise to two cells, the smaller being the generative cell and the larger the vegetative. Further, the generative cell loosens itself from the wall of the pollen grain and divides either before or after the germination of the pollen grain, while the vegetative or tube nucleus remains undivided. Thus, the pollen tube eventually shows three nuclei, one vegetative and two generative[3].

On the basis of his studies on the embryo sac of *Monotropa* and some other plants, Strasburger further showed that the pollen tube discharges its nuclei into the sac (previous to this it was believed that fertilization occurred merely by the diffusion of the cell sap from the tube) and that one of the two male nuclei fuses with the nucleus of the egg, thus providing actual proof of the nature of fertilization and its importance in the life cycle of a plant (Fig. 14).

In the concluding part of his memoir, Strasburger made the following generalizations, which are now almost axiomatic with us: (1) the process of fertilization comprises the union of the nucleus of the male gamete with that of the egg; (2) the cytoplasm of the gametes is not concerned in the process; and (3) the sperm nucleus and the egg nucleus are true nuclei.

Fig. 15. Melchior Treub. (*Photograph obtained through the courtesy of Dr. F. Verdoorn.*)

Chalazogamy. Strasburger's work opened the way to a more detailed study of the process of fertilization in angiosperms. Prior to 1891, it was believed that the pollen tube always enters the ovule through the micropyle. Treub, in that year, reported that in *Casuarina* it enters through the chalaza (Fig. 16). This was thought to be so strange that he proposed a new classification of the angiosperms into two classes: the chalazogams and the porogams, with *Casuarina* as the only representative of the former. Later investigations showed, however, that there is no uniformity in the mode of entry of the pollen tube into the embryo sac, and in *Ulmus* (Nawaschin, 1898*a*) its behavior was found to be particularly varied and irregular. The phenomenon of chalazogamy,

[3] These two are now called the male gametes.

therefore, lost the great phylogenetic importance which had been attached to it by Treub. Today it is considered to be more of physiological than of phylogenetic significance, although it does have a certain taxonomic value in narrow circles of affinity.

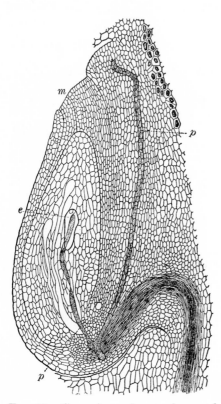

FIG. 16. *Casuarina suberosa*, l.s. ovule, showing chalazogamy (*m* = micropyle; *p* = pollen tube; *e* = embryo sac). (*After Treub, 1891*.)

Double Fertilization. The fate of the second male gamete discharged by the pollen tube was not known so far. In a study of *Lilium martagon* and *Fritillaria tenella*, S. G. Nawaschin (1898*b*) showed that in angiosperms both male gametes are concerned in fertilization, one fusing with the egg (syngamy) and the other with the two polar nuclei (triple fusion). A few months later L. Guignard (1899) also reported the same phenomenon in *Lilium* and *Fritillaria* and presented a series of beautiful drawings to illustrate it (Fig. 19). These discoveries attracted widespread attention and were followed by a series of similar investigations dealing with other species of angiosperms. Double fertilization was soon demonstrated in several plants and within a few years it began to be considered as of universal occurrence in angiosperms. It is interesting to note that a year earlier D. M. Mottier (1897) had seen the second male nucleus in close proximity to one of the polar nuclei, but that he had considered this proximity to be accidental and had failed to realize its true significance. Of considerable interest in this connection is Finn's (1931) report on a preparation of *Scilla sibirica* (= *S. cernua*) made by a Russian botanist, W. Arnoldi, a number of years before Nawaschin's announcement of 1898. Finn found both syngamy and triple fusion to be so clear in one of the sections on this slide (Fig. 20) that it is surprising that the process could have been missed at all. As it was, however, Arnoldi mistook the male gametes for displaced nuclei (of the nucellus?) which had in some way entered into the embryo sac during the process of sectioning, and he therefore ignored them altogether.

FIG. 17.

Sergius Nawaschin. (*Photograph obtained through the courtesy of Dr. A. W. Haupt.*)

FIG. 18.

Leon Guignard.

One of the results of Nawaschin's discovery was that it gave a plausible explanation of "xenia." This term had been coined by Focke (1881) to denote those cases in which the pollen produced a visible influence on the hereditary characters of those parts of the ovule which surround the embryo. It now became clear that just as the fertilized egg gives rise to an embryo combining the characters of the two parents, so does the triple fusion nucleus give rise to a tissue containing the potentialities of both the parents.

A controversy soon started, however, on the morphological nature of the endosperm, which is neither n nor $2n$ but $3n$. Some claimed that it was a continuation of the old gametophytic tissue, while others (Sargant, 1900) thought it to be a second embryo which took a monstrous and highly abnormal shape because of the intrusion of the lower polar nucleus.   Strasburger (1900) suggested that only the fusion of the male gamete with the egg was to be regarded as true or "generative" fertilization, while the fusion of the polar nuclei

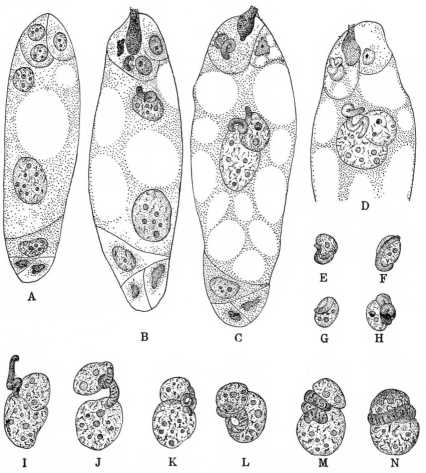

FIG. 19.   Double fertilization in *Lilium martagon*.   *A*, mature embryo sac.   *B*, same, showing discharge of pollen tube.   One male nucleus has entered the egg and the other is in contact with the upper polar nucleus; the nucleus of one of the synergids is in process of degeneration.   *C*, one male nucleus in contact with the egg nucleus and the other in contact with the two polar nuclei.   *D*, same, slightly more advanced stage.   *E–H*, stages in fusion of egg nucleus and one male nucleus. *I–N*, stages in triple fusion.   (*After Guignard, 1899.*)

with the second male nucleus was in the nature of a growth stimulus and could therefore be called "vegetative" fertilization.

Parthenogenesis. About the same time that Nawaschin made his discovery of double fertilization, two Swedish botanists, H. O.

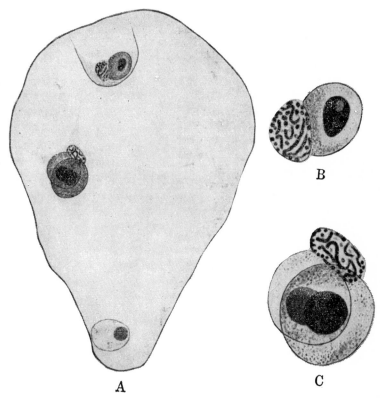

Fig. 20. Double fertilization in *Scilla sibirica*. *A*, one male nucleus in contact with egg nucleus, another in contact with the two polar nuclei. *B*, sperm and egg nuclei, more highly magnified. *C*, sperm nucleus in contact with two polar nuclei, more highly magnified. (*After Finn, 1931.*)

Juel (1898, 1900) and S. Murbeck (1897, 1901), were engaged in studying the mechanism of parthenogenesis in *Antennaria* and *Alchemilla*. Some years earlier Kerner (1876) had noted that in *Antennaria alpina* male plants were extremely rare in nature but that even unpollinated female plants were able to form seeds. Juel made a thorough study of the development and showed that even when staminate plants do occur, the pollen is either lacking or only feebly developed.   In the ovules the megaspore mother cell develops directly into the embryo sac without any reduction in the chromosome number and the diploid egg produces an embryo without fertilization (Fig. 21).   Murbeck similarly showed that some species of

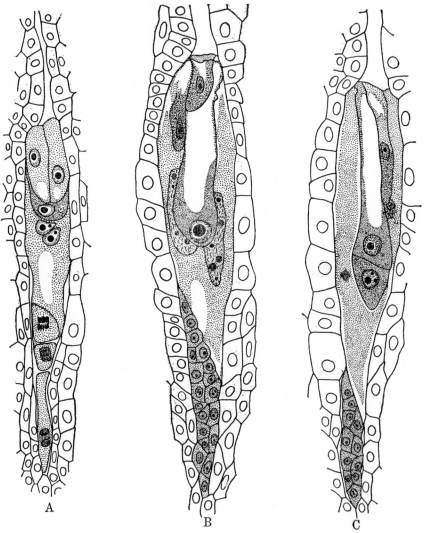

A   B   C

FIG. 21. Apomixis in *Antennaria alpina*.   *A*, mature embryo sac.   *B*, later stage, showing enlargement of egg and increase in number of antipodal cells; polar nuclei preparing to divide.   *C*, embryo two-celled; polar nuclei in division.   (*Redrawn after Juel, 1900*.)

Alchemilla, belonging to the section Eualchemilla, develop partheno-genetically without any chromosome change in the life cycle.

The Twentieth Century. The year 1900 marked the beginning of a new era in angiosperm embryology. By this time most of the facts on the development of the gametophytes and embryo had been discovered, and an able summary of the literature was given by Coulter and Chamberlain (1903) in their book entitled "Morphology of Angiosperms." The stage was now set for more detailed inves-tigations of special topics to clear up previous obscurities, and for studies of a comparative nature on whole families and orders to determine what light embryo-logy could throw on problems of taxonomy.

To outline the contributions of the numerous individuals who have been engaged in such studies during recent years is out of place in this brief and introductory sketch but will be attempted in the following chapters. Mention may be made here of the names of a few whose contributions have been especially noteworthy.

Among modern students of the subject, the name of the late Karl Schnarf of Vienna stands

FIG. 22. Karl Schnarf.

preeminent. His two works entitled "Embryologie der Angio-spermen" (1929) and "Vergleichende Embryologie der Angiosper-men" (1931) are the most important and exhaustive treatises in this field, and still serve as valuable works of reference. E. C. R. Souèges of France has distinguished himself by his painstaking studies on the development of the embryo in several families and genera of both dicotyledons and monocotyledons; and W. W. Finn in the Ukraine has similarly engaged himself in a study of the development and structure of the male gametophyte. In Swe-den, Sv. Murbeck, O. Rosenberg, and the late H. O. Juel in-spired a flourishing school of research on all phases of embryology (especially gametogenesis and apomixis), work on which is being continued at present by K. V. O. Dahlgren, F. Fagerlind, A. Håkansson, H. Stenar, and Å. Gustafsson. Among workers from other countries may be mentioned the names of A. Chiarugi and the late E. Carano from Italy; A. Ernst from Switzerland; H. D. Wulff from Germany; and the late J. M. Coulter and D. S. Johnson from the United States. During recent years there has also been considerable activity in this field in India, Japan, and Australia.

Of particular interest is the origin of the new science of experimental embryology, dealing with problems of storage and viability of pollen, effect of environmental factors on pollen tube growth, control of fertilization, production of seedless fruits, embryo culture, and artificial induction of parthenogenesis and adventive embryony. Here embryology stands in intimate relation with physiology and genetics, and promises to offer many opportunities and openings for the future.

References

Amici, G. B.   1824.   Observations microscopiques sur diverses espèces de plantes. Ann. des Sci. Nat., Bot. **2:** 41–70, 211–248.

———.   1830.   Note sur le mode d'action du pollen sur le stigmate. Extrait d'une lettre d'Amici à Mirbel. Ann. des Sci. Nat., Bot. **21:** 329–332.

———.   1844.   Quatrieme réunion des naturalistes italiens. Padua, 1843. Flora **1:** 359.

———.   1847.   Sur la fécondation des Orchidées. Ann. des Sci. Nat., Bot. **7/8:** 193–205.

Aristotle.   "The Works of Aristotle." Engl. transl. by J. A. Smith and W. D. Ross.   Oxford, 1913.

Braun, A.   1859.   Über Polyembryonie und Keimung von *Coelobogyne*. Abh. Königl. Akad. Wiss. Berlin, phys. Kl., pp. 107–263.

Brongniart, A.   1827.   Mémoire sur la génération et le développement de l'embryon dans les végétaux phanérogamiques. Ann. des Sci. Nat., Bot. **12:** 14–53, 145–172, 225–298.

Brown, R.   1831.   Observations on the organs and mode of fecundation in Orchideae and Asclepiadeae. Trans. Linn. Soc. London **16:** 685–745.

———.   1833.   "The Miscellaneous Botanical Works of Robert Brown." London, 1866–1868.

Camerarius, R. J.   1694.   "De sexu plantarum epistola." Tubingen.

Coulter, J. M., and Chamberlain, C. J.   1903.   "Morphology of Angiosperms." New York.

Elfving, F.   1879.   Studien über die Pollenkörner der Angiospermen. Jenaische Ztschr. f. Naturw. **13:** 1–28.

Famintzin, A. 1879. Embryologische Studien. Mém. Acad. Imp. des Sci. St. Petersburg VII, **26**(10): 1–19.

Finn, W. W. 1931. Zur Geschichte der Entdeckung der doppelten Befruchtung. Ber. deutsch. bot. Gesell. **49**: 153–157.

Focke, W. O. 1881. "Die Pflanzen-Mischlinge, ein Beitrag zur Biologie der Gewächse." Berlin.

Grew, N. 1682. "The Anatomy of Plants." London.

Guignard, L. 1881. Recherches d'embryogénie végétale comparée. I. Légumineuses. Ann. des Sci. Nat., Bot. **12**: 5–166.

———. 1899. Sur les anthérozoides et la double copulation sexuelle chez les végétaux angiospermes. Rev. Gén. de Bot. **11**: 129–135.

Hanstein, J. 1870. Die Entwickelung des Keimes der Monocotylen und Dicotylen. Bot. Abhandl. Bonn **1**: 1–112.

Hegelmaier, F. 1897. Zur Kenntnis der Polyembryonie von *Allium odorum*. Bot. Ztg. **55**: 133–140.

Herodotus. circa 484–425 B.C. "Historiae." Engl. transl. by A. D. Godley. London, 1921.

Hertwig, O. 1918. "Dokumente zur Geschichte der Zeugungslehre. Eine historische Studie." Bonn.

Hofmeister, W. 1847. Untersuchungen des Vorgangs bei der Befruchtung der Oenotheren. Bot. Ztg. **5**: 785–792.

———. 1848. Über die Entwicklung des Pollens. Bot. Ztg. **6**: 425–434, 649–658, 670–674.

———. 1849. "Die Entstehung des Embryo der Phanerogamen." Leipzig.

———. 1859. Neue Beiträge zur Kenntnis der Embryobildung der Phanerogamen. I. Dikotyledonen mit ursprünglich einzelligem, nur durch Zelltheilung wachsendem Endosperm. Abh. Königl. Sachs. Gesell. Wiss. 1859, pp. 535–672.

———. 1861. Neue Beiträge zur Kenntnis der Embryobildung der Phanerogamen. II. Monokotyledonen. Abh. Königl. Sächs. Gesell. Wiss. **7**: 629–760.

Juel, H. O. 1898. Parthenogenesis bei *Antennaria alpina* (L) R.Br. Vorläufige Mittheilung. Bot. Centbl. **74**: 369–372.

———. 1900. Vergleichende Untersuchungen über typische und parthenogenetische Fortpflanzung bei der Gattung *Antennaria*. K. Svenska Vet.-Akad. Handl. **33** (5): 1–59.

Kerner, A. 1876. Parthenogenesis bei einer angiospermen Pflanze. Sitzber. Math., Nat. Kl. Akad. der Wiss. Wien 1, **74**: 469.

Kölreuter, J. C. 1761–1766. "Vorläufige Nachricht von einigen das Geschlecht der Pflanzen betreffenden Versuchen und Beobachtungen."

Leeuwenhoek, A. v. 1677. "Observations. . . . de natis e semine genitali animalculis."

———. "The Secret Works of Antony van Leeuwenhoek, Containing his Microscopical Discoveries in Many of the Works of Nature." Engl. transl. by Samuel Hoole. London, 1800.

Mottier, D. M.   1897.   Über das Verhalten der Kerne bei der Entwicklung des Embryosackes und die Vorgänge bei der Befruchtung.   Jahrb. f. wiss. Bot. **31:** 125–158.

Murbeck, S.   1897.   Om vegetativ embryobildning hos flertalet Alchemillar och den flörkläring öfver formbeständigheten inom slägtet, som densamma innebär. Bot. Notiser 1897, pp. 273–277.

———.   1901.   Parthenogenetische Embryobildung in der Gattung *Alchemilla*. Lunds Univ. Årsskr., Afd. II, **36**(7): 1–41.

Nawaschin, S. G.   1898*a*.   Über das Verhalten des Pollenschlauches bei der Ulme. Bul. Acad. Imp. des Sci. St. Petersburg **8:** 345–357.

———.   1898*b*.   Resultate einer Revision der Befruchtungsvorgänge bei *Lilium martagon* und *Fritillaria tenella*.   Bul. Acad. Imp. des Sci. St. Petersburg **9:** 377–382.

Pliny (Plinius Secundus, Gaius).   "The Historie of the World: Commonly Called the Naturall Historie of G. Plinius Secundus."   Engl. Transl.   London, 1635.

Pringsheim, N.   1855.   Über die Befruchtung der Algen.   Ber. Preuss. Akad. der Wiss. Berlin 1855, pp. 133–165.

———.   1856.   Über die Befruchtung und der Generationswechsel der Algen. Monatsber. Königl. Preuss. Akad. der Wiss. Berlin 1856, pp. 225–237.

Radlkofer, L.   1856.   "Die Befruchtung der Phanerogamen.   Ein Beitrag zur Entscheidung des darüber bestehenden Streites."   W. Engelmann, Leipzig.

Sachs, J.   1874.   "Lehrbuch der Botanik."   Leipzig.

Sargant, E.   1900.   Recent work on the results of fertilization in angiosperms. Ann. Bot. **22:** 121–186.

Schacht, H.   1850.   "Entwicklungsgeschichte der Pflanzenembryo."   Amsterdam.

Schleiden, M. J.   1837.   Einige Blicke auf die Entwicklungsgeschichte des vegetablischen Organismus bei den Phanerogamen.   Arch. Bwl. Naturgeschichte III, **1:** 289–320.

———.   1845.   Über Amicis letzten Beitrag zur Lehre von der Befruchtung der Pflanzen.   Flora: 593–600.

Schnarf, K.   1929.   "Embryologie der Angiospermen."   Berlin.

———.   1931.   "Vergleichende Embryologie der Angiospermen."   Berlin.

Sharp, L. W.   1943.   "Fundamentals of Cytology."   McGraw-Hill Book Company.

Strasburger, E.   1877.   Über Befruchtung und Zelltheilung.   Jenaische Ztschr. f. Naturw. **11:** 435–536.

———.   1878.   Über Polyembryonie.   Jenaische Ztschr. f. Naturw. **12:** 647–670.

———.   1879.   "Die Angiospermen und die Gymnospermen."   Jena.

———.   1884.   "Neue Untersuchungen über den Befruchtungsvorgang bei den Phanerogamen."   Jena.

———.   1900.   Einige Bemerkungen zur Frage nach der "doppelten Befruchtung" bei Angiospermen.   Bot. Ztg. II, **58:** 293–316.

Thuret, G.   1854.   Recherches sur la fécondation des Fucacées, suivies d'observations sur les anthéridies des algues.   Ann. des Sci. Nat., Bot. **2:** 196–214.

Tretjakow, S.   1895.   Die Beteilung der Antipoden in Fallen der Polyembryonie bei *Allium odorum*.   Ber. deutsch bot. Gesell. **13:** 13–17.

Treub, M. 1879. Notes sur l'embryogénie de quelques Orchidées. Natuurk. Verh. Koninkl. Akad. Amsterdam **19**: 1–50.

———. 1891. Sur les Casuarinées et leur place dans le système naturel. Ann. Jard. Bot. Buitenzorg **10**: 145–231.

——— and Mellink, J. 1880. Notice sur le développement du sac embryonnaire dans quelques Angiospermes. Arch. Néerland. **15**: 452–457.

Von Mohl, H. 1863. Giambattista Amici. Bot. Ztg. **21** (Beilage 34): 1–8.

CHAPTER 2

THE MICROSPORANGIUM

In considering the course of events leading to the origin of the embryo, we must first deal with the development of the micro- and megasporangia. It is the microsporangium which produces the microspores and eventually the male gametophyte. Similarly, the megasporangium, or ovule, is the place of formation of the megaspores and the female gametophyte. The latter, after fertilization,

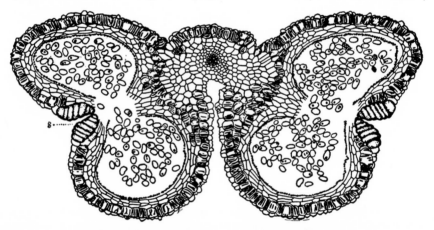

Fig. 23. T.s. anther of *Lilium philadelphicum*, showing dissolution of cells separating the two microsporangia on each side. Note the fibrous endothecium and stomium *s*. The minute punctate markings lining the inner wall of the anther probably represent remnants of tapetum. (*After Coulter and Chamberlain, 1903.*)

produces the embryo and endosperm, while the entire megasporangium with its enclosed structures becomes the seed and the progenitor of the next generation.

A typical anther comprises four elongated microsporangia, but at maturity the two sporangia of each side become confluent owing to the breaking down of the partition between them (Fig. 23). A cross section of a very young anther shows a mass of homogeneous meristematic cells surrounded by the epidermis (Fig. 24*A,B*). It soon becomes slightly four-lobed, and rows of hypodermal cells become differentiated in each lobe by their larger size, radial elongation, and more conspicuous nuclei. These form the archesporium. The extent of the archesporial tissue varies considerably both lengthwise and breadthwise. Either a single archesporial cell may be seen in each lobe in a cross section of the anther, as in *Sansevieria* (Guérin, 1927), *Dionaea* (Smith, 1929), and *Boerhaavia* (Maheshwari, 1929), or a plate of such cells, as in *Ophiopogon* (Maheshwari, 1934), *Urginea* (Capoor, 1937a), and most other plants. In longitudinal section also the row may comprise only one cell as in

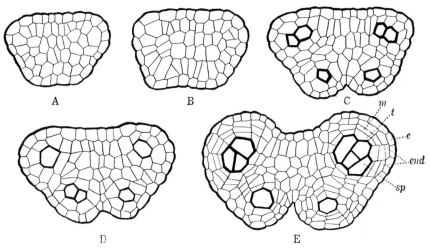

F$_{IG}$. 24.   *A–E*, differentiation of parietal and sporogenous tissue in anthers of *Chrysanthemum leucanthemum* (*e* = epidermis; *end* = endothecium; *m* = middle layer; *t* = tapetum; *sp* = sporogenous cell). (*After Warming, 1873*.)

Enalus (Kausik, 1941), or two cells as in *Boerhaavia* (Maheshwari, 1929), or several cells as in *Urginea* (Capoor, 1937a).

Figure 24*C–E* shows the stages leading to the origin of the sporogenous tissue. The archesporial cells divide to form a primary parietal layer toward the outside and a primary sporogenous layer toward the inside. The cells of the former divide by periclinal and anticlinal walls to give rise to a series of concentric layers, usually three to five, composing the wall of the anther. The primary sporogenous cells either function directly as the spore mother cells or undergo further divisions to form a larger number of cells.

In a few plants a hypodermal archesporium has not been clearly distinguished and more deep-seated cells are said to give rise to the sporogenous tissue.   In *Doryanthes* (Newman, 1928), *Pholisma* (Copeland, 1935), and *Holoptelea* (Capoor, 1937b) it is stated that there is no definite system of periclinal divisions separating the parietal tissue from the archesporium and that the sporogenous function is gradually taken over by a group of cells about three or four layers below the epidermis.   It is probable, however, that such appearances are due to the difficulty of obtaining a sharp differentiation between the cells during the early stages of development of the anther, and further studies may reveal the hypodermal origin of the archesporium in these plants also.

The Wall Layers.   The epidermis, which is the outermost layer of the anther, undergoes only anticlinal divisions.   Its cells become greatly stretched and flattened in order to keep pace with the enlargement of the anther, and in many plants, especially those of dry habitats, they eventually lose contact with each other so that only their withering remains can be seen at maturity.

The layer of cells lying immediately beneath the epidermis is the endothecium.   Its maximum development is attained at the time when the pollen grains are about to be shed (Fig. 23).   The cells become radially elongated, and from their inner tangential walls fibrous bands run upward, ending near the outer wall of each cell. In aquatics with aerial flowers like *Utricularia* (Kausik, 1938) and even such reduced forms as *Wolffia* (Gupta, 1935) the fibrous thickenings occur as usual, but in several members of the Hydrocharitaceae (Ernst-Schwarzenbach, 1945; Maheshwari and Johri, 1950), and in some cleistogamous forms whose flowers never open, they fail to develop and there is no special mode of dehiscence.   In those plants, also, whose anthers open by apical pores, the endothecium may not develop any fibrous thickenings and dehiscence takes place here by the dissolution of certain cells at the apex of the anther. In *Erica*, which is an example of this kind, there is a further peculiarity in that the "apical" pores are in fact basal.   Figure 25 shows some stages in the curvature of the anther which bring about this inversion (Matthews and Taylor, 1926).

Among other exceptions may be cited *Musa* (Juliano and Alcala, 1933), *Sesamum* (Nohara, 1934), *Anona* (Juliano, 1935a), *Ipomoea*, (Juliano, 1935b), *Aeginetia* (Juliano, 1935c), and *Melastoma* (Subramanyam, 1948) in which the fibrous thickening are absent but the walls of the epidermal cells undergo a general cutinization and lignification over the entire surface. *Oryza* (Juliano and Aldama, 1937), *Ditepalanthus* (Fagerlind, 1938), and *Balanophora* (Fagerlind, 1945) are peculiar in that the parietal layers, one or two in number, become crushed and disorganized during the development of the anther so that a fibrous layer is absent and the epidermis abuts directly on the tapetum.[1]

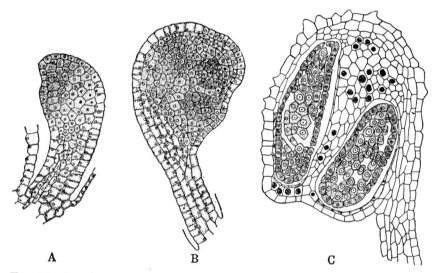

A   **B**   **C**

Fig. 25. Development of anther of *Erica hirtiflora*. *A, B,* l.s. young stamens, showing gradual inversion of anther. *C,* l.s. stamen at spore mother cell stage, showing almost complete inversion of anther, so that its lower end comes to lie toward the upper side. (*After Matthews and Taylor, 1926.*)

Next to the endothecium there are usually one to three "middle" layers. As a rule, all of them become flattened and crushed at the time of the meiotic divisions in the microspore mother cells, but there are a few exceptions. In *Holoptelea* (Capoor, 1937*b*) there are three to four middle layers, of which the outermost persists for a long time. In *Ranunculus* (Singh, 1936) there are two middle layers, of which the inner soon disappears but the outer persists;

---

[1] In *Styphelia* (Brough, 1924), *Arceuthobium* (Pisek, 1924) and some members of the Ericales it is the epidermis which is said to develop fibrous thickenings and function as an endothecium, but this deserves confirmation.

occasionally its cells become densely protoplasmic and simulate those of the tapetum. In *Lilium* there are several middle layers, of which those lying adjacent to the endothecium persist for a long time (Fig. 23), and in *Gloriosa* (Eunus, 1949) the outermost middle layer develops fibrous thickenings similar to those of the endothecium.

Rarely, a middle layer may be absent as in the anthers of *Wolffia* (Gupta, 1935) and *Vallisneria* (Witmer, 1937), but some previous reports of the absence of a middle layer have been shown to be mis-

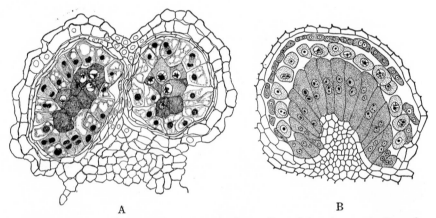

A   B

FIG. 26.   Anthers, showing microspore mother cells and tapetum.   *A, Bougainvillea*, t.s. portion of anther, showing mitotic divisions in tapetal cells.   (*After Cooper, 1931.*)   *B, Salvia mellifera*, t.s. portion of anther lobe.   The tapetal cells lying toward the connective are considerably larger than those on the outer side. (*After Carlson and Stuart, 1936.*)

interpretations caused by its ephemeral nature and early disappearance.   Johri (1934) has demonstrated the presence of a middle layer in *Cuscuta* where it was formerly reported to be absent (Peters, 1908).

The innermost wall layer or tapetum is of considerable physiological significance, for all the food materials entering into the sporogenous cells must pass through it.[2]   Its cells are full of dense cytoplasm, and at the beginning of meiosis the tapetal nuclei may also undergo some divisions (Fig. 26).[3]   Because of these similarities of

[2] Typically the tapetum is a single layer of cells but in *Nicolaia* and *Costus* (Boehm, 1931) it is composed of several layers.

[3] Rarely, tapetal nuclei may even pass through a condition resembling the prophase of a meiotic division.   Gates and Rees (1921) figure some tapetal

appearance and behavior between the cells of the tapetum and the microsporogenous tissue, earlier botanists supposed that the former is derived by a sterilization of the outer sporogenous cells. Developmental studies of a precise nature have, however, nearly always confirmed its parietal origin.[4]

The nuclear divisions in the tapetum were formerly believed to be amitotic, but recent studies (Bonnet, 1912; Cooper, 1933; Witkus, 1945) have shown that this is incorrect and that appearances suggesting amitosis are really caused by mitotic irregularities and

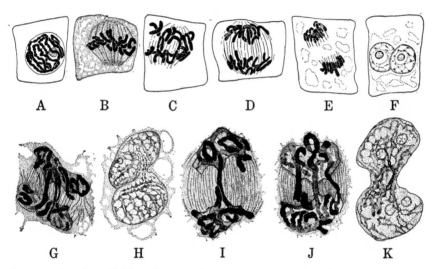

FIG. 27. Nuclear divisions in tapetal cells of *Zea mays* (*A–F*), *Lilium canadense* (*G–H*), and *Podophyllum peltatum* (*I–K*). (*After Cooper, 1933.*)

nuclear fusions. According to present conceptions, the nucleus of a tapetal cell may divide in any of the following ways:[5]

1. *By normal mitosis.* The division takes place in the ordinary

nuclei of *Lactuca* in the synizesis stage, and Moissl (1941) reports a similar condition in some members of the Caprifoliaceae.

[4] Recently, Capoor (1937*b*) has reported that in *Holoptelea* the tapetal cells are almost indistinguishable from the adjacent cells of the sporogenous tissue. He cautiously adds, however, that this fact alone is insufficient to justify any inference regarding the sporogenous origin of the tapetum.

[5] It is to be noted that in a few families and orders, *viz.*, Mimosaceae, Crassulaceae, Gentianaceae, Boraginaceae, Hydrophyllaceae, Juncaceae, Orchidaceae, and Helobiales, the tapetal cells usually remain uninucleate from the time of their formation to their eventual disintegration.

way, but no cell plate is laid down. The two daughter nuclei, which are diploid, remain inside the cell (Fig. 27 *A–F*).

2. *By a "sticky" type of division.* Here the chromosomes behave normally up to the early anaphase stage. After this, one or more of them fail to separate, forming chromosome bridges which persist during the telophase as well as the resting stage. As a result a single dumbbell-shaped tetraploid nucleus is formed whose middle portion may be broad or narrow depending on the number of chromosome bridges present (Fig. 27 *G–K*).

3. *By endomitosis.*[6] Here the nucleolus and the nuclear membrane remain intact and there is no spindle formation. The chro-

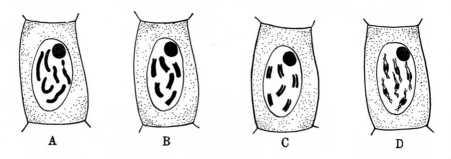

Fɪɢ. 28.   Diagrams showing "endomitosis" in tapetal cells of *Spinacia oleracea.* *A*, endoprophase. *B*, endometaphase. *C*, endo-anaphase. *D*, endotelophase. (*Drawing supplied by Dr. E. R. Witkus.*)

mosomes contract and split longitudinally, but all of them remain within the same nucleus, which becomes tetraploid (Fig. 28).

The first nuclear division in a tapetal cell is often followed by further divisions. Some of the divisions may be accompanied by nuclear fusions, resulting in one or more large polyploid nuclei. The latter may, however, divide again and give rise to smaller nuclei. Since this type of behavior is very frequent in tapetal cells, it is unnecessary to give specific instances.

An interesting condition has been reported in certain haploid and

[6] This type of division was first postulated by Meyer (1925). In the tapetal cells of *Leontodon* he found diploid nuclei in younger stages and polyploid nuclei in older stages. Since no spindle fibers were observed, he concluded that there was an "internal division" of the chromosomes without any nuclear division. See also Brown (1949) who has recently given a detailed account of endomitosis in the tapetal cells of tomato.

diploid plants of *Oenothera rubricalyx* (Gates and Goodwin, 1930). In the former the tapetal cells are uninucleate and in the latter they are binucleate—a fact which is no doubt related to the general reduction of tissues in haploid individuals. More difficult to explain is the marked difference in shape and structure of the tapetal cells belonging to the same anther. In *Lathraea* (Gates and Latter, 1927), *Salvia* (Carlson and Stuart, 1936) (Fig. 26B), and *Moringa* (Puri, 1941) the tapetal cells on the inner side of the loculus show a marked radial elongation and are much larger than those on the outer side. Further, in *Lathraea* the cells on the outer side are uninucleate while those adjacent to the connective are binucleate. In *Lactuca sativa* (Gates and Rees, 1921) the tapetal cells lying on one side of the loculus may be quadrinucleate while those on the other are binucleate. The binucleate cells are nearly always shorter and broader than the quadrinucleate. Possibly these differences are related to the varying amounts of nutritive materials passing into the cells.

Toward the close of the meiotic divisions in the microspore mother cells, the tapetal cells begin to lose contact with each other. Large vacuoles appear in the cytoplasm and the nuclei begin to show signs of degeneration.[7] Finally the cells are entirely absorbed at the time when the microspores begin to separate from one another. This type of tapetum, in which the cells remain *in situ*, is called the glandular or secretory tapetum and is of common occurrence in angiosperms. However, there are several genera and families (see Juel, 1915; Tischler, 1915; Mascré, 1919 *a*, *b*) in which the walls of the tapetal cells break down but the protoplasts, which remain intact, protrude and "wander" inside the loculus, where they may coalesce to form a continuous mass called the tapetal periplasmodium (Fig. 29). Clausen (1927), who has reviewed the previous literature in this connection, classifies this kind of tapetum (often called the "amoeboid" tapetum) into four subtypes:

1. *Sagittaria type.* The tapetal cells lose their walls by the time the microspore tetrads have been formed, and their protoplasts begin to project inward as soon as the microspores have separated. Later the periplasmodium becomes continuous. Examples: *Sagittaria, Alisma, Limnocharis, Hydrocharis.*

---

[7] At this stage the anther loculi frequently show a densely staining jelly-like or mucilaginous fluid which disappears at maturity. As suggested by Nietsch (1941), this is probably a secretion from the tapetal cells.

2. *Butomus type.*   In this case the formation of the periplasmo-dium occurs a little earlier, when the microspores are still grouped in tetrads.   Examples: *Butomus, Stratiotes,* and *Ouvirandra.*

3. *Sparganium type.*   Here also the fusion of protoplasts begins at the tetrad stage but the tapetal cells are multinucleate.   Examples: *Sparganium, Typha, Tradescantia.*

4. *Triglochin type.*   In a few plants the tapetum begins its activity while the microspore mother cells are still undergoing the meiotic divisions.   The tapetal protoplasts and nuclei protrude into the

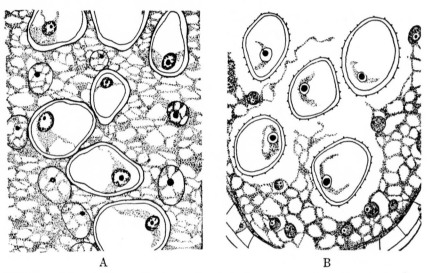

A   B

FIG. 29.   Tapetal plasmodium in *Symphoricarpos racemosus (A)* and *Lonicera pyrenaica (B). (After Moissl, 1941.)*

spaces between the mother cells so that the periplasmodium is formed at a very early stage.   Examples: *Triglochin, Potamogeton,* and several members of the Araceae.

Like the glandular or secretory tapetum, the amoeboid tapetum also serves for the nutrition of the spores, and is probably more effective for this purpose.   As some authors (see Mezzetti-Bamba-cioni, 1941) have suggested, it seems probable that the periplas-modium contributes to the formation of the exine, but this point deserves further study.   A curious feature which has been observed in several plants (see Ubisch, 1927; Kosmath, 1927; Kajale, 1940; Puri, 1941; Singh, 1950) is the appearance of small granular markings on the inner surface of the tapetum (Fig. 30) and later on the inner surface of the middle layers or the endothecium. They give the same staining reactions as the exine of the pollen grains and probably contribute to the development of the latter. This seems to be supported by Gorczyński's (1934) observations on *Cardamine*, according to which the exine first begins to develop on that side of the pollen grains which lies towards the tapetum.

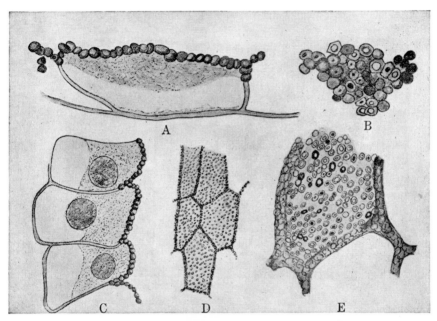

Fig. 30. Tapetal cells, showing cutinization of inner walls. *A, Magnolia youlan,* tapetal cell, showing prominent thickenings on inner surface. *B,* the thickenings as seen in surface view. *C, Lilium tigrinum,* thickenings on inner walls of tapetal cells. *D,* same in surface view. *E,* more highly magnified than *D.* (*After Kosmath, 1927.*)

Sporogenous Tissue. The primary sporogenous cells give rise to the microspore mother cells. In some plants the sporogenous cells undergo several divisions, in others only a few divisions, and rarely there are no divisions at all, so that the primary sporogenous cells function directly as the microspore mother cells. *Alangium, Sansevieria, Knautia,* and some members of the Malvaceae and Cucurbitaceae are examples of the third kind, showing a single row of microspore mother cells in each anther lobe.

A peculiar feature met with in some members of the Mimosaceae is the development of transversely placed sterile septa in the anther lobes (Fig. 31). In some members of the Loranthaceae also, *viz.*, *Dendrophthoe* (Rauch, 1936), *Elytranthe*, and *Amyema* (Schaeppi

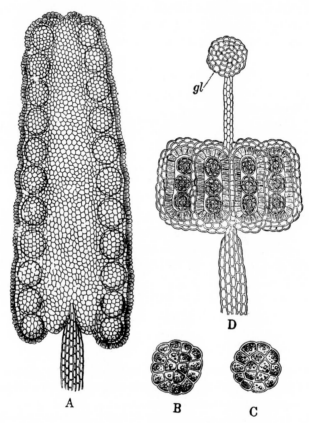

Fig. 31. Structure of anther in some members of the Mimosaceae. *A*, *Parkia*, l.s. anther showing two rows of pollinia. *B,C*, pollinia dissected out from anther. *D*, *Dichrostachys*, l.s. anther, showing pollinia; note stalked gland *gl* at apex of anther. (*After Engler, 1876.*)

and Steindl, 1942), the microsporangia become vertically partitioned by the formation of sterile septa, and in *Viscum* (Schaeppi and Steindl, 1945) such partitions arise not only in the vertical plane but also in the horizontal one so that each anther has as many as 50 loculi.

Formation of sterile septa is also known in a few other plants. Caldwell (1899) reports that in *Lemna* the archesporial tissue originally comprises a single mass of cells. After the usual wall layers have been cut off, a plate of sterile cells divides this mass into two and then into four. In *Limnophyton* (Johri, 1935) and *Ranunculus* (Singh, 1936) a cross section of the young anther shows an oval or somewhat dumbbell-shaped outline with a plate of archesporial cells on each side. Both of these become partitioned by the appearance of a sterile septum resulting in the usual tetralocular condition. In *Quamoclit* (Fedortschuk, 1932) there is a single row of sporogenous cells in each lobe of the anther but one or two of these fail to keep pace with the others and become nonfunctional. These give rise to sterile partitions separating the loculus into two or three parts.

In some plants there are fewer than four groups of sporogenous cells. In the family Malvaceae (Stenar, 1925) the anthers are uniformly bisporangiate and the two loculi eventually fuse to form a single loculus. In *Elodea* (Wylie, 1904), *Styphelia* (Brough, 1924), *Circaeaster* (Junell, 1931), *Phoradendron* (Billings, 1932), *Wolffia* (Gupta, 1935), and *Moringa* (Puri, 1941) also, there are two microsporangia which may later become confluent by the breaking down of the intervening cell layers. The anthers of *Naias* (Campbell, 1897) are said to be unilocular, but the developmental stages have not been traced satisfactorily. In *Vallisneria* (Witmer, 1937) there are all gradations from a unilocular to a tetralocular condition. Typically two loculi are formed, owing to the appearance of a sterile septum in the sporogenous tissue, but sometimes the septum is incomplete, resulting in a unilocular condition, and frequently each of the two loculi becomes bisected so as to form four loculi.

The stamens of *Piper betle* (Johnson, 1910) are peculiar in that the number of microsporangia in an anther may be four, three, two, or one, and it remains constant from the time of initiation of the sporangia to the maturation of the anther. There is no secondary fusion of the sporogenous tissue.

In *Korthalsella* (Stevenson, 1934; Rutishauser, 1935) there are three stamens, each of which consists of two microsporangia, but since all the anthers fuse to form a synandrium, a cross section of the flower shows six microsporangia arranged in a ring. At maturity the partitions between the sporangia break down and the loculi become continuous.

The genus *Arceuthobium* is unique in having a single annular pollen sac forming a continuous ring around a central column of sterile cells called "columella" (Städtler, 1923; Pisek, 1924; Thoday and Johnson, 1930; Dowding, 1931). Regarding the origin of this condition there is, however, some difference of opinion. Städtler (1923) thinks that the anther is at first multilocular but the partitions break down at maturity. Pisek (1924), on the other hand, contends that it is unilocular from the commencement, and this is supported by Thoday and Johnson (1930) who state that even in the youngest anthers there is a ring-shaped archesporium surrounding the central columella. Dowding (1931) agrees regarding the continuity of the archesporium but finds that the columella exhibits a considerable amount of variation. It frequently forms a sort of flange dividing the anther into two halves; sometimes the first flange tends to disappear, and a new one arises at right angles to it. Rarely, the flanges give out branches extending outwards to the anther wall. In Dowding's opinion these flanges of the columella are to be regarded as remnants of the septa which once separated four distinct archesporia.

Although all the sporogenous cells in the anther are potentially capable of giving rise to microspores, some of them frequently degenerate and become absorbed by the remaining cells. In *Ophiopogon* (Maheshwari, 1934) and *Holoptelea* (Capoor, 1937b) some of the sporogenous cells do not reach even the mother cell stage and probably serve to nourish the remaining cells. In *Zostera* (Rosenberg, 1901) most of the sporogenous cells divide longitudinally to form the numerous long microspore mother cells but others interspersed between them undergo transverse divisions and give rise to sterile cells which are later crushed and used up by the functioning cells. In certain members of the Gentianaceae (Guérin, 1926) which are devoid of any well-formed tapetum, the nutritive function is taken over by some of the sporogenous cells themselves. These become sterile and do not go through the reduction divisions (Fig. 32). In *Kigelia* (Venkatasubban, 1945) degeneration takes place at a later stage; some of the microspores in a tretrad fail to develop further and become functionless.

Cytomixis. While making a study of *Oenothera gigas* and *O.*

biennis, Gates (1911) observed a frequent migration of chromatic material from one microspore mother cell into another and called it cytomixis. Since then it has been reported in several other plants, and while it is most frequent between the synizesis and diakinesis stages, it may sometimes occur even during the interkinesis stage, *i.e.*, after the first meiotic division has been completed. In *Lathraea* (Gates and Latter, 1927), which is an instance of this kind, the microspore mother cells do not round up but remain in close contact with one another. During interkinesis the nuclei of the two dyad cells occupy an eccentric position near the cell wall so that the

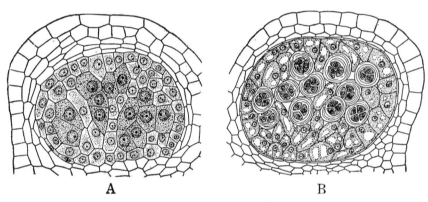

A **B**

Fig. 32. Sterilization of part of sporogenous tissue in anthers of *Swertia perennis*. *A*, anther lobe at microspore mother cell stage. *B*, same, at microspore tetrad stage. (*After Guérin, 1926*.)

chances of cytomixis are increased. In *Coreopsis tripteris* (Gelin, 1934) cytomixis may also occur at the close of the meiotic divisions but the multinucleate cells formed in this way again break up into smaller units consisting of one or two nuclei.

In some plants individual chromosomes, or groups of chromosomes, or even whole spindles are said to be carried from one cell into another. It is believed, however, that it is a pathological phenomenon, or that such appearances are caused by faulty fixation. Woodworth (1931), who used smear preparations of anthers, states that cytomixis was common when a little extra pressure was used in squeezing out the microspore mother cells. Further, such abnormalities were found to be more frequent in hybrids than in other plants, and he attributes this to an "innate unbalance" in the heterozygous cytoplasm which makes it more susceptible to pressures and other similar treatments.

Mention may also be made here of fusions of entire cells of the sporogenous tissue. Matsura (1935) reported that in *Phacellanthus* the separating walls between adjacent microspore mother cells sometimes dissolve and fuse in pairs to form giant cells, which may either give rise to polyploid gametes or degenerate without completing the meiotic divisions. In two haploid plants of *Phleum pratense*, Levan (1941) observed the fusion of as many as 30 microspore mother cells, giving rise to large plasmodia or "syncytes." A similar behavior has also been reported by Stern (1946) in sugar suspensions of the microspore mother cells of *Trillium erectum*. Here the extent of the fusions appeared to be unlimited, although the maximum number of nuclei actually observed in a cell was 32.

Cytokinesis. The divisions of the microspore mother cells may be of the successive or the simultaneous type.[8] In the former a cell plate is laid down immediately after the first meiotic division and another in each of the two daughter cells after the second meiotic division. In the simultaneous type, on the other hand, no wall is laid down after the first division and the mother cell becomes separated all at once into four parts after both the meiotic divisions are over.

The investigations of C. H. Farr (1916) and others have shown that there is also another difference in the mechanism of cytokinesis. In the successive type the cell plate is laid down in the center and then extends centrifugally on both sides, dividing the cell into two equal halves. In the simultaneous type, on the other hand, the division usually occurs by centripetally advancing constriction furrows, which meet in the center and divide the mother cell into four parts.

Farr (1916) studied *Nicotiana tabacum* in special detail. At first there is an enlargement of the nucleus of the microspore mother cell, accompanied by a thickening of the mother cell wall. No cell plate is laid down after Meiosis I, and the spindle fibers of this division disappear during the metaphases of Meiosis II. After the four daughter nuclei have become organized, they assume a tetrahedral arrangement and a spindle is re-formed between every two nuclei,

---

[8] For an account of the nuclear changes in meiosis, see Sharp (1943) and other works on cytology.

making a total of six spindles. However, these spindles have nothing to do with the quadripartition of the mother cell, and there is no laying down of centrifugally growing cell plates such as are characteristic of other dividing cells. Instead, constriction furrows now start at the periphery and proceed inward until they meet at the center, so that there is a simultaneous division of the protoplast into four cells, *i.e.*, the microspores.

In *Melilotus alba* (Castetter, 1925) vacuoles seem to play a conspicuous part in cytokinesis (Fig. 33). After Meiosis II, hyaline areas develop between the four nuclei, apparently as the result of a migration of the denser cytoplasm toward the nuclei and an extrusion of sap into the regions between them. The small vacuoles arising in this manner soon fuse to form larger ones which virtually split the cytoplasm into four masses. Furrows originating at the surface now grow inward and soon meet the vacuoles. Meanwhile, the mother cell rounds up and secretes a thick layer of callose or some other gelatinous material, which extends inward with the cleavage furrows and eventually completes the division of the cell into the four microspores.[9]

Zea mays (Reeves, 1928) may be taken as an example of the successive type of microspore formation (Fig. 34). At the end of Meiosis I, thickenings are formed on the spindle fibers at the equatorial region of the cell. They gradually increase in size, coming in contact with each other and fusing to form the cell plate. Additional spindle fibers continue to appear just beyond the periphery of the plate so as to increase the diameter of the spindle. At the same time the cell plate extends centrifugally and joins the wall of the mother cell, so as to complete the division of the protoplast into two halves. Now the second meiotic division follows, and a new partition wall develops in each cell in the same way as after Meiosis I, resulting in a tetrad showing the bilateral arrangement of microspores.

The question as to which of the two modes of tetrad formation is primitive and which is the more advanced is difficult to decide. It seems, however, that since a division by furrowing is common

---

[9] The mode of origin of this gelatinous layer has been a subject of much discussion. Beer (1906), Gates (1925), and Castetter (1925) have expressed the view that it is secreted by the cytoplasm of the mother cell, while Farr (1922), Bowers (1931), and Capoor (1937a) believe that it is the result of a swelling of the secondary lamellae of the cell wall.

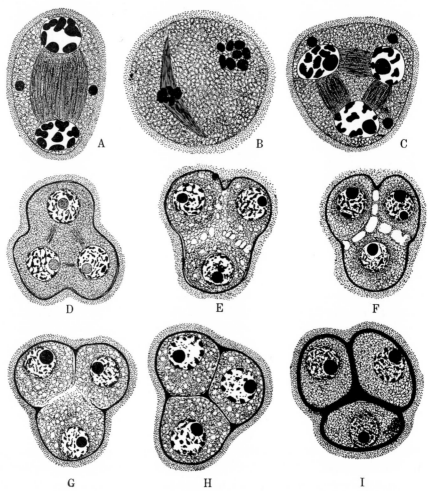

FIG. 33.   Cytokinesis in microspore mother cells of *Melilotus alba*.   *A*, telophase
of Meiosis I.   *B*, metaphase of Meiosis II.   *C*, end of Meiosis II, showing three
of the four microspore nuclei.   Note large extranuclear "centrosome-like bodies"
seen here and in *A*.   *D*, microspore nuclei in resting stage.   Spindles have almost
disappeared and protoplast has begun to invaginate at the periphery, at points
equidistant from the nuclei.   Note origin of special wall, shown in black.   *E,F*,
formation of vacuoles in portions of cytoplasm lying between nuclei.   *G*, special
wall entering furrows.   *H*, special walls have met in center, forming partitions between microspore nuclei.   *I*, fully formed microspores.   (*After Castetter, 1925*.)

in the Thallophytes and other lower plants, the simultaneous type is the more ancient and the successive type the derived. In general, the former is prevalent in the majority of dicotyledons and the latter in the majority of monocotyledons. There is no hard and fast rule, however, and exceptions are frequent. Thus the successive type is found in a few dicotyledonous families like the Asclepiadaceae, Podostemonaceae, and Apocynaceae, and the simultaneous type in a few monocotyledonous families, *viz.*, the Iridaceae, Taccaceae, Juncaceae, and Dioscoreaceae, and in several genera of the Liliaceae, Palmaceae, and Orchidaceae.

In *Magnolia* (Farr, 1918) there are isobilateral tetrads formed by furrowing instead of by cell plates. A cleavage furrow starts after

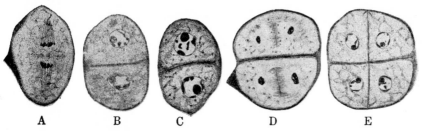

A   B   C   D   E

Fig. 34. Cytokinesis in microspore mother cells of *Zea mays*. *A*, anaphase of Meiosis I. *B,C*, laying down of partition wall after Meiosis I. *D*, telophase of Meiosis II. *E*, isobilateral tetrad. (*After Reeves, 1928.*)

Meiosis I, but its development is arrested during the second meiotic division. It resumes growth at the end of Meiosis II and forms a partition through the equatorial region of the mother cell. At the same time additional furrows originate at the periphery, and the two dyad cells now become subdivided to give rise to the four microspores. A similar condition occurs in *Anona* (Juliano, 1935a) and *Asimina* (Locke, 1936).

The Microspore Tetrad. As mentioned above, the microspores are usually arranged in a tetrahedral (Fig. 35A) or isobilateral (Fig. 35B) fashion, but there are exceptions (Fig. 35C–E). A decussate arrangement of the cells has been recorded in *Magnolia* (Farr, 1918), *Atriplex* (Billings, 1934), *Cornus* (D'Amato, 1946), and many other plants. In some genera of the Asclepiadaceae (Gager, 1902) and in the genus *Halophila* of the Hydrocharitaceae (Kausik and Rao, 1942) the mother cells divide transversely so as to give rise to

linear tetrads (Fig. 36*A–D*). T-shaped tetrads also occur sometimes as in *Aristolochia* (Samuelsson, 1914) and *Butomopsis* (Johri,
1936). In *Zostera* (Rosenberg, 1901) the elongated microspore
mother cells, measuring 5 by 60 microns at the time of meiosis,
divide in a plane parallel to the longitudinal axis of the cell, resulting in a group of four filiform cells which undergo further elongation
and become approximately 2000 microns long when mature.[10] Of
considerable interest are *Musa* (Juliano and Alcala, 1933), *Neottia*
(Goebel, 1933), *Agave* (Vignoli, 1936, 1937), *Nicolaia* (Boehm, 1931),
Habenaria (Swamy, 1946), *Laurus* (Battaglia, 1947), and *Ottelia*
(Islam, 1950) in which two or three types of dispositions may be
found in one and the same species.

Occasionally there are either fewer than four spores resulting from
the divisions of the microspore mother cell, or more than four.

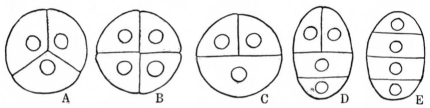

Fig. 35.   Diagram showing different types of microspore tetrads.   *A*, tetrahedral.
B, isobilateral.   *C*, decussate.   *D*, T-shaped.   *E*, linear.   (*B–E, after Boehm, 1931.*)

The former condition originates as the result of a failure of one
division, or the formation of a "restitution nucleus" after the first
division, or an irregular wall formation giving rise to one binucleate
and two uninucleate spores.   The latter condition, *i.e.*, the formation of more than four spores (polyspory), usually results from the
occurrence of lagging chromosomes which organize into micronuclei.
In general, however, such abnormalities in the number of microspores are found only in hybrids characterized by a high degree of
sterility and the pollen grains arising in this way are nonfunctional.

Usually the microspores soon separate from one another but in
some plants they adhere in tetrads to form the so-called "compound" pollen grains.[11]   As examples may be cited *Drimys, Anona,*

[10] Filiform pollen grains also occur in *Phyllospadix* and *Cymodocea*, but the
method by which they arise does not seem to have been studied so far.

[11] For detailed information on such variations of external form, see Wodehouse
(1936) and Erdtman (1943, 1945).

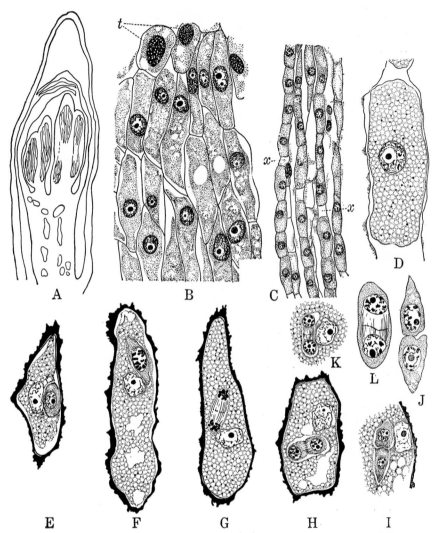

Fig. 36. Development of microspores and male gametophyte of *Halophila ovata*. *A*, l.s. of young staminate flower. *B*, microspore mother cells with a few tapetal cells *t*. *C*, chains of microspores; note vacant spaces *x* separating individual tetrads. *D*, single microspore. *E*, microspore, showing tube and generative cells. *F*, older stage, showing spindle-shaped generative cell lying inside vegetative cytoplasm. *G*, pollen grain, showing division of generative cell. *H*, same, more advanced stage. Note formation of constriction furrow across generative cell. *I,J*, formation of sperm cells completed. *K,L*, division of generative cell, showing formation of transitory cell plate. (*After Kausik and Rao, 1942.*)

Drosera, Elodea, Typha, Furcraea, and several members of the Ericaceae, Apocynaceae, Asclepiadaceae, Juncaceae, and Orchidaceae.
In the Mimosaceae there are larger units composed of 8 to 64 cells,
and in a number of genera belonging to the Asclepiadaceae all the
microspores in a sporangium remain together to form a single mass
called the pollinium.   The family Orchidaceae is especially interesting in this connection (see Swamy, 1948).   In some genera, such as
Cypripedium and *Vanilla,* the microspores separate from one another
and become free.   In *Pogonia* the four cells of a tetrad adhere and
form a compound pollen grain.   In the tribes Ophrydeae and Neot-
tieae this tendency is carried further and the compound grains are
themselves held together in small units known as massulae.   Finally, in *Coelogyne* and *Pholidota* all the microspore mother cells and
their derivatives remain together and continue their development
as a single unit.

References

Battaglia, E.   1947.   Meiosi anormale nella microsporogenesi di *Laurus nobilis* L.
    Atti d. Società Toscana Sci. Nat. **54**: 1–22.
Beer, R.   1906.   On the development of the pollen grain and anther of some
    Onagraceae.   Beihefte bot. Centbl. **19A**: 286–313.
Billings, F. H.   1932.   Microsporogenesis in *Phoradendron.*   Ann. Bot. **46**: 979–
    992.
————.   1934.   Male gametophyte of *Atriplex hymenelytra.*   Bot. Gaz. **95**:
    477–484.
Boehm, K.   1931.   Embryologische Untersuchungen an Zingiberaceen.   Planta
    14: 411–440.
Bonnet, F.   1912.   Recherches sur l'évolution des cellules nourricières du pollen
    chez les Angiospermes.   Arch. f. Zellforsch. **7**: 605–722.
Bowers, C. G.   1931.   The development of pollen and viscin strands in *Rhododen-
    dron catawbiense.*   Bul. Torrey Bot. Club **57**: 285–314.
Brough, P.   1924.   Studies in the Epacridaceae.   I. The life history of *Styphelia
    longifolia.*   Proc. Linn. Soc. N. S. Wales **49**: 162–178.
Brown, S. W.   1949.   Endomitosis in the tapetum of tomato.   Amer. Jour. Bot.
    36: 703–716.
Caldwell, O. W.   1899.   On the life history of *Lemna minor.*   Bot. Gaz. **27**:
    37–66.
Campbell, D. H.   1897.   A morphological study of *Naias* and *Zannichellia.*   Proc.
    Calif. Acad. Sci. III. Bot. **1**: 1–71.
Capoor, S. P.   1937a.   Contributions to the morphology of some Indian Liliaceae.
    II. The gametophytes of *Urginea indica* Kunth.   Beihefte bot. Centbl. **57A**:
    156–170.

Capoor, S. P. 1937*b*. The life history of *Holoptelea integrifolia* Planch. Beihefte bot. Centlbl. **57A**: 233–249.

Carlson, E. M., and Stuart, B. C. 1936. Development of spores and gametophytes in certain New World species of *Salvia*. New Phytol. **35**: 68–91.

Castetter, E. F. 1925. Studies on the comparative cytology of the annual and biennial varieties of *Melilotus alba*. Amer. Jour. Bot. **12**: 270–286.

Claussen, P. 1927. Über das Verhalten des Antherentapetums bei einigen Monocotylen und Ranales. Bot. Arch. **18**: 1–27.

Cooper, D. C. 1931. Microsporogenesis in *Bougainvillaea glabra*. Amer. Jour. Bot. **18**: 337–358.

———. 1933. Nuclear divisions in the tapetal cells of certain angiosperms. Amer. Jour. Bot. **20**: 358–364.

Copeland, H. F. 1935. The structure of the flower of *Pholisma arenarium*. Amer. Jour. Bot. **22**: 366–383.

Coulter, J. M., and Chamberlain, C. J. 1903. "Morphology of Angiosperms." New York.

D'Amato, F. 1946. Osservazioni cito-embryologiche su *Cornus mas* L. con particolare riguardo alla sterilità di un biotipo triploide. Nuovo Gior. Bot. Ital. N.S. **53**: 170–210.

Dowding, E. S. 1931. Floral morphology of *Arceuthobium americanum*. Bot. Gaz. **91**: 42–54.

Engler, A. 1876. Beiträge zur Kenntnis der Antherenbildung der Metaspermen. Jahrb. f. wiss. Bot. **10**: 275–316.

Erdtman, G. 1943. "An Introduction to Pollen Analysis." Chronica Botanica Company.

———. 1945. Pollen morphology and plant taxonomy. V. On the occurrence of tetrads and dyads. Svensk Bot. Tidskr. **39**: 286–297.

Ernst-Schwarzenbach, M. 1945. Zur Blütenbiologie einiger Hydrocharitaceen. Ber. schweiz. bot. Gesell. **55**: 33–69.

Eunus, A. M. 1949. Contributions to the embryology of the Liliaceae (*Gloriosa superba*). Proc. 36th Indian Sci. Cong. Allahabad, Bot. Sect. No. 25.

Fagerlind, F. 1938. *Ditepalanthus*, eine neue Balanophoraceen Gattung aus Madagaskar. Arkiv för Bot. **29A**: 1–15.

———. 1945. Blüte und Blütenstand der Gattung *Balanophora*. Bot. Notiser 1945, pp. 330–350.

Farr, C. H. 1916. Cytokinesis of the pollen mother cells of certain dicotyledons. Mem. N. Y. Bot. Gard. **6**: 253–317.

———. 1918. Cell division by furrowing in *Magnolia*. Amer. Jour. Bot. **5**: 379–395.

———. 1922. Quadripartition by furrowing in *Sisyrinchium*. Bul. Torrey Bot. Club **49**: 51–61.

Fedortschuk, W. 1932. Entwicklung und Bau des männlichen Gametophyten bei den Arten der Convolvulaceen-Gattung *Quamoclit*. Planta **16**: 554–574.

Gager, C. S. 1902. The development of the pollinium and sperm cells in *Asclepias cornuti* Decne. Ann. Bot. **16**: 123–148.

Gates, R. R.   1911.   Pollen formation in *Oenothera gigas*.   Ann. Bot. **25**: 909–940.

———.   1925.   Pollen tetrad wall formation in *Lathraea*.   Cellule **35**: 47–60.

——— and Goodwin, K. M.   1930.   A new haploid *Oenothera*, with some considerations on haploidy in plants and animals.   Jour. Genet. **23**: 123–156.

——— and Latter, J.   1927.   Observations on the pollen development of two species of *Lathraea*.   Jour. Roy. Micros. Soc. 1927, pp. 209–224.

——— and Rees, E. M.   1921.   A cytological study of pollen development in *Lactuca*.   Ann. Bot. **16**: 123–148.

Gelin, O. E. V.   1934.   Embryologische und cytologische Studien in Heliantheae-Coreopsidinae.   Acta Horti Bergiani **11**: 99–128.

Goebel, K.   1933.   "Organographie der Pflanzen. III. Samenpflanzen."   3d ed. Jena.

Gorczyński, T.   1934.   Zytologische Analyse einiger Pollenentwicklungs vorgänge bei der Apfelsorte "Schöner von Boskoop."   Acta Soc. Bot. Poloniae **11**: 103–118.

Guérin, P.   1926.   Le développement de l'anthère chez les Gentianacées.   Bul. Soc. Bot. de France **73**: 5–18.

———.   1927.   Le développement de l'anthère et du pollen chez les Liliacées (*Sansevieria, Ophiopogon, Peliosanthes*).   Bul. Soc. Bot. de France **74**: 102–107.

Gupta, B. L.   1935.   Studies in the development of the pollen grain and embryo sac of *Wolffia arrhiza*.   Current Sci. [India] **4**: 104–105.

Islam, A. S.   1950.   The embryology of *Ottelia alismoides* Pers.   Jour. Indian Bot. Soc. **29**: 79–91.

Johnson, D. S.   1910.   Studies in the development of Piperaceae.   I. The suppression and extension of sporogenous tissue in the flower of *Piper betle* L. var. *monoicum* C. DC.   Jour. Expt. Zool. **9**: 715–749.

Johri, B. M.   1934.   The development of the male and female gametophytes in *Cuscuta reflexa* Roxb.   Proc. Indian Acad. Sci. Sect. B. **1**: 233–289.

———.   1935.   Studies in the family Alismaceae.   I. *Limnophyton obtusifolium* Miq.   Jour. Indian Bot. Soc. **14**: 49–66.

———.   1936.   The life history of *Butomopsis lanceolata* Kunth.   Proc. Indian Acad. Sci. Sect. B. **4**: 139–162.

Juel, H. O.   1915.   Untersuchung über die Auflösung der Tapetenzellen in den Pollensäcken der Angiospermen.   Jahrb. f. wiss. Bot. **56**: 337–364.

Juliano, J. B.   1935*a*.   Morphological contribution on the genus *Anona*.   Philippine Agr. **24**: 528–541.

———.   1935*b*.   Morphology of the sweet potato, *Ipomoea batatus* (Linn.) Poir.   Philippine Agr. **23**: 833–858.

———.   1935*c*.   Anatomy and morphology of the Bunga *Aeginetia indica* L.   Philippine Jour. Sci. **56**: 405–451.

——— and Alcala, P. E.   1933.   Floral morphology of *Musa errans* (Blanco) Teodoro var. *Botoan* Teodoro.   Philippine Agr. **22**: 91–126.

——— and Aldama, M. J.   1937.   Morphology of *Oryza sativa* L.   Philippine Agr. **26**: 1–134.

Junell, S. 1931. Die Entwicklungsgeschichte von *Circaeaster agrestis*. Svensk Bot. Tidskr. **25**: 238–270.

Kajale, L. B. 1940. A contribution to the embryology of the Amaranthaceae. Proc. Natl. Inst. Sci. India **6**: 597–625.

Kausik, S. B. 1938. Pollen development and seed formation in *Utricularia coerulea* L. Beihefte bot. Centbl. **58A**: 365–378.

———. 1941. Structure and development of the staminate flower and male gametophyte of *Enalus acoroides* (L. fil) Steud. Proc. Indian Acad. Sci. Sect. B. **14**: 1–16.

——— and Rao, P. V. K. 1942. The male gametophyte of *Halophila ovata* Gaudich. Jour. Mysore Univ. Sect. *B*. **3**: 43–49.

Kosmath, L. 1927. Studien über das Antherentapetum. Österr. bot. Ztschr. **76**: 235–241.

Levan, A. 1941. Syncyte formation in the pollen mother cells of haploid *Phleum pratense*. Hereditas **27**: 243–252.

Locke, J. F. 1936. Microsporogenesis and cytokinesis in *Asimina triloba*. Bot. Gaz. **98**: 159–168.

Maheshwari, P. 1929. Contributions to the morphology of *Boerhaavia diffusa*. I. Jour. Indian Bot. Soc. **8**: 219–234.

———. 1934. Contributions to the morphology of some Indian Liliaceae. I. The gametophytes of *Ophiopogon wallichianus* Hook. f. Proc. Indian Acad. Sci. Sect. B. **1**: 197–204.

——— and Johri, B. M. 1950. The embryology of *Hydrilla verticillata* (in press).

Mascré, M. 1919*a*. Sur le rôle de l'assise nourricière du pollen. Compt. Rend. Acad. des Sci. Paris **168**: 1120–1122.

———. 1919*b*. Nouvelles remarques sur le rôle de l'assise nourricière du pollen. Compt. Rend. Acad. des Sci. Paris **168**: 1214–1216.

Matthews, J. R., and Taylor, G. 1926. The structure and development of the stamen in *Erica hirtiflora*. Trans. and Proc. Bot. Soc. Edinb. **29**: 235–242.

Meyer, K. 1925. Über die Entwicklung des Pollens bei *Leontodon autumnalis* L. Ber. deutsch. bot. Gesell. **43**: 108–114.

Mezzetti-Bambacioni, V. 1941. Ricerche morfologiche sulle Lauraceae. Embriologia della *Umbellularia californica* Nutt. Ann. di Bot. **22**: 99–116.

Moissl, E. 1941. Vergleichende embryologische Studien über die Familie der Caprifoliaceae. Osterr. bot. Ztschr. **90**: 153–212.

Newman, I. V. 1928. The life history of *Doryanthes excelsa*. I. Some ecological and vegetative features and spore production. Proc. Linn. Soc. N. S. Wales **53**: 499–538.

Nietsch, H. 1941. Zur systematischen Stellung von *Cyanastrum*. Osterr. bot. Ztschr. **90**: 31–52.

Nohara, S. 1934. Gametogenesis and embryogeny of *Sesamum indicum* L. Jour. Col. Agr. Tokyo Imp. Univ. **13**: 19–25.

Peters, K. 1908. "Vergleichende Untersuchungen über die Ausbildung der sexuellen Reproduktionsorgane bei *Convolvulus* und *Cuscuta*." Diss. Zürich.

Pisek, A. 1924. Antherenentwicklung und meiotische Teilung bei der Wacholdermistel (*Arceuthobium oxycedri* [D.C.] M.B.); Antherenbau und Chromosomen zahlen von *Loranthus europaeus* Jacq. Sitzber. math., nat. Kl. Akad. der Wiss. Wien 1 **133**: 1–15.

Puri, V. 1941. Life history of *Moringa oleifera* Lamk. Jour. Indian Bot. Soc. **20**: 263–284.

Rauch, K. V. 1936. Cytologische-embryologische Untersuchungen an *Scurrula atropurpurea* Dans. und *Dendrophthoe pentandra* Miq. Ber. schweiz. bot. Gesell. **45**: 5–61.

Reeves, R. G. 1928. Partition wall formation in the pollen mother cells of *Zea mays*. Amer. Jour. Bot. **15**: 114–122.

Rosenberg, O. 1901. Über die Embryologie von *Zostera marina* L. Bihang Till K. Svenska Vet.-Akad. Handl., III, **27**(6): 1–24.

Rutishauser, A. 1935. Entwicklungsgeschichtliche und zytologische Untersuchungen an *Korthalsella dacrydii* (Ridl.) Danser. Ber. schweiz. bot. Gesell. **44**: 389–436.

Samuelsson, G. 1914. Über die Pollenentwicklung von *Anona* und *Aristolochia* und ihre systematische Bedeutung. Svensk Bot. Tidskr. **8**: 181–189.

Schaeppi, H., and Steindl, F. 1942. Blütenmorphologische und embryologische Untersuchungen an Loranthoideen. Vrtljschr. naturf. Gesell. Zürich **87**: 301–372.

——— and ———. 1945. Blütenmorphologische und embryologische Untersuchungen an einigen Viscoideen. Vrtljschr. naturf. Gesell. Zürich **90**: 1–46.

Sharp, L. W. 1943. "Fundamentals of Cytology." McGraw-Hill Book Company.

Singh, Bahadur. 1936. The life history of *Ranunculus sceleratus* Linn. Proc. Indian Acad. Sci. Sect. B. **4**: 75–91.

———. 1950. The embryology of *Dendrophthoe falcata* (Linn. fil.) Ettingshausen. Proc. 37th Indian Sci. Cong. Sect. Bot.

Smith, C. M. 1929. Development of *Dionaea muscipula*. I. Flower and seed. Bot. Gaz. **87**: 507–530.

Städtler, G. 1923. Über Reduktionserscheinungen im Bau der Antherenwand von Angiospermen. Flora **16**: 85–108.

Stenar, H. 1925. "Embryologische Studien. I. Zur Embryologie einiger Columniferen. II. Die Embryologie der Amaryllidaceen." Diss. Uppsala.

Stern, H. 1946. The formation of polynucleated pollen mother cells. Jour. Hered. **37**: 47–50.

Stevenson, G. B. 1934. The life-history of the New Zealand species of the parasitic genus *Korthalsella*. Trans. and Proc. Roy. Soc. New Zeal. **64**: 175–190.

Subramanyam, K. 1948. An embryological study of *Melastoma malabathricum* L. Jour. Indian Bot. Soc. **27**: 1–9.

Swamy, B. G. L. 1946. Embryology of *Habenaria*. Proc. Natl. Inst. Sci. India **12**: 413–426.

———. 1948. Embryological studies in Orchidaceae. I. Gametophytes. Amer. Midland Nat. **41**: 184–201.

Thoday, D., and Johnson, E. T. 1930. On *Arceuthobium pusillum* Peck. II. Flowers and fruit. Ann. Bot. **44**: 813–824.

Tischler, G. 1915. Die Periplasmodienbildung in den Antheren der Commelinaceen und Ausblicke auf das Verhalten der Tapetenzellen bei den übrigen Monocotylen. Jahrb. f. wiss. Bot. **55**: 52–90.

Ubisch, G. V. 1927. Zur Entwicklungsgeschichte der Antheren. Planta **3**: 490–495.

Venkatasubban, K. R. 1945. Cytological studies in Bignoniaceae. The cytology of *Dolichandrone rheedii* Seem. and allied genera. Proc. Indian Acad. Sci. Sect. B. **21**: 77–92.

Vignoli, L. 1936. Cariologia del genre *Agave*. I. Lavori, R. Ist. Bot. Palermo **7**.

———. 1937. Cariologia del genre *Agave*. II. Lavori f. R. Ist. Bot. Palermo **8**.

Warming, E. 1873. Untersuchungen über Pollenbildende Phyllome und Kaulome. Hanstein's Bot. Abhandl. **2**: 1–90.

Witkus, E. R. 1945. Endomitotic tapetal cell divisions in *Spinacia*. Amer. Jour. Bot. **32**: 326–330.

Witmer, S. W. 1937. Morphology and cytology of *Vallisneria*. Amer. Midland Nat. **18**: 309–327.

Wodehouse, R. P. 1936. "Pollen Grains." McGraw-Hill Book Company.

Woodworth, R. H. 1931. Cytomixis. Jour. Arnold Arboretum **12**: 23–25.

Wylie, R. B. 1904. The morphology of *Elodea canadensis*. Bot. Gaz. **37**: 1–22.

CHAPTER 3

THE MEGASPORANGIUM

The megasporangium or ovule consists of the nucellus and one or two integuments. It may have various forms, which sometimes intergrade into one another, and very often the same ovule changes its form during the course of its development. Mature ovules are usually classed under five types. In the orthotropous or atropous type the micropyle lies directly in line with the hilum and above it (Fig. 37A) as in Polygonaceae, Urticaceae, Cistaceae and Piperaceae. In the anatropous type the body of the ovule becomes completely inverted so that the micropyle and hilum come to lie very close to each other (Fig. 37B). This form is universal in almost all members of the Sympetalae and is also found in several other families belonging to both dicotyledons and monocotyledons. When the ovule is curved, as in some of the Resedaceae and Leguminosae, it is called campylotropous (Fig. 37C); when the curvature is more pronounced and also affects the embryo sac, so that the latter becomes bent like a horseshoe, as in the Alismaceae, Butomaceae, and Centrospermales, the ovule is called amphitropous (Fig. 37E); and when the nucellus and integuments lie more or less at right angles to the funiculus as in *Ranunculus*, *Nothoscordum*, and *Tulbaghia*, it is called hemianatropous or hemitropous (Fig. 37D). Ovules may also be designated as epitropous, apotropous, or pleurotropous, according as the inversion or bending is directed towards the top, bottom, or sides of the ovary.

A very peculiar type of ovule is seen in some members of the Plumbaginaceae (Fig. 38). Here the nucellar protuberance is at first in the same line as the axis, but the rapid growth on one side causes it to become anatropous. The curvature does not stop but continues until the ovule has turned over completely so that the micropylar end again points upwards. It has been suggested that this kind of ovule, also seen in *Opuntia* (Fig. 39), is distinctive enough to merit a separate name, circinotropous (Archibald, 1939).

54

Integuments. Ordinarily the ovule has either one or two integuments. The number is constant in most families, and only in rare cases do unitegmic and bitegmic ovules occur in the same family. In the Sympetalae a single massive integument is almost universal,

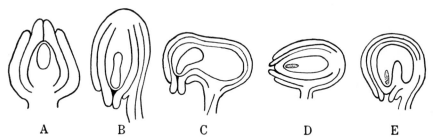

FIG. 37. Types of ovules as seen in vertical longitudinal section. *A*, atropous or orthotropous. *B*, anatropous. *C*, campylotropous. *D*, hemianatropous. *E*, amphitropous. (*After Prantl.*)

the Plumbaginales and Primulales being the only important exceptions. In the Archichlamydeae and the monocotyledons most genera have two integuments but a few have only one. There is evidence that in many cases the single integument has originated

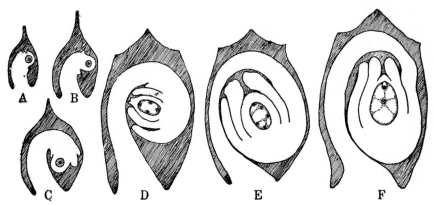

FIG. 38. Development of ovule of *Plumbago capensis*. (*After Haupt, 1934.*)

by a fusion of two separate primordia. Transitional types have been observed in some members of the Ranunculaceae, Rosaceae, Connaraceae, and Icacinaceae.

The unitegmic condition may also arise by an elimination of one

of the two integuments.   In *Cytinus*, a member of the Rafflesia-ceae, the outer integument is arrested in its development.   In the Salicaceae (see Schnarf, 1929) *Populus tremula* has a single integument, while *P. canadensis* and *P. candicans* also possess a weakly developed inner integument which is apparently on its way to extinction.   In the Icacinaceae (Fagerlind, 1945c) *Gomphandra* and *Gonocaryum* are unitegmic but *Phytocrene* shows two primordia.
   In some plants there is also a third integument or aril.[1]   In *Ulmus*

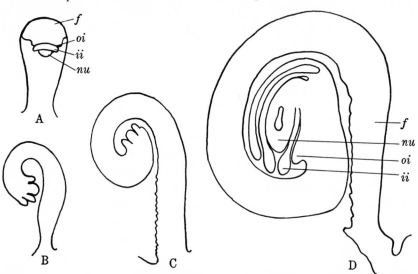

FIG. 39.   Development of ovule of *Opuntia aurantiaca*.   *A*, front view of young ovule.   *B–D*, longitudinal sections of progressively older ovules (*nu* = nucellus; *ii* = inner integument; *oi* = outer integument; *f* = funiculus).   (*After Archibald, 1939.*)

(Shattuck, 1905) it is said to originate by the splitting of the outer integument, but in most other cases it is a new structure arising from the base of the ovule.   Good examples of this kind are seen in *Asphodelus* (Fig. 40*A,B*) and *Trianthema* (Fig. 40*C*).   Of a different origin is the "caruncle," found in several members of the Euphorbiaceae, which arises by a proliferation of the integumentary cells at the micropylar region (Landes, 1946).   Sometimes this prolifera-

---

[1] In *Canangium, Mezzettia,* and *Xylopia* Corner (1949) records the presence of a "middle integument" arising between the outer and inner integuments.   In *Canangium* and *Xylopia,* which also have an aril, the middle integument becomes the fourth integument of the seed.

tion becomes more pronounced and takes the form of a backwardly
directed process (Fig. 40D–G) which resembles an aril in later
stages. A very peculiar condition occurs in *Opuntia* (Archibald,
1939), where the extremely long funiculus completely surrounds the
ovule and looks like a third integument (Fig. 39).

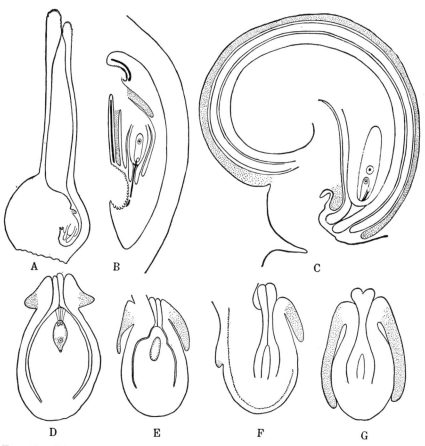

Fig. 40. Diagrams of ovules showing origin of aril or third integument (*A–C*) and
caruncle (*D–G*). *A,B, Asphodelus fistulosus. (After Stenar, 1928.) C, Trianthema monogyna. (After Bhargava, 1935.) D, Brachychilum horsfieldii. (After
Mauritzon, 1936.) E, Burbidgea schizocheila. (After Mauritzon, 1936.) F,G,
Careya arborea. (After Mauritzon, 1939.)*

Whatever may be the condition of the integuments in the younger
stages, they often present a very different and a more complicated
aspect in the mature seed. Frequently several layers of cells are

completely absorbed and do not take any part in the formation of the seed coat. In the Umbelliferae only two or three of the outer layers persist at maturity; in the Compositae most of the cells disappear, leaving only a thin layer of crushed and disorganized tissue; and in *Circaeaster* (Junell, 1931), *Thesium* (Rutishauser, 1937), and *Zea* (Randolph, 1936) practically nothing remains of the seed coat. In *Symplocarpus* (Rosendahl, 1909) both integuments and endosperm are consumed so that the embryo lies naked inside the ovary wall. So variable is the nature of the cell layers surrounding the embryo that only a thorough study of the developmental stages can reveal their true nature.

Mention must be made of a few records of the occurrence of chlorophyll in the integuments. Hofmeister (1861) observed this in *Brunsvigia minor* and *Amaryllis belladonna*, and Treub (1879) in *Sobralia micrantha*. Later, Berg (1898) and Puri (1941) reported the presence of chlorophyll in the outer integument and a portion of the chalaza in *Gladiolus communis*, *Lilium martagon*, and *Moringa oleifera*. Schlimbach (1924) observed the presence of stomata on the outer integument of *Nerine curvifolia*, and Flint and Moreland (1943) have described the occurrence of an elaborate chlorophyllous tissue with stomata in *Hymenocallis occidentalis*. Stomata have also been found on the outer integument of *Gossypium*, but they are believed to be concerned with respiration rather than transpiration or photosynthesis (Seshadri Ayyangar, 1948).[1a]

Micropyle. When two integuments are present, the micropyle may be formed either by the inner integument as in the Centrospermales and Plumbaginales (Fig. 38) or by both inner and outer integuments as in the Pontederiaceae (Fig. 142). Less frequently, as in the Podostemonaceae, Rhamnaceae, and Euphorbiaceae, it may be formed by the outer integument alone (Fig. 67A). When both the integuments take part in the formation of the micropyle, the passage formed by the outer integument (exostome) may not be in line with that formed by the inner integument (endostome) so that the micropylar canal has a somewhat zigzag outline. Good examples of this kind are seen in the Resedaceae (Oksijuk, 1937) and in some members of the Melastomaceae (Subramanyam, 1948). In *Leitneria* (Pfeiffer, 1912) and *Malpighia* (Subba Rao, 1941) there

[1a] See Boursnell (1950) on the occurrence of a fungus in the funiculus and outer integument of *Helianthemum chamaecistus*.

is an excessive development of the upper portion of the integuments so that the micropylar canal lies in folds over the nucellus. Rarely, as in *Ficus* (Condit, 1932), *Fouquieria* (Khan, 1943), and *Cynomorium* (Steindl, 1945), the integumentary cells come in such intimate contact with each other that the micropylar canal is extremely narrow and imperceptible.

Nucellus.[1b] Depending on the extent of development of the nucellus, ovules are called crassinucellate or tenuinucellate.[2] In the first type, there is a well-developed parietal tissue and the megaspore mother cell is separated from the nucellar epidermis by one or several layers of cells. In the second type, parietal cells are absent and the megaspore mother cell lies directly below the nucellar epidermis.[3]

In the crassinucellate forms the nucellus may enlarge either by an increase in the number of the parietal cells or by periclinal divisions of the nucellar epidermis. In some plants like *Zizyphus* (Kajale, 1944) and *Quisqualis* (Fagerlind, 1941) (Fig. 41) both these processes take place simultaneously.

Several members of the Salicaceae, Nyctaginaceae, Euphorbiaceae, Polygonaceae, and Cucurbitaceae are characterized by having a beak-shaped nucellus which reaches out into the micropyle. In one species, *Polygonum persicaria* (Souèges, 1919), the beak forms a very conspicuous structure protruding upward to the base of the style (Fig. 42).

The tenuinucellate forms are of two kinds: (1) those in which the nucellus is short and the primordia of the integument or integu-

[1b] For more detailed information on the nucellus, see Dahlgren (1927).

[2] It should be noted that the above distinction between crassinucellate and tenuinucellate ovules, although convenient and useful, is not always sharp and clear-cut and there are various intergradations between them. Further, both types may sometimes occur in one and the same species. To mention only two examples, in *Butomus* (Holmgren, 1913) and *Ophiopogon* (Maheshwari, 1934) in some ovules the megaspore mother cell is situated directly below the nucellar epidermis while in others it is separated from the latter by a wall cell.

[3] Even in those plants in which the ovules are usually tenuinucellate and devoid of parietal cells, some of the cells of the nucellar epidermis may undergo one or two periclinal divisions. Svensson (1925) and Dahlgren (1927) have figured this in *Helioptropium* and *Cobaea*. Here the epidermal cells just above the megaspore tetrad undergo a radial elongation followed by a periclinal division which may give the false impression of the cutting off of parietal cells.

ments arise near its apex (Fig. 43*B*), and (2) those in which the nucellus is elongated and the integuments arise near its base (Fig. 43*A*). The Asclepiadaceae, Orobanchaceae, and Rubiaceae are good examples of the first condition, and the Orchidaceae of the second.

As the embryo sac matures, the nucellar cells gradually become

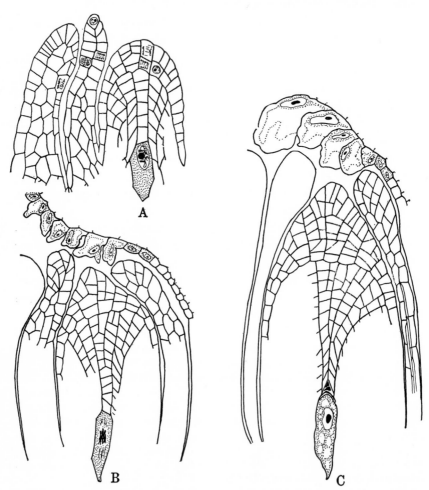

FIG. 41. L.s. ovules of *Quisqualis indica* showing progressively increasing amount of parietal tissue, arising partly by divisions of the wall layers and partly by divisions of cells of nucellar epidermis. *A,B,* megaspore mother cell stage. *C,* functioning megaspore stage. In *B* and *C,* note enlarging cells of obturator. (*After Fagerlind, 1941.*)

used up.[4]   In the tenuinucellate forms this takes place at such an early stage (even before fertilization) that some workers have misinterpreted the integument as the nucellus.   Schleiden (1837) wrote long ago that in the Rubiaceae the ovules are naked.   Lloyd (1902) demonstrated the presence of an integument in all the genera studied by him excepting *Houstonia.*   Owing to its narrow and incon-

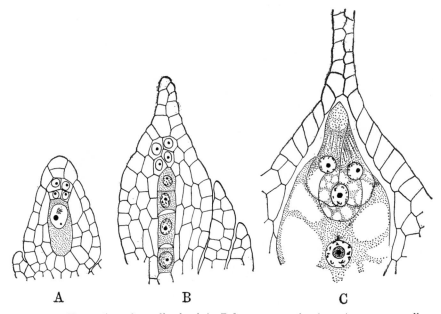

A   B   C

FIG. 42.   Formation of nucellar beak in *Polygonum persicaria.*   *A*, young nucellus, showing megaspore mother cell and four wall cells; note periclinal division of a cell of the nucellar epidermis.   *B*, older stage, showing megaspore tetrad, wall cells, and nucellar beak.   *C*, mature embryo sac with part of nucellar beak; wall cells have degenerated and disappeared.   (*After Souèges, 1919.*)

spicuous micropyle, Schleiden mistook the integument for the nucellus, while the latter escaped his notice altogether.   More recently, Fagerlind (1937) has shown that even in *Houstonia* an integument is present as usual and it is really the nucellus which is on its way to extinction.   He presents a series of stages to show how this condition has been derived (Fig. 44).   In *Phyllis,* which is at the begin-

[4] It is only in a few families like the Piperaceae and Scitamineae that the nucellus persists in the seed; it is then known as the perisperm.

ning of the series, the nucellus comprises a single layer of cells (the epidermis) surrounding the archesporium (Fig. 44*A*). This is in accordance with the general condition in the Sympetalae.   In *Bouvardia* and *Vaillantia*, which represent the next stage, the nucellar epidermis is reduced to a few cells lying immediately above the sporogenous tissue (Fig. 44*B,C*).   In *Rubia olivieri* there is further

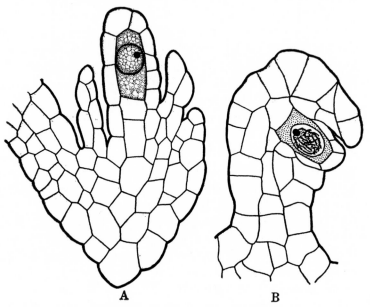

A   B

FIG. 43.   Young ovules of *Orchis maculatus* (*A*) and *Aeginetia indica* (*B*).   Note that in *Orchis* the integuments arise near base of megaspore mother cell, while in *Aeginetia* the single integument arises near apical end of nucellus.   (*A, after Hagerup, 1944; B, after Juliano, 1935.*)

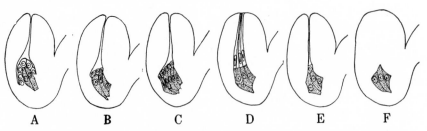

A   B   C   D   E   F

FIG. 44.   Diagram illustrating different types of nucelli found in the Rubiaceae. *A, Phyllis. B, Bouvardia. C, Vaillantia. D, Rubia. E, Oldenlandia. F, Houstonia. (After Fagerlind, 1937.*)

reduction in their number, although this is accompanied by a pronounced radial elongation of the walls (Fig. 44D). In *Oldenlandia* the nucellar epidermis is represented by one or two cells only (Fig. 44E), and in *Houstonia*, which is the last member of the series, there is no distinguishable epidermis and the ovule consists of only the sporogenous cells and the integument (Fig. 44F).

Fagerlind's series is so clear and convincing that there is no longer any doubt about the true relationships of the nucellus and integument in the Rubiaceae. Houk's (1938) statement that in *Coffea* there is no distinction between the tissues of the integument and nucellus is therefore incorrect (see also Mendes, 1941).

Woodcock's (1943) report that in *Ipomoea* the ovule has no distinct integument and the micropyle is formed by an "invagination" is also due to a misinterpretation. As in other members of the Convolvulaceae (see Maheshwari, 1944), an integument is present and it is the nucellus which soon disappears. The micropyle is not an invagination but a continuous passage, which begins to be more or less occluded in postfertilization stages and is therefore difficult to demonstrate in nonmedian sections.

Formerly the Olacaceae were also believed to have naked ovules. A recent study by Fagerlind (1947) has shown that an integument is present as usual but the nucellus is extremely reduced and ephemeral and is represented by only a few epidermal cells lying just above the megaspore mother cell.

A complete absence of the integuments is known only in some members of the Loranthaceae and Balanophoraceae, but it seems probable that this is a derived condition. Fagerlind (1945d) has given a series of illustrations showing the stages by which this may have been brought about (Fig. 45). The case of *Crinum* (Amaryllidaceae), in which the nucellus is ephemeral and the integuments are said to be absent (Tomita, 1931), deserves further study.

Integumentary Tapetum. In those plants in which the nucellus is soon disorganized, the embryo sac comes in direct contact with the inner layer of the seed coat. The cells of this layer frequently become specially differentiated from the rest by their form and contents (Fig. 46). They show a pronounced radial elongation and sometimes become binucleate. Owing to these similarities with the cells of the anther tapetum, this layer of cells is known as the integumentary tapetum or endothelium.

There seems to be no doubt that the endothelium is a nutritive layer whose chief function is to serve as an intermediary for the transport of food materials from the integument to the embryo sac.

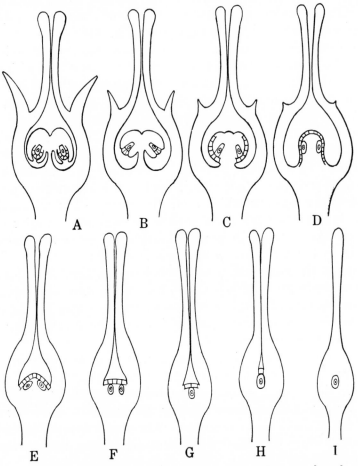

FIG. 45.   Diagram illustrating derivation of the female flower and ovule of *Balanophora*. *A*, l.s. hypothetical ovary showing two ovules. *B*, ovary of *Thesium*. *C*, ovary, as in *Osyris*, *Santalum* and *Myzodendron*. *D*, as in *Arceuthobium* and *Helosis*. *E*, as in *Korthalsella*. *F*, as in *Viscum* and *Dendrophthoe*. *G,H*, as in *Scurrula*. *I*, as in *Balanophora*. (*After Fagerlind, 1945d*.)

Some writers also claim that it contains diastase and other enzymes which convert the food into a suitable form for the use of the embryo sac. In later stages, when the embryo is approaching maturity, the inner surface of the endothelium becomes cutinized and this layer seems to take up a protective instead of a nutritive function.

Hypostase.[5] Just at the level of origin of the two integuments and directly below the embryo sac, there is often a well-defined but

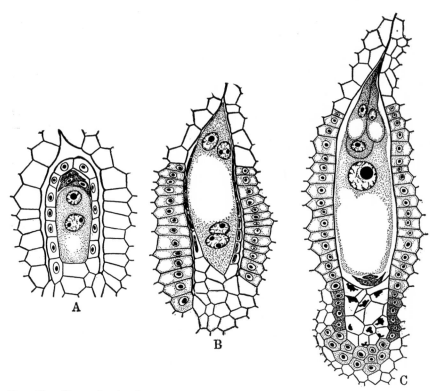

Fig. 46. Stages in the formation of integumentary tapetum in *Lobelia trigona*. *A*, two-nucleate embryo sac with remains of degenerating megaspores; nucellar epidermis still intact. *B*, Four-nucleate embryo sac, showing degeneration of nucellar epidermis and formation of integumentary tapetum from inner layer of integument. *C*, mature embryo sac bounded by cells of integumentary tapetum. (*After Kausik, 1935.*)

irregularly outlined group of nucellar cells which are usually poor in cytoplasmic contents but have partially lignified or suberized walls composed of a highly refractive material. Van Tieghem (1901),

[5] Dahlgren (1940) has reviewed the literature on the occurrence of the hypostase in angiosperms and also recommended some changes of terminology. Reference should be made to this paper for fuller information on the subject.

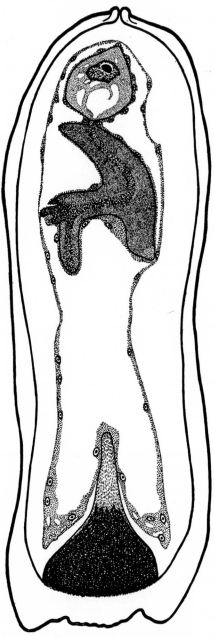

FIG. 47. *Zostera marina*, l.s. young seed, showing prominent hypostase and well-developed embryo. (*After Dahlgren, 1939.*)

who first called attention to this patch of cells, gave it the name hypostase, and believed that it formed a sort of barrier or boundary for the growing embryo sac and prevented it from pushing into the base of the ovule. Goebel (1933) says, however, that the peculiar position of this tissue—directly above the termination of the vascular supply of the ovule—is indicative of its relation to the water economy of the embryo sac. While the function of the hypostase is still in doubt, morphologically it is a very characteristic feature of certain families and genera. *Zostera* (Dahlgren, 1939) offers an especially good instance of a well-developed hypostase (Fig. 47). The hypostase may not always consist of thick-walled cells. In *Knautia* (Lavialle, 1925) it comprises a group of small thin-walled cells having a number of schizogenous cavities which branch and anastomose and become filled with a yellowish substance, which also spreads into the antipodal cells and other adjacent tissue. In *Dionaea* (Smith, 1929) some of the thin-walled cells in the chalaza become disorganized and replaced by airspaces. In *Allium odorum* (Haberlandt, 1923) the cells become richly protoplasmic and the hypostase has an appearance similar to that of the epithem of many hydathodes. Haberlandt considers it to be a sort of glandular tissue secreting some hormone or enzyme required for the growth of the embryo sac.

Epistase. Van Tieghem also reported the occasional presence of a similar well-marked tissue in the micropylar part of the ovule and called it the epistase. Usually it originates from the apical cells of the nucellar epidermis, which show a marked radial elongation and become somewhat thickened or suberized. Occasionally the cells undergo one or more periclinal divisions to form the so-called nucellar cap, which persists as a hood over the apex of the embryo sac even after the cells at the sides have disorganized and disappeared.[6] In *Castalia* (Cook, 1906) the epidermal cells lying at the apex of the embryo sac show "a very pronounced sclerification," and in *Costus* (Boehm, 1931) the inner tangential walls of these cells become conspicuously thickened. In *Nicolaia* (Boehm, 1931) the walls surrounding the megaspore tetrad become cutinized and form a firm covering, which becomes ruptured and separated into two parts only with the continued enlargement of the embryo sac. The thickenings at the micropylar end disappear but are seen once again at the time of organization of the mature embryo sac.

In some plants the apical cells of the integuments give rise to a proliferation usually called the "operculum." To mention a few examples, in *Lemna* (Caldwell, 1899) the cells forming the micropylar portion of the two integuments enlarge and divide to form a compact tissue lying just above the nucellus (Fig. 48). In *Dionaea* (Smith, 1929) a similar tissue is formed by the cells of the inner integument. In *Acorus* (Buell, 1935) the cells become elongated and coiled around one another, so as to form a plug in the lower part of the micropyle.

Vascular Supply of Ovule. As a rule the vascular bundle entering the ovule terminates at the chalaza but in some plants it gives out branches, a few of which enter the integument. If two integuments are present, the branches may enter only the outer integument or both the outer and the inner integuments. Since integumentary vascular bundles are common in gymnosperms, their presence is usually considered to be a primitive feature and the loss of the con-

[6] Dahlgren (1940) designates a persistent nucellar cap of this kind by the name "petasus."

ducting tissue to be an advanced one.   There is, however, no definite evidence in favor of this view.   Integumentary vascular bundles are now known to occur in a number of families, both primitive
(Betulaceae, Euphorbiaceae, Ranunculaceae, and Berberidaceae)
and specialized (Moringaceae, Leguminosae, Punicaceae, Rhamnaceae, Convolvulaceae, Cuscutaceae, Boraginaceae, Caprifoliaceae,
Compositae, and Cyanastraceae).   In *Zizyphus* (Kajale, 1944) the
vascular strands extend far up into the tip of the outer integument.
In the large succulent seeds of *Hymenocallis occidentalis* (Whitehead

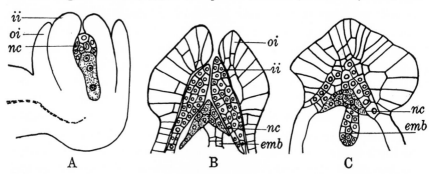

Fig. 48.   Development of "operculum" in *Lemna minor*.   *A*, ovule showing two
integuments, *oi* and *ii*, nucellar cap *nc*, and young embryo sac.   *B*, upper part of
ovule showing portion of embryo *emb*, nucellar cap, and two integuments; note
enlargement of cells of outer integument.   *C*, embryo, nucellus, and thickened tips
of integuments which form the so-called "operculum."   (*After Caldwell, 1899.*)

and Brown, 1940) four bundles enter the ovule and during their
upward course they freely branch and anastomose so that a cross
section of a large seed shows from 14 to 18 bundles in the seed coat.
The inner integument of *Croton* (Landes, 1946) shows a network of
tracheids which remain conspicuous even after the other cells of the
integument have become flattened and crushed.

The occurrence of vascular elements in the nucellus is much rarer.
Benson (1894), Frye (1902), and Benson, Sanday, and Berridge
(1906) identified some nucellar tracheids in *Castanea*, *Asclepias*,
and *Carpinus* respectively, but they showed no connection with the
vascular bundle of the funiculus.   Guérin (1915) described the occurrence of connecting nucellar tracheids in some genera of the
Thymelaeaceae,[7] and Orr (1921*a*, *b*) reported the same in a few members of the Capparidaceae and Resedaceae.

[7] According to Mauritzon (1939) all statements of the occurrence of xylem ele-

Among recent records, in *Agave* (Grove, 1941) and *Strombosia* (Fagerlind, 1947), the vascular strand of the ovule is said to penetrate into the nucellus up to the base of the embryo sac, and in *Magnolia* (Earle, 1938) it gives out short branches in the chalaza, one of which is directed towards the embryo sac. In *Acalypha* (Landes, 1946) the main bundle of the ovule proceeds up to the hypostase and forms a number of short branches whose ultimate ramifications extend into the nucellus up to a distance about one-fifth of the length of the ovule. More striking still is the condition recently reported in *Casuarina* (Swamy, 1948), where the funicular strand extends up to the base of the sporogenous tissue, some of whose cells elongate and themselves assume a conducting function instead of giving rise to embryo sacs (Fig. 51).

The occurrence of vascular elements in the nucellus is of considerable theoretical importance, as such a condition has been considered by some authors to be a relic of the highly developed "tracheidal envelope" found in some fossil gymnosperms. A few years ago integumentary vascular bundles were considered to be very uncommon in angiosperms, but now they are known to occur in several families. Possibly the occurrence of xylem elements in the nucellus may also be found to be more frequent than the few reports just mentioned may seem to indicate.

Archesporium. The archesporial tissue is of hypodermal origin. In general, one cell of the nucellus, situated directly below the epidermis, becomes more conspicuous than the others owing to its larger size, denser cytoplasm, and more prominent nucleus. This is the primary archesporial cell. Frequently the cells situated below it lie in a row so that the archesporial cell appears as the terminal member of a series of nucellar cells (Fig. 43*A*).

The archesporial cell may divide to form a primary parietal cell and a primary sporogenous cell (Fig. 49*A–B*), or it may function directly as the megaspore mother cell (Fig. 50*H*). The primary parietal cell may remain undivided or it may undergo periclinal and anticlinal divisions to form a variable number of wall layers. The

ments in the nucellus or inner integument of the Thymelaeaceae are due to misinterpretations. In his opinion these tracheids really belong to the chalazal tissue which, by "vigorous growth," extends around the endosperm and thus forms a part of the seed coat. Fuchs (1938) and Kausik (1940) also failed to observe any nucellar tracheids in the species studied by them.

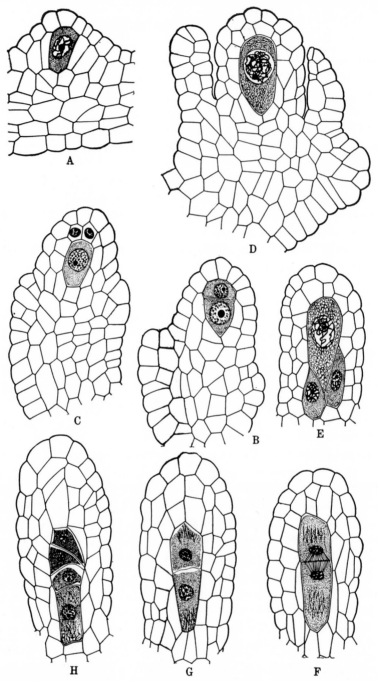

ғɪɢ. 49. *Hydrilla verticillata*, formation of megaspores. *A*, hypodermal arche-sporial cell. *B*, cutting off of primary parietal cell. *C*, anticlinal division of pri-mary parietal cell. *D*, ovule at megaspore mother cell stage. *E*, megaspore mother cell in prophase of Meiosis I; two other cells of the nucellus lying below it simulate sporogenous cells. *F,G*, first division of megaspore mother cell resulting in formation of dyad cells. *H*, tetrad of megaspores.

primary sporogenous cell usually functions as the megaspore mother cell without undergoing any further divisions.

The outline presented above is subject to many variations. In some plants the archesporial cell is said to originate from the third layer of cells in the nucellus, but this is probably a misinterpretation caused by the difficulty in distinguishing the archesporial cell at an earlier stage of development. Sometimes, as in the Onagraceae (Khan, 1942), the archesporium may comprise a small group of half a dozen cells or more (Fig. 50E). Of these usually the central cell alone is functional, but frequently one or two of the other cells also reach the megaspore mother cell stage. In the Malvaceae (Stenar, 1925) the primary sporogenous cell divides to form a few accessory cells in addition to the functional megaspore mother cell. In some members of the Rubiaceae and Compositae there are several sporogenous cells, all of which may go through the meiotic divisions (Fig. 50B–C). In *Scurrula* (Rauch, 1936) and *Dendrophthoe* (Singh, 1950), which have a very massive archesporium, the sporogenous cells undergo further division to give rise to a still larger number of cells. These begin to elongate very actively and become so closely interlocked that the whole tissue gives an appearance suggestive of the hymenial layer of an ascomycete.

In *Hydrilla* there are sometimes two or three archesporial cells in a single row (Fig. 50A). In *Ruppia* (Murbeck, 1902), *Butomus* (Holmgren, 1913), and *Urginea* (Capoor, 1937) the primary parietal cell may also assume a sporogenous function so that two megaspore tetrads are formed in the same row (Fig. 52D). In *Oncidium praetextum* (Afzelius, 1916) a cell of the nucellar epidermis may function as a megaspore mother cell (Fig. 50F), and in *Solanum* (Bhaduri, 1932) and *Limnanthes* (Fagerlind, 1939) some of the integumentary cells may behave similarly (Fig. 50D,G).

In the Sympetalae a parietal cell is absent, the only important exceptions being the Plumbaginales and some members of the family Convolvulaceae. Since this is also the condition in some other advanced families like the Umbelliferae and Orchidaceae, the presence of a massive parietal tissue is regarded as a primitive feature and its absence as advanced. An objection to this view is that parietal cells are often absent even in some admittedly primitive families like the Ranunculaceae (Häfliger, 1943).

In the Casuarinaceae (Fig. 51), and some other families (see

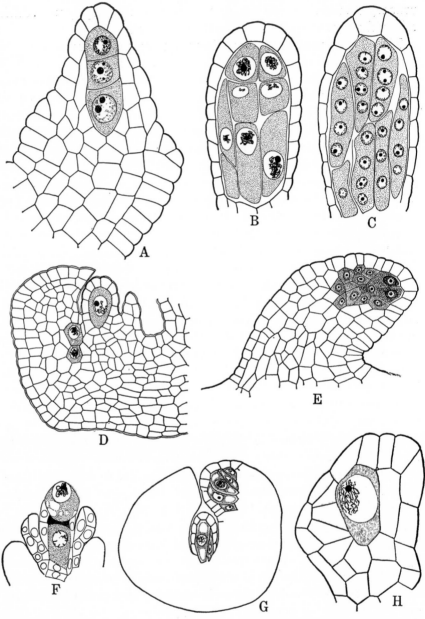

FIG. 50. Variations in origin and extent of sporogenous tissue in ovule. *A,*
Hydrilla verticillata, young ovule, showing a row of three sporogenous cells. *B,*
Achillea millefolium, nucellus, showing a number of megaspore mother cells in

Schnarf, 1929) there is a multicellular archesporium and also an extensive parietal tissue. In some members of the Rosaceae the cells of the nucellar epidermis also divide periclinally and thus add to the wall tissue (see also page 60).

Megasporogenesis. The megaspore mother cell undergoes the usual meiotic divisions to form a tetrad of four cells. The first division is always transverse and gives rise to two dyad cells (Fig. 49*F–G*). Typically the second division is also transverse and results in a linear tetrad of four megaspores (Fig. 52*A*). Frequently the micropylar dyad cell divides in a plane at right angles to that of the chalazal dyad cell. This results in a T-shaped tetrad in which the two outer megaspores lie in contact with the third megaspore which separates them both from the chalazal megaspore (Fig. 52*B*). Since both linear and T-shaped tetrads may occur in ovules of one and the same ovary, it is unnecessary to give specific examples. Tetrads of an intermediate type (Fig. 49*H*), in which the wall separating the two micropylar megaspores lies at an angle of approximately 45° with respect to the chalazal megaspores, are also not infrequent.

Rarely, the two upper megaspores of a tetrad lie in a line parallel to the long axis of the ovule but the lower two lie at right angles to it. Such ⊥-shaped tetrads are sometimes found in the Onagraceae and have been reported in *Zauschneria* (Johansen, 1931*a*), *Anogra* (Johansen, 1931*b*), and *Ludwigia* (Maheshwari and Gupta, 1934).[8] Among other examples of a similar kind may be cited *Drimiopsis* (Baranow, 1926), *Tacca* (Paetow, 1931), *Styrax* (Cope-

---

[8] The occurrence of ⊥-shaped tetrads in the Onagraceae is probably related to the fact that here the micropylar megaspore gives rise to the embryo sac, while the three chalazal megaspores are nonfunctional (see Chap. 4).

---

prophase. (*After Dahlgren, 1927.*) *C, Chrysanthemum corymbosum*, nucellus, showing megaspore mother cells each with four megaspore nuclei; one cell at the bottom has lagged behind. (*After Dahlgren, 1927.*) *D, Solanum melongena*, ovule showing hypodermal megaspore mother cell and two other such cells in the tissues of the integument. (*After Bhaduri, 1932.*) *E, Jussieua repens*, nucellus, showing multicellular archesporium. (*After Khan, 1942.*) *F, Oncidium praetextum*, ovule, showing supernumerary archesporial cell arising from the nucellar epidermis. (*After Afzelius, 1916.*) *G, Limnanthes douglasii*, normal archesporial cells in nucellus and supernumerary archesporial cell in integument. (*After Fagerlind, 1939.*) *H, Machaerocarpus californicus*, megaspore mother cell in prophase. (*After Maheshwari and Singh, 1943.*)

land, 1938), *Cyathula* (Kajale, 1940), *Costus* (Banerji, 1940), and *Desmodium* (Pantulu, 1941).

An isobilateral or a tetrahedral arrangement of megaspores is very rare and has been reported only as an abnormality (Fig. 52C).

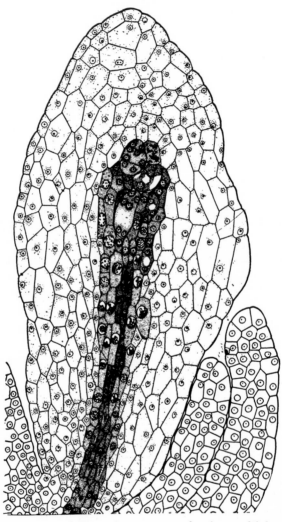

Fig. 51. Part of ovule of *Casuarina montana*, showing multiple archesporium. Some of the sporogenous cells are in prophase; others have gone through meiotic divisions to form megaspore tetrads; and a few have formed two- and four-nucleate embryo sacs. Note that in tetrad at upper end, all megaspores are binucleate. (*After Swamy, 1948.*)

The genus *Musa* is of special interest, for here tetrads of four different kinds—linear, T-shaped, ⊥-shaped and isobilateral—may occur in the same species (Dodds, 1945). Tetrads of very variable appearances have also been described in *Poa alpina* (Håkansson, 1943).

Frequently a row of only three cells is seen in place of the usual four. This is due to an omission of the second meiotic division in one of the two dyad cells, usually the upper.[9] All intermediate stages leading towards this condition have been seen. In some plants the division in the upper dyad cell merely lags behind that

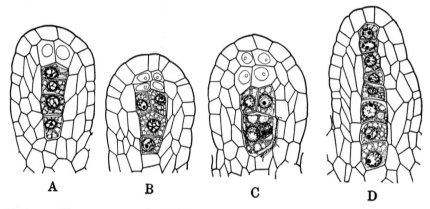

A   **B**   **C**   **D**

FIG. 52. Megaspore tetrads in *Urginea indica*. *A*, linear tetrad. *B*, T-shaped tetrad. *C*, tetrad showing decussate arrangement of megaspores. *D*, two tetrads lying in same row. (*After Capoor, 1937*.)

in the lower dyad cell, and all four cells are formed as usual; in others the nucleus divides normally, but a separating wall is not laid down; in still others the division is abortive and merely gives rise to two degenerating clumps of chromosomes; and in a few cases the nucleus degenerates without undergoing any division.

Functioning Megaspore. Normally it is the chalazal megaspore of the tetrad which functions and gives rise to the embryo sac, while the remaining three megaspores degenerate and disappear. But

[9] It is to be noted that sometimes one gets a false impression of the occurrence of a row of three cells either because of the plane of the section or because of the orientation of the wall between the two upper megaspores so that one of the cells lies superposed over the other. In such cases more careful focusing, or a study of the adjacent section, reveals the presence of the fourth megaspore (see Graves, 1908).

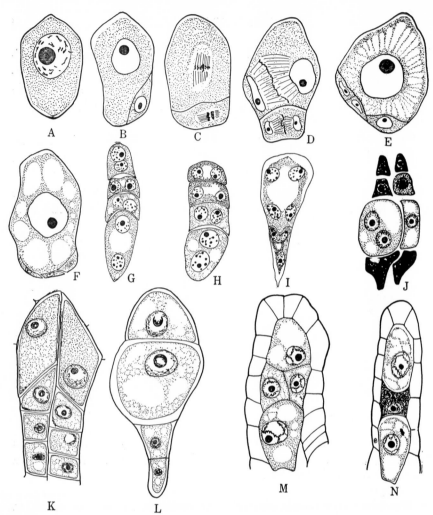

F<small>IG</small>. 53. Formation of megaspore tetrads in various angiosperms. *A, Balano-phora elongata*, megaspore mother cell. *B*, dyad stage; lower dyad cell is much smaller than upper. *C,D*, both dyad cells dividing. *E,F*, tetrad stage; note that uppermost megaspore functions, while the other three degenerate and disappear. (*After Fagerlind, 1945b.*) *G,H, Gloriosa virescens*, megaspore tetrads in which every cell is binucleate. *I*, one of the megaspores has developed to four-nucleate stage and another to two-nucleate. (*After Afzelius, 1916.*) *J, Aristotelia racemosa*, two tetrads with third megaspore functioning. (*After Mauritzon, 1934.*) *K, Rosa*, two tetrads with micropylar megaspores functioning. *L*, same, megaspore tetrad with both micropylar and submicropylar megaspores enlarging. (*After Hurst, 1931.*) *M, Senecio abrotanifolius*, megaspore tetrad, showing two middle mega-spores lying side by side. (*After Afzelius, 1924.*) *N, Culcitium reflexum*, mega-spore tetrad, showing micropylar as well as chalazal megaspore enlarging. (*After Afzelius, 1924.*)

in *Elytranthe* (Schaeppi and Steindl, 1942), *Langsdorffia* (Fagerlind, 1945*a*), and *Balanophora* (Fagerlind, 1945*b*) (Fig. 53 *A–F*) the micropylar megaspore gives rise to the embryo sac and the other three soon degenerate. A similar condition occurs in the Onagraceae and in a few members of the Compositae, although here it is not unusual to find both the terminal megaspores, micropylar and chalazal, growing concurrently (Fig. 53*M,N*). In *Rosa* (Hurst, 1931)

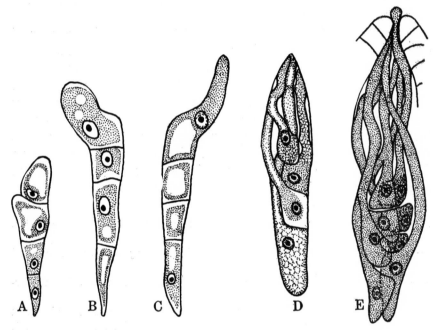

Fig. 54. Formation of megaspore haustoria in *Galium lucidum (A–C)*, *Sedum sempervivoides (D)*, and *Rosularia pallida (E)*. (*A–C* after *Fagerlind, 1937; D–E after Mauritzon, 1933.*)

it is usually the micropylar megaspore which functions (Fig. 53*K*) but sometimes it is the second (Fig. 53*L*). In *Aristotelia* (Mauritzon, 1934), belonging to the Elaeocarpaceae, it is the third megaspore from the micropylar end which gives rise to the embryo sac (Fig. 53*J*). Rarely, as in *Gloriosa* (Afzelius, 1918; Eunus, 1949) (Fig. 53*G–I*), *Ostrya* (Finn, 1936), *Poa* (Håkansson, 1943), and *Casuarina* (Swamy, 1948) (Fig. 51) all or any of the four megaspores may begin to enlarge and divide. A peculiar condition occurs in *Rosularia*, *Sedum* (Mauritzon, 1933), *Laurus* (Bambacioni-Mezzetti,

1935), *Potentilla* (Rutishauser, 1945), and some members of the Rubiaceae (Fagerlind, 1937), in which the megaspores give out lateral tubes which subsequently begin to grow upward and are in a state of competition with one another (Fig. 54). In *Putoria* and *Galium* the tubes enter the tissues of the integument. In *Rosularia* two to three megaspore tetrads may be formed, and as every megaspore can give rise to a haustorium, the upper part of the nucellus often shows quite a tangle of haustorial processes competing with one another.

Failure of Wall Formation during Meiosis. The functioning of only one megaspore out of four is the commonest condition in angiosperms, but in several plants only the first of the two meiotic divisions is accompanied by wall formation, so that after the meiotic divisions are over each of the dyad cells is binucleate. In others wall formation fails altogether, or if walls are laid down they soon disappear, so that all the four megaspore nuclei lie within the same cell. Such differences in the mode of origin of the megaspores form the basis for a classification of the types of embryo sacs in angiosperms.

References

Afzelius, K. 1916. Zur Embryosackentwicklung der Orchideen. Svensk Bot. Tidskr. **10**: 183–227.

———. 1918. Zur Entwicklungsgeschichte der Gattung *Gloriosa*. Acta Horti Bergiani **6**(3): 3–12.

———. 1924. Embryologische und zytologische Studien in *Senecio* und verwandten Gattungen. Acta Horti Bergiani **8**: 123–219.

Archibald, E. E. A. 1939. The development of the ovule and seed of jointed cactus (*Opuntia aurantiaca* Lindley). South African Jour. Sci. **36**: 195–211.

Bambacioni-Mezzetti, V. 1935. Ricerche morfologiche sulle Lauraceae. Lo sviluppo dell'ovulo e dei sacchi pollinici nel *Laurus nobilis* L. Ann. di Bot. **21**(1): 1–19.

Banerji, I. 1940. A contribution to the life history of *Costus speciosus* Smith. Jour. Indian Bot. Soc. **19**: 181–196.

Baranow, P. 1926. Zytologische und embryologische Untersuchungen an *Drimiopsis maculata* Lindl. Ztschr. f. Zellforsch. und Mikros. Anat. **3**: 131–148.

Benson, M. 1894. Contribution to the embryology of the Amentiferae. I. Trans. Linn. Soc. London, II. Bot. **3**: 409–424.

———, Sanday, E., and Berridge, E. 1906. Contribution to the embryology of the Amentiferae. II. *Carpinus betulus*. Trans. Linn. Soc. London, II. Bot. **7**: 37–44.

Berg, O. 1898. "Beitrag zur Kenntnis der Entwicklung des Embryosackes der Angiospermen." Diss. Erlangen.

Bhargava, H. R. 1935. The life history of *Trianthema monogyna* L. Proc. Indian Acad. Sci. Sect. B. **2**: 49–58.

Boehm, K. 1931. Embryologische Untersuchungen an Zingiberaceen. Planta **14**: 411–440.

Bhaduri, P. N. 1932. The development of ovule and embryo sac in *Solanum melongena* L. Jour. Indian Bot. Soc. **11**: 202–224.

Boursnell, J. G. 1950. The symbiotic seed-borne fungus in the Cistaceae. Ann. Bot. **14**: 217–243.

Buell, M. F. 1935. Seed and seedling of *Acorus calamus*. Bot. Gaz. **96**: 758–765.

Caldwell, O. W. 1899. On the life history of *Lemna minor*. Bot. Gaz. **27**: 37–66.

Capoor, S. P. 1937. Contributions to the morphology of some Indian Liliaceae. II. The gametophytes of *Urginea indica* Kunth. Beihefte bot. Centbl. **56A**: 156–170.

Condit, I. J. 1932. The structure and development of flowers in *Ficus carica* L. Hilgardia **6**: 443–481.

Cook, M. T. 1906. The embryology of some Cuban Nymphaeaceae. Bot. Gaz. **42**: 376–392.

Copeland, H. F. 1938. The *Styrax* of Northern California and the relationships of the Styracaceae. Amer. Jour. Bot. **25**: 771–780.

Corner, E. J. H. 1949. The annonaceous seed and its four integuments. New Phytol. **48**: 332–364.

Dahlgren, K. V. O. 1927. Die Morphologie des Nuzellus mit besonderer Berücksichtigung der deckzellosen Typen. Jahrb. f. wiss. Bot. **67**: 347–426.

———. 1939. Endosperm und Embryobildung bei *Zostera marina*. Bot. Notiser 1939, pp. 607–615.

———. 1940. Postamentbildungen in den Embryosäcken der Angiospermen. Bot. Notiser 1940, pp. 347–369.

Dodds, K. S. 1945. Genetical and cytological studies of *Musa*. VI. The development of female cells of certain edible diploids. Jour. Genet. **46**: 161–179.

Earle, T. T. 1938. Embryology of certain Ranales. Bot. Gaz. **100**: 257–275.

Eunus, A. M. 1949. Contributions to the embryology of the Liliaceae (*Gloriosa superba*). Proc. 36th Indian Sci. Cong. Allahabad, Bot. Sect. No. 25.

Fagerlind, F. 1937. Embryologische, zytologische und Bestäubungs-experimentelle Studien in der Familie Rubiaceae nebst Bemerkungen über einige Polploiditäts-probleme. Acta Horti Bergiani **11**: 195–470.

———. 1939. Kritische und revidierende Untersuchungen über das Vorkommen des Adoxa ("Lilium")-Typus. Acta Horti Bergiani **13**: 1–49.

———. 1941. Der Bau der Samenanlage und des Makrogametophyten bei *Quisqualis indica*. Bot. Notiser 1941, pp. 217–222.

———. 1945a. Bau der floralen Organe bei der Gattung *Langsdorffia*. Svensk Bot. Tidskr. **39**: 197–210.

——— 1945b. Bildung und Entwicklung des Embryosacks bei sexuellen und agamospermischen *Balanophora*-Arten. Svensk Bot. Tidskr. **39**: 65–82.

Fagerlind, F. 1945c. Bau des Gynöceums, der Samenanlage und des Embryosackes bei einigen Repräsentaten der Familie Icacinaceae. Svensk Bot. Tidskr. **39**: 346–364.

———. 1945d. Blüte und Blütenstand der Gattung *Balanophora*. Bot. Notiser 1945, pp. 330–350.

———. 1947. Gynöceummorphologische und embryologische Studien in der Familie Olacaceae. Bot. Notiser 1947, pp. 207–230.

Finn, W. W. 1936. Zur Entwicklungsgeschichte der Chalazogamen, *Ostrya carpinifolia* Scop. Jour. Inst. Bot. Acad. Sci. Ukraine **8**: 15–25.

Flint, L. H., and Moreland, C. G. 1943. Notes on photosynthetic activity in seeds of the spider lily. Amer. Jour. Bot. **30**: 315–317.

Frye, T. C. 1902. A morphological study of certain Ascelpiadaceae. Bot. Gaz. **34**: 389–413.

Fuchs, A. 1938. Beiträge zur Embryologie der Thymelaeaceae. Österr. bot. Ztschr. **87**: 1–41.

Goebel, K. 1933. "Organographie der Pflanzen. III. Samenpflanzen." 3d ed. Jena.

Graves, A. H. 1908. The morphology of *Ruppia maritima*. Trans. Conn. Acad. Arts and Sci. **14**: 59–170.

Grove, A. R. 1941. Morphological study of *Agave lechuguilla*. Bot. Gaz. **103**: 354–365.

Guérin, P. 1915. Reliquiae Treubinae. I. Recherches sur la structure anatomique de l'ovule et de la graine des Thyméléacées. Ann. Jard. Bot. Buitenzorg **14**: 1–35.

Haberlandt, G. 1923. Zur Embryologie von *Allium odorum*. Ber. deutsch. bot. Gesell. **41**: 174–179.

Häfliger, E. 1943. Zytologisch-embryologische Untersuchungen pseudogamer Ranunkeln der Auricomus-Gruppe. Ber. schweiz. bot. Gesell. **53**: 317–382.

Hagerup, O. 1944. On fertilisation, polyploidy and haploidy in *Orchis maculatus* L. sens. lat. Dansk Bot. Arkiv **11**(5): 1–26.

Håkansson, A. 1943. Die Entwicklung des Embryosackes und die Befruchtung bei *Poa alpina*. Hereditas **28**: 25–61.

Haupt. A. W. 1934. Ovule and embryo sac of *Plumbago capensis*. Bot. Gaz. **95**: 649–659.

Hofmeister, W. 1861. Neue Beiträge zur Kenntnis der Embryobildung der Phanerogamen. II. Monokotyledonen. Abh. Königl. Sächs. Gesell. Wiss. **7**: 629–760.

Holmgren, J. 1913. Zur Entwicklungsgeschichte von *Butomus umbellatus* L. Svensk Bot. Tidskr. **7**: 58–77.

Houk, W. G. 1938. Endosperm and perisperm of coffee with notes on the morphology of the ovule and seed development. Amer. Jour. Bot. **25**: 56–61.

Hurst, C. C. 1931. Embryo sac formation in diploid and polyploid species of Roseae. Proc. Roy. Soc. London Ser. B. **109**: 126–148.

Johansen, D. A. 1931a. Studies on the morphology of the Onagraceae. V. *Zauschneria latifolia*, typical of a genus characterized by irregular embryology. Ann. N. Y. Acad. Sci. **33**: 1–26.

———. 1931b. Studies on the morphology of the Onagraceae. VI. *Anogra pallida*. Amer. Jour. Bot. **18**: 854–863.

Juliano, J. B. 1935. Anatomy and morphology of the Bunga, *Aeginetia indica* L. Philippine Jour. Sci. **56**: 405–451.

Junell, S. 1931. Die Entwicklungsgeschichte von *Circaeaster agrestis*. Svensk Bot. Tidskr. **25**: 238–270.

Kajale, L. B. 1940. A contribution to the embryology of the Amarantaceae Proc. Nat. Inst. Sci. India **6**: 597–625.

——. 1944. A contribution to the life history of *Zizyphus jujuba* Lamk. Proc Nat. Inst. Sci. India **10**: 387–391.

Kausik, S. B. 1935. The life history of *Lobelia trigona* Roxb. with special reference to the nutrition of the embryo sac. Proc. Indian Acad. Sci. Sect. B. **2**: 410–418.

——. 1940. Structure and development of the ovule and embryo sac of *Lasiosiphon eriocephalus* Dcne. Proc. Natl. Inst. Sci. India **6**: 117–132.

Khan, R. 1942. A contribution to the embryology of *Jussieua repens* L. Jour. Indian Bot. Soc. **21**: 267–282.

——. 1943. The ovule and embryo sac of *Fouquieria*. Proc. Natl. Inst. Sci. India **9**: 253–256.

Landes, M. 1946. Seed development in *Acalypha rhomboidea* and some other Euphorbiaceae. Amer. Jour. Bot. **33**: 562–568.

Lavialle, P. 1925. Sur la nutrition du sac embryonnaire chez *Knautia arvensis*. Compt. Rend. Acad. des Sci. Paris **180**: 2055–2056.

Lloyd, F. E. 1902. The comparative morphology of the Rubiaceae. Mem. Torrey Bot. Club **8**: 1–112.

Maheshwari, P. 1934. Contributions to the morphology of some Indian Liliaceae. I. The gametophytes of *Ophiopogon wallichianus* Hook f. Proc. Indian Acad. Sci. Sect. B. **1**: 197–204.

——. 1944. The seed structure of *Ipomoea*, a criticism. Sci. and Culture **9**: 557.

—— and Gupta, B. L. 1934. The development of the female gametophyte of *Ludwigia parviflora* Roxb. and *Jussieua repens* Linn. Current Sci. [India] **3**: 107–108.

—— and Singh, Balwant. 1943. Studies in the family Alismaceae. V. The embryology of *Machaerocarpus californicus* (Torr.) Small. Proc. Natl. Inst. Sci. India **9**: 311–322.

Mauritzon, J. 1933. "Studien über die Embryologie der Familien Crassulaceae und Saxifragaceae." Diss. Lund.

——. 1934. Zur Embryologie der Elaeocarpaceae. Arkiv för Bot. **26A**: 1–8.

——. 1936. Samenbau und Embroyologie einiger Scitameen. Lunds Univ. Årsskr. N. F. Avd. II, **31**(9): 1–31.

——. 1939. Contributions to the embryology of the orders Rosales and Myrtales. Lunds Univ. Årsskr. N.F. Avd. II, **35**(2): 1–120.

Mendes, A. J. T. 1941. Cytological observations in *Coffea*. VI. Embryo and endosperm development in *Coffea arabica* L. Amer. Jour. Bot. **28**: 784–789.

Murbeck, S. 1902. Über die Embryologie von *Ruppia rostellata*. K. Svenska Vet.-Akad. Handl. **36**(5): 1–21.

Oksijuk, P. 1937. Vergleichende zytologisch-embryologische Untersuchung der

Familie Resedaceae. I. *Reseda* und *Astrocarpus*. Jour. Inst. Bot. Acad. Sci. Ukraine **12**: 3–81.

Orr, M. Y. 1921*a*. The occurrence of tracheids in the nucellus of *Steriphoma cleomides* Spreng. Notes Roy. Bot. Gard. Edinb. **12**: 241–242.

———. 1921*b*. The occurrence of a tracheal tissue enveloping the embryo in certain Capparidaceae. Notes Roy. Bot. Gard. Edinb. **12**: 249–257.

Paetow, W. 1931. Embryologische Untersuchungen an Taccaceen, Meliaceen und Dilleniaceen. Planta **14**: 441–470.

Pantulu, J. V. 1941. Some unusual megaspore tetrads in the Leguminosae. Current Sci. [India] **10**: 175–176.

Pfeiffer, W. M. 1912. The morphology of *Leitneria floridana*. Bot. Gaz. **53**: 189–203.

Puri, V. 1941. Life history of *Moringa oleifera* Lamk. Jour. Indian Bot. Soc. **20**: 263–284.

Randolph, L. F. 1936. Developmental morphology of the caryopsis in maize. Jour. Agr. Res. **53**: 881–916.

Rauch, K. V. 1936. Cytologisch-embryologische Untersuchungen an *Scurrula atropurpurea* Dans. und *Dendrophthoe pentandra* Miq. Ber. schweiz. bot. Gesell. **45**: 5–61.

Rosendahl, C. O. 1909. Embryo sac development and embryology of *Symplocarpus foetidus*. Minn. Bot. Studies **4**: 1–9.

Rutishauser, A. 1937. Entwicklungsgeschichtliche Untersuchungen an *Thesium rostratum*. Mitt. naturf. Gesell. Schaffhausen **13**: 25–47.

———. 1945. Zur Embryologie amphimiktischer Potentillen. Ber. schweiz. bot. Gesell **55**: 19–32.

Schaeppi, H., and Steindl, F. 1942. Blütenmorphologische und embryologische Untersuchungen an Loranthoideen. Vtljschr. naturf. Gesell. Zürich **87**: 301–372.

Schleiden, M. J. 1837. Einige Blicke auf die Entwicklungsgeschichte der vegetablischen Organismus bei den Phanerogamen. Wiegmanns Archiv **3**: 289–320.

Schlimbach, H. 1924. Beiträge zur Kenntnis der Samenanlagen und Samen der Amaryllidaceen mit Berücksichtigung des Wassergehaltes der Samen. Flora **117**: 41–54.

Schnarf, K. 1929 "Embryologie der Angiospermen." Berlin.

Seshadri Ayyangar, G. 1948. Some observtions on stomata found on cotton ovules. Indian Cotton Growing Rev. **2**: 187–192.

Shattuck, C. H. 1905. A morphological study of *Ulmus americana*. Bot. Gaz. **40**: 209–223.

Singh, Bahadur. 1950. The embryology of *Dendrophthoe falcata* (Linn. fil.) Ettingshausen. Proc. 37th Indian Sci. Cong. Sect. Bot.

Smith, C. M. 1929. Development of *Dionaea muscipula*. I. Flower and seed. Bot. Gaz. **87**: 508–530.

Souèges, E. C. R. 1919. Recherches sur l'embryogénie des Polygonacées. Bul. Soc. Bot de France **66**: 168–199; **67**: 1–11, 75–85.

Steindl, F. 1945. Beitrag zur Pollen- und Embryobildung bei *Cynomorium coccineum* L. Arch. Julius Klaus-Stift. f. Vererbungsforsch. **20**: 342–355.

Stenar, H. 1925. "Embryologische Studien. I. Zur Embryologie der Columniferen. II. Die Embryologie der Amaryllideen." Diss. Uppsala.

———. 1928. Zur Embryologie der Asphodeline-Gruppe. Ein Beitrag zur systematischen Stellung der Gattungen *Bulbine* und *Paradisia*. Svensk. Bot. Tidskr. **22**: 145–159.

Subba Rao, A. M. 1941. Studies in the Malpighiaceae. II. Structure and development of the ovules and embryo sacs of *Malpighia coccifera* Linn. and *Tristellateia australis*. Proc. Natl. Inst. Sci. India **7**: 393–404.

Subramanyam, K. 1948. An embryological study of *Melastoma malabathricum* L. Jour. Indian Bot. Soc. **27**: 1–9.

Svensson, H. G. 1925. "Zur Embryologie der Hydrophyllaceen, Borraginaceen und Heliotropiaceen." Diss. Uppsala.

Swamy, B. G. L. 1948. A contribution to the life history of *Casuarina*. Proc. Amer. Acad. Arts and Sci. **77**: 1–32.

Tomita, K. 1931. Über die Entwicklung des nackten Embryos von *Crinum latifolium* L. Sci. Rpt. Tôhoku Imp. Univ. **6**: 163–169.

Treub, M. 1879. Notes sur l'embryogénie de quelques Orchidées. Natuurk. Verh. Koninkl. Akad. Amsterdam **19**: 1–50.

Van Tieghem, Ph. 1901. L'hypostase, sa structure et son rôle constantes, sa position et sa forme variables. Bul. Mus. Hist. Nat. **7**: 412–418.

Whitehead, M. R., and Brown, C. A. 1940. The seed of the spider lily, *Hymenocallis occidentalis*. Amer. Jour. Bot. **27**: 199–203.

Woodcock, E. F. 1943. Seed development in morning-glory (*Ipomoea rubro caerulea* Hook). Papers Mich. Acad. Sci. Arts and Letters **28**: 209–212.

CHAPTER 4

THE FEMALE GAMETOPHYTE[1]

Depending on the number of megaspore nuclei taking part in the development, the female gametophytes of angiosperms may be classified into three main types: *monosporic, bisporic,* and *tetrasporic.* In the first, only one of the four megaspores takes part in the development of the gametophyte. In the second, two megaspore nuclei take part in its formation; and in the third, all four of them. A further subdivision is based on the number of nuclear divisions intervening between the time of megaspore formation and the time of differentiation of the egg, and the total number of nuclei present in the gametophyte at the moment when such differentiation takes place. A secondary increase in their number, which sometimes takes place at a later stage, is not taken into account in this classification.

The *monosporic* female gametophytes or embryo sacs fall under two types: 8-nucleate and 4-nucleate. In the development of the 8-nucleate embryo sacs, the first division of the functioning megaspore gives rise to 2 nuclei: the primary micropylar and the primary chalazal. The second division produces one pair of nuclei at the micropylar end and one at the chalazal, and the third results in two groups of 4 nuclei lying at the opposite poles of the elongated embryo sac. The micropylar quartet differentiates into a three-celled egg apparatus and the upper polar nucleus, and the chalazal quartet into a group of three antipodal cells (or nuclei) and the lower polar nucleus. The 2 polar nuclei fuse to give rise to a secondary nucleus.

This type of embryo sac is the most common and is, therefore, commonly designated as the "Normal type." However, since the others are by no means so infrequent as was once supposed, it will be designated here as the "Polygonum type," for it was in *Polygonum divaricatum* that Strasburger (1879) gave the first clear and well-

---

[1] In writing this chapter the author has drawn freely upon some of his review articles (Maheshwari, 1937, 1941, 1946a,b; 1947, 1948), to which reference may be made for fuller information.

84

illustrated account of the development of a monosporic 8-nucleate embryo sac.

In certain other monosporic embryo sacs, the megaspore nucleus undergoes only two divisions and a micropylar quartet alone is formed. This quartet gives rise to a normal egg apparatus and a single polar nucleus. The lower polar nucleus and antipodal nuclei are absent. This type of development is known as the "Oenothera type" and has so far been reported only in the family Onagraceae.

The *bisporic* embryo sacs are typically 8-nucleate ("Allium type") and arise from one of the two dyad cells formed after Meiosis I. Since no wall is laid down after Meiosis II and both the megaspore nuclei formed in the functional dyad cell take part in the development of the embryo sac, only two further divisions are necessary to give rise to the 8-nucleate stage. A doubtful 4-nucleate type ("Podostemon type") has been reported in a few members of the Podostemonaceae but this is questionable and will not receive detailed consideration.

The *tetrasporic* embryo sacs present a great deal of variation. In several cases 16 nuclei are formed as the result of two divisions following megasporogenesis. These are classified under the following types, depending on the polarity and organization of the nuclei in the sac: "Peperomia type," "Penaea type," "Drusa type."

In some plants, owing to a crowding of 3 of the megaspore nuclei into the chalazal end of the cell (1 + 3 arrangement), there is a fusion of their spindles in the next division, resulting in a secondary 4-nucleate stage with 2 haploid nuclei at the micropylar end and 2 triploid ones at the chalazal. The next division results in 8 nuclei, 4 of which are haploid and 4 triploid. This mode of development is known as the "Fritillaria type."

The "Plumbagella type," reported only in *Plumbagella micrantha*, is similar to the Fritillaria type, except that here the development stops at the secondary 4-nucleate stage, which is at once followed by the organization of the embryo sac.

Finally, there are the "Adoxa" and "Plumbago" types, in both of which the 4 megaspore nuclei divide once to give rise to 8 nuclei. In *Adoxa*, however, the organization is bipolar and in *Plumbago* it is tetrapolar.

All the variations of embryo sac development described above are shown diagrammatically in Fig. 55.

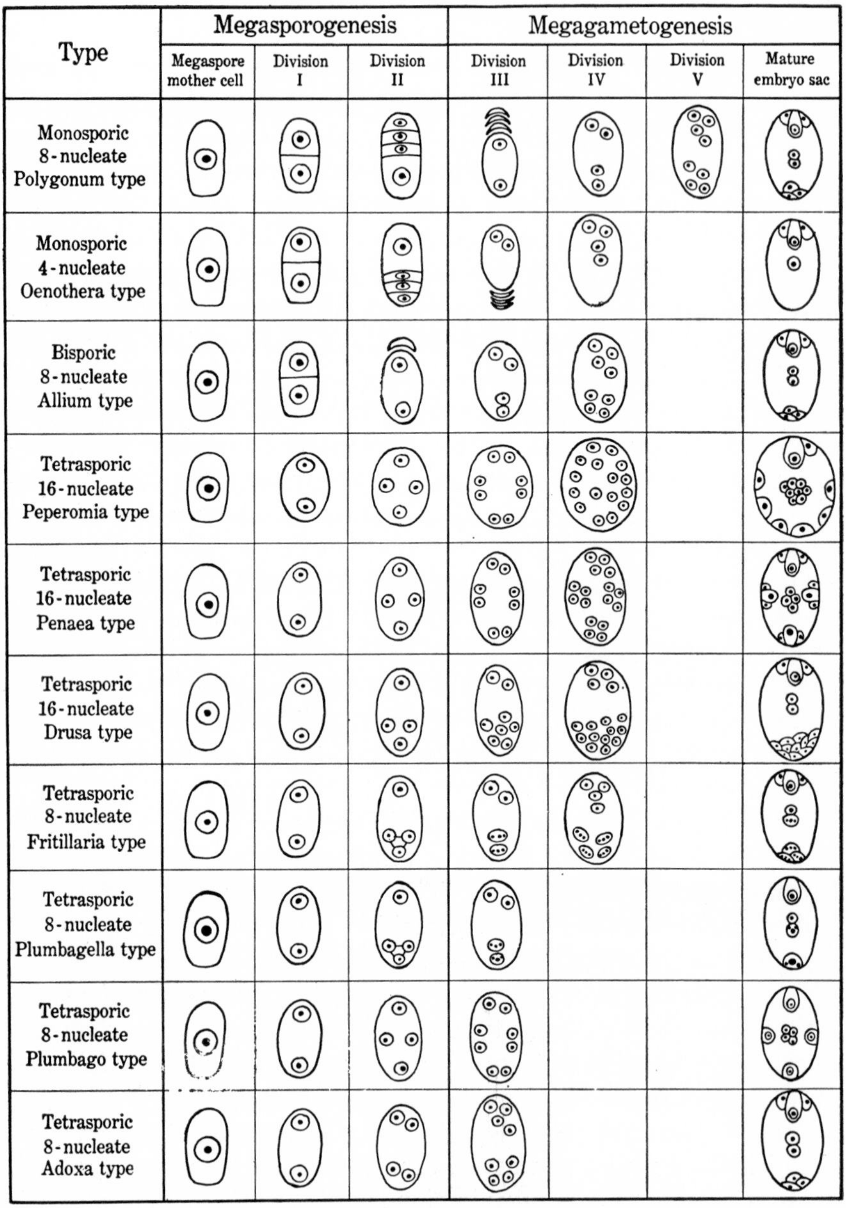

Type	Megasporogenesis			Megagametogenesis			
	Megaspore mother cell	Division I	Division II	Division III	Division IV	Division V	Mature embryo sac
Monosporic 8-nucleate Polygonum type							
Monosporic 4-nucleate Oenothera type							
Bisporic 8-nucleate Allium type							
Tetrasporic 16-nucleate Peperomia type							
Tetrasporic 16-nucleate Penaea type							
Tetrasporic 16-nucleate Drusa type							
Tetrasporic 8-nucleate Fritillaria type							
Tetrasporic 8-nucleate Plumbagella type							
Tetrasporic 8-nucleate Plumbago type							
Tetrasporic 8-nucleate Adoxa type							

FIG. 55. Diagram showing important types of embryo sacs in angiosperms.

MONOSPORIC EMBRYO SACS

Polygonum type. The monosporic 8-nucleate embryo sac, formed by three divisions of the functioning megaspore, occurs in at least 70 per cent of the angiosperms now known. The enlargement of the megaspore is always accompanied by increased vacuolation, one large vacuole usually appearing on either side of the nucleus in the direction of the long axis of the cell (Fig. 56A). After the first division has taken place, the two daughter nuclei move apart to opposite poles. Most of the cytoplasm is aggregated around them and the rest forms a thin peripheral layer, the center being occupied by a large vacuole (Fig. 56B). The next division gives rise to a 4-nucleate stage (Fig. 56C) which is followed by the 8-nucleate stage comprising a micropylar and a chalazal quartet.

Of the 8 nuclei arising in this manner, 3 at the micropylar end give rise to the egg and two synergids; 3 at the chalazal end give rise to antipodal cells;[2] and the remaining 2, one from each pole, fuse in the center to form a secondary nucleus (Fig. 56D).

Occasionally embryo sacs are found with less than the normal quota of 8 nuclei. This is usually because of an early degeneration of the antipodals, which obscures the true nature of the embryo sac. Even when the antipodals are present, they are sometimes overlooked because of their being situated in the narrow chalazal end of the embryo sac, which is seen only in median sections (Puri, 1939, 1941).

In some cases there is a genuine reduction in the number of nuclei. In certain species of *Phajus*, *Corallorhiza*, *Broughtonia* (Sharp, 1912), *Chamaeorchis*, *Oncidium* (Afzelius, 1916), *Elatine* (Frisendahl, 1927) (Fig. 57A), *Thesium* (Rutishauser, 1937a), *Calypso* (Stenar, 1940), and *Bulbophyllum* and *Geodorum* (Swamy, 1949a) the embryo sacs are 6-nucleate owing to a suppression of division of the two chalazal nuclei of the 4-nucleate stage. In *Orchis morio* (Afzelius, 1916) the primary chalazal nucleus of the 2-nucleate stage may degenerate without undergoing any division, so as to result in a 5-nucleate embryo sac.

A reduction in the number of nuclei may also be brought about in a different way. In *Epipactis pubescens* (Brown and Sharp, 1911)

[2] In several plants, like *Thesium rostratum* (Rutishauser, 1937a), cell formation does not occur at the chalazal end and the antipodal nuclei remain free.

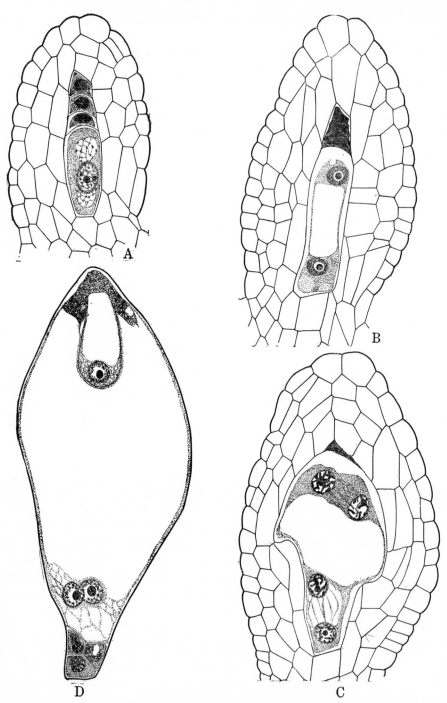

Fig. 56. Development of embryo sac in *Hydrilla verticillata*. *A*, tetrad of mega-spores with chalazal cell functioning. *B,C,* two-nucleate and four-nucleate embryo sacs. *D*, mature embryo sac; synergids have degenerate d.

and *Paphiopedilum insigne* (Afzelius, 1916) it has been noted that sometimes the two chalazal spindles of the last division come to lie more or less parallel and very close to each other and eventually coalesce to form a single large spindle which produces 2 diploid nuclei instead of the 4 haploid ones which would have been formed

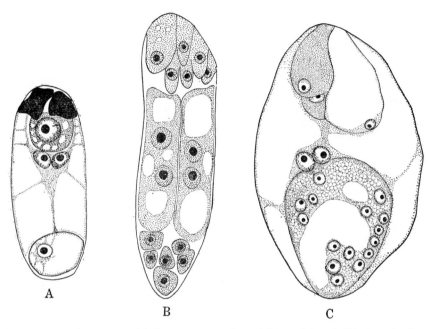

A   B   C

FIG. 57. Embryo sacs with fewer or more than eight nuclei. *A, Elatine triandra,* six-nucleate embryo sac which has arisen by omission of last division at chalazal end; the two black masses represent degenerated synergids. *B, E. hydropiper,* fusion of two eight-nucleate embryo sacs, resulting in 16-nucleate compound embryo sac. (*After Frisendahl, 1927.*) *C, Sandoricum koetjape,* embryo sac containing cytoplasmic vesicle with several nuclei. (*After Juliano, 1934.*)

in the ordinary way. This results in a 6-nucleate embryo sac with a haploid micropylar quartet, a diploid lower polar nucleus, and a single diploid antipodal cell (Fig. 58).

The reverse condition, *i.e.*, the occurrence of more than 8 nuclei in the embryo sac, is less frequent and may arise in three ways: (1) fusion of two embryo sacs (2) migration of the nuclei of nucellar cells into the embryo sac; and (3) occurrence of secondary divisions of some of the first-formed 8 nuclei.

In plants having a multicellular archesporium, several megaspore tetrads are formed and a number of megaspores may begin to enlarge. As examples may be mentioned the Casuarinaceae, Loranthaceae, and Rosaceae, and some members of the Rhamnaceae, Rubiaceae, and Compositae.[3] Commonly most of the embryo sacs become arrested in their development at a comparatively early stage and only a few reach maturity. Rarely the separating walls between the sacs may dissolve so that the contents become included

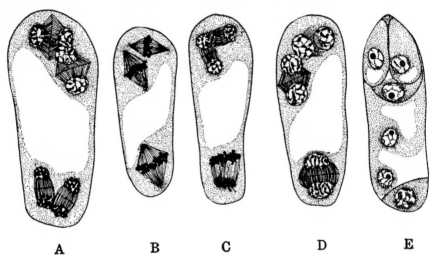

A	**B**	**C**	**D**	**E**

FIG. 58. Some stages in development of embryo sac of *Epipactis pubescens*. *A*, telophase of last division in embryo sac; note that two chalazal spindles show tendency to lie parallel to each other. *B*, metaphase of similar division; two chalazal spindles have coalesced to form single large spindle. *C,D*, later stages of division. *E*, mature embryo sac, showing egg apparatus, two polar nuclei, and single antipodal cell. (*After Brown and Sharp, 1911.*)

in a common cavity. A very good example of this kind has been figured in *Elatine hydropiper* (Frisendahl, 1927), showing an embryo sac with two egg apparatuses, two pairs of polar nuclei, and two groups of three antipodal cells each (Fig. 57*B*). This must clearly have originated by a fusion of two normally growing sacs. Similar "compound" sacs have been noted by Oksijuk (1937) in *Reseda alba* and *R. inodora*. Sometimes he found less than 16 nuclei, which is

[3] In *Potentilla heptaphylla* (Rutishauser, 1945) as many as nine embryo sacs were seen in one ovule.

quite possible if one of the fusing gametophytes is at a younger stage of development than the other.

In a *Musa* variety known as "I.R. 53," Dodds (1945) has recently described one compound embryo sac with three egg apparatuses and two pairs of polar nuclei; and another with two egg apparatuses, one pair of polar nuclei, and an additional group of 7 large "polar-like" nuclei at the chalazal end. Juliano (1934) has figured a peculiar embryo sac in a fallen flower of *Sandoricum koetjape* with a normal egg apparatus, two polar nuclei, and a large cytoplasmic vesicle extending from the chalazal end of the sac to its middle and containing more than a dozen nuclei (Fig. 57C). Since the antipodals are very ephemeral in this species, it is considered probable that the embryo sac proper was formed from the third megaspore and that the multinucleate vesicle arose as a result of some free nuclear divisions in the fourth megaspore.[4]

In some plants there is a migration of the nucellar nuclei into the embryo sac. This migration is due to the fact that during the growth and enlargement of the latter, the adjacent cells of the nucellus become flattened and crushed. Their walls, which are very thin and delicate, get ruptured, and the contents—both cytoplasm and nuclei, or only the latter—may "wander" into the embryo sac and become incorporated in it.[5] Two instances of this nature deserve special mention. In *Hedychium gardnerianum* (Madge, 1934) the nuclei of the nucellar cells lying just below the hypostase migrate "from cell to cell" through a small hole in the walls until they reach the hypostase. Here their progress is stopped for a time and groups of 20 or 30 nuclei collect together, surrounded by the ragged cell walls of the ruptured cells. Some of the nuclei now make their way around the hypostase into the cavity of the embryo sac, where they are believed to serve a nutritive function. In *Pandanus* (Fagerlind, 1940), which has no thick-walled hypostase, the nucellar cells lying directly beneath and on the sides of the young embryo sac show a marked tendency to enlarge. Their nuclei become swollen and the plasma assumes an appearance simi-

[4] Another possibility, not mentioned by Juliano, is that the embryo sac proper arose normally from the chalazal megaspore and the vesicle was of aposporic origin.

[5] This is comparable to the condition in many gymnosperms in which the nuclei of the jacket cells often make their way inside the egg.

lar to that of the embryo sac (Fig. 59*A*). The enlarged nuclei soon approach the embryo sac wall, which becomes perforated at such points. Gradually the pores become wider and finally the entire separating wall is absorbed. The embryo sac now encroaches upon these areas and soon incorporates them, coming in contact with newer cells which may also meet the same fate (Fig. 59*B*,*C*).[6] Even at the 4-nucleate stage, as many as 10 or more nucellar cells may become included inside the embryo sac in this fashion. Their nuclei divide synchronously with the sac nuclei, resulting in the formation of 8 haploid and a variable number of diploid nuclei (Fig. 59*D*). The secondary nucleus attains varying degrees of polyploidy, depending not only on the number of the nuclei which take part in the fusion but also on their chromosome content. In the mature embryo sac (Fig. 59*F*), the egg apparatus contains haploid nuclei only; some of the antipodal cells contain haploid nuclei, others diploid; most of the lateral cells (Fig. 59*E*) are diploid.

The third possibility, *i.e.*, an increase in the number of nuclei caused by further divisions of the original nuclei of the sac, is rare except with regard to the antipodal nuclei or cells, for which see page 134. To mention some examples from recent literature, in *Crassula schmidtii* and *Umbilicus intermedius* (Mauritzon, 1933) it is reported that occasionally there is a fourth division in the embryo sac, resulting in the formation of 16 nuclei, which organize to form four synergids, two eggs, six antipodal cells, and four polar nuclei. In *Crepis capillaris* (Gerassimova, 1933) some supernumerary egg cells were occasionally seen in addition to the other and usual components of the embryo sac, but their origin could not be traced and eventually they were found to degenerate and disappear. In *Nicotiana*, Goodspeed (1947) has recently reported some embryo sacs having 9 to 16 nuclei,—"obviously the result of division of from one to all of the normal eight nuclei." Here 3 to 5 nuclei were found to take part in polar fusion.

Special mention may be made of the development of the embryo sac in *Balanophora* and *Langsdorffia* (Fagerlind, 1945*a*,*b*). In both cases the micropylar megaspore functions and the three chalazal megaspores degenerate at a very early stage, although their re-

[6] Harling (1946) reports that in *Carludovica* the nucellar cells enlarge and push against the wall of the embryo sac, but in this case their contents do not actually enter the sac.

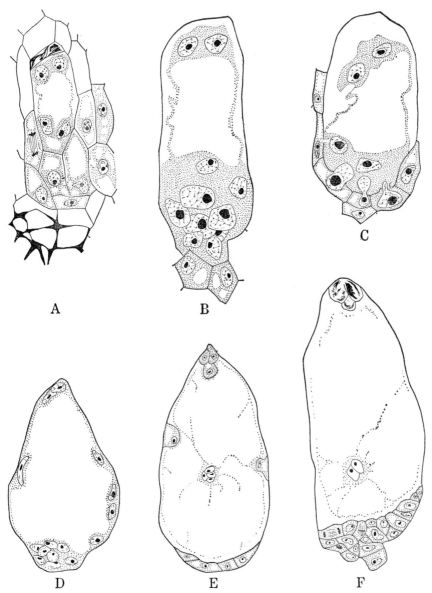

Fig. 59. Development of embryo sac in *Pandanus*. *A, P. ornatus*, four-nucleate stage; note enlargement of nucellar cells in chalazal region. *B*, same, with some nucellar cells incorporated inside embryo sac. *C, P. dubius*, four-nucleate stage, showing nucellar nuclei entering into embryo sac. *D, P. oleiocephalus*, embryo sac, showing several nuclei some of which are apparently derived from nucellus. *E*, same, mature embryo sac, showing two lateral cells and supernumerary polar nuclei. *F, P. ornatus*, mature embryo sac, showing large number of antipodal cells. *(After Fagerlind, 1940.)*

93

mains can be recognized for a considerable time (Fig. 60*B,C*; Fig. 61*A–C*). In *Balanophora* even the dyad cells show a marked difference in size, the micropylar cell being much larger than the chalazal (Fig. 60*A*). At the 2- or 4-nucleate stage a tubular out-

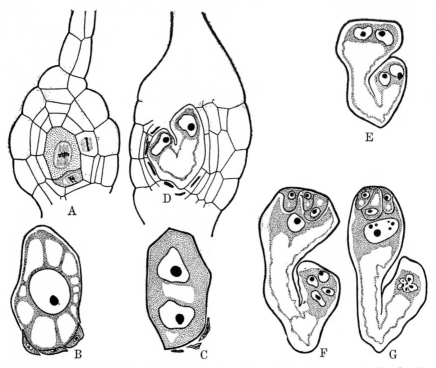

Fig. 60.   Development of embryo sac in *Balanophora elongata*. *A*, dyad cells undergoing second meiotic division. *B*, functioning megaspore, with remains of three degenerating megaspores at its base. *C,D*, two-nucleate embryo sacs; note lateral outgrowth from basal part of embryo sac in *D*. *E*, four-nucleate embryo sac. *F*, eight-nucleate embryo sac; note that egg apparatus has organized in morphologically lower end of embryo sac. *G*, older stage of same, showing fusion of four nuclei at antipodal end. (*After Fagerlind, 1945a.*)

growth arises from the embryo sac and then grows upward. In *Balanophora* it originates near the basal end of the sac (Fig. 60*D*) and in *Langsdorffia* near its apical end (Fig. 61*A*). In both cases it grows very quickly and soon comes to lie at a higher level than the originally upper end of the embryo sac (Fig. 60*E*, Fig. 61*B,C*). The 4 nuclei of the sac now undergo the last division to form the usual 8 nuclei, of which those belonging to the morphologically basal end give rise to the egg apparatus and one polar nucleus (Fig. 60*G*) and those belonging to the upper end fuse to form an irregularly lobed nucleus which usually degenerates *in situ.* A similar fusion takes place in *Langsdorffia* (Fig. 61*F–I*) except that some-

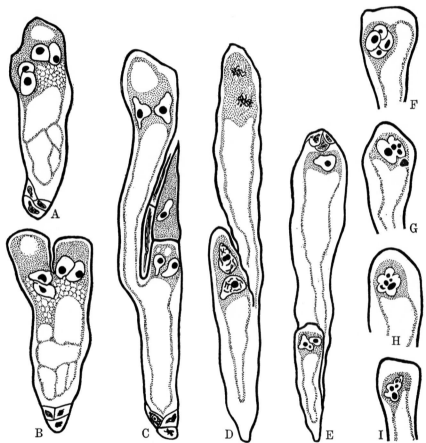

FIG. 61. Development of embryo sac in *Langsdorffia hypogaea.* *A*, four-nucleate stage; note three degenerating megaspores at lower end and formation of lateral protuberance near upper end. *B*, older stage, showing entry of two basal nuclei of sac into lateral arm. *C*, more advanced stage, showing pronounced upward growth of lateral arm, which is now situated at a higher level than morphologically upper end of sac; note three degenerating megaspores at lower end. *D*, two upper nuclei of the sac, dividing. *E*, mature embryo sac. *F–I*, stages in fusion of four nuclei belonging to antipodal end of embryo sac. (*After Fagerlind, 1945b.*)

times the last division fails to occur at this end of the embryo sac (Fig. 61*D*), so that only 6 nuclei are formed (Fig. 61*E*).

Oenothera Type. About a hundred years ago, Hofmeister (1847, 1849) published some remarkably accurate figures of the embryo sac of a few members of the Onagraceae, but because of the crude technique of those days he was unable to give a full account of the development. Geerts, in 1908, found that in *Oenothera lamarckiana* the embryo sac is usually formed by the micropylar megaspore of the tetrad, which undergoes only two nuclear divisions instead of the usual three occurring in the Polygonum type of embryo sac. In this way, 4 nuclei are produced which organize into the two synergids, the egg, and a single polar nucleus. Since the third division is omitted and all the nuclei are situated in the micropylar part of the developing embryo sac, there is neither a lower polar nucleus nor any antipodal cells. Modilewski (1909) independently studied species of *Oenothera, Epilobium,* and *Circaea* and confirmed the observations of Geerts in all essential respects. These two investigations were soon followed by several others and this mode of development, known as the Oenothera type, has been found to be a characteristic and constant feature of the entire family Onagraceae, having been demonstrated in more than 16 genera. The only exception is *Trapa,* which has an 8-nucleate embryo sac of the Polygonum type, but this genus, as most systematists now agree, is best assigned to a separate family, the Hydrocaryaceae or Trapaceae.

A noteworthy feature in the development of the Oenothera type of embryo sac is the concurrent growth of more than one cell of the tetrad. Eventually it is the micropylar megaspore which functions, but sometimes it may be the chalazal and occasionally both grow simultaneously forming "twin" embryo sacs (Fig. 62).

Rarely, more than 4 nuclei may be seen in an embryo sac. Usually this condition results from the incorporation of an adjacent megaspore and its contents, but it appears that sometimes there may be further division or divisions of the nuclei of the embryo sac. In *Anogra pallida*[7] Johansen (1931*a*) reported repeated ami-

[7] This plant is a native of the arid regions of southern Arizona and California. It shows little or no seed production, and propagation occurs by means of offshoots at the ends of subterranean stolons.

totic divisions of the polar nucleus, and in one embryo sac as many
as 140 nuclei were formed by this method. In a few instances he
found a synergid containing about 20 nuclei. In *Zauschneria latifolia* (Johansen, 1931*b*) the nuclei of the nucellar cells are said to

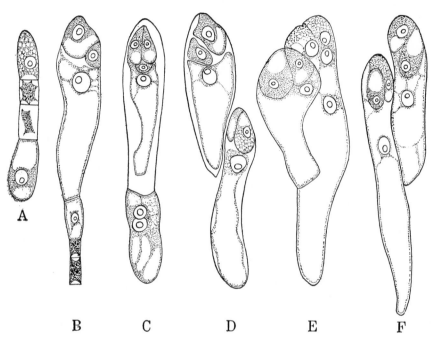

Fig. 62. Development of embryo sac in *Oenothera suaveolens*. *A*, tetrad of megaspores; both micropylar and chalazal megaspores are enlarging. *B*, embryo sac
formed from micropylar megaspore; the three chalazal megaspores in process of
degeneration. *C*, embryo sac formed from micropylar megaspore; one of chalazal
megaspores has also developed up to two-nucleate stage. *D–F*, twin embryo sacs
formed by concurrent growth of two megaspores. (*After Hoeppener and Renner,
1929.*)

migrate into the embryo sac to form a variable number of bodies
looking like micronuclei of different sizes.

Embryo sacs with fewer than 4 nuclei are rare, but in *Hartmannia
tetraptera* (Johansen, 1929) and *Jussieua repens*, Khan (1942) saw
two 3-nucleate embryo sacs having a single synergid, an egg, and a
polar nucleus. Their origin is probably to be explained by a lack
of division of the primary synergid nucleus of the 2-nucleate stage.

BISPORIC EMBRYO SAC

Allium Type.   A bisporic embryo sac was first described in *Allium fistulosum* (Strasburger, 1879) and has since been confirmed in several species of this genus (Weber, 1929; Messeri, 1931; Jones and Emsweller, 1936; and others).   The megaspore mother cell (Fig. 63*A*) divides to form two dyad cells, of which the upper is much smaller and soon degenerates (Fig. 63*B*).   The nucleus of the lower divides to form 2 (Fig. 63*C*), 4 (Fig. 63*D*) and then 8 nuclei, which give rise to an embryo sac with the usual organization.

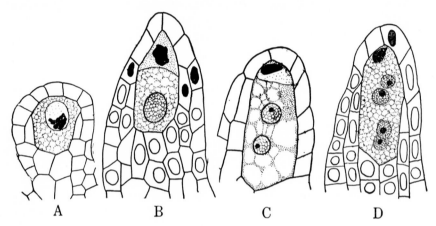

| A | B | C | D |

FIG. 63.   Early stages in development of embryo sac of *Allium cepa*.   *A*, megaspore mother cell.   *B*, dyad cells, upper degenerating.   *C*, two-nucleate embryo sac.   *D*, four-nucleate embryo sac.   (*After Jones and Emsweller, 1936.*)

Treub and Mellink (1880) independently described the same type of development in *Agraphis patula* (= *Scilla hispanica*), and this has also been found to be true of other species of *Scilla* (see Hoare, 1934).   The chief difference between *Allium* and *Scilla* lies in the fact that while in *Allium* it is the lower dyad cell which gives rise to the embryo sac, in *Scilla* it is usually the upper.   The lower does not degenerate at once, however, but often develops up to the 4-nucleate stage forming the so-called "antigone," which probably serves for the nutrition of the functional embryo sac.

During the last seven decades the Allium type has been reported in several plants belonging to diverse groups and it appears to be quite characteristic of certain families, *viz.*, Podostemonaceae, Butomaceae (except *Butomus*), Alismaceae, and the tribe Viscoideae of the Loranthaceae. It is also found in several members of the Balanophoraceae, Liliaceae, Amaryllidaceae, and Orchidaceae, but in other groups its occurrence is more or less sporadic.

The chief variation in development is a tendency toward reduction in the number of nuclei at the chalazal end. This has been very clearly demonstrated in the Alismaceae (Dahlgren, 1928*b*, 1934; Johri, 1935*a,b,c*, 1936*a*; Maheshwari and Singh, 1943), Butomaceae (Johri, 1936*b*, 1938*a,b*), Podostemonaceae (Went, 1910, 1912, 1926), and some members of the Orchidaceae (see Swamy, 1949*a*). In the Alismaeae, of which *Machaerocarpus californicus* (Maheshwari and Singh, 1943) may be cited as an example (Fig. 64), the development usually proceeds normally up to the 4-nucleate stage. After this only the 2 micropylar nuclei divide again, resulting in a 6-nucleate stage comprising an egg apparatus, two polar nuclei, and a single antipodal nucleus. In those plants in which reduction has gone still further, only 5 nuclei are formed, four at the upper end and the undivided primary chalazal nucleus at the lower. The mature embryo sac therefore comprises an egg apparatus, an upper polar nucleus, and a single antipodal nucleus; a lower polar nucleus is absent.

Special mention may be made of a few plants following the Allium type of development.

In the tribe Viscoideae, belonging to the Loranthaceae, this mode of development seems to be of general occurrence and has recently been described in some detail in *Ginalloa* (Rutishauser, 1937*b*), *Korthalsella* (Rutishauser, 1935, 1937*b*; Schaeppi and Steindl, 1945), and *Viscum* (Steindl, 1935; Schaeppi and Steindl, 1945). In all these genera the central ovarian papilla has two or more archesporial cells, each of which divides to form two dyad cells (Fig. 65*A–C*). Of these, the upper dyad cell is the larger and functions, while the lower soon degenerates (Fig. 65*D*). A peculiar feature is that after the 4-nucleate stage there is a slow but steady curvature of the embryo sac, which causes its lower end to bend out of the papilla and proceed upward into the carpellary tissue (Fig. 65*E*). Meanwhile, the 4 nuclei divide to form 8, one quartet being situated at each pole of the embryo sac. The egg apparatus differentiates in the originally lower pole, which is, however, now situated at a higher level than the upper (Fig. 65*F*).

In *Convallaria majalis* (Stenar, 1941) the first division of the megaspore mother cell results in the formation of the usual dyad cells (Fig. 66*A,B*). Walls are also laid down after the second division (Fig. 66*C*), but these soon break down so that the dyad cells are again restored although each of them is now binucleate

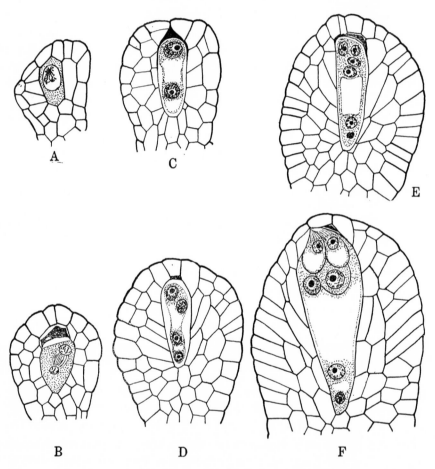

Fig. 64.   Development of embryo sac in *Machaerocarpus californicus*.   *A*, megaspore mother cell.   *B*, dyad stage; nucleus of lower dyad cell dividing.   *C*, twonucleate embryo sac with remains of degenerated upper dyad cell.   *D*, fournucleate embryo sac.   *E*, six-nucleate embryo sac; lower two nuclei of four-nucleate stage have remained undivided.   *F*, mature embryo sac, showing two synergids, egg, two polar nuclei, and single antipodal nucleus.   (*After Maheshwari and Singh, 1943.*)

(Fig. 66*D*). The micropylar dyad cell is at first the larger and more vacuolated (Fig. 66*E*) but gradually the chalazal dyad cell increases in size and plays the more dominant role (Fig. 66*F*). The

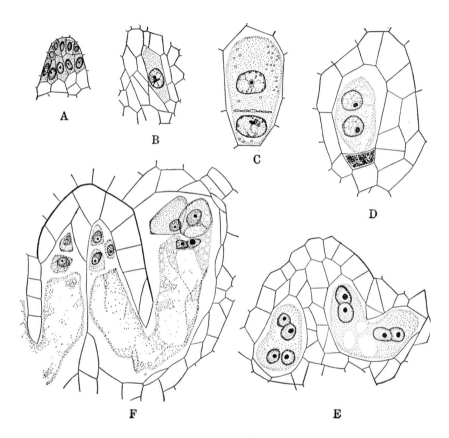

Fig. 65. Development of embryo sac in *Korthalsella dacrydii*. *A*, l.s. central papilla. *B*, portion of older papilla, showing a megaspore mother cell. *C*, telophase of Meiosis I. *D*, two-nucleate embryo sac formed from upper dyad cell; note degenerating lower dyad cell. *E*, central papilla showing two four-nucleate embryo sacs; note beginning of curvature in embryo sac on right. *F*, mature embryo sac; egg apparatus has differentiated in originally basal end, which has now penetrated upward into tissues of carpel. (*After Rutishauser, 1935.*)

2 nuclei of this cell divide to form 4 (Fig. 66*G–H*) and then the 8 nuclei of the mature stage (Fig. 66*I*). The interesting point in the development is that it starts like that of a monosporic form

but is actually bisporic as a result of an early dissolution of the cell walls laid down after the second meiotic division.

In 1907, Pace published an interesting paper on the development of the embryo sac in four species of *Cypripedium*. According

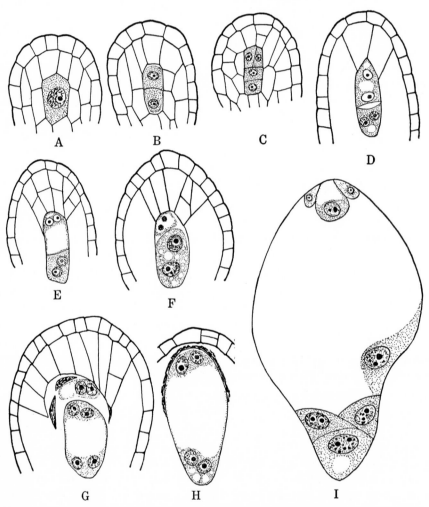

Fig. 66.   Development of embryo sac in *Convallaria majalis. A*, l.s. nucellus, showing megaspore mother cell. *B*, dyad stage. *C*, T-shaped tetrad. *D*, wall separating the two megaspores of each dyad cell has disappeared. *E*, the two dyad cells, each binucleate. *F*, upper dyad cell degenerating; lower enlarging. *G*, four-nucleate embryo sac formed from lower dyad cell. *H*, same, more advanced stage. *I*, mature embryo sac. (*After Stenar, 1941*.)

to her account, the megaspore mother cell divides to form two dyad cells, of which the lower develops normally up to the 4-nucleate stage. One of the micropylar nuclei is now said to form the egg and the other a synergid; the second synergid is formed by one of the chalazal nuclei which migrates upward; and the remaining nucleus functions as the single polar. At the time of fertilization, one of the synergid nuclei is said to become displaced by the incoming pollen tube and forced, as it were, to take part in triple fusion. Owing to its unique and distinctive nature, this mode of development was designated as the "Cypripedium type."

The reinvestigations made by Prosina (1930), Francini (1931), Carlson (1945), and Swamy (1945) have, however, shown that the development does not end at the 4-nucleate stage but continues further. Occasionally all 8 nuclei may be formed, but in any case at least the 2 micropylar nuclei go through the next division, so that the embryo sacs are 6 nucleate.

The ovules and embryo sacs of the Podostemonaceae show several interesting features to which a brief reference may be made here, using *Podostemon ceratophyllum* (Hammond, 1937) as an example. The outer integument appears first and forms the micropyle (Fig. 67*A*). The megaspore mother cell (Fig. 67*B,C*), which is situated directly below the epidermis, divides to form the two dyad cells (Fig. 67*D*), of which the micropylar soon aborts although its nucleus may occasionally divide (Fig. 67*E*). The nucleus of the chalazal dyad cell divides to form 2 nuclei (Fig. 67*F–H*), of which the lower promptly degenerates and disappears (Fig. 67*G*). The remaining nucleus undergoes two divisions, resulting in 4 nuclei (Fig. 67*I*), which organize to form two synergids, an egg, and a polar nucleus. Occasionally the primary chalazal nucleus persists up to this stage so that the 5-nucleate nature of the embryo sac is easily recognized. More commonly, however, only 4 nuclei are seen and the fifth is no longer recognizable at this stage (see also Razi, 1949).

The following members of the Podostemonaceae are reported to have tetranucleate embryo sacs: *Podostemon subulatus*, *Hydrobium* (= *Zeylanidium*) *olivaceum*, *Farmeria metzgerioides* (Magnus, 1913), and *Weddelina squamulosa* (Chiarugi, 1933). Here the lower dyad cell is said to undergo only two divisions, resulting in 4 nuclei which organize into the egg apparatus and a single polar nucleus (Fig. 67*J–K*, 68*A–F*). This type of development, sometimes called

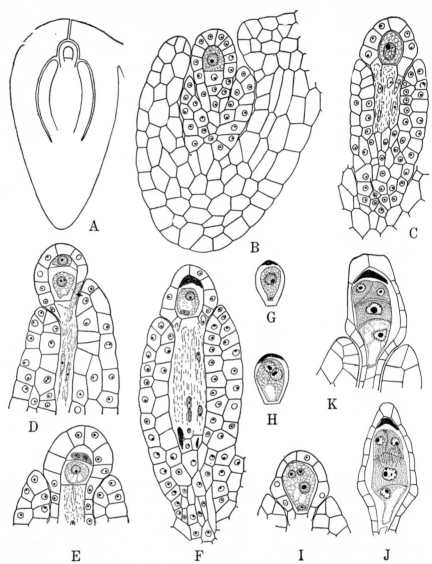

Fig. 67. Development of embryo sac in *Podostemon ceratophyllum* (*A–I*) and *Weddelina squamulosa* (*J,K*). *A, Podostemon*, l.s. ovule, diagrammatic. *B*, l.s. young ovule, showing archesporial cell. *C*, older stage, showing formation of psuedo embryo sac by disintegration of nucellar cells lying just below the mega-spore mother cell. *D*, formation of dyad cells. *E*, degeneration of upper dyad cell. *F*, two-nucleate embryo sac; note enlarging pseudo embryo sac. *G*, two-nucleate embryo sac; primary chalazal nucleus disorganizing. *H*, primary micro-pylar nucleus divided into two daughter nuclei; primary chalazal nucleus has disap-peared. *I*, five-nucleate stage in which the primary chalazal nucleus has degenerated and disappeared. (*After Hammond, 1937.*) *J,K, Weddelina*, stages corresponding to *I*. (*After Chiarugi, 1933.*)

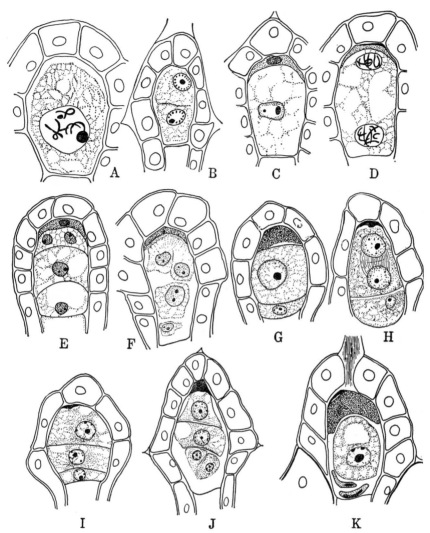

FIG. 68. Development of embryo sac in *Podostemon subulatus* (*A–F*) and *Dicraea elongata* (*G–K*). *A*, *Podostemon*, megaspore mother cell. *B*, dyad cells. *C*, lower dyad cell enlarging; upper in course of degeneration. *D*, two-nucleate embryo sac formed from lower dyad cell. *E*, four-nucleate stage with accompanying wall formation. *F*, mature embryo sac showing two synergids, egg, and a polar nucleus. *G*, *Dicraea*, upper dyad cell degenerating; lower divided into two cells. *H–J*, upper dyad cell crushed and disorganized; of the other two cells, upper has divided transversely and lower has divided vertically. *K*, embryo sac after fertilization, showing degeneration of all the cells except the zygote. (*After Magnus, 1913.*)

the "Podostemon type", has, however, always been considered doubtful, and the four plants named above deserve to be re-investigated.

An even more doubtful case is that of *Dicraea elongata* (Magnus, 1913), in which the chalazal dyad cell is said to divide transversely to form two cells (Fig. 68*G*). Of these the upper, which is larger, again divides in the same plane (Fig. 68*H,I*) to produce one synergid and an egg cell, and the lower divides anticlinally to form two antipodal cells (Fig. 68*J*). According to this interpretation the polar nuclei are absent, and all the cells except the zygote degenerate after fertilization (Fig. 68*K*). These observations need to be confirmed before they can be accepted.

TETRASPORIC EMBRYO SACS[8]

Peperomia Type. Campbell (1899*a,b*; 1901) and Johnson (1900) reported that in *Peperomia pellucida* each of the 4 megaspore nuclei divides twice, resulting in a total of 16 nuclei which become more or less uniformly distributed in the rather thick layer of cytoplasm lying at the periphery of the embryo sac. According to Johnson, 2 nuclei at the micropylar end now become organized to form the egg and a synergid, 8 fuse to form the secondary nucleus, and the remaining 6 are cut off at the periphery of the embryo sac. According to Campbell, on the other hand, 1 to 3 nuclei in the vicinity of the egg show a more or less evident aggregation of cytoplasm around them and are to be regarded as the equivalents of synergids; approximately 8 nuclei enter into the formation of the secondary nucleus; and the remaining 4 to 6 nuclei are cut off as antipodal cells.

Subsequent studies, made by others on several species of *Peperomia*, have confirmed Johnson's account. The chief variations concern the number of nuclei which fuse to form the secondary nucleus, and the number left over to form the antipodals. In every case only one synergid was observed.

A recent study of *Peperomia pellucida* (Fagerlind, 1939*a*) has shown that after the meiotic divisions are over (Fig. 69*A–C*), the coenomegaspore[9] may either retain its more or less spherical form or become slightly pear-shaped with a little protuberance at the

---

[8] See Fagerlind (1944) for fuller information on tetrasporic embryo sacs.

[9] This term is used to denote the cell containing the four free megaspore nuclei.

micropylar end. The 4 megaspore nuclei are usually arranged tetrahedrally, but in the embryo sacs of the pear-shaped type one nucleus projects rather conspicuously towards the upper papillate

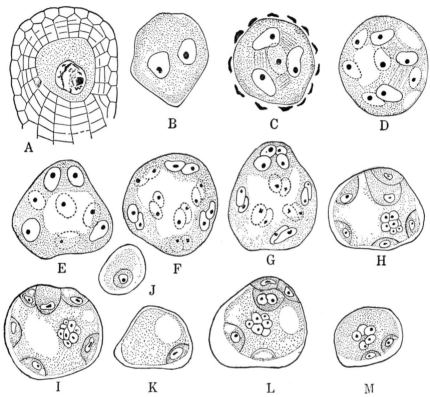

Fig. 69. Development of embryo sac in *Peperomia pellucida*. *A*, megaspore mother cell. *B*, two-nucleate stage. *C*, four-nucleate stage. *D,E*, eight-nucleate stage as seen in spherical and pear-shaped types of embryo sacs respectively. *F,G*, 16-nucleate stage. *H*, mature embryo sac of spherical type, showing a single synergid, six lateral cells, and eight polar nuclei (all nuclei of sac are not seen in this section). *I*, same, showing one lateral cell in close proximity to egg and therefore simulating a second synergid. *J–M*, successive sections through a pear-shaped embryo sac, showing a three-celled egg apparatus. (*After Fagerlind, 1939a.*)

end. In the next stage, the 8 nuclei are either distributed more or less symmetrically around the periphery of the embryo sac (Fig. 69*D*), or 2 nuclei may lie somewhat closer to each other at its upper end (Fig. 69*E*). The fourth and the last division now gives rise to

16 nuclei, which may form either eight groups of 2 nuclei each (in the spherical embryo sacs) (Fig. 69*F*) or six groups of 2 and a micropylar group of 4 nuclei (in the pear-shaped embryo sacs) (Fig. 69*G*). In the former case the egg apparatus is usually two-celled (egg and one synergid); 8 nuclei fuse in the center to form the secondary nucleus; and 6 nuclei are cut off at the periphery (Fig. 69*H*). Only occasionally, because of slight displacements and the small size of the embryo sac, one may find another peripheral cell lying so close to the egg that the egg apparatus may be said to comprise three cells (Fig. 69*I*). In the pear-shaped embryo sacs, however, a three-celled egg apparatus is the rule, the fourth nucleus from the micropylar end and one member from each of the six peripheral pairs form the seven polars, and 6 nuclei are cut off to form the lateral cells (Fig. 69*K–M*).

Fagerlind's observations help us to understand the slight divergence between the account of Johnson (1900) and that of Campbell (1899*a,b*; 1901). The former saw only one synergid, while the latter believed that there were more than one. Now it appears that both these conditions are possible, depending on the form which the embryo sac takes during its growth and development. In the pear-shaped type there are invariably two synergids; in the spherical type there is usually only one synergid unless another peripheral cell accidentally happens to lie so close to the egg as to look like a second synergid.

Johnson (1914) discovered a different type, however, in *P. hispidula*. At the 8-nucleate stage, 2 nuclei are seen at the micropylar and 6 at the chalazal end (Fig. 70*A*); at the 16-nucleate stage, 4 lie at the micropylar end and 12 at the chalazal (Fig. 70*B*). Two nuclei of the micropylar group now form the egg and single synergid, as in other species, but the remaining 2 nuclei of this group and all the remaining 12 nuclei meet near the center and fuse to form a single large secondary nucleus (Fig. 70*C,D*).

The embryo sac of *Gunnera* (Haloragidaceae) is essentially similar to that of *Peperomia pellucida*. Two species have been studied: *G. macrophylla* (Ernst, 1908; Samuels, 1912) and *G. chilensis* (Modilewski, 1908). After the 16-nucleate stage, 3 of the micropylar nuclei form the egg apparatus, the fourth descends and fuses with 6 other nuclei to form a large secondary nucleus, and the remaining 6 are cut off as antipodal cells. It is possible that if the

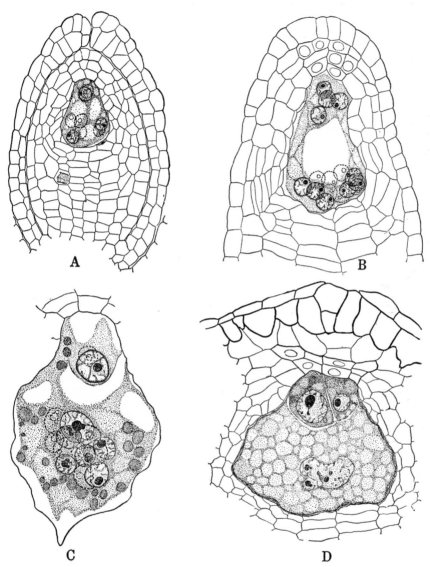

Fig. 70. Some stages in development of embryo sac of *Peperomia hispidula.*
A, eight-nucleate embryo sac; nuclei shown in dotted outline have been included
from adjacent sections of sac. *B*, l.s. ovule, showing 16-nucleate embryo sac. *C*,
embryo sac, showing egg, one synergid, and 12 polar nuclei. *D*, embryo sac with
egg, single synergid, and large lobed secondary nucleus. (*After Johnson, 1914.*)

embryo sac of *Gunnera* were to be studied again and a sufficient quantity of material examined, it would show a range of variation similar to that in *Peperomia*.

Penaea Type.   Stephens (1909) described an interesting mode of development in three genera of the Penaeaceae, *viz.*, *Penaea*, *Brachysiphon*, and *Sarcocolla* (Fig. 71).   Here the 16 nuclei lie in four distinct quarters which are arranged crosswise, one at each end of the embryo sac and two at the sides.   Now 3 nuclei of each quartet become cut off as cells, while the fourth remains free and

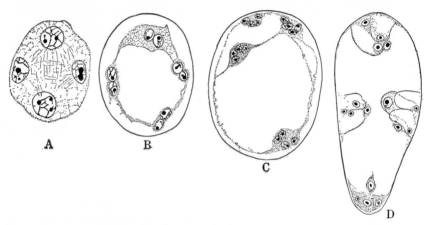

FIG. 71.   Development of embryo sac in Penaeaceae.   *A, Sarcocolla minor*, four megaspore nuclei at close of the second meiotic division.   *B, S. formosa*, eight-nucleate stage.   *C, S. squamosa*, 16-nucleate stage, showing four groups of four nuclei each.   *D, Penaea mucronata*, mature embryo sac.   (*After Stephens, 1909.*)

moves to the center.   There are thus four "triads" and four polar nuclei.   As a rule, the egg cell of the micropylar "triad" alone is functional, although the others often look very similar.

Embryo sacs of this type have since been described in several members of the Malpighiaceae (see Stenar, 1937; Subba Rao, 1940, 1941) and Euphorbiaceae (Modilewski, 1910, 1911; Arnoldi, 1912; Tateishi, 1927; and others) and in a few scattered genera belonging to other families.

Special mention may be made of the embryo sac of *Acalypha indica* (Maheshwari and Johri, 1941), which, although similar, does not entirely fit into the type described above.   Up to the 16-nu-

cleate stage (Fig. 72*A–D*) the development corresponds with that
of the Penaeaceae and other species of *Acalypha*, but the organization of the mature embryo sac presents a great variation. The
commonest condition found was that 2 nuclei of each quartet remain free and migrate to the center of the embryo sac, while the
other two organize into cells. Thus there are four groups of two
cells each at the periphery and 8 free nuclei in the center (Fig.
72*E*).

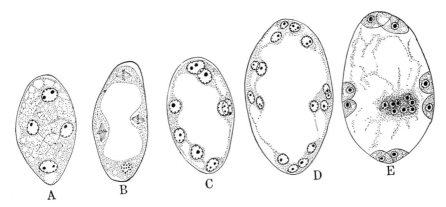

Fɪɢ. 72. Development of embryo sac in *Acalypha indica*. *A*, megaspore mother
cell with four megaspore nuclei. *B*, megaspore nuclei in division. *C*, eight-
nucleate stage. *D*, sixteen-nucleate stage. *E*, mature embryo sac, showing four
peripheral pairs of cells and eight polar nuclei. (*After Maheshwari and Johri,
1941*.)

This was not the only kind of organization, however. Some
ovules showed a micropylar group of three cells and three other
groups of two cells each, leaving only 7 nuclei (instead of the usual
8) to fuse in the center. In one embryo sac, the chalazal group
had three cells and all the rest had two cells each. Another embryo sac showed three two-celled groups, one lateral cell, and 9 free
nuclei meeting in the center. In a third and very peculiar embryo
sac, one lateral group was entirely missing, the second had only one
cell, the micropylar had three cells, and the chalazal had two cells,
leaving 10 free nuclei to take part in polar fusion.

A few cases were noted in which it seemed that fewer than 16
nuclei had been formed, and others with slightly more than this

number. These counts could not be regarded as certain, however, since such embryo sacs ran into three or four sections and their exact reconstruction was a matter of doubt.

Abnormalities of a somewhat similar nature have also been recorded in *Combretum* (Mauritzon, 1939), but it has to be seen how far these are related to differences of environment.

Drusa Type. A 16-nucleate embryo sac of a different nature was recorded by Håkansson (1923) in *Drusa oppositifolia*, a member of the family Umbelliferae (Fig. 73*A*). After the meiotic divisions are over, three of the megaspore nuclei pass down to the basal end of the embryo sac, and only one remains at the micropylar end. This 1+3 arrangement is followed by a 2+6 and then a 4+12 stage. The four micropylar nuclei give rise to the egg apparatus and upper polar nucleus, and the 12 chalazal nuclei to a lower polar nucleus and 11 antipodal cells.

During recent years this type of development has been recorded in *Mallotus japonicus* (Ventura, 1934), *Maianthemum bifolium* and *M. canadense* (Stenar, 1934; Swamy, 1949*b*[9a]), *Crucianella latifolia*, *Rubia olivieri* (Fagerlind, 1937), *Tanacetum vulgare*, *Chrysanthemum parthenium* (Fagerlind, 1941), *Ulmus* (Ekdahl, 1941; Walker, 1950), and a few other plants. A few of these deserve special mention and are briefly discussed below.

Shattuck (1905) reported an 8-nucleate embryo sac of the Adoxa type in *Ulmus americana*, but he observed that frequently there seemed to be a further nuclear division. Several embryo sacs were found to contain as many as 12 or more nuclei, rather evenly dis-

---

[9a] In *M. canadense*, according to Swamy (1949*b*), in about 13 per cent of the ovules the chalazal spindles of the last division fuse in pairs so that the mature embryo sac comes to possess 4 haploid nuclei at the micropylar end and 6 diploid nuclei at the chalazal end.

FIG. 73. Development of embryo sac in *Drusa oppositifolia* (*A*), *Chrysanthemum parthenium* (*B–H*), and *Crucianella latifolia* (*I–M*). *A*, *Drusa*, 16-nucleate embryo sac, showing four nuclei at micropylar end and twelve at chalazal. (*After Håkansson, 1923.*) *B,C*, *Chrysanthemum*, young embryo sacs showing varying arrangements of the four megaspore nuclei. *D–F*, eight-nucleate stage; note degeneration of basal nucleus in *E*. *G*, last division in embryo sac, basal nucleus degenerating. *H*, mature embryo sac, showing 12 nuclei. (*After Fagerlind, 1941.*) *I*, *Crucianella*, megaspore nuclei. *J*, same, in division. *K*, fourth division in embryo sac; some of nuclei at chalazal end have failed to divide. *L*, embryo sac, showing 15 nuclei. *M*, mature embryo sac. (*After Fagerlind, 1937.*)

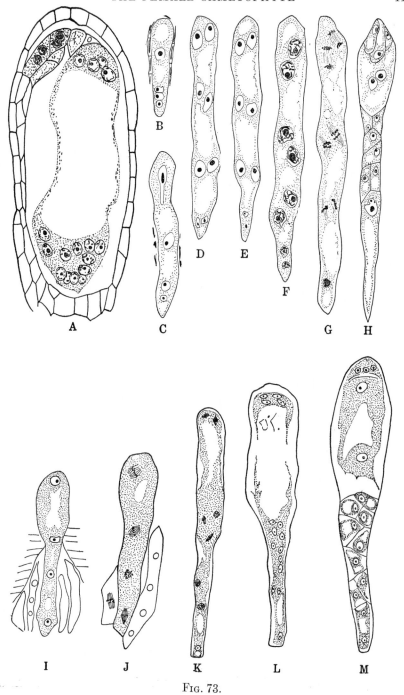

F<small>IG</small>. 73.

tributed and very similar to one another in appearance. Some other workers also obtained similar results, and noted that the mature embryo sacs occasionally showed more than three antipodals. D'Amato (1940a), Ekdahl (1941), and Walker (1950), working on several species of *Ulmus*, have clarified the position by showing that as a rule four divisions intervene between the megaspore mother cell stage and the organization of the embryo sac, and not three. The coenomegaspore shows a 1 + 3 arrangement of the megaspore nuclei, each of which undergoes two further divisions, resulting in the formation of 4 nuclei at the micropylar end and 12 at the chalazal end. Frequently, however, some of the chalazal nuclei fail to undergo the fourth division, resulting in a total of 14, 12, or only 10 nuclei, of which 4 are at the micropylar end and the rest at the chalazal. Several of the latter degenerate soon after their formation, so that there is a further decrease in the number of nuclei, and eventually only two to four antipodal cells may be differentiated. Also, in certain cases the 4 megaspore nuclei divide only once, so as to give rise to an 8-nucleate embryo sac of the Adoxa type.

The embryo sac of *Chrysanthemum parthenium* presents a range of variation which seems to indicate that there are several races of this plant which behave somewhat differently from one another, although possibly the differences are related to environmental conditions. According to Palm (1915), who gave the first detailed account of the embryo sac of this species, each of the 4 megaspore nuclei divides twice. The 16 nuclei arising in this way organize to form a three-celled egg apparatus, two polar nuclei, and eight antipodal cells of which the basal cell is four-nucleate.

Fagerlind (1941) studied two specimens of the same species. In specimen 1 the 4 megaspore nuclei were observed to take up the most variable positions, and frequently the 3 basal nuclei were seen to lie in close contact (Fig. 73B). With the subsequent elongation of the sac the nuclei became separated from one another by vacuoles, the micropylar nucleus being larger than the rest (Fig. 73C). All the nuclei now divided simultaneously, resulting in 8 nuclei, of which the 2 basal were the smallest and soon began to degenerate (Fig. 73D–F). When the next division (Fig. 73G) was over, there were 14 nuclei in the sac, of which 3 organized into an egg apparatus, 2 functioned as polar nuclei, and the rest formed the antipodal cells (Fig. 73*H*). The basal antipodal cell contained a variable number of nuclei, which subsequently fused to form 1 nucleus. Embryo sacs with fewer than 14 nuclei were also seen, but this was due to a degeneration and disappearance of some of the nuclei at the chalazal end.

In specimen 2, collected from a different locality in Sweden, the megaspore mother cells as well as the developing embryo sacs and their nuclei were found to be of a larger size than in the first plant. The chalazal megaspore nucleus degenerated soon after its formation. The remaining 3 nuclei divided to form 6 and then 12 nuclei. In the mature embryo sac the basal antipodal cell was observed to have more than one nucleus, while the remaining antipodal cells were uninucleate.

Material of the same species collected from the Brooklyn Botanical Gardens, New York (Maheshwari and Haque, 1949), showed the usual 4- and 8-nucleate stages, after which all the nuclei were found to divide again, resulting in 16 nuclei, 4 at the micropylar end and 12 at the chalazal. These organize to form a three-celled egg apparatus, two polar nuclei, and eleven uninucleate antipodal cells.

The embryo sac of *Tanacetum vulgare* (Fagerlind, 1941) is fundamentally similar to that of *Chrysanthemum*. The megaspore mother cell (Fig. 74*A*) undergoes the usual reduction divisions to produce 2 (Fig. 74*B*) and then 4 nuclei (Fig. 74*C*) which become arranged in a linear fashion (Fig. 74*D*). Vacuoles soon appear between the nuclei, which now increase in size and prepare for the next division (Fig. 74*E*), resulting in the formation of 8 nuclei (Fig. 74*H*). In many cases, however, the basal nucleus does not take part in the division and soon begins to degenerate (Fig. 74*G*), and sometimes the subbasal nucleus also remains undivided (Fig. 74*F*). At this stage the embryo sac may, therefore, contain 8, 7, or only 6 nuclei. If all of them take part in the next division, the mature embryo sacs may be 16-, 14-, or 12-nucleate (Fig. 74*I*). But frequently there is a further degeneration of one or two of the chalazal nuclei so that embryo sacs with fewer than 12 nuclei are not uncommon (Fig. 74*J*).

Crucianella latifolia (Fagerlind, 1937), a member of the Rubiaceae, also belongs to the Drusa type. After the reduction divisions are over, the coenomegaspore shows a pronounced elongation, rupturing the nucellar epidermis at its micropylar end (Fig. 73*I*). The next division proceeds normally (Fig. 73*J*), but of the 8 nuclei now formed the basal nucleus remains undivided (Fig. 73*K*) so that the mature embryo sac shows only 15 nuclei (Fig. 73*L*) which become organized to form a three-celled egg apparatus, two polar nuclei, and 10 antipodals (Fig. 73*M*).

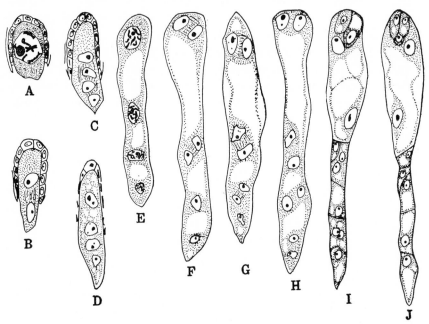

FIG. 74.   Development of embryo sac in *Tanacetum vulgare*.   *A*, megaspore mother cell.   *B,C*, end of first and second meiotic division, respectively.   *D*, megaspore nuclei.   *E*, same, older stage, showing vacuolation.   *F–H*, first postmeiotic division; two megaspore nuclei dividing in *F*, three in *G*, and all four in *H*.   *I,J*, mature embryo sacs with varying number of nuclei.   (*After Fagerlind, 1941.*)

In *Maianthemum bifolium* (Stenar, 1934) both the reduction divisions are accompanied by the formation of cell plates (Fig. 75 *A–C*). They soon become absorbed, however, resulting in a common tetranucleate cell (Fig. 75*D*). The four megaspore nuclei take up a 1+3 arrangement, so that the next stage shows 2 nuclei at the micropylar pole and 6 at the chalazal pole (Fig. 75*E–F*). There is one more division, resulting in 16 nuclei (Fig. 75*G*). These organize into an egg apparatus, two polar nuclei, and 11 antipodal cells.

Most of the antipodal cells soon degenerate, and only a few may be seen in the mature embryo sac (Fig. 75*H*).

Fritillaria Type. Following the work of Treub and Mellink

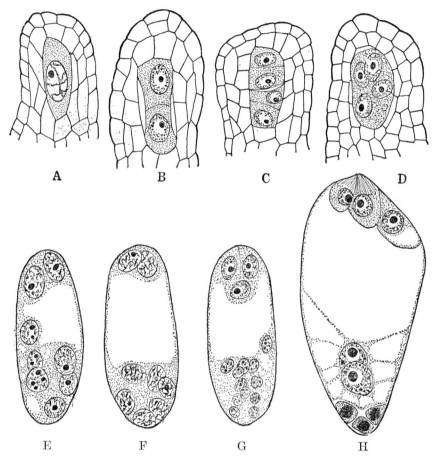

Fig. 75. Development of embryo sac in *Maianthemum bifolium.* *A*, l.s. nucellus, showing megaspore mother cell. *B*, dyad stage. *C*, tetrad. *D*, four-nucleate embryo sac formed by dissolution of walls separating megaspores. *E*, eight-nucleate stage. *F*, same, nuclei in prophase of next division. *G*, embryo sac with 16 nuclei. *H*, mature embryo sac. *(After Stenar, 1934.)*

(1880) on *Lilium bulbiferum,* several other investigators, notably Strasburger, Mottier, Guignard, Coulter, and Sargant, studied a number of species of this genus and repeatedly confirmed that the

4 megaspore nuclei undergo only one division to give rise to the 8 nuclei of the mature embryo sac. They no doubt observed certain peculiarities and curious appearances which could not be explained on this interpretation, but these were disregarded as abnormal or even "pathological" conditions.

Bambacioni (1928*a,b*) showed that in *Fritillaria* and *Lilium* the formation of the 4 megaspore nuclei is not followed directly by the 8-nucleate stage but by a *secondary 4-nucleate* stage, in which the 2 chalazal nuclei are much larger than the micropylar. This comes about in a very peculiar manner. At first there is a 1+3 arrangement of the megaspore nuclei (Fig. 76*A–D*) so that the 3 chalazal nuclei come to lie very close to each other. During the next stage the micropylar nucleus divides normally, but the three chalazal spindles fuse to form a single common spindle (Fig. 76*E–F*), so that at the close of the division there are two haploid nuclei at the micropylar end and two triploid nuclei at the chalazal (Fig. 76 *G–H*). One more division occurs, resulting in 8 nuclei, of which the 4 chalazal nuclei are triploid and the 4 micropylar are haploid (Fig. 76*I*). The mature embryo sac thus consists of three haploid cells (the egg and two synergids), three triploid cells (the antipodals), and a tetraploid secondary nucleus formed by the fusion of the two polar nuclei, one haploid and the other triploid (Fig. 76*J*). Of the antipodals, the two lowest frequently show a flattened and degenerated appearance—a condition originating from the fact that the basal nucleus of the secondary 4-nucleate stage often divides in a more or less abortive fashion.

Cooper (1935*a*) extended the observations of Bambacioni to several other species of *Lilium*, and since then the Fritillaria type has been demonstrated in a general way for the entire tribe Lilioideae and several other genera belonging to diverse families; *Piper*, *Heckeria*, *Myricaria*, *Tamarix*, *Cornus* (some spp.), *Armeria*, *Statice* (most spp.), *Rudbeckia* (most spp.), *Gaillardia*, *Cardiocrinum*, *Gagea*, *Erythronium* (most spp.), *Tulipa* (some spp.), and *Clintonia* (see Maheshwari, 1946*b*, for detailed information).

It may be noted that the fusion of the 3 chalazal megaspore nuclei may take place when they are either in the prophase stage or in early metaphase. In the former case the secondary 4-nucleate stage is preceded by a secondary 2-nucleate one, and the sequence then is as follows: megaspore mother cell, primary 2-nucleate stage, primary 4-nucleate, secondary 2-nucleate, secondary 4-nucleate, and last of all the 8-nucleate stage.

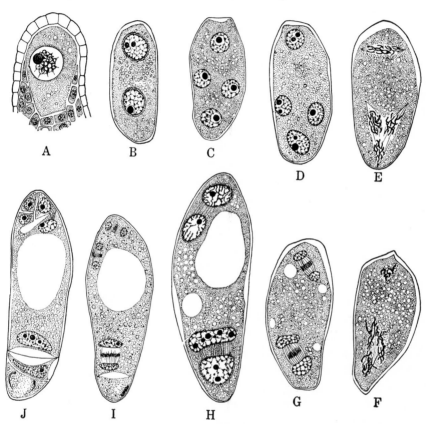

Fig. 76. Development of embryo sac in *Fritillaria persica*. *A*, l.s. nucellus, showing megaspore mother cell in prophase of Meiosis I. *B*, two-nucleate stage. *C*, primary four-nucleate stage. *D*, megaspore nuclei, showing 1+3 arrangement. *E*, megaspore nuclei dividing. *F*, same, showing fusion of three chalazal spindles. *G*, telophase of same division. *H*, secondary four-nucleate stage in which the two micropylar nuclei are haploid and chalazal nuclei are triploid. *I*, four nuclei dividing to form eight. *J*, eight-nucleate embryo sac. (*After Bambacioni, 1928a.*)

Normally all the 4 megaspore nuclei are of the same size, but in some plants the micropylar nucleus is the largest and the other 3 nuclei are considerably smaller. When this happens, the nuclei of the secondary 2-nucleate and secondary 4-nucleate stages show no appreciable difference in size, and rarely the chalazal nuclei are smaller than the micropylar in spite of the triploid nature of the former.

Finally, the basal nucleus of the secondary 4-nucleate stage sometimes fails to divide, resulting in a 7-nucleate gametophyte with two antipodal cells instead of three, as in some species of *Gagea* (Romanov, 1936); or, both the basal as well as the subbasal nucleus remain undivided and the embryo sac is 6-nucleate, as in *Statice* (Fagerlind, 1939*b*). In *Tulipa maximovicii* (Romanov, 1939) the 3 chalazal megaspore nuclei undergo an abnormal division in which all the telophase chromosome groups become included in a common membrane, so that the mature embryo sac is 5-nucleate. In one genus, *Clintonia* (R. W. Smith, 1911; F. H. Smith, 1943; Walker, 1944), the chalazal megaspore nuclei degenerate as soon as they are formed, without undergoing any division at all.

Plumbagella Type. In this type also, which has so far been reported only in *Plumbagella micrantha* (Fagerlind, 1938*b*; Boyes, 1939), the 4 megaspore nuclei take up a 1+3 arrangement (Fig. 77*A–C*), and a large vacuole separates the 3 chalazal nuclei from the micropylar nucleus (Fig. 77*D*). The former gradually approach one another and eventually fuse to give rise to a single triploid nucleus (Fig. 77*E*). This results in a secondary 2-nucleate stage, followed by a secondary 4-nucleate one, in which the 2 micropylar nuclei are haploid and the chalazal are triploid (Fig. 77*F–G*). There are no further divisions. The nucleus nearest the micropylar end organizes into the egg; the triploid nucleus nearest the chalazal end forms the single antipodal cell; and the remaining 2 nuclei, one haploid and the other triploid, fuse to form a tetraploid secondary nucleus (Fig. 77*H–I*).

This mode of development shows an evident relationship with

F$_{IG}$. 77. Development of embryo sac in *Plumbagella micrantha*. *A*, megaspore mother cell. *B*, second meiotic division in megaspore mother cell. *C*, megaspore nuclei showing 1+3 arrangement; the three chalazal nuclei are of a smaller size. *D*, chalazal nuclei in process of fusion. *E*, fusion of the three chalazal nuclei is completed, resulting in formation of secondary two-nucleate stage. *F,G*, formation of secondary four-nucleate stage. *H*, wall formation in embryo sac. *I*, mature embryo sac showing egg, secondary nucleus, and single antipodal cell. (*After Fagerlind, 1938b.*)

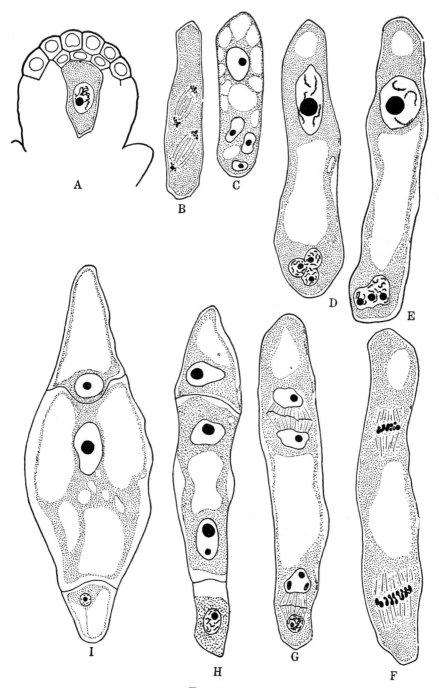

FIG. 77.

the Fritillaria type, the only difference being that in *Plumbagella* the development is arrested at the secondary 4-nucleate stage and the fourth division is omitted.

Adoxa Type. The Adoxa type, formerly known as "Lilium type," is characterized by all 4 megaspore nuclei undergoing just one more division to form an 8-nucleate embryo sac having a normal egg apparatus, three antipodal cells, and two polar nuclei (Fig. 78). It was described for the first time by Jönsson (1879–1880) in *Adoxa moschatellina* and later by Lagerberg (1909) and Fagerlind (1938a).

Until only a few years ago there was a long list of plants under the Adoxa type. With the publication of Bambacioni's work and the consequent reinvestigation of *Lilium, Fritillaria,* and several other genera, its ranks have steadily diminished and there are now only five genera in which its occurrence is a more or less regular feature: *Adoxa, Sambucus,* and some species of *Erythronium*[10], *Tulipa,* and *Ulmus.*

An interesting variation has been reported in some species of *Tulipa.* In *T. sylvestris* (Bambacioni-Mezzetti, 1931) vacuolation frequently commences even at the megaspore mother cell stage, and all the 4 megaspore nuclei gather at the micropylar end of the cell, where they divide to give rise to a group of six cells (one of which is to be interpreted as the egg) and 2 free nuclei. *T. tetraphylla* (Romanov, 1938) is essentially similar. After the meiotic divisions are over, 3 nuclei go to the micropylar pole and one to the chalazal (Fig. 79*A–D*). All of them divide again (Fig. 79*E*), so that there are 6 daughter nuclei in the upper part of the sac and 2 in the lower. Cell plates are laid down at the conclusion of the division, resulting in the formation of five cells at the micropylar end (one of these is to be regarded as the egg) and one cell at the chalazal, leaving 2 free nuclei (the polars) in the center (Fig. 79*F*).

Since this peculiar mode of development occurs only in the Eriostemones section of the genus *Tulipa,* it is known as the "Eriostemones form" of the Adoxa type. Other species of the genus come under the Fritillaria or the Drusa type (see Maheshwari, 1948).

[10] Haque's (1950) observations on *E. americanum* and Walker's (1950) on *U. fulva, U. racemosa,* and *U. glabra* show that the development sometimes follows the Adoxa type and sometimes the Fritillaria type.

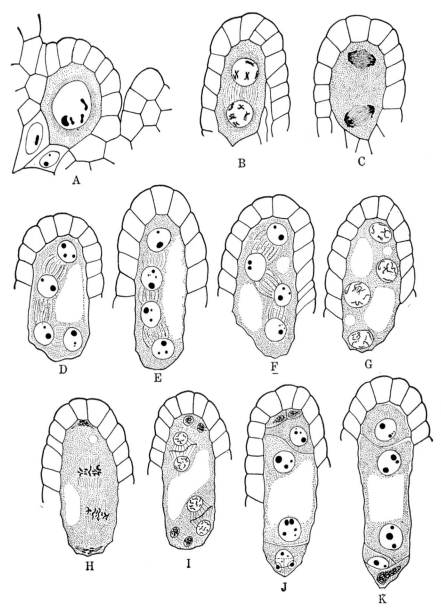

FIG. 78. Development of embryo sac in *Adoxa moschatellina.* *A*, megaspore mother cell. *B*, two-nucleate stage. *C*, two nuclei dividing. *D–G*, four-nucleate embryo sacs. *H*, division of four nuclei. *I*, same, telophase. *J,K*, mature embryo sacs. (*After Fagerlind, 1938a.*)

One species of *Leontodon*, *L. hispidus*, also deserves mention in this connection (Bergman, 1935). Ordinarily a row of four megaspores is formed, and the embryo sac is of the Polygonum type. But in more than 50 per cent of the ovules of one plant the separating walls between the megaspore nuclei frequently dissolved and disappeared, and all the 4 nuclei divided only once to give rise to the 8-nucleate stage (Fig. 80). Since here only three divisions intervened between the megaspore mother cell stage and the differentiation of the egg, this mode of development comes under the Adoxa type.

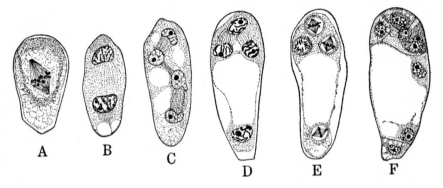

FIG. 79. Development of embryo sac in *Tulipa tetraphylla*. *A–C*, formation of megaspore nuclei. *D*, 3+1 arrangement of megaspore nuclei. *E*, all four nuclei dividing. *F*, mature embryo sac. (*After Romanov, 1938.*)

Plumbago Type. The embryo sac of *Plumbago capensis*, described by Haupt (1934), may be presented as a representative of the Plumbago type. The 2- and 4-nucleate stages (Fig. 81*A–B*) are normal, and the 4 megaspore nuclei, which are arranged in a crosswise fashion, undergo a further division (Fig. 81*C*) resulting in 8 free nuclei arranged in four pairs (Fig. 81*D*). One nucleus of the micropylar pair is now cut off to form the lenticular egg cell (Fig. 81*E*). Of the remaining 7 nuclei, 4 (presumably one member of each of the original four pairs) undergo a slight increase in size and gradually approach one another, functioning as polar nuclei (Fig. 81*F*). The remaining 3 nuclei degenerate at their original places, but occasionally 1, 2, or all 3 of them are cut off at the periphery to form cells which may persist and assume an egg-like appearance; synergids are entirely absent (Fig. 81*G–H*).

The Plumbago type occurs not only in other species of the genus *Plumbago* (Dahlgren, 1937; Fagerlind, 1938*b*) but also in two other genera of the Plumbaginaceae, *viz.*, *Ceratostigma* (D'Amato, 1940*b*) and *Vogelia* (Mathur and Khan, 1941). It is so far unknown outside this family.

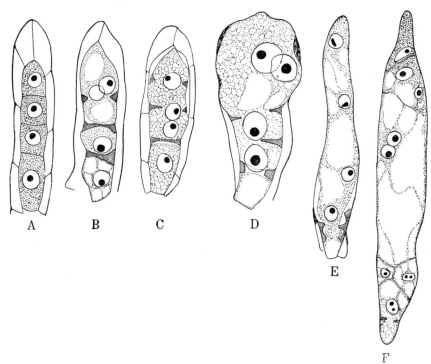

Fig. 80. Development of embryo sac in *Leontodon hispidus*. *A*, tetrad of megaspores. *B–E*, dissolution of separating walls between megaspore nuclei. *F*, mature eight-nucleate embryo sac. (*After Bergman, 1935.*)

ABERRANT AND UNCLASSIFIED TYPES

In addition to the above fairly distinct and well-established types of embryo sac development, there are a few which appear to be more or less isolated. The more important of them are mentioned below.

Limnanthes douglasii. The embryo sac of this plant has been investigated by three different workers but without any complete agreement regarding the mode of development. Stenar (1925*a*) reported an Adoxa type of embryo sac and called attention to the

reduced size of the nuclei at the chalazal end. Eysel (1937) confirmed this report but noted an occasional reduction in the number
of nuclei at the chalazal end of the embryo sac, owing to a failure

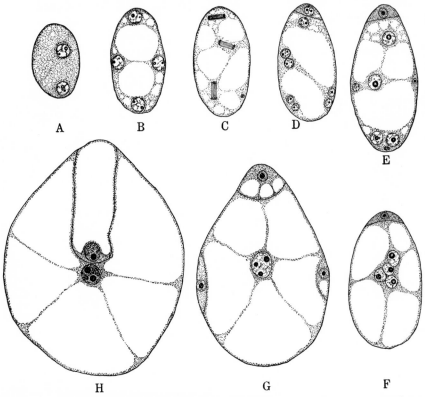

Fig. 81. Development of embryo sac in *Plumbago capensis*. *A*, two-nucleate
stage derived from first division of megaspore mother cell. *B*, four-nucleate stage.
C, all four nuclei dividing; one of the mitotic figures is oriented at right angles to
plane of sectioning. *D*, eight-nucleate stage, showing cutting off of egg cell. *E*,
differentiation of the four polar nuclei. *F*, fusion of polar nuclei. *G,H*, later
stages, showing egg at micropylar end and secondary nucleus in center. The two
lateral cells in *G* are derived from nuclei which ordinarily disappear in earlier stages.
(*After Haupt, 1934.*)

of the basal nucleus of the 4-nucleate stage to undergo the last
division. In other cases he observed a disappearance of the wall
separating the megaspore mother cell from the nucellar cell situated
directly below it and the consequent incorporation of the latter
into the embryo sac. One embryo sac showed 9 nuclei, of which

7 had organized into cells (four looking like synergids, two looking like eggs, and one of an undecided nature) and 2 resembled polar nuclei; antipodals were absent.

Fagerlind's (1939c) observations differ from those of both Stenar and Eysel. The megaspore mother cell has a highly vacuolated cytoplasm (Fig. 82A).[11] As a result of the first division, 2 nuclei are formed of which the lower promptly degenerates and is reduced

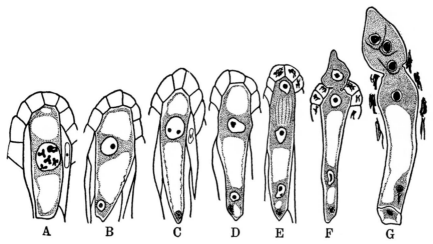

FIG. 82. Development of embryo sac in *Limnanthes douglasii*. *A*, megaspore mother cell. *B,C*, two-nucleate embryo sacs; note degeneration of primary chalazal nucleus. *D*, three-nucleate stage originating by division of primary micropylar nucleus. *E*, division of micropylar nucleus. *F*, embryo sac piercing the nucellar epidermis; note two nuclei at micropylar end, one nucleus in middle, and degenerated nucleus at chalazal end. *G*, mature embryo sac showing egg apparatus, upper polar nucleus, lower polar nucleus (?), and degenerating antipodal cell. (*After Fagerlind, 1939c.*)

to a densely staining homogeneous blob which lies at the bottom of the embryo sac and takes no further part in the development (Fig. 82B–C). The upper nucleus divides to form 2 daughter nuclei, of which the lower is much smaller and usually incapable of further division (Fig. 82D). Following meiosis, we thus have a 3-nucleate stage showing a micropylar nucleus, a middle nucleus, and a chalazal nucleus. Of these the micropylar nucleus divides

[11] In the majority of angiosperms vacuolation takes place only after the meiotic divisions are over.

twice, to give rise to a group of 4 nuclei which form the egg apparatus and the upper polar nucleus (Fig. 82*E–G*). Of the remaining 2 nuclei, one may be considered as an antipodal and the other as the lower polar nucleus.

Several variations in the development and organization of the embryo sac were found, however. Most of these seemed to have their origin in the behavior of the middle nucleus. In some cases it was found to take part in the third or fourth division, resulting in a 7-nucleate embryo sac with two antipodal nuclei instead of one. Less frequently it divided synchronously with the micropylar nucleus, but only one of its daughter nuclei divided again, resulting in an 8-nucleate embryo sac.

It is probable that at least some of the variations reported by Stenar, Eysel, and Fagerlind are due to environmental influences, and a more detailed study is necessary to decide the point.[11a]

Balsamita vulgaris. A recent investigation of the embryo sac of this plant (Fagerlind, 1939*c*) has revealed several interesting features. As in other Compositae, the ovules are tenuinucellate. The archesporium is usually two-celled (Fig. 83*A*), but sometimes three cells may be present and occasionally there is only one. After the first meiotic division 2 nuclei are formed of which the upper soon becomes larger than the lower (Fig. 83*B*). Both divide again without wall formation and the resulting 4 nuclei take up a 1+3 arrangement (Fig. 83*C–D*). Only the micropylar nucleus functions, while the other 3 nuclei soon begin to degenerate. Vacuolation takes place at this stage and is followed by the appearance of a lateral vesicular outgrowth, which assumes a tubular form and gradually makes its way upward into the micropyle (Fig. 83*E–F*). The functioning megaspore nucleus, which has by this time moved

[11a] Mason (1949), who has made a recent study of *Limnanthes*, regards the embryo sac as bisporic.

FIG. 83. Development of embryo sac in *Balsamita vulgaris*. *A*, l.s. nucellus showing two-celled archesporium. *B*, mother cell on right has two nuclei (end of Meiosis I); that on left has four nuclei (end of Meiosis II). *C,D*, megaspore nuclei take up 1+3 position; micropylar nucleus has enlarged; smaller chalazal nuclei are on way to degeneration. *E*, formation of vesicular outgrowth from chalazal end of the cell. *F*, functional megaspore nucleus has entered vesicle. *G–H*, two- and four-nucleate stages. *I*, eight-nucleate embryo sac; note three nonfunctioning megaspore nuclei at base. *J*, mature embryo sac, showing egg apparatus, secondary nucleus, and multinucleate antipodal cells. (*After Fagerlind, 1939c.*)

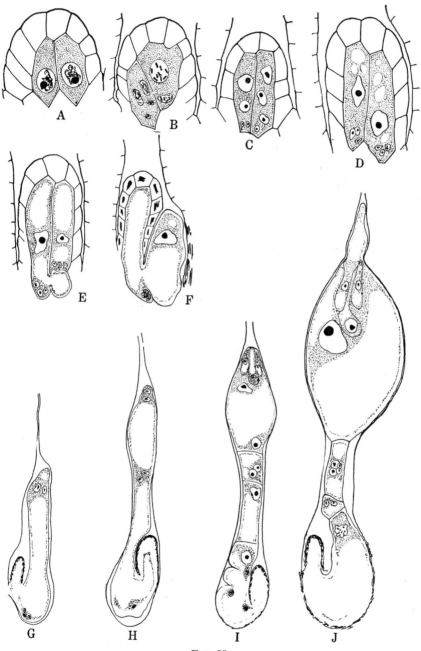

Fig. 83.

into the apex of the tube, undergoes two divisions to form 4 nuclei, which lie in two pairs, one at each end of a large vacuole (Fig. 83*G–H*). The next division gives rise to 8 nuclei, of which the upper 4 form the egg apparatus and the upper polar nucleus, and the lower 4 give rise to the three antipodal cells and the lower polar nucleus (Fig. 83*I–J*). The lowest antipodal cell connects the vesicular outgrowth with the body of the old megaspore mother cell in which the three degenerated megaspore nuclei are sometimes still distinguishable. The nuclei of the antipodal cells frequently undergo a few divisions but the daughter nuclei fuse once again to form a single lobed nucleus.

Chrysanthemum cinerariaefolium. Martinoli (1939) has discovered a peculiar mode of development in this plant. The embryo sac is tetrasporic and the megaspore nuclei take up a $1+2+1$ arrangement so that there is 1 nucleus at each pole and 2 nuclei lie in the middle (Fig. 84*A–C*). The two central nuclei become separated from the terminal nuclei by vacuoles and may either fuse to form a single diploid nucleus (Fig. 84*H*) or may merely remain close to one another without undergoing any fusion (Fig. 84*D*). The subsequent development differs, depending on which of the two conditions is present.

In the first case the next division gives rise to 6 nuclei (a haploid pair at either end and a diploid pair in the center) (Fig. 84*I*) which divide again to form three groups of 4 nuclei each (Fig. 84*J*). The micropylar quartet now produces the egg apparatus and upper polar nucleus, all haploid. The chalazal quartet gives rise to four antipodal cells, also haploid. The central quartet is composed of diploid nuclei; one of these functions as the lower polar nucleus and the remaining 3 organize as additional antipodal cells (Fig. 84*K*). Sometimes less than 12 nuclei are formed (10 or 7), either because of a failure of some divisions at the chalazal end or because the central diploid nucleus of the 3-nucleate stage undergoes only one division instead of two.

In the second of the two previously mentioned alternatives, *i.e.*, when the two central megaspore nuclei do not fuse but only lie in contact with each other, neither undergoes any further divisions and both function directly as the polar nuclei. Meanwhile the micropylar megaspore nucleus divides twice, to give rise to the micropylar quartet, but there is no regularity in the behavior of the chalazal nucleus. The total number of nuclei in the mature embryo sac may therefore be 10 or 9 or even as few as 6, depending upon two divisions, or a single division, or a complete failure of division, of this nucleus (Fig. 84*E–G*).

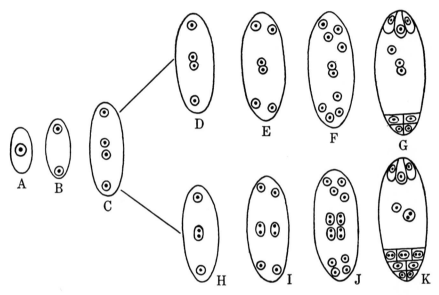

FIG. 84. Two modes of development of embryo sac of *Chrysanthemum cinerariae-folium*. *A–C*, formation of the four megaspore nuclei. *D–G*, first type of development, in which the two central megaspore nuclei remain undivided and function directly as polar nuclei. *H–K*, second type of development, in which two central megaspore nuclei fuse to form diploid nucleus which undergoes two divisions to give rise to four nuclei; of these, one functions as polar nucleus and three form antipodal cells. For details, see text. (*Adapted from Martinoli, 1939.*)

ORGANIZATION OF MATURE EMBRYO SAC

Although the origin of the mature embryo sac may differ, its eventual organization shows a surprisingly uniform pattern in the majority of angiosperms. The Polygonum, Allium, Fritillaria, and Adoxa types of embryo sacs all have a similar appearance at the time of fertilization (three-celled egg apparatus, three antipodals, and two polar nuclei). Even in the remaining types an egg apparatus, at least, is almost always present and it is only in a few genera like *Peperomia*, *Plumbago*, *Plumbagella*, and *Acalypha indica* that we see a radical departure from the basic plan. Ignoring for the present the origin of the embryo sac (whether mono-, bi-, or tetrasporic), we shall now confine our attention to the organization of the mature stage only.

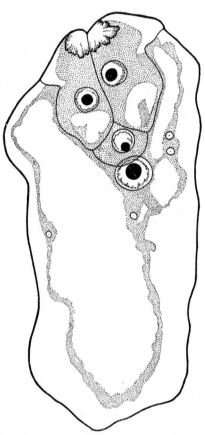

Fig. 85.   Mature embryo sac of *Oeno-thera nutans*, showing synergids with fili-form apparatus and indentations. Note that nucleus of synergids lies towards upper end of cell, and vacuole towards lower end.   (*After Ishikawa, 1918.*)

The Egg Apparatus. Typically the egg apparatus is composed of an egg and two synergids. As a rule each of the synergids is notched by an indentation resulting in the formation of a prominent hook (Fig. 85). The upper part of the cell is occupied by the so-called "filiform apparatus" which shows a number of striations converging towards the apex. The nucleus lies in or just below the region of the hook and the lower part of the cell contains a large vacuole (Dahlgren, 1928*a*, 1938). In the egg, on the other hand, the nucleus and most of the cytoplasm lie in the lower part of the cell and the vacuole in the upper. Hooks and indentations are usually absent, having been described only in *Plumbagella*, *Ditepalanthus*, *Helosis*, and a few members of the Ulmaceae and Urticaceae (Fagerlind, 1943).

Usually the synergids are ephemeral structures which degenerate and disappear soon after fertilization or even before it. In some cases, however, one or both of them may persist for a time and show signs of considerable activity. In *Allium unifolium* and *A. rotundum* (Weber, 1929) this behavior is particularly pronounced, and one of the synergids begins to degenerate only after the development of the embryo is well under way. *Nothoscordum* (Stenar, 1932), *Limnanthes* (Fig. 86*B*) (Fagerlind in 1939c), and *Albuca* (Eunus, 1950) are essentially similar; and in some Cucurbitaceae (Fig. 86A) both the synergids become large and prominent and seem to play an important role in the nutrition of the embryo sac.

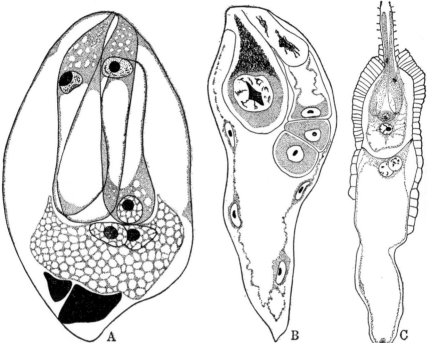

Fig. 86. Modifications of synergids. *A, Luffa acutangula*, embryo sac, showing extremely long synergids reaching down to level below middle of sac. (*After Kirkwood, 1905.*) *B, Limnanthes douglasii*, embryo sac showing three-celled embryo and persisting synergid. (*After Fagerlind, 1939c.*) *C, Ursinia anthemoides*, beak-shaped synergids protruding through micropyle. (*After Dahlgren, 1924.*)

In none of the plants cited above do the synergids extend beyond the limits of the embryo sac wall. This condition has so far been noted to a pronounced extent only in the Compositae. Dahlgren (1924) found that in *Ursinea* (Fig. 86C) and *Calendula* the synergids elongate so much that their tips project to a considerable distance into the micropyle and outside it, sometimes reaching as far as the funiculus.

Certain other reports of the occurrence of synergid haustoria, as in *Lathraea, Lobelia,* and *Angelonia,* have, however, to be interpreted differently, for there is now no doubt that the cells in question are really endosperm derivatives. The confusion was caused by the fact that the micropylar cells of the endosperm sometimes show an appearance identical with that of the synergids—a vacuole lying in the lower part of the cell and the nucleus and cytoplasm in the tapering upper part (see Rosén, 1947). In *Myriophyllum* (Stolt, 1928; Souèges, 1940) and *Hypecoum* (Souèges, 1943) even suspensor cells are known to show a surprising resemblance to synergids.

Antipodal Cells. Although usually short-lived, the antipodals frequently show a considerable increase in size or number. In some members of the Gentianaceae (Stolt, 1921) the three antipodal cells divide to form about 10 to 12 cells (Fig. 87*D*), and in the Gramineae a still larger number of cells is produced (Fig. 87*C*). In *Sasa paniculata* (Yamaura, 1933), a member of the Bambusae, an many as 300 antipodal cells have been reported.

In several genera of the Rubiaceae, like *Putoria* (Fagerlind, 1936*a*) and *Galium* (Fagerlind, 1937), the basal antipodal cell is often greatly elongated and acts as an aggressive haustorium (Fig. 87 *B, E*). In *Phyllis* (Fagerlind, 1936*b*) all three of the antipodal cells are swollen; the basal becomes 8-nucleate and each of the upper two becomes 4-nucleate (Fig. 87*G,H*).

An increase in the number of antipodal cells and the number of nuclei per antipodal cell is well known in the Compositae (Fig. 87*A,F*). In *Grindelia squarrosa,* according to Howe (1926), only two antipodal cells are formed, the one nearer the micropyle being binucleate. One or both of these cells undergo further development, growing laterally into the integument for a considerable distance. In *Artemisia* (Diettert, 1938) the number of antipodal cells varies from three to six and each cell may have 2 or more nuclei. The basal antipodal cell frequently elongates and penetrates through the chalazal tissue, finally entering the ovarian chamber. *Rudbeckia bicolor* (Maheshwari and Srinivasan, 1944), whose embryo sac follows the Fritillaria type of development, has triploid antipodal cells which attain a much larger size than the cells of the egg apparatus (Fig. 88). The central antipodal cell, in particular, persists for a long time, being recognizable even during embryonal development.

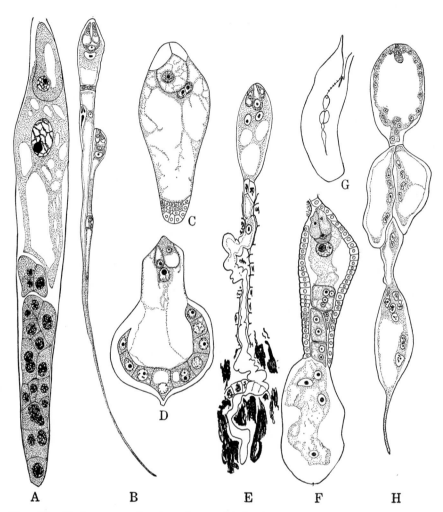

FIG. 87. Embryo sacs showing abnormal behavior of antipodal cells. *A, Ligularia sibirica*; embryo sac showing increase in number of antipodal cells, some of which are binucleate. (*After Afzelius, 1924.*) *B, Putoria calabrica*, three embryo sacs of which two are well organized; note extreme elongation of basal antipodal cell. (*After Fagerlind, 1936a.*) *C, Zea mays*, embryo sac showing mass of antipodal cells at lower end. (*After Randolph, 1933.*) *D, Gentiana campestris*, embryo sac showing increase in number of antipodal cells. (*After Stolt, 1921.*) *E, Galium mollugo*, embryo sac showing elongation of basal antipodal cell. (*After Fagerlind, 1937.*) *F, Aster novae-anglieae*, several multinucleate antipodal cells, of which basal has undergone considerable enlargement. (*After Chamberlain, 1895.*) *G, Phyllis nobla*, l.s. ovule. *H*, embryo sac of same enlarged to show young embryo, endosperm, and three haustorial antipodal cells. (*After Fagerlind, 1936b.*)

The antipodal cells of some members of the Ranunculaceae become greatly enlarged and assume a glandular appearance (Fig. 89). Grafl (1941) has shown that in *Caltha palustris* they attain a

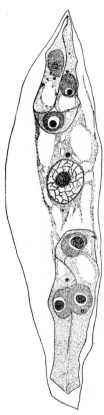

high degree of polyploidy. At first each antipodal cell becomes binucleate. The two nuclei now divide again, but the spindles fuse during this process so that there are again only two nuclei which, however, possess the diploid number of chromosomes. This process may be repeated, leading to the formation of tetraploid and even octoploid nuclei. It gives an indication of the high metabolic activity in these cells and offers a close analogy with the behavior of the anther tapetum.

Polar Nuclei. The central portion of the embryo sac containing the polar nuclei eventually gives rise to the endosperm and has therefore been called the *Endospermanlage* or "endosperm mother cell." Usually the two nuclei are so similar to each other that once they have come together it is difficult to distinguish the micropylar from the chalazal. When there is a difference in size between the two, it is usually the micropylar which is the larger. In embryo sacs of the Fritillaria type, however, the chalazal polar nucleus is the larger (see page 118).

The fusion of the polar nuclei may occur either before, or during, or sometimes after, the entry of the pollen tube inside the embryo sac. The secondary nucleus formed after fusion usually lies just below the egg and is separated from the antipodal cells by a large vacuole. In those plants in which it lies near the center, it is connected with the egg apparatus by a conspicuous cytoplasmic strand. A chalazal position is less frequent except in those plants which are characterized by a Helobial type of endosperm (see page 245).

Fig. 88. Embryo sac of *Rudbeckia bicolor*, showing three large antipodal cells which are arranged like cells of egg apparatus. (*After Maheshwari and Srinivasan, 1944.*)

Embryo Sacs with Disturbed Polarity. Rarely, embryo sacs may be found in which the usual polarity and organization are absent.

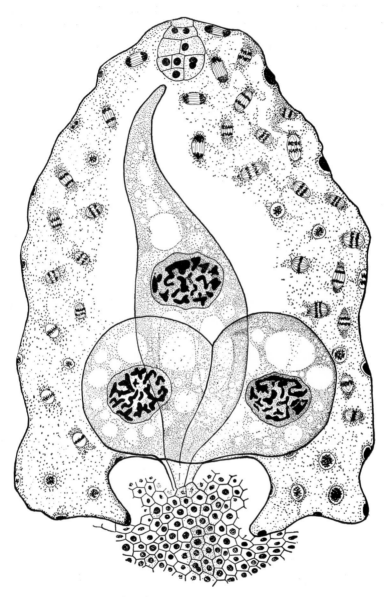

FIG. 89. Embryo sac of *Aconitum napellus* showing three large antipodal cells. Note young embryo at micropylar end and endosperm nuclei in various stages of division. (*After Osterwalder, 1898.*)

Sometimes one or all of the antipodal nuclei move up and function as supernumerary polar nuclei; or the secondary nucleus fragments to form a group of micronuclei of varying sizes. Supernumerary egg cells and synergids have also been noted. Very rarely, the embryo sac shows a reversed polarity, with the egg apparatus differentiating at the chalazal end and the antipodals at the micropylar. As examples may be cited *Atamosco texana* (Pace, 1913), *Fuchsia marinka* (Täckholm, 1915), *Lindelofia longiflora* (Svensson, 1925), *Saccharum officinarum* (Dutt and Subba Rao, 1933; Narayanaswami, 1940), *Woodfordia floribunda* (Joshi and Venkateswarlu, 1935), *Eriodendron anfractuosum* (Thirumalachar and Khan, 1941), *Heptapleurum venulosum* (Gopinath, 1943), and *Crinum asiaticum* (Swamy, 1946). In certain other plants, a normal egg apparatus is differentiated at the micropylar end, but two of the antipodal cells also look like synergids and the third resembles an egg, (Fig. 94*A*) so that the embryo sac apparently shows two egg apparatuses, one at each end. *Poa alpina* (Håkansson, 1943) sometimes shows the reverse condition, *i.e.*, the occurrence of two groups of antipodal cells, one at the micropylar end and the other at the chalazal. Embryo sacs of the latter type are functionless, however, and do not produce embryos.[12]

The embryo sacs of the Viscoideae (Fig. 65), some members of the Balanophoraceae (Figs. 60, 61), and a few saprophytic genera of the Gentianaceae (Fig. 90) also appear to be inverted. Oehler (1927) has given the correct explanation when he says that the ovules of *Leiphaimos* and *Cotylanthera*, although seemingly orthotropous, are in fact anatropous, and that the inversion in the polarity of the embryo sac is only apparent but not real.

Food Reserves in the Embryo Sac. It is usually taken for granted that the angiosperm embryo sac is devoid of any appreciable food reserves. While this is generally true, there are now several records of the occurrence of starch in embryo sacs, and in the families Aizoaceae, Cactaceae, Portulacaceae, Bruniaceae, Tiliaceae, Crassulaceae, and Asclepiadaceae this is a common phenomenon. Dahlgren (1927, 1939) who has reviewed the subject in recent years, states that the reason why starch grains have not been re-

[12] A fertilization of antipodal cells seems to have been recorded only in *Nigella arvensis* (Derschau, 1918), but it is quite likely that it also occurs sometimes in *Ulmus* (Shattuck, 1905; Ekdahl, 1941).

ported more frequently in embryo sacs is that they are not very
distinct in the usual balsam mounts, and very few workers take the
trouble of removing the coverslip and testing the sections with
an iodine solution.

While reference must be made to Dahlgren's papers for fuller
information on the subject, a few noteworthy cases of the occurrence of starch grains in the embryo sac may be mentioned here.

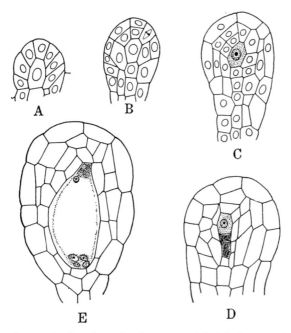

Fig. 90.   Development of ovule and embryo sac of *Leiphaimos spectabilis*.   (*After
Oehler, 1927.*)

In *Arachis* (Reed, 1924), *Tilia* (Stenar, 1925b), *Pentstemon* (Evans,
1919), and *Acacia* (Newman, 1934) the embryo sacs are so full of
starch that it becomes difficult to study the nuclei inside them.
In *Styphelia* (Brough, 1924) starch grains are so abundant in the
vicinity of the egg that the latter is obscured by them.   In *Dendrophthora* (York, 1913) their crowding is said to cause a degeneration and disappearance of the nuclei.

The stage at which the starch makes its appearance in the embryo
sac varies in different plants.   In *Loranthus pentandrus*, Treub
(1883) saw starch grains even at the megaspore mother cell stage;

in *Psychotria* (Fagerlind, 1937) starch appears at the dyad cell stage; in *Castalia* (Cook, 1902), *Acacia* (Guignard, 1881), *Sedum* (D'Hubert, 1896), *Pentas*, *Richardsonia*, and *Cephalantus* (Fagerlind, 1937) at the functioning megaspore stage; in *Portulaca oleracea* (Cooper, 1940) at the binucleate stage; and in *Corchorus trilocularis* (Stenar, 1925b), *Cynanchum acutum* (Francini, 1927), and *Medicago sativa* (Cooper, 1935b) at the 4-nucleate stage.   In the majority of

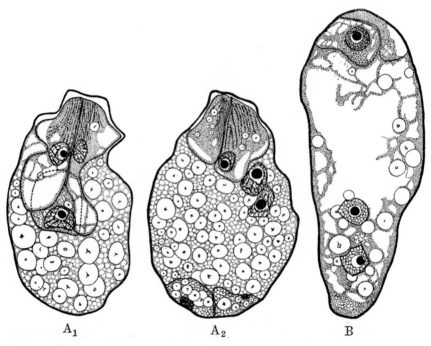

A_1 A_2 B

FIG. 91.   Embryo sacs of *Acacia baileyana*, showing starch grains. A_1, A_2, successive sections of unfertilized embryo sac. B, postfertilization stage. (*After Newman, 1934.*)

plants, however, the starch appears when the embryo sac is mature and reaches a maximum shortly after fertilization, gradually decreasing in postfertilization stages. *Xyris indica* (Weinzieher, 1914), *Acacia baileyana* (Newman, 1934) (Fig. 91), and *Petunia* (Cooper, 1946) (Fig. 112) are peculiar in having large quantities of starch even during endosperm formation.

A few cases are on record in which the starch occurs not merely in the cavity of the embryo sac but also in the cells of the egg apparatus and rarely even in the antipodal cells. The following are some examples of the occurrence of starch grains in the egg: *Astilbe grandis* (Dahlgren, 1930), *Aspidistra elatior* (Golaszewska, 1934), *Acacia baileyana* (Newman, 1934), *Medicago sativa* (Cooper, 1935b; Cooper, Brink, and Albrecht, 1937), *Korthalsella opuntia* (Rutishauser, 1937b), *Zea mays, Euchlaena mexicana* (Cooper, 1938), *Portulaca oleracea* (Cooper, 1940), and *Phryma leptostachya* (Cooper, 1941). In *Korthalsella* (Rutishauser, 1937b) starch is also found in antipodal cells.

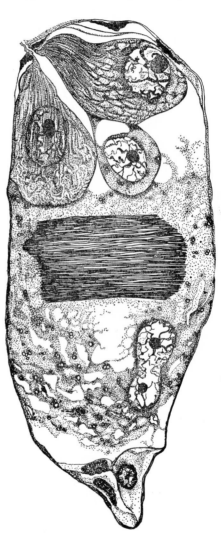

In *Sonneratia* (Venkateswarlu, 1937; Mauritzon, 1939) certain oily bodies of an unknown nature persist from the megaspore mother cell stage to the formation of the mature embryo sac, and in *Aspidistra* (Fig. 92) (Golaszewska, 1934) large raphides have been seen in the mature stages. The significance of these structures in the economy of the embryo sac has not been elucidated up to this time.

Embryo Sac Haustoria. In the majority of angiosperms the entire surface of the embryo sac serves an absorptive function, demolishing the adjacent cells of the nucellus and even the inner layers of the integument. In some plants, however, more active growth is seen at the ends of the sac. In *Phaseolus* (Fig. 93A) (Wein-

FIG. 92. Embryo sac of *Aspidistra elatior*, showing starch grains and a large raphide. (*After Golaszewska, 1934.*).

stein, 1926) and *Melilotus*, (Cooper, 1933) the embryo sac ruptures the nucellar epidermis and grows beyond it, so that more than one-third of it lies in direct contact with the cells lining the micropylar canal. In *Arechavaletaia* (Ventura, 1937) and *Kirengeshoma* (Mauritzon, 1939) it protrudes out of the endostome and comes to lie in the exostome. In *Philadelphus* (Mauritzon, 1933), *Thesium* (Schulle, 1933), *Galium* (Fagerlind, 1937), *Utricularia* (Kausik,

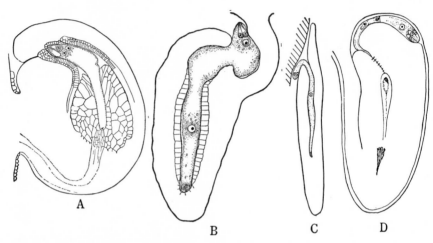

A   B   C   D

FIG. 93. Some instances of embryo sacs protruding into and beyond micropyle. *A, Phaseolus vulgaris,* upward elongation of embryo sac, resulting in rupture of nucellar tissue; nucellar epidermis is intact, however, at apex of embryo sac. (*After Weinstein, 1926.*) *B, Torenia hirsuta,* embryo sac protruding out of micropyle. (*After Krishna Iyengar, 1941.*) *C, Philadelphus coronarius,* embryo sac protruding out of micropyle. (*After Mauritzon, 1933.*) *D, Galium lucidum,* one embryo sac completely outside micropyle; another in position, but in process of degeneration. (*After Fagerlind, 1937.*)

1938), and certain members of the Scrophulariaceae like *Vandellia* and *Torenia* (Krishna Iyengar, 1940, 1941) the nucellus breaks down completely at a rather early stage and the naked embryo sac protrudes out of the ovule, establishing direct contact with the placenta and digesting its way into the tissue of the latter (Fig. 93*B–D*). Strangest of all are some genera of the Loranthaceae, like *Scurrula* and *Dendrophthoe* (Rauch, 1936; Singh, 1950), in which ovules and integuments are absent in the usual sense and the embryo sacs undergo a remarkable elongation toward both the top and the bottom. At the lower end they are soon stopped by a pad of collenchymatous cells, but the upper part continues to grow, sometimes reaching a considerable distance into the style. Fertilization occurs here by the incoming pollen tubes and the embryos are thrust down again by the elongating suspensors. The observations of Schaeppi and Steindl (1942), who have recently studied several other genera of the family, show that in *Macrosolen* the upper end of the embryo

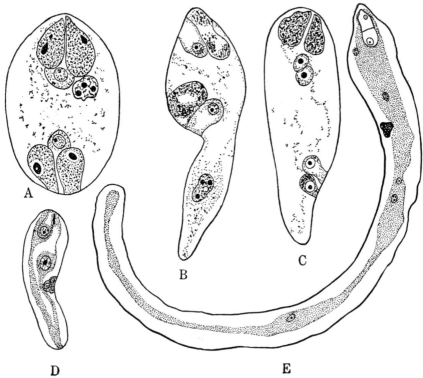

Fig. 94. Formation of embryo sac caeca in *Allium paniculatum* (*A–C*), and *Digera arvensis* (*D, E*). (*A–C, after Modilewski, 1928; D–E, after Joshi, 1936.*)

sac reaches up to the base of the style, in *Elythranthe* it grows beyond its base, in *Lepeostegeres* it is at about one-fourth of the height of the style, in *Amyema* somewhere near its middle region, in *Taxillus*, slightly above the middle, and in *Helixanthera*[12a] just below the papillate layer of the stigma.

In other plants it is a downward growth which is more striking.

[12a] See also Johri and Maheshwari (1950).

In several members of the Centrospermales (Oksijuk, 1927; Art-schwager and Starrett, 1933; Joshi, 1936; Cooper, 1949) the embryo sac pushes forward at the chalazal end and digests its way through the nucellus, while the antipodal cells remain *in situ* and are left behind in a lateral position (Fig. 94*E*). This "caecum," which is also known in *Allium* (Modilewski, 1928) (Fig. 94*A–C*), *Elegia* (Borwein, *et al.*, 1949), *Macrosolen* (Maheshwari and Singh, 1950), and certain other plants (see Finn, 1936), seems to be a very effective haustorial organ.

In *Veltheimia* (Stiffler, 1925; Buchner, 1948), *Paradisia* (Stenar, 1928), and *Eucomis* (Buchner, 1948) the haustorium arises laterally rather than from the pole of the embryo sac. As a rule, however, such a condition is met with only in postfertilization stages and will therefore be considered in the chapter on the endosperm.

References

Afzelius, K. 1916. Zur Embryosackentwicklung der Orchideen. Svensk Bot. Tidskr. **10**: 183–227.

———. 1924. Embryologische und zytologische Studien in *Senecio* und ver-wandten Gattungen. Acta Horti Bergiani 8(7): 123–219.

Arnoldi, W. 1912. Zur Embryologie einiger Euphorbiaceen. Trav. Mus. Bot. Acad. St. Petersburg **9**: 136–154.

Artschwager, E., and Starrett, R. C. 1933. The time factor in fertilization and embryo development in the sugar beet. Jour. Agr. Res. **47**: 823–847.

Bambacioni, V. 1928*a*. Ricerche sulla ecologia e sulla embriologia di *Fritillaria persica* L. Ann. di Bot. **18**: 7–37.

———. 1928*b*. Contributo alla embriologia di *Lilium candidum* L. R. C. Accad. Naz. Lincei **8**: 612–618.

Bambacioni-Mezzetti, V. 1931. Nouve ricerche sull'embriologia delle Gigliaceae. Ann. di Bot. **19**: 365–382.

Bergman, B. 1935. Zytologische Studien über die Fortpflanzung bei den Gat-tungen *Leontodon* und *Picris*. Svensk Bot. Tidskr. **29**: 155–301.

Borwein, B., Coetsee, M. L., and Krupko, S. 1949. Development of the embryo sac of *Restio dodii* and *Elegia racemosa*. Jour. South Afri. Bot. **15**: 1–11.

Boyes, J. W. 1939. Development of the embryo sac of *Plumbagella micrantha*. Amer. Jour. Bot. **26**: 539–547.

Brough, P. 1924. Studies in the Epacridaceae. I. The life history of *Styphelia longifolia* (R.Br.). Proc. Linn. Soc. N. S. Wales **49**: 162–178.

Brown, W. H., and Sharp, L. W. 1911. The embryo sac of *Epipactis*. Bot. Gaz. **52**: 439–452.

Buchner, L. 1949. Vergleichende embryologische Studien an Scilloideae. Österr. bot. Zeitschr. **95**: 428–450.

Campbell, D. H. 1899*a*. Die Entwicklung des Embryosackes von *Peperomia pellucida*. Ber. deutsch. bot. Gesell. **17**: 452–456.

———. 1899*b*. A peculiar embryo sac in *Peperomia pellucida*. Ann. Bot. **13**: 626.

———. 1901. The embryo sac of *Peperomia*. Ann. Bot. **15**: 103–117.

Carlson, M. C. 1945. Megasporogenesis and development of the embryo sac of *Cypripedium parviflorum*. Bot. Gaz. **107**: 107–114.

Chamberlain, C. J. 1895. Contributions to the embryology of *Aster novae-angliae*. Bot. Gaz. **20**: 205–212.

Chiarugi, A. 1933. Lo sviluppo del gametofito femmineo della *Weddelina squamulosa* Tul. (Podostemonaceae). R. C. Accad. Naz. Lincei **17**: 1095–1100.

Cook, M. T. 1902. Development of the embryo sac and embryo of *Castalia odorata* and *Numphaea advena*. Bul. Torrey Bot. Club **29**: 211–220.

Cooper, D. C. 1933. Macrosporogenesis and embryology of *Melilotus*. Bot. Gaz. **95**: 143–155.

———. 1935*a*. Macrosporogenesis and development of the embryo sac of *Lilium henryi*. Bot. Gaz. **97**: 364–355.

———. 1935*b*. Macrosporogenesis and embryology of *Medicago*. Jour. Agr. Res. **51**: 471–477.

———. 1938. Macrosporogenesis and embryo sac development in *Euchlaena mexicana* and *Zea mays*. Jour. Agr. Res. **55**: 539–551.

———. 1940. Macrosporogenesis and embryo ogy of *Portulaca oleracea*. Amer. Jour. Bot. **27**: 326–330.

———. 1941. Macrosporogenesis and the development of the seed of *Phryma leptostachya*. Amer. Jour. Bot. **28**: 755–761.

———. 1946. Double fertilization in *Petunia*. Amer. Jour. Bot. **33**: 53–57.

———. 1949. Flower and seed development in *Oxybaphus nyctagineus*. Amer. Jour. Bot. **36**: 348–355.

———, Brink, R. A., and Albrecht, H. R. 1937. Embryo mortality in relation to seed formation in alfalfa (*Medicago sativa*). Amer. Jour. Bot. **24**: 203–213.

Dahlgren, K. V. O. 1924. Studien über die Endospermbildung der Kompositen. Svensk Bot. Tidskr. **18**: 177–203.

———. 1927. Über das Vorkommen von Stärke in den Embryosäcken der Angiospermen. Ber deutsch. bot. Gesell. **45**: 374–384.

———. 1928*a*. Hakenförmige Leistenbildungen bei Synergiden. Ber. deutsch. bot. Gesell. **46**: 434–443.

———. 1928*b*. Die Embryologie einiger Alismataceae. Svensk Bot. Tidskr. **22**: 1–17.

———. 1930. Zur Embryologie der Saxifragagoideen. Svensk Bot. Tidskr. **24**: 429–448.

———. 1934. Die Embryosackentwicklung von *Echinodorus macrophyllus* und *Sagittaria sagittifolia*. Planta **21**: 602–612.

———. 1937. Die Entwicklung des Embryosackes bei *Plumbago zeylanica*. Bot. Notiser 1937, pp. 487–498.

Dahlgren, K.V.O. 1938. Hakenbildungen bei Synergiden. Zweite Mitteilung. Svensk Bot. Tidskr. **52**: 221–237.

———. 1939. Sur la présence d'amidon dans le sac embryonnaire chez les angiospermes. Bot. Notiser 1939, pp. 487–498.

D'Amato, F. 1940*a*. Embriologia di *Ulmus campestris* L. Nuovo Gior. Bot. Ital. N.S. **47**: 247–263.

———. 1940*b*. Contributo all'embriologia delle Plumbaginaceae. Nuovo Gior. Bot. Ital. N.S. **47**: 349–382.

Derschau, M. v. 1918. Über disperme Befruchtung der Antipoden von *Nigella arvensis*. Ber. deutsch. bot. Gesell. **36**: 260–262.

D'Hubert, E. 1896. Recherches sur le sac embryonnaire des plantes grasses. Ann. des Sci. Nat., Bot. **2**: 37–128.

Diettert, R. A. 1938. The morphology of *Artemisia tridentata* Nutt. Lloydia **1**: 3–74.

Dodds, K. S. 1945. Genetical and cytological studies of *Musa*. VI. The development of female cells of certain edible diploids. Jour. Genet. **46**: 161–179.

Dutt, N. L., and Subba Rao, K. S. 1933. Observations on the cytology of the sugarcane. Indian Jour. Agr. Sci. **3**: 37–56.

Ekdahl, I. 1941. Die Entwicklung von Embryosack und Embryo bei *Ulmus glabra* Huds. Svensk Bot. Tidskr. **35**: 143–156.

Ernst, A. 1908. Ergebnisse neurer Untersuchungen über den Embryosack der Angiospermen. Verh. schweiz. naturf. Ges. **91,** Jahresv. I: 230–263.

Eunus, A. M. 1950. Contributions to the embryology of the Liliaceae. X. *Albuca transvalensis* Moss-Verdoorn. Jour. Indian Bot. Soc. **29**: 68–78.

Evans, A. T. 1919. Embryo sac and embryo of *Pentstemon secundiflorus*. Bot. Gaz. **67**: 426–437.

Eysel, G. 1937. "Die Embryosackentwicklung von *Limnanthes douglasii* R. Br." Diss. Marburg.

Fagerlind, F. 1936*a*. Die Embryologie von *Putoria*. Svensk Bot. Tidskr. **30**: 362–372.

———. 1936*b*. Embryologische Beobachtungen über die Gattung *Phyllis*. Bot. Notiser 1936, pp. 577–584.

———. 1937. Embryologische, zytologische und bestäubungsexperimentelle Studien in der Familie Rubiaceae nebst Bemerkungen über einige Polyploiditätsprobleme. Acta Horti Bergiani **11**: 195–470.

———. 1938*a*. Wo kommen tetrasporische durch drei Teilungsschritte vollenentwickelte Embryosäcke unter den Angiospermen vor? Bot. Notiser 1938, pp. 461–498.

———. 1938*b*. Embryosack von *Plumbagella* und *Plumbago*. Arkiv. för Bot. **29B**: 1–8.

———. 1939*a*. Die Entwicklung des Embryosackes bei *Peperomia pellucida*. Arkiv. för Bot. **29A**: 1–15.

———. 1939*b*. Drei Beispiele des Fritillaria-Typus. Svensk Bot. Tidskr. **33**: 188–204.

Fagerlind, F. 1939c. Kritische und revidierende Untersuchungen über das Vorkommen des Adoxa ("Lilium")-Typus. Acta Horti Bergiani **13**: 1–49.

——. 1940. Stempelbau und Embryosackentwicklung bei einigen Pandanazeen. Ann. Jard. Bot. Buitenzorg **49**: 55–78.

——. 1941. Die Embryosackentwicklung bei *Tanacetum vulgare* und einigen *Chrysanthemum*-Arten. Svensk Bot. Tidskr. **35**: 157–176.

——. 1943. Vorkommen und Entstehung von Hakenleisten an Synergiden und Eizellen. Svensk Bot. Tidskr. **37**: 339–351.

——. 1944. Der tetrasporische Angiospermen-Embryosack und dessen Bedeutung für das Verhältnis der Entwicklungsmechanik und Phylogenie des Embryosacks. Arkiv. för Bot. **31A**: 1–71.

——. 1945a. Bildung und Entwicklung des Embryosacks bei sexuellen und agamospermischen *Balanophora*-Arten. Svensk Bot. Tidskr. **39**: 65–82.

——. 1945b. Bau der floralen Organe bei der Gattung *Lanjsdorffia*. Svensk Bot. Tidskr. **39**: 197–210.

Finn, W. W. 1936. Zur Entwicklungsgeschichte der chalazogamen *Ostrya carpinifolia* Scop. Jour. Inst. Bot. Acad. Sci. Ukraine **8**: 15–25.

Francini, D. E. 1927. L'embriologia del *Cynanchum acutum* L. Nuovo Gior. Bot. Ital. N.S. **34**: 381–395.

——. 1931. Ricerche embriologichee cariologiche sul genere *Cypripedium*. Nuovo Gior. Bot. Ital. N.S. **38**: 155–212.

Frisendahl, A. 1927. Über die Entwicklung chasmogamer und kleistogamer Blüten bei der Gattung *Elatine*. Acta Hort. Gothoburg. **3**: 99–142.

Geerts, J. M. 1908. Beiträge zur Kenntnis der cytologischen Entwicklung von *Oenothera lamarckiana*. Ber. deutsch. bot. Gesell. **26A**: 608–614.

Gerassimova, H. 1933. Fertilisation in *Crepis capillaris*. Cellule **42**: 103–148.

Golaszewska, Z. 1934. Die Entwicklung des Embryosackes bei *Aspidistra elatior*. Acta Soc. Bot. Poloniae **11**: 399–407.

Goodspeed, T. H. 1947. Maturation of the gametes and fertilization in *Nicotiana*. Madroño **9**: 110–120.

Gopinath, D. M. 1943. Reversed polarity in the embryo sac of *Heptapleurum venulosum* Seem. Current Sci. [India] **12**: 58.

Grafl, I. 1941. Über das Wachstum der Antipodenkerne von *Caltha palustris*. Chromosoma **2**: 1–11.

Guignard, L. 1881. Recherches d'embryogénie végétale comparée. I. Legumineuses. Ann. des Sci. Nat., Bot. **12**: 5–166.

Håkansson, A. 1923. Studien über die Entwicklungsgeschichte der Umbelliferen. Acta Univ. Lund N.F. Avd. II, **18**(7): 1–120.

——. 1943. Die Entwicklung des Embryosacks und die Befruchtung bei *Poa alpina*. Hereditas **29**: 25–61.

Hammond, B. L. 1937. Development of *Podostemon ceratophyllum*. Bul. Torrey Bot. Club **64**: 17–36.

Haque, A. 1950. The embryo sac of *Erythronium americanum*. (In press.)

Harling, G. 1946. Studien über den Blutenbau und die Embryologie der Familie Cyclanthaceae. Svensk Bot. Tidskr. **40**: 257–272.

Haupt, A. W. 1934. Ovule and embryo sac of *Plumbago capensis*. Bot. Gaz. **95:** 649–659.

Hoare, G. 1934. Gametogenesis and fertilization in *Scilla nonscripta*. Cellule **42:** 269–292.

Hoeppener, E., and Renner, O. 1929. Genetische und zytologische Oenotheren-studien. II. Bot. Abh. Goebel **15:** 1–66.

Hofmeister, W. 1847. Untersuchungen des Vorgangs bei der Befruchtung der Oenotheren. Bot. Ztg. **5:** 785–792.

————. 1849. "Die Entstehung des Embryo der Phanerogamen." Leipzig.

Howe, T. D. 1926. Development of embryo sac in *Grindelia squarrosa*. Bot. Gaz. **81:** 280–296.

Ishikawa, M. 1918. Studies on the embryo sac and fertilisation in *Oenothera*. Ann. Bot. **32:** 279–317.

Jönsson, B. 1879–80. Om embryosäckens utveckling hos angiospermerna. Lunds Univ. Årskr. **16:** 1–86.

Johansen, D. A. 1929. Studies on the morphology of the Onagraceae. I. The megagametophyte of *Hartmannia tetraptera*. Bul. Torrey Bot. Club **56:** 285–298.

————. 1931*a*. Studies on the morphology of the Onagraceae. II. *Anogra pallida*. Amer. Jour. Bot. **18:** 854–863.

————. 1931*b*. Studies on the morphology of the Onagraceae. V. *Zauschneria latifolia*, typical of a genus characterised by irregular embryology. Ann. N. Y. Acad. Sci. **33:** 1–26.

Johnson, D. S. 1900. On the endosperm and embryo of *Peperomia pellucida*. Bot. Gaz. **80:** 1–11.

————. 1914. Studies in the development of the Piperaceae. II. The structure and seed development of *Peperomia hispidula*. Amer. Jour. Bot. **1:** 323–339, 357–397.

Johri, B. M. 1935*a*. Studies in the family Alismaceae. I. *Limnophyton obtusi-folium* Miq. Jour. Indian Bot. Soc. **14:** 49–66.

————. 1935*b*. Studies in the family Alismaceae. II. *Sagittaria sagittifolia* L. Proc. Indian Acad. Sci. Sect. B. **1:** 340–348.

————. 1935*c*. Studies in the family Alismaceae. III. *Sagittaria guayanensis* H.B.K. and *S. latifolia* Willd. Proc. Indian Acad. Sci. Sect. B. **2:** 33–48.

————. 1936*a*. Studies in the family Alismaceae. IV. *Alisma plantago* L.; *A. plantago-aquatica* L., and *Sagittaria graminea* Mich. Proc. Indian Acad. Sci. Sect. B. **4:** 128–138.

————. 1936*b*. The life history of *Butomopsis lanceolata* Kunth. Proc. Indian Acad. Sci. Sect. B. **4:** 139–162.

————. 1938*a*. The embryo sac of *Limnocharis emarginata* L. New Phytol. **37:** 279–285.

————. 1938*b*. The embryo sac of *Hydrocleis nymphoides* Buchen. Beihefte bot. Centbl. **48A:** 165–172.

Johri, B. M. and Maheshwari, P. 1950. The development of the embryo sac, embryo, and endosperm in *Helixanthera ligustrina* (Wall.) Dans. (In press.)

Jones, H. A., and Emsweller, S. L. 1936. Development of the flower and macro-gametophyte of *Allium cepa*. Hilgardia **10**: 415–454.

Joshi, A. C. 1936. A note on the antipodals of *Digera arvensis* Forsk. Current Sci. [India] **4**: 741–742.

—— and Venkateswarlu, J. 1935. A case of reversed polarity in the embryo sac. Ann. Bot. **49**: 841–843.

Juliano, J. B. 1934. Studies on the morphology of the Meliaceae. II. Sterility in santol, *Sandoricum kootjape* (Burm. F.) Merill. Philippine Jour. Agr. **23**: 253–266.

Kausik, S. B. 1938. Pollen development and seed formation in *Utricularia coerulea* L. Beihefte bot. Centbl. **58A**: 365–578.

Khan, R. 1942. A contribution to the embryology of *Jussieua repens* Linn. Jour. Indian Bot. Soc. **21**: 267–282.

Kirkwood, J. E. 1905. The comparative embryology of the Cucurbitaceae. Bul. N. Y. Bot. Gard. **3**: 313–402.

Krishna Iyengar, C. V. 1940. Development of embryo sac and endosperm-haustoria in some members of Scrophularineae. IV. *Vandellia hirsuta* Ham. and *V. scabra* Benth. Jour. Indian Bot. Soc. **18**: 179–189.

———. 1941. Development of the embryo sac and endosperm haustoria in *Torenia cordifolia* Roxb. and *T. hirsuta* Benth. Proc. Natl. Inst. Sci. India **7**: 61–71.

Lagerberg, T. 1909. Studien über die Entwicklungsgeschichte und systematische Stellung von *Adoxa moschatellina* L. Svenska Vet.-Akad. Handl. **44**(4): 1–86.

Madge, M. 1934. Nuclear migrations in *Hedychium*. Proc. Linn. Soc. London **146**: 108–109.

Magnus, W. 1913. Die atypische Embryosackentwicklung der Podostomaceen. Flora **105**: 275–336.

Maheshwari, P. 1937. A critical review of the types of embryo sacs in angiosperms. New Phytol. **36**: 359–417.

———. 1941. Recent work on the types of embryo sacs in angiosperms—a critical review. Jour. Indian Bot. Soc. **20**: 229–261.

———. 1946*a*. The Fritillaria type of embryo sac: a critical review. Jour. Indian Bot. Soc., M. O. P. Iyengar Comm. Vol., pp. 101–119.

———. 1946*b*. The Adoxa type of embryo sac—a critical review. Lloydia **9**: 73–113.

———. 1947. Tetranucleate embryo sacs in angiosperms. Lloydia **10**: 1–18.

———. 1948. The angiosperm embryo sac. Bot. Rev. **14**: 1–56.

—— and Haque, A. 1949. The embryo sac of *Chrysanthemum parthenium* L. (Bernh). New Phytol. **48**: 255–258.

—— and Johri, B. M. 1941. The embryo sac of *Acalypha indica* L. Beihefte bot. Centbl. **61A**: 125–136.

Maheshwari, P. and Singh, Bahadur. 1950. The embryology of *Macrosolen cochinchinensis* Van Tieghem. (In press.)

—— and Singh, Balwant. 1943. Studies in the family Alismaceae. V. The embryology of *Machaerocarpus californicus* (Torr.) Small. Proc. Natl. Inst. Sci. India **9**: 311–322.

Maheshwari and Srinivasan, A. R. 1944. A contribution to the embryology of *Rudbeckia bicolor* Nutt. New Phytol. **43**: 135–142.

Martinoli, G. 1939. Contributo all'embriologia delle Asteraceae. I–III. Nuovo Gior. Bot. Ital. N.S. **46**: 259–298.

Mason, C. T. 1949. Development of the embryo sac in the genus *Limnanthes*. Amer. Jour. Bot. **36**: 799.

Mathur, K. L., and Khan, R. 1941. The development of the embryo sac in *Vogelia indica* Lamk. Proc. Indian Acad. Sci. Sect. B. **13**: 330–368.

Mauritzon, J. 1933. "Studien über die Embryologie der Familien Crassulaceae und Saxifragaceae." Diss. Lund.

———. 1939. Contributions to the embryology of the orders Rosales and Myrtales. Lunds Univ. Årsskr. N.F. Avd. II, **35**(2): 1–120.

Messeri, A. 1931. Ricerche embriologiche e cariologiche sopra i genri *Allium* e *Nothoscordum*. Nuovo Gior. Bot. Ital. N.S. **33**: 409–441.

Modilewski, J. 1908. Zur Embryobildung von *Gunnera chilensis*. Ber. deutsch. bot. Gesell. **26A**: 550–556.

———. 1909. Zur Embryobildung von einiger Onagraceen. Ber. deutsch. bot. Gesell. **27**: 287–291.

———. 1910. Weitere Beiträge zur Embryobildung einiger Euphorbiaceen. Ber. deutsch. bot. Gesell. **28**: 414–418.

———. 1911. Über die abnormale Embryosackentwicklung bei *Euphorbia palustris* L. und anderen Euphorbiaceen. Ber. deutsch. bot. Gesell. **29**: 430–436.

———. 1918. [Cytological and embryological studies on *Neottia nidus avis* (L.) Rich.] Verh. Kiewer Ges. Naturf. **26**: 1–55.

———. 1928. Weitere Beiträge zur Embryologie und Cytologie von *Allium*-Arten. Bul. Jard. Bot. de Kieff **7/8**: 57–64.

Narayanaswami, S. 1940. Megasporogenesis and the origin of triploids in *Saccharum*. Indian Jour. Agr. Sci. **10**: 534–551.

Newman, I. V. 1934. Studies in the Australian acacias. IV. The life history of *Acacia baileyana* F.v.M. Proc. Linn. Soc. N. S. Wales **59**: 277–313.

Oehler, E. 1927. Entwicklungsgeschichtlich-zytologische Untersuchungen an einigen saprophytischen Gentianaceen. Planta **3**: 641–733.

Oksijuk, P. 1927. Entwicklungsgeschichte der Zuckerrübe (*Beta vulgaris*). Bul. Jard. Bot. de Kieff **5/6**: 145–164.

———. 1937. Vergleichende zytologisch-embryologische Untersuchung der Familie Resedaceae. I. *Reseda* und *Astrocarpus*. Jour. Inst. Bot. Acad. Sci. Ukraine **12**: 3–81.

Osterwalder, A. 1898. Beiträge zur Embryologie von *Aconitum napellus* L. Flora **85**: 254–292.

Pace, L. 1907. Fertilization in *Cypripedium*. Bot. Gaz. **44**: 353–374.

———. 1913. Apogamy in *Atamosco*. Bot. Gaz. **56**: 376–394.

Palm, B. 1915. "Studien über Konstruktionstypen und Entwicklungswege des Embryosackes der Angiospermen." Diss. Stockholm.

Prosina, M. N. 1930. Über die vom Cypripedilum-Typus abweichende Embryosackentwicklung von *Cypripedium guttatum* SW. Planta **12**: 532–544.

Puri, V. 1939. Studies in the order Parietales. II. A contribution to the morphology of *Garcinia livingstonii* T. Anders. Proc. Indian Acad. Sci. Sect. B. **9**: 74–86.

———. 1941. Life history of *Moringa oleifera* Lamk. Jour. Indian Bot. Soc. **20**: 263–284.

Randolph, L. F. 1936. Developmental morphology of the caryopsis in Maize. Jour. Agr. Res. **53**: 881–916.

Rauch, K. V. 1936. Cytologisch-embryologische Untersuchungen an *Scurrula atropurpurea* Dans. und *Dendrophthoe pentandra* Miq. Ber. schweiz. bot. Gesell. **45**: 5–61.

Razi, B. A. 1949. Embryological studies of two members of the *Podostomaceae*. Bot. Gaz. **111**: 211–218.

Reed, E. L. 1924. Anatomy, embryology and ecology of *Arachis hypogea*. Bot. Gaz. **78**: 289–310.

Romanov, I. D. 1936. Die Embryosackentwicklung in der Gattung *Gagea* Salisb. Planta **25**: 438–459.

———. 1938. Eine neue Form des Embryosackes von Adoxa-Typus bei *Tulipa tetraphylla* und *T. ostrovskiana*. Compt. Rend. (Dok.) Acad. des Sci. U.R.S.S. **19**: 113–115.

———. 1939. Two new forms of embryo sac in the genus *Tulipa*. Compt. Rend. (Dok.) Acad. des Sci. U.R.S.S. **22**: 139–141.

Rosén, W. 1947. The female gametophyte in *Nolana* and endosperm development in Tubiflorae. Bot. Notiser 1947, pp. 372–382.

Rutishauser, A. 1935. Entwicklungsgeschichtliche und zytologische Untersuchungen an *Korthalsella dacrydii* (Ridl.) Danser. Ber. schweiz. bot. Gesell. **44**: 389–436.

———. 1937*a*. Entwicklungsgeschichtliche Untersuchungen an *Thesium rostratum* M.u.K. Mitt. Naturf. Gesell. Schaffhausen **13**: 25–47.

———. 1937*b*. Blütenmorphologische und cytologische Untersuchungen an den Viscoideen *Korthalsella opuntia* Morr. und *Ginalloa linearis* Dans. Ber. schweiz. bot. Gesell. **47**: 5–28.

———. 1945. Zur Embryologie amphimiktischer Potentillen. Ber. schweiz. bot. Gesell. **55**: 19–32.

Samuels, J. A. 1912. Études sur le développement du sac embryonnaire et sur la fécondation du *Gunnera macrophylla* Bl. Arch. f. Zellforsch. **8**: 52–120.

Schaeppi, H., and Steindl, F. 1942. Blütenmorphologische und embryologische Untersuchungen an Loranthoideen. Vrtljschr. naturf. Gesell. Zürich **87**: 301–372.

——— and ———. 1945. Blütenmorphologische und embryologische Untersuchungen an einigen Viscoideen. Vrtljschr. naturf. Gesell. Zürich **90**: 1–46.

Schulle, H. 1933. Zur Entwicklungsgeschichte von *Thesium montanum* Ehrh. Flora **27**: 140–184.

Sharp, L. W. 1912. The orchid embryo sac. Bot. Gaz. **54**: 373–385.

Shattuck, C. H. 1905. A morphological study of *Ulmus americana*. Bot. Gaz. **49**: 209–223.

Singh, Bahadur. 1950. The embryology of *Dendrophthoe falcata* (Linn. fil.) Ettingshausen. Proc. 37th Indian Sci. Cong. Sect. Bot.

Smith, R. W. 1911. The tetranucleate embryo sac of *Clintonia*. Bot. Gaz. **52**: 209–217.

Smith, F. H. 1943. Megagametophyte of *Clintonia*. Bot. Gaz. **105**: 233–267.

Souéges, E. C. R. 1940. Embryogénie des Haloragacées. Développement de l'embryon chez le *Myriophyllum alterniflorum* DC. Compt. Rend. Acad. des Sci. Paris **211**: 185–188.

———. 1943. Embryogénie des Fumariacées. L'origine et les premières divisions de la cellule embryonnaire proprement dite chez l'*Hypecoum procumbens* L. Compt. Rend. Acad. des Sci. Paris **216**: 310–311.

Steindl, F. 1935. Pollen- und Embryosackentwicklung bei *Viscum album* L. und *V. articulatum* Burm. Ber. schweiz. bot. Gesell. **44**: 343–388.

Stenar, H. 1925a. Embryologische und zytologische Studien über *Limnanthes douglassi* R.Br. Svensk Bot. Tidskr. **19**: 133–152.

———. 1925b. "Embryologische Studien. I. Zur Embryologie der Columniferen. II. Die Embryologie der Amaryllideen." Diss. Upsala.

———. 1928. Zur Embryologie der Asphodeline-Gruppe. Ein Beitrag zur systematischen Stellung der Gattungen *Bulbine* und *Paradisia*. Svensk Bot. Tidskr. **22**: 145–159.

———. 1932. Studien über die Entwicklungsgeschichte von *Nothoscordum fragrans* Kunth u. *N. striatum* Kunth. Svensk Bot. Tidskr. **26**: 25–44.

———. 1934. Embryologische und zytologische Beobachtungen über *Majanthemum bifolium* und *Smilacina stellata*. Arkiv. för Bot. **26**: 1–20.

———. 1937. Zur Embryosackentwicklung einiger Malpighiazeen. Bot. Notiser 1937, pp. 110–118.

———. 1940. Biologiska och embryologiska notiser rörande *Calypso bulbosa* (L) Oakes. Jämten Heimbygdas Förlag, Östersund 1940, pp. 184–189.

———. 1941. Über die Entwicklung des Embryosackes bei *Convallaria majalis* L. Bot. Notiser 1941, pp. 123–128.

Stephens, E. L. 1909. The embryo sac and embryo of certain Penaeaceae. Ann. Bot. **23**: 363–378.

Stiffler, E. G. 1925. Development of embryo sac in *Gasteria, Cyrtanthus* and *Veltheimia*. Bot. Gaz. **79**: 207–216.

Stolt, K. A. H. 1921. Zur Embryologie der Gentianaceen und Menyanthaceen. K. Svenska Vet.-Akad. Handl. **61**(14): 1–56.

———. 1928. Die Embryologie von *Myriophyllum alterniflorum* DC. Svensk Bot. Tidskr. **22**: 305–319.

Strasburger, E. 1879. "Die Angiospermen und die Gymnospermen." Jena.

Subba Rao, A. M. 1940. Studies in the Malpighiaceae. I. Embryo sac development and embryogeny in the genera *Hiptage, Banisteria* and *Stigmatophyllum*. Jour. Indian Bot. Soc. **18**: 145–156.

———. 1941. Studies in the Malpighiaceae. II. Structure and development of the ovules and embryo sacs of *Malpighia coccigera* Linn. and *Tristellateia australis*. Proc. Natl. Inst. Sci. India **7**: 393–404.

Svensson, H. G. 1925. "Zur Embryologie der Hydrophyllaceen, Borraginaceen und Heliotropiaceen." Diss. Upsala.

Swamy, B. G. L. 1945. Embryo sac and fertilization in *Cypripedium spectabile.* Bot. Gaz. **107**: 291–295.

———. 1946. Inverted polarity of the embryo sac of angiosperms and its relation to the archegonium theory. Ann. Bot. **9**: 171–183.

———. 1949*a.* Embryological studies in the Orchidaceae. I. Gametophytes. Amer. Midland Nat. **41**: 184–201.

———. 1949*b.* A reinvestigation of the embryo sac of *Maianthemum canadense.* Bul. Torrey Bot. Club **76**: 17–23.

Täckholm, G. 1915. Beobachtungen über die Samenentwicklung einiger Onagraceen. Svensk Bot. Tidskr. **9**: 294–361.

Tateishi, S. 1927. On the development of the embryo sac and fertilization of *Acalypha australis* L. (preliminary note). Bot. Mag. [Tokyo] **51**: 477–485.

Thirumalachar, M. J., and Khan, B. A. 1941. Megasporogenesis and endosperm formation in *Eriodendron anfractuosum* DC. Proc. Indian Acad. Sci. Sect. B. **14**: 461–465.

Treub, M. 1883. Observations sur les Loranthacées. IV. *Loranthus pentandrus* L. Ann. Jard. Bot. Buitenzorg **3**: 184–189.

——— and Mellink, J. 1880. Notice sur le développement du sac embryonnaire dans quelques angiospermes. Arch. Néerld. des Sci. **15**: 452–457.

Venkateswarlu, J. 1937. A contribution to the embryology of the Sonneratiaceae. Proc. Indian Acad. Sci. Sect. B. **5**: 206–223.

Ventura, M. 1934. Sulla poliembryonia di *Mallotus japonicus* Muell. Arg. Ann. di Bot. **20**: 568–578.

———. 1937. Osservazioni embryologiche su *Arechavaletaia uruguayensis* Speg. Ann. di Bot. **21**: 527–533.

Walker, R. I. 1944. Chromosome number, megasporogenesis and development of embryo sac of *Clintonia.* Bul. Torrey Bot. Club **71**: 529–535.

Walker, R. I. 1950. Megasporogenesis and development of megagametophyte in *Ulmus.* Amer. Jour. Bot. **37**: 47–52.

Weber, E. 1929. Entwicklungsgeschichtliche Untersuchungen über die Gattung *Allium.* Bot. Arch. **25**: 1–44.

Weinstein, A. J. 1926. Cytological studies on *Phaseolus vulgaris.* Amer. Jour. Bot. **13**: 248–263.

Weinzieher, S. 1914. Beiträge zur Entwicklungsgeschichte von *Xyris indica* L. Flora **106**: 393–432.

Went, F. A. F. C. 1910. Untersuchungen über Podostomaceen. I. Verhandel. K. Akad. van Wetensch. te Amsterdam II, **16**(1).

———. 1912. Untersuchungen über Podostomaceen. II. Verhandel. K. Akad. van Wetensch. te Amsterdam II, **17**(2).

———. 1926. Untersuchungen über Podostomaceen. III. Verhandel. K. Akad. van Wetensch. te Amsterdam II, **25**(1).

Yamaura, A. 1933. Karyologische und embryologische Studien über einige *Bambusa*-Arten. (Vorläufige Mitteilung). Bot. Mag. [Tokyo] **47**: 551–555.

York, H. H. 1913. The origin and development of the embryo sac and embryo of *Dendrophthora opuntioides* and *D. gracile.* I and II. Bot. Gaz. **56**: 89–111, 200–216.

CHAPTER 5

THE MALE GAMETOPHYTE[1]

The development of the male gametophyte is remarkably uniform in angiosperms. The microspore, which is the first cell of the gametophyte generation, undergoes only two divisions. The first division gives rise to a large vegetative cell and a small generative cell (Fig. 95*A–F*). The second, which concerns only the generative cell, may take place either in the pollen grain (Fig. 95*G–H*) or in the pollen tube (Fig. 95*I–J*) and gives rise to the two male gametes. Details of the process may be considered under the following heads: microspore, formation of the vegetative and generative cells, division of the generative cell, male "cells" or "nuclei," and vegetative nucleus.

Microspore. The newly formed microspore has a very dense cytoplasm with a centrally situated nucleus, but the cell rapidly increases in volume and the accompanying vacuolation is followed by a displacement of the nucleus from the center to a place adjacent to the wall. In most tropical plants the nucleus begins to divide almost immediately, but in plants belonging to colder regions there is often a resting stage lasting from a few days to several weeks. To mention a few instances, in *Tradescantia reflexa* the resting period of the microspore is about four days or less, in *Styrax obassia* about a week, and in *Himantoglossum hircinum* between two to three weeks. In *Uvularia sessilifolia*, *Empetrum nigrum*, and *Betula odorata*, the microspores are said to pass the entire winter in the uninucleate stage (for further information, see Dahlgren, 1915; Finn, 1937*a*).

Formation of Vegetative and Generative Cells. The first division of the microspore gives rise to the vegetative and generative cells. Geitler (1935) noted that the metaphase spindle usually shows a

---

[1] For more detailed information on the development and organization of the male gametophyte, see Wulff and Maheshwari (1938) and Maheshwari (1949). The technique for the study of the male gametophyte has been reviewed in another paper by Maheshwari and Wulff (1937).

pronounced asymmetry, the wallward pole being blunt and the free pole acute. More recent studies (Brumfield, 1941) seem to indicate that this asymmetry is associated with the form of the prophase nucleus. In *Allium*, where the nucleus is strongly flattened on the

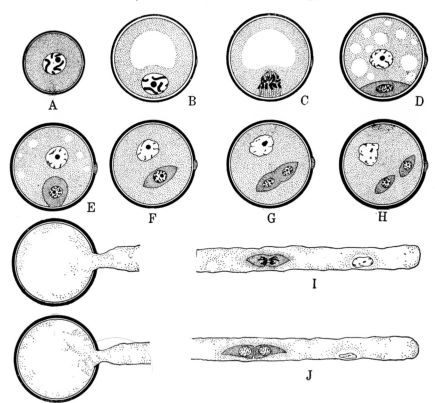

FIG. 95. Diagram to illustrate the more important stages in development of male gametophyte. *A*, newly formed microspore. *B*, older stage, showing vacuolation and wallward position of microspore nucleus. *C*, microspore nucleus dividing. *D*, division completed; two-celled stage, showing vegetative and generative cells. *E*, generative cell losing contact with wall. *F*, generative cell lying free in cytoplasm of vegetative cell. *G, H*, division of generative cell in pollen grain. *I, J*, division of generative cell in pollen tube. (*After Maheshwari, 1949.*)

wallward side, the asymmetry is extreme (Fig. 96); in *Pancratium*, where it is only slightly flattened, the asymmetry is much less pronounced; and *Tradescantia* shows an intermediate condition. The direct cause of the asymmetry has been attributed to a difference in

the time of development of the two spindle poles, the wallward or
generative pole developing more slowly than the vegetative, presumably because of the smaller amount of cytoplasm associated
with the former.   With the onset of the anaphase, the asymmetry
becomes less pronounced.   In the telophase the generative chromosomes are arranged in a plane surface parallel to the inner wall of
the microspore, while the vegetative ones form a somewhat hemi-
spherical pattern.

Symmetrical spindles have been observed only occasionally.   To
mention a few examples, in *Asclepias* (Gager, 1902) and *Anthericum*
(Geitler, 1935) both the poles of the spindle are blunt; in *Adoxa*
(Lagerberg, 1909) both are more or less pointed; and in *Podophyllum*

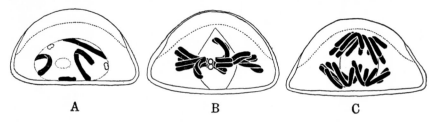

| A | B | C |

FIG. 96.   *Allium cernuum*, first division of microspore.   *A*, prophase.   *B*, metaphase.   *C*, end of anaphase.   (*After Brumfield, 1941.*)

(Darlington, 1936) both symmetrical and asymmetrical spindles are
said to occur in the same loculus.   Further, in *Adoxa* (Lagerberg,
1909), *Myricaria* (Frisendahl, 1912), *Sambucus* (Schürhoff, 1921),
Cotylanthera (Oehler, 1927), and *Uvularia* (Geitler, 1935) the spindle
is not situated near the wall of the pollen grain but occupies almost
the entire width of the latter.   In any case the cells formed by the
division are always unequal, although the conditions which bring
about this result are not clearly understood.   In *Cuscuta* (Fedortschuk, 1931) and *Strychnos* (Mohrbutter, 1936), where the daughter
cells are sometimes of the same size, this is clearly an abnormality
leading to the formation of double microspores, each of which is destined to divide again to give rise to the vegetative and generative cells
(Fig. 99*F*).   Double pollen grains comprising two units, each with its
own generative and vegetative cells, have also been figured in *Podostemon subulatus* (Magnus, 1913) (Fig. 99*H, I*).   The separating wall
between the two pollen grains is pitted (Fig. 99*J*) and only one of them

produces a pollen tube, the other presumably serving as a source of food material.

It may be noted that unlike the reduction divisions, which occur more or less simultaneously in all the microspore mother cells of an anther, the microspores usually divide without any such synchronization, and the same loculus may show different although not widely separated stages of division and development. In those plants in which the microspores remain together in a tetrad, all

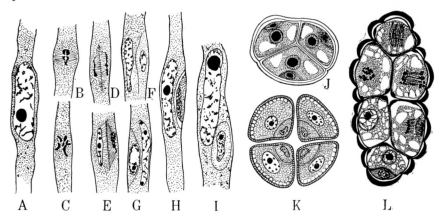

A   C   E   G   H   I   K   L

Fig. 97. *A–I, Zostera marina,* division of microspore to form vegetative and generative cells. Pollen grains are so long that only a part of each is shown. (*After Rosenberg, 1901.*) *J, Vaccinium vitis idaea,* pollen tetrad showing generative cell cut off toward outer side of each microspore. (*After Samuelsson, 1913.*) *K, Xyris indica,* pollen tetrad, showing generative cell cut off toward inner side of each microspore. (*After Weinzieher, 1914.*) *L, Acacia baileyana,* pollinium, showing various stages in division of microspore. (*After Newman, 1934.*)

four cells in a tetrad are usually in the same stage of division, but not all the tetrads of an anther. A complete synchronization may perhaps be expected only where the microspores are united into pollinia (Mimosaceae, Asclepiadaceae, and Orchidaceae), for here the cells probably exercise some influence over one another through the uncuticularized walls which lie between them (Barber, 1942). Exceptions do occur, however, even in such cases. Figure 97*L* of the pollinium of *Acacia baileyana* (Newman, 1934) shows one of the microspores in prophase, another with the tube and generative cells already formed, and the rest in various intermediate stages.

Goebel (1933) thought that in the angiosperms the generative cell is always cut off on the distal (*i.e.*, ventral) side of the microspore. Geitler (1935) showed, however, that there is no such uniformity and that the generative cell may be cut off either on the outer side (Fig. 97*J*, *L*), or on the inner side (Fig. 97*K*, 98), or on a radial wall (Fig. 97*A–I*), or in a corner instead of the middle of the radial wall. To cite a few examples, the first-named condition has

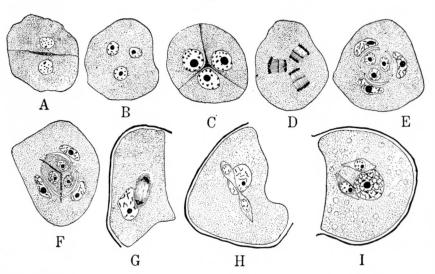

Fig. 98. Microsporogenesis and development of male gametophyte in *Juncus filiformis* (*A–F*) and *J. squarrosus* (*G–I*). *A*, interkinesis after Meiosis I, showing formation of ephemeral cell plate. *B*, microspore nuclei. *C*, microspore nuclei in prophase; note intervening plasma membranes. *D*, microspore nuclei in anaphase. *E*, *F*, formation of vegetative and generative cells. *G*, one member of tetrad, showing generative cell in late anaphase. *H*, same, division nearly completed. *I*, older stage, showing vegetative nucleus and two sperm cells. (*After Wulff, 1939a.*)

been reported in *Elodea* (Wylie, 1904), *Vaccinium* (Samuelsson' 1913), *Albizzia* (Maheshwari, 1931), *Acacia* (Newman, 1934), *Asimina* (Locke, 1936), and most members of the Orchidaceae (Swamy, 1949); the second in *Symplocarpus* (Duggar, 1900), *Xyris* (Weinzieher, 1914), *Erica* (Geitler, 1935), *Juncus* (Wulff, 1939a), *Cyanastrum* (Nietsch, 1941), and most members of the Cyperaceae (Piech, 1928); the third in *Allium* (Geitler, 1935); and the fourth in *Lilium* (Strasburger, 1908), *Anthericum,* and *Convallaria* (Geitler, 1935).

Whatever the position may be, it is usually constant in individuals of the same species and sometimes in all the species of a genus or family and is thus a character of some systematic significance. Unfortunately, it can be recognized most clearly only in those plants in which the pollen grains remain together in tetrads. In most genera the microspores round up at such an early stage that it becomes impossible to distinguish one side from the other, although even here the position of the germ pores and furrows often serves as a useful guide. An important point to keep in mind, however, is that very soon the generative cell loses contact with the wall of the microspore, and after this has happened it may change its position in the pollen grain and come to lie in almost any part of it.[2]

There is considerable variation in the form of the generative cell. Usually it is elliptical, lenticular, or spindle-shaped, but in *Cuscuta* (Finn, 1937b) and *Ottelia* (Islam, 1950) it becomes long enough to occupy the entire width of the pollen grain, coming quite close to the inner wall of the latter on either side. In *Monochoria* (Banerji and Haldar, 1942) it is one and a half times as long as the diameter of the pollen grain and is accommodated in the latter only by the incurving of its whip-like ends. In *Campanula ranunculoides* (Schnarf, 1937) the two ends are dissimilar, one being pointed and the other more or less blunt and swollen so as to look like a "head." There are also occasional reports of changes in the form of the generative cell. More frequently, however, such appearances are merely due to the plane of sectioning. A spindle-shaped cell appears round when cut across and oval when cut obliquely.

In fixed material the cytoplasm of the generative cell is usually distinguishable from that of the vegetative by its hyaline appearance and general lack of food materials. Plastids (Ruhland and Wetzel, 1924; Krupko, 1926) (Fig. 99O) and chondriosomes have, however, been demonstrated in a few cases, and some recent studies on living pollen grains and pollen tubes (Benetskaia, 1939; Kostriukova, 1939a, b; Kostriukova and Benetskaia, 1939) have confirmed the

---

[2] This gradual extension of the vegetative cytoplasm around the generative cell and the consequent "engulfing" of the latter has been referred to by several workers, *viz.,* Friemann (1910), Wefelscheid (1911), Capoor (1937a), and others.

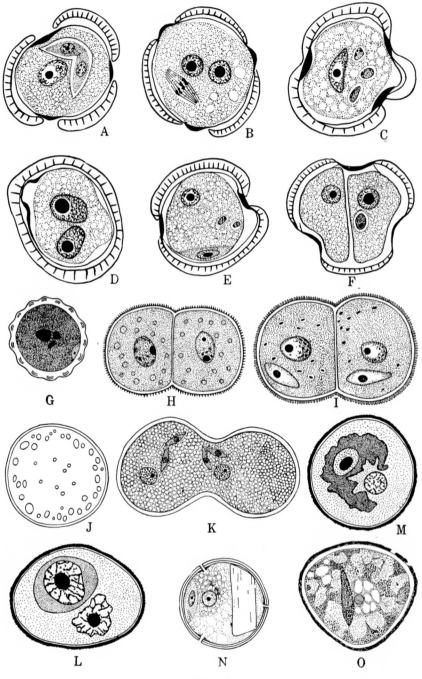

FIG. 99.

presence of a vacuome and mitochondria in the generative as well as the sperm cells of *Narcissus, Asclepias, Vinca, Crinum,* and *Lilium.* Mention may also be made of the "colored bodies" described by Kostriukova (1939*b*) in living pollen tubes of *Lilium martagon.* He saw two structures of a pale greenish color, one at each end of the generative nucleus. In older stages these bodies were found to divide and occupy similar positions in the sperm cells (Fig. 100). They were not recognizable in fixed material, but in their places small areolae were seen which stained black with osmic acid. The author concludes that they probably correspond with the structures described as Golgi bodies, but a further study is of course necessary to confirm this.[3]

Regarding the contents of the vegetative cell, starch and fat are the most conspicuous substances. The distinction between starchy and fatty pollen has been recognized for a long time and their possible ecological significance has been a subject of much interest (see Tischler, 1917; Kühlwein, 1937). Luxemburg (1927) traced the origin of the starch grains and fat bodies from plastids in the pollen grains of several members of the Malvaceae, and believes that the

[3] In his book "The Cytoplasm of the Plant Cell" Guilliermond (1941) remarks that "there is no Golgi apparatus in plants" and that all formations described as Golgi apparatus are elements belonging either to the vacuolar system or to the chondriome.

Fig. 99. Pollen grains of various angiosperms. *A, Cuscuta epithymum,* mature pollen grain, showing vegetative nucleus and two male cells. *B,* pollen grain, showing two vegetative nuclei and dividing generative nucleus. *C,* vegetative nucleus and three sperms. *D,* two vegetative nuclei. *E,* vegetative nucleus, two sperms, and prothallial cell. *F,* microspore has divided into two parts, of which one on right shows vegetative as well as generative nucleus. (*After Fedortschuk, 1931.*) *G, Atriplex hymenelytra,* pollen grain showing prothallial cell (?), vegetative nucleus, and two male nuclei. (*After Billings, 1934.*) *H, Podostemon subulatus,* double pollen grain. *I,* older stage, in which microspore nucleus of each has divided to form vegetative and generative nuclei; small bodies outside nuclei are starch grains. *J,* partition wall between the two cells, showing pits. (*After Magnus, 1913.*) *K, Vinca herbacea,* dumbbell-shaped pollen grain with two pairs of sperm cells and two vegetative nuclei. (*After Finn, 1928.*) *L, Erythronium americanum,* pollen grain, showing vegetative and generative cells. *M,* same, showing amoeboid nature of generative cell. (*After Schaffner, 1901.*) *N, Wormia suffruticosa,* pollen grain, showing large crystal. (*After Paetow, 1931.*) *O, Lupinus luteus,* pollen grain, showing chloroplasts in generative cell as seen after silver impregnation. (*Ruhland and Wetzel, 1924.*)

plastids in turn arise either from preexisting plastids or from chondriosomes. In very young pollen grains the reserve food consists almost entirely of droplets of fat, and starch formation begins only after the pollen grains have increased in size.

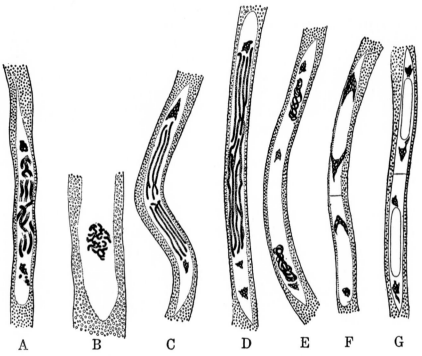

A   B   C   D   E   F   G

Fig. 100.   Portions of pollen tubes of *Lilium martagon* showing behavior of "colored bodies" inside generative cell and sperm cells, as seen in living condition. *A*, generative cell in division, showing colored body at either end. *B*, enlarged view of one end of generative cell, showing detail of colored body. *C–E*, stages in division of generative cell. *F*, *G*, sperm cells, showing the colored bodies. (*After Kostriukova, 1939b.*)

Certain proteinaceous bodies have also been reported in pollen grains and pollen tubes (Fig. 101), but their exact origin remains unknown. They probably arise in plastids but soon become liberated in the general cytoplasm of the pollen grain and pollen tube. Most remarkable of all are the large transparent protein crystals of *Wormia suffruticosa* (Paetow, 1931) (Fig. 99*N*), although these are of a transitory nature and disappear during the later stages in the maturation of the pollen grain.

Division of Generative Cell. The generative cell may divide either in the pollen grain (Fig. 95*G–H*) or in the pollen tube (Fig. 95*I–J*). Formerly the second condition was believed to be the more frequent, but during recent years three-celled pollen grains

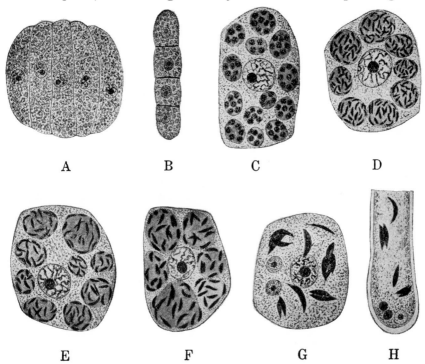

A   B   C   D

E   F   G   H

FIG. 101. Stages in development of male gametophyte of *Asclepias*, showing protein granules inside cytoplasm of pollen grain and pollen tube. *A*, microspore mother cells. *B*, tetrad of microspores. *C–F*, microspores. *G*, pollen grain, showing vegetative nucleus and two sperm nuclei. *H*, terminal portion of pollen tube. (*After Guignard, 1922.*)

have been reported in several genera (see Schnarf, 1939) and it seems certain that many of the older records were based on a study of immature pollen.[4]

[4] As the pollen grain grows older, the vacuoles become smaller and more evenly distributed and finally they disappear almost entirely so that with the usual methods of fixing and staining the mature pollen grain, like the young microspore, again shows a dense cytoplasm devoid of all conspicuous vacuolation. This is such a constant feature in most angiosperms (excluding some aquatics) that it serves as a useful check for judging whether a pollen grain is fully mature or not (see Schnarf, 1937).

There is also considerable evidence to indicate that even in those plants in which the pollen grains are shed in the two-celled condition, the generative nucleus is already in the prophase stage and the process of division is merely continued in the pollen tube. Sometimes the nucleus may even show a pro-metaphase stage which is distinguishable from a typical metaphase only by the delay in the dissolution of the nuclear membrane and the organization of the spindle. This has been demonstrated very clearly in *Impatiens* (Wulff, 1934; Heitz and Resende, 1936), *Bulbine* (Geitler, 1942) and other plants.

Occasionally both two- and three-celled pollen grains have been reported in the same plant, as in the cleistogamous flowers of *Viola* (West, 1930), in *Dionaea* (Smith, 1929), *Circaeaster* (Junell, 1931), *Nicotiana* (Poddubnaja-Arnoldi, 1936), *Epimedium*, and *Iris* (Schnarf, 1937), but this is probably due to environmental influences. Poddubnaja-Arnoldi (1936) found that, in several kinds of pollen grains which are normally two-celled, the generative nucleus divided before germination if the grains were kept for some time on a sugar-agar substrate. Eigsti (1941) was similarly able to induce a precocious division of the generative cell in the pollen grains of *Polygonatum canaliculatum*. In *Holoptelea integrifolia* (Capoor, 1937b) the pollen grains are shed at the two-celled stage, but the generative cell divides on the surface of the stigma before the pollen tube has started to grow.[5]

Details of the division of the generative cell vary depending on whether it takes place in the pollen grain or in the pollen tube. In the former case, spindle fibers and a normal metaphase plate have been regularly observed, and the process does not seem to differ in any essential way from a normal mitosis. Cytokinesis, resulting in a bipartitioning of the cell, may take place either by a process of furrowing as in *Juncus* (Wulff, 1939a) (Fig. 98H), or by the laying down of a cell plate as in *Asclepias* (Finn, 1925) and *Portulaca* (D. C. Cooper, 1935). Witmer (1937), who observed both cell plates and constriction furrows in *Vallisneria*, states that in his material these two factors varied in importance.[6] In some pollen

[5] In *Euphorbia terracina* (D'Amato, 1947), which is at the other extreme, the division occurs only after the pollen tube has entered the embryo sac and its tip has come to lie by the side of the egg.

[6] See also Kausik and Rao (1942).

grains a definite cell plate was laid down in the beginning, but it soon faded away, leaving the final separation of the sperms to a constriction furrow which arose soon afterwards. In others the cell plate persisted, and the progress of the constriction furrow was arrested in this region although evident on either side of it; here the splitting of the cell plate divided the generative cell before the constriction could make much progress.

It has proved more difficult to understand the mechanism of the division when it occurs in the pollen tube. The chief points in question are: (1) whether a regular metaphase plate is formed during the division, (2) whether spindle fibers are present or absent, and (3) whether cytokinesis takes place by constriction or by cell-plate formation.

Nawaschin (1910), O'Mara (1933), Wulff and Raghavan (1937), Raghavan *et al.* (1939), and several other workers failed to find any regular metaphase plates in the plants studied by them, *viz.*, *Lilium martagon*, *L. regale*, *Nemophila insignis*, and *Impatiens balsamina*. On the other hand, Cooper (1936) reported their occurrence to be a regular feature in *Lilium regale*, *L. auratum*, and *L. philippinense* (Fig. 102), and believes that O'Mara's (1933) figures of an "irregular metaphase" really represent a late prophase, the true metaphase having been missed by him. Upcott (1936) and Madge (1936) also found a metaphase plate in *Tulipa* and *Hedychium* respectively, the only important difference being its oblique orientation which gives more space to the chromosomes for their proper alignment. More recently, well-differentiated metaphase plates have been recorded in *Eichhornia* (Banerji and Gangulee, 1937), *Tulipa*, *Amaryllis*, *Nicotiana*, *Forsythia*, *Camellia*, *Bryophyllum* (Johnston, 1941), and *Eschscholtzia* (Beatty, 1943) (Fig. 103).

Regarding the presence or absence of spindle fibers, Nawaschin (1909) in *Lilium martagon*, Welsford (1914) in *L. auratum* and *L. martagon*, O'Mara (1933) in *L. regale*, Trankowsky (1931) in *Convallaria majalis* and *Galanthus nivalis*, Fuchs (1936) in *Elaeagnus angustifolius*, Wunderlich (1937) in *Muscari racemosum* and *M. comosum*, Finn (1939) in *Phlomis tuberosa*, Raghavan *et al.* (1939) in *Impatiens balsamina*, and several other workers failed to find a spindle. On the other hand, Trankowsky (1931) in *Hemerocallis fulva*, Cooper (1936) in *Lilium auratum*, *L. regale*, and *L. philippinense* (Fig. 102), Madge (1936) in *Hedychium gardnerianum*,

Upcott (1936) in several species of *Tulipa*, Eigsti (1939) in *Lilium canadense*, *L. speciosum*, *L. auratum*, *Polygonatum commutatum*, *Convallaria majalis*, and *Tradescantia reflexa*, Johnston (1941) in *Tulipa gesneriana*, *Amaryllis* spp., *Nicotiana tabacum*, *Forsythia viridissima*, *Camellia japonica*, and *Bryophyllum pinnatum*, and

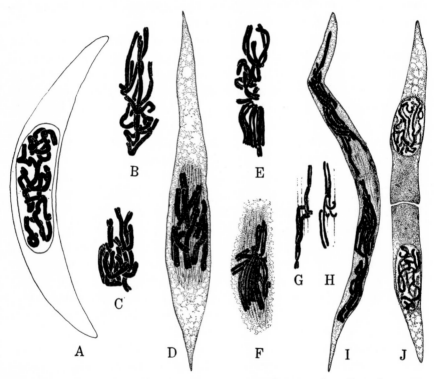

F<small>IG</small>. 102.   Division of generative cell of *Lilium regale* as seen in pollen tubes grown in culture.   *A*, prophase.   *B–C*, metaphase chromosomes advancing to equatorial plate.   *D–F*, metaphase.   *G*, three chromosomes at metaphase.   *H*, two chromosomes at early anaphase.   *I*, late anaphase showing cell-plate formation.   *J*, two male gametes; cell plate completed.   (*After Cooper, 1936.*)

Beatty (1943) in *Eschscholtzia californica* (Fig. 103) have emphasized that spindle fibers are present and perform the same functions as in normal mitosis.

Coming finally to the mode of cytokinesis, Raghavan *et al.* (1939) in *Impatiens*, Banerji and Gangulee (1937) in *Eichhornia*, and several other authors have reported that the division of the generative cell occurs by a constriction.   Eigsti (1940) also states that cell plates are difficult to find and are temporary structures without any special significance. On the other hand, very distinct cell plates have been figured in *Lilium regale* (Cooper, 1936) (Fig. 102*J*) and a number of other plants, and their occurrence has also been confirmed from studies on living pollen tubes of *Crinum hildebrandtii* (Kostriukova, 1939*a*), *Lilium martagon* (Kostriukova, 1939*b*), and *Narcissus poeticus* (Kostriukova and Benetskaia, 1939).

In an important and extensive work on pollen tubes, Johnston (1941) suggests that the inability to see cell plates is to be attributed

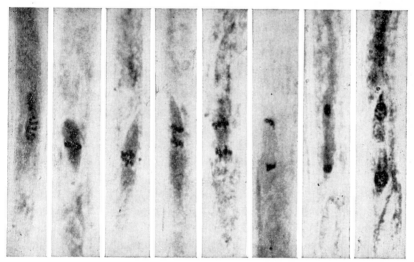

FIG. 103.   Division of generative cell in *Eschscholtzia californica*. (*After Beatty, 1943.*)

to the exclusive use of nuclear stains in most studies of this type. The same explanation holds good for the frequently reported absence of spindle fibers in the division of the generative cell. Delafield's haematoxylin, he says, is much superior to Heidenhain's haematoxylin for such purposes and should always be used for comparison.

As far as present evidence goes, it may therefore be concluded that the division of the generative cell, whether it takes place in the pollen grain or in the pollen tube, occurs in a fairly regular fashion. However, in cases in which the tube is very narrow and the chromosomes are rather large, there may be some disturbance of the metaphasic alignment, resulting in their crowding or buckling. It is also probable that the metaphase stage, owing to its very short duration, has been entirely missed in some plants, thereby creating the false impression that the nucleus passes directly from the prophase into the anaphase. Regarding the spindle, an intensity of staining which is adequate or just right for the chromosomes often fails to bring out the fibers, which are more clearly seen in overstained material. Finally, the division of the cell may take place either by means of a constriction furrow or by the laying down of a cell plate.

Male "Cells" or "Nuclei." Formerly it was believed that whenever the division of the generative cell occurs in the pollen grain it is followed by the formation of sperm *cells*, but if it takes place in the streaming cytoplasm of the pollen tube only *nuclei* are formed. Recent work has shown, however, that in all cases the male gametes are definite cells and the cytoplasmic sheath persists throughout their course in the pollen tube (see Schnarf, 1941).

Considering first the case of *Lilium*, which has been the favorite object for such studies, Guignard (1889) figured the male gametes of *L. martagon* as cells, but Koernicke (1906), Strasburger (1908) and Nawaschin (1910) believed that the cytoplasmic sheath is lost during the division of the generative cell. As to the exact time of disappearance of the sheath, however, these authors are not in agreement with one another. According to Koernicke it is lost when the generative cell is in prophase; according to Strasburger, at the metaphase stage; and according to Nawaschin, only during the telophase. Later, Welsford (1914) and O'Mara (1933) reported that in *L. martagon* and *L. auratum* definite sperm cells are formed, although eventually the cytoplasm dissolves away so that only the naked nuclei enter the embryo sac. Cooper (1936) showed, however, that the male gametes persist as cells right up to the time they enter the embryo sac. This has received further confirmation from the work of Anderson (1939), who finds that the cytoplasmic sheath around the male nuclei possesses all the inclusions normally present in the vegetative cytoplasm. He explains that the failure of other workers to see the sheath is due to their use of nuclear stains, which are not suited for bringing out the cytoplasm to the best advantage.

Not only in *Lilium* but also in other plants, the cytoplasmic sheath around the male nuclei has been followed up to the time of their discharge in the embryo sac. Nawaschin and Finn (1913) figured a clear space around the male nuclei of *Juglans*, which, as Finn (1925) subsequently explained, represents a thin layer of cytoplasm around them. Tschernojarow (1915), Dahlgren (1916) and Ishi-kawa (1918) demonstrated the occurrence of male cells in *Myosurus*, *Plumbagella*, and *Oenothera* respectively. Wulff (1933) and Finn (1935, 1940, 1941), who are the most active workers in this field, categorically state that the occurrence of male cells may be assumed in all angiosperms, and assert that in those plants in which only male nuclei have been reported, proper methods of fixing and staining will eventually reveal the thin cytoplasmic sheath around them.

Vegetative Nucleus. Earlier authors took it for granted that the vegetative nucleus (often called "tube" nucleus) had an important role in directing the growth of the pollen tube. Present evidence seems to indicate, however, that its functional importance had been greatly exaggerated.

The vegetative nucleus is not always in the distal end of the pollen tube (where it would be most expected if it had any important function in directing the growth of the tube) but frequently lies considerably behind the male gametes. When the tube becomes branched as in *Aconitum*, *Cucurbita*, and *Papaver* (Poddubnaja-Arnoldi, 1936), the individual branches continue their growth for an appreciable period, although only one of them contains the vegetative nucleus. In *Ulmus* (Shattuck, 1905), *Senecio*, *Crepis*, and *Secale* (Poddubnaja-Arnoldi, 1936) it degenerates even before the pollen grains begin to germinate and does not enter the tube at all; nevertheless the tube continues to function normally.[7] In *Cheno-podium*, *Atriplex*, and *Salsola* it seems to break up and diffuse into the surrounding cytoplasm (G. O. Cooper, 1935), and in *Musa* (Juliano and Alcala, 1933) and *Senecio* (Poddubnaja-Arnoldi, 1933) it fragments into small bits which seem to be quite functionless. In some other plants also the vegetative nucleus assumes a very abnormal appearance. For instance, in the pollen tubes of *Viola odorata* (Madge, 1929) it becomes 4 times, in *Cymbidium bicolor* (Swamy, 1941) 18 times, and in *Vallisneria americana* (Wylie, 1923) 27 times longer than broad. In a few members of the Labiatae (Finn, 1939) and in *Nicotiana* (Goodspeed, 1947) the elongation is sufficiently pronounced to give it a filamentous outline.

On the basis of these and other data Poddubnaja-Arnoldi (1936) regards the vegetative nucleus as a vestigial structure without any important function in the growth of the pollen tube. This view is

[7] See Hewitt (1939) for other examples of an early degeneration of the vegetative nucleus.

supported by Suita (1936, 1937a, b), who studied the pollen grains of *Crinum* with the Feulgen method. He states that soon after its formation the vegetative nucleus increases in size and becomes amoeboid. Later it begins to stain very faintly, indicating a decomposition of the chromatin. He agrees, therefore, that it is a degenerating structure without any important function in the life of the pollen tube.

While further evidence would be welcome, it seems safe to conclude that the old view attributing a leading role to the vegetative nucleus in the growth and direction of the pollen tube now needs modification. It is likely that these functions are really discharged by the nucleus of the generative cell itself and later by the nuclei of the two male cells formed by its division.

Development of Pollen in the Cyperaceae. The course of development described above is generally characteristic of all angiosperms, dicotyledons as well as monocotyledons, the family Cyperaceae being the only notable exception. Juel (1900), Stout (1912), Piech (1928) and others have shown that, of the four microspore nuclei produced after meiosis, only one develops further, while the other three become pushed toward one end of the mother cell (Fig. 104A, B). The functional nucleus, which lies in the center, divides with its spindle oriented in the direction of the long axis of the cell (Fig. 104C, D). The cell plate, which is laid down between the vegetative nucleus and generative nucleus, extends around the latter so as to give rise to a continuous plasma membrane. The generative cell (Fig. 104E) soon becomes spindle-shaped and divides to form the two sperm cells (Fig. 104F).

A few doubtful points, which need further clarification, are the following: (1) whether the functioning microspore nucleus is separated from the three nonfunctioning nuclei by a wall, (2) whether the nonfunctioning nuclei are separated from one another by walls, and (3) what the fate of the nonfunctioning nuclei may be. Tanaka (1940, 1941), who has recently discussed these questions, believes that normally a plasma membrane separates the functioning microspore nucleus from the three nonfunctioning nuclei and that subsequently similar membranes arise between the latter. The nonfunctioning nuclei sometimes undergo one division, resulting in a pair of daughter nuclei in each of the three cells. No separating wall is formed between them, however, and they are soon absorbed.

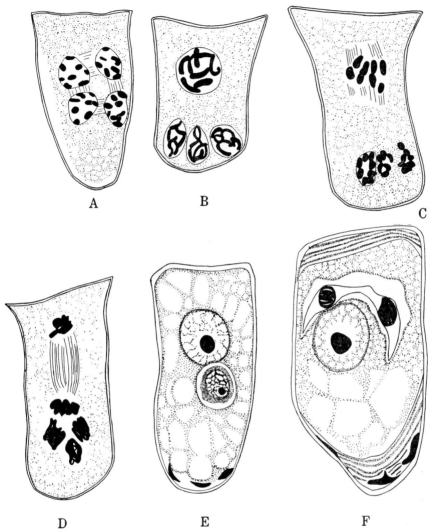

A   B   C

D   E   F

Fig. 104.   Development of male gametophyte of *Scirpus paluster*.   *A*, telophase
of Meiosis II resulting in formation of four microspore nuclei.   *B*, three of microspore nuclei pushed to one end of pollen grain; functioning nucleus in center.   *C, D*,
functioning nucleus dividing; remaining three nuclei in process of degeneration.
E, pollen grain, showing vegetative and generative cells.   *F*, generative cell dividing
to form two male cells.   (*After Piech, 1928.*)

Embryo-sac-like Pollen Grains.   In 1898 Némec noted that in
the petaloid anthers of *Hyacinthus orientalis* the pollen grains sometimes form large eight-nucleate structures showing a surprising
resemblance to embryo sacs.   He believed that they arose as the

result of a degeneration of the generative nucleus and three divisions of the vegetative nucleus.

De Mol (1923) observed this so-called "Némec-phenomenon" in the anthers of other varieties of *Hyacinthus orientalis* which had been subjected to certain special conditions in order to obtain early flowering. He attributed the origin of the abnormality to a duplication of the generative nuclei.

Stow (1930, 1934) found similar embryo-sac-like pollen grains or "pollen-embryo sacs" in the anthers of a variety called "La Victor" whose bulbs had been subjected to a temperature of 20°C. at the time of meiosis and were further "forced" in a greenhouse. He traced their development more fully than either Némec or De Mol. At first the microspores increase in size to form large sac-like bodies (Fig. 105*A*, *B*), after which the nucleus undergoes three successive divisions (Fig. 105*C–F*) to form 8 daughter nuclei. Of these, 3 lie at the end where the exine is still intact, 3 at the opposite end, and 2 in the middle. The 6 nuclei at the two poles organize into cells, while the remaining two fuse in the center (Fig. 105*G*). Since the three cells at the exine end were found to remain healthy for a much longer time than those at the opposite end, Stow regards the former as corresponding to the egg and synergids, and the latter to the antipodals. In addition certain abnormal pollen-embryo sacs were also seen, showing the following types of organization: (1) 8 nuclei forming an egg, two polars, and five antipodal cells; (2) 4 nuclei forming an egg, two polars, and one antipodal cell; (3) 4 nuclei forming a polar and three antipodal cells but no egg; (4) 16 nuclei forming a 5- to 10-celled egg apparatus, one or two polars, and a few antipodal cells; and (5) more than 16 nuclei without any definite arrangement.

According to Stow, it is not the divisions of the vegetative or generative nucleus which give rise to the pollen-embryo sacs but those of the microspore nucleus itself. Once the vegetative and

---

Fig. 105. Development of pollen–embryo sacs in *Hyacinthus orientalis*. *A*, microspore in metaphase of first division. *B*, microspore showing tendency toward formation of pollen–embryo sac; nucleus is in metaphase. *C*, second nuclear division in pollen–embryo sac; on right, young pollen–embryo sac with undivided nucleus. *D*, four- and two-nucleate pollen–embryo sacs. *E*, division of four nuclei; metaphase. *F*, same; anaphase. *G*, well-developed pollen–embryo sac. (*After Stow, 1930.*)

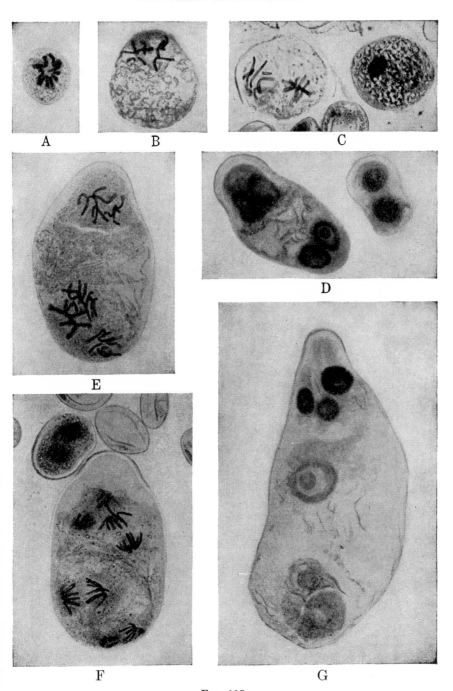

A   B   C

D

E

F   G

Fig. 105.

generative cells have been differentiated, further development is quite normal and no pollen-embryo sacs are formed. Further, the pollen-embryo sacs were always accompanied by a large number of dead pollen grains, leading Stow to suggest that the latter secrete a "necrohormone" which causes an abnormal growth of the surviving pollen grains.

Stow also observed that when the pollen-embryo sacs were placed on an agar medium, together with some normal pollen grains of another variety, the pollen tubes formed from the latter coiled

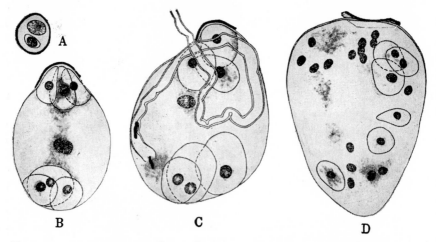

Fig. 106. Fertilization of pollen–embryo sacs in *Hyacinthus orientalis*. *A*, normal pollen grain, showing vegetative and generative cells. *B*, pollen–embryo sac. *C*, pollen–embryo sac affected by pollen tube from pollen grain of another variety. *D*, fertilized pollen–embryo sac; the smaller nuclei are presumed to be products of division of triple fusion nucleus. (*After Stow, 1934*.)

around the former (Fig. 106). Once a sperm nucleus was observed to be in process of entering the pollen-embryo sac; and in another case the pollen-embryo sac showed 16 nuclei, believed to have been derived from the divisions of a triple fusion nucleus.

In conclusion Stow says that all pollen grains are potentially capable of assuming either the male or the female form. Under normal conditions the "male potency" is dominant over the "female potency" leading to the formation of the generative cell and the male gametes; but under abnormal conditions, when there is a release of necrohormones, the female potency gets the upper hand resulting in the formation of embryo-sac-like structures.

Shortly after the publication of Stow's papers, Naithani (1937) found embryo-sac-like pollen grains in the variety "Yellow Hammer" whose bulbs had been treated for early flowering. He confirms Stow's observations regarding the mode of development of these abnormal pollen grains, but believes their formation to be a temperature effect and not the result of a liberation of necrohormones. According to him, the degeneration of the other pollen grains is not the cause but the effect of a hypertrophied growth of the more favored ones, which use up all the available food for their own growth.

More recently, pollen-embryo sacs with 8 and 16 nuclei have also been observed in another plant, *Ornithogalum nutans* (Geitler, 1941). Those with 8 nuclei showed the typical embryo-sac-like organization, but, contrary to Stow, Geitler interprets the three cells at the exine end of the pollen grain as the equivalents of antipodals and the other three as equivalents of the egg and synergids.

References

Anderson, L. E. 1939. Cytoplasmic inclusions in the male gametes of *Lilium·* Amer. Jour. Bot. **26:** 761–766.

Banerji, I., and Gangulee, H. C. 1937. Spermatogenesis in *Eichhornia crassipes* Solms. Jour. Indian Bot. Soc. **16:** 289–296.

———— and Haldar, S. 1942. A contribution to the morphology and cytology of *Monochoria hastaefolia* Presl. Proc. Indian Acad. Sci. Sect. B. **16:** 91–106.

Barber, H. N. 1942. The pollen grain division in the Orchidaceae. Jour. Genet. **43:** 97–103.

Beatty, A. V. 1943. The division of the generative nucleus in *Eschscholtzia*. Amer. Jour. Bot. **30:** 378–382.

Benetskaia, G. K. 1939. Observations in vivo des gamètes mâles dans les tubes polliniques d'*Asclepias cornutii* Decsn., de *Vinca major* L. et de *Vinca minor* L. Jour. Bot. de l'U.R.S.S. **24:** 273–281.

Billings, F. H. 1934. Male gametophyte of *Atriplex hymenelytra*. Bot. Gaz. **95:** 477–484.

Brumfield, R. T. 1941. Asymmetrical spindles in the first microspore division of certain angiosperms. Amer. Jour. Bot. **28:** 713–722.

Capoor, S. P. 1937a. Contributions to the morphology of some Indian Liliaceae. II. The gametophytes of *Urginea indica* Kunth. Beihefte bot. Centbl. **56A:** 156–170.

————. 1937b. The life history of *Holoptelea integrifolia* Planch. Beihefte bot. Centbl. **57A:** 233–249.

Cooper, D. C. 1935. Microsporogenesis and the development of the male gametes in *Portulaca oleracea*. Amer. Jour. Bot. **22:** 453–459.

————. 1936. Development of the male gametes in *Lilium*. Bot. Gaz. **98:** 169–177.

Cooper, G. O. 1935. Cytological studies in the Chenopodiaceae. I. Microsporogenesis and pollen development. Bot. Gaz. **97:** 169–178.

Dahlgren, K. V. O. 1915. Über die Überwinterungsstadien der Pollensäcke und der Samenanlagen bei einigen Angiospermen. Svensk Bot. Tidskr. **9:** 1–12.

————. 1916. Zytologische und embryologische Studien über die Reihen Primulales und Plumbaginales. K. Svenska Vet.-Akad. Handl. **56**(4): 1–80.

D'Amato, F. 1947. Nuove ricerche embriologiche e cariologiche sul genere *Euphorbia*. Nuovo Gior. Bot. Ital. N.S. **53:** 405–436.

Darlington, C. D. 1936. The analysis of chromosome movements. I. *Podophyllum versipella*. Cytologia **7:** 242–247.

De Mol, W. E. 1923. Duplication of generative nuclei by means of physiological stimuli and its significance. Genetica **5:** 225–272.

Duggar, B. M. 1900. Studies in the development of the pollen grain in *Symplocarpus foetidus* and *Peltandra undulata*. Bot. Gaz. **29:** 81–98.

Eigsti, O. J. 1939. The morphology of pollen tubes in angiosperms. Proc. Okla. Acad. Sci. **19:** 105–107.

————. 1940. The effects of colchicine upon the division of the generative cell in *Polygonatum, Tradescantia* and *Lilium*. Amer. Jour. Bot. **27:** 512–524.

————. 1941. The occurrence of a pollen tube with four sperms and two tube nuclei in *Polygonatum*. Proc. Okla. Acad. Sci. **21:** 134–136.

Fedortschuk, W. 1931. Embryologische Untersuchung von *Cuscuta monogyna* Vahl. und *Cuscuta epithymum* L. Planta **14:** 94–111.

Finn, W. W. 1925. Male cells in angiosperms. I. Spermatogenesis and fertilization in *Asclepias cornutii*. Bot. Gaz. **80:** 1–25.

————. 1928. Spermazellen bei *Vinca minor* und *V. herbacea*. Ber. deutsch. bot. Gesell. **46:** 235–246.

————. 1935. Einige Bemerkungen über den männlichen Gametophyten der Angiospermen. Ber. deutsch. bot. Gesell. **53:** 679–686.

————. 1937*a*. Entwicklungsgeschwindigkeit des männlichen Gametophyten bei den Angiospermen. Trav. Inst. Rech. Sci. Biol., Univ. Kiew 1937, pp. 71–86.

————. 1937*b*. Vergleichende Embryologie und Karyologie einiger *Cuscuta*-Arten. Jour. Inst. Bot. Acad. Sci. Ukraine **12:** 83–99.

————. 1939. On the history of the development of the male gametophyte in Labiatae. Jour. Inst. Bot. Acad. Sci. Ukraine **20:** 77–96.

————. 1940. Spermazellen bei Angiospermen. Jour. Bot. de l'U.R.S.S. **25:** 155–175.

————. 1941. Männlichen Gameten bei Angiospermen. Compt. Rend. (Dok.) Acad. des Sci. U.R.S.S. **30:** 451–458.

Friemann, W. 1910. "Über die Entwicklung der generativen Zelle im Pollenkorn der monocotylen Pflanzen." Diss. Bonn.

Frisendahl, A. 1912. Cytologische und Entwicklungsgeschichtliche Studien an *Myricaria germanica* Desv. K. Svenska Vet.-Akad. Handl. **48**(7): 1–62.

Fuchs, A. 1936. Untersuchungen über den männlichen Gametophyten von *Elaeagnus angustifolia*. Österr. bot. Ztschr. **85:** 1–16

Gager, C. S. 1902. The development of the pollinium and sperm cells in *Asclepias cornutii* Decaine. Ann. Bot. **16**: 123–148.

Geitler, L. 1935. Beobachtungen über die erste Teilung im Pollenkorn der Angiospermen. Planta **24**: 361–386.

———. 1941. Embryosäcke aus Pollenkörnern bei *Ornithogalum*. Ber. deutsch. bot. Gesell. **59**: 419–423.

———. 1942. Über die Struktur des generativen Kerns im zweikernigen Angiospermenpollen. Planta **32**: 187–195.

Goebel, K. 1933. "Örganographie der Pflanzen. III. Samenpflanzen." 3d ed. Jena.

Goodspeed, T. H. 1947. Maturation of the gametes and fertilization in *Nicotiana*. Madroño **9**: 110–120.

Guignard, L. 1889. Études sur les phénomènes morphologiques de la fécondation. Bul. Soc. Bot. de France **36**: 100–146.

———. 1922. Sur l'existence de corps proteiques dans le pollen de diverses Angiospermes. Compt. Rend. Acad. Sci. Paris **175**: 1015–1020.

Guilliermond, A. 1941. "The Cytoplasm of the Plant Cell." Chronica Botanica Company.

Heitz, E., and Résende, F. 1936. Zur Methodik der Pollenkorn- und Pollenschlauch-untersuchung. Bol. Soc. Broteriana, Coimbra II, **11**: 5–15.

Hewitt, W. C. 1939. Seed development of *Lobelia amoena*. Jour. Elisha Mitchel Sci. Soc. **55**: 63–82.

Ishikawa, M. 1918. Studies on the embryo sac and fertilization in *Oenothera*. Ann. Bot. **32**: 279–317.

Islam, A. S. 1950. The embryology of *Ottelia alismoides* Pers. Jour. Indian Bot. Soc. **28**: 79–91.

Johnston, G. W. 1941. Cytological studies of male gamete formation in certain angiosperms. Amer. Jour. Bot. **28**: 306–319.

Juel, H. O. 1900. Beiträge zur Kenntnis der Tetradenteilung. Jahrb. f. wiss. Bot. **35**: 626–649.

Juliano, J. B., and Alcala, P. E. 1933. Floral morphology of *Musa errans* (Blanco) Teodoro var. *Botoan* Teodoro. Philippine Agr. **22**: 91–126.

Junell, S. 1931. Die Entwicklungsgeschichte von *Circaeaster agrestis*. Svensk Bot. Tidskr. **40**: 111–126.

Kausik, S. B., and Rao, P. V. K. 1942. The male gametophyte of *Halophila ovata* Gaudich. Jour. Mysore Univ. B. **3**: 43–49.

Koernicke, M. 1906. Zentrosomen bei Angiospermen? Zugleich ein Beitrag zur Kenntnis der generativen Elemente im Pollenschlauch. Flora **96**: 501–522.

Kostriukova, K. 1939a. Spermatogenesis in *Crinum hildebrandtii* Vatke. Observations in vivo. Jour. Inst. Bot. Acad. Sci. Ukraine **21/22**: 157–164.

———. 1939b. Observations *in vivo* on the formation of the male sex cells in *Lilium martagon* L. Compt. Rend. (Dok.) Acad. des Sci. U.R.S.S. **22**: 444–447.

——— and Benetskaia, G. 1939. Spermatogenesis in *Narcissus poeticus* L. Observations in vivo. Jour. Bot. de l'U.R.S.S. **24**: 209–220.

Krupko, S. 1926. Les plastides et le chondriome pendant la gonogenèse dans le *Gagea lutea*. Acta Soc. Bot. Poloniae **4**: 77–86.

Kühlwein, H. 1937. Zur Physiologie der Pollenkeimung, insbesondere der Frage nach dem Befruchtungsverzug bei Gymnospermen. Beihefte bot. Centbl. **57A.**

Lagerberg, T. 1909. Studien über die Entwicklungsgeschichte und systematische Stellung von *Adoxa moschatellina* L. K. Svenska Vet.-Akad. Handl. **44**(4): 1–86.

Locke, J. F. 1936. Microsporogenesis and cytokinesis in *Asimina triloba*. Bot. Gaz. **98:** 159–168.

Luxemburg, A. 1927. Recherches cytologiques sur les grains de pollen chez les Malvacées. Bul. Internatl. Acad. Polonaise Sci. et Lettr.: Cl. Sci. Math. et Nat. B. 1927, pp. 363–396.

Madge, M. 1929. Spermatogenesis and fertilisation in the cleistogamous flowers of *Viola odorata* var. *praecox*. Ann. Bot. **43:** 545–577.

———. 1936. Division of the generative cell in *Hedychium gardnerianum*. Cellule **45:** 171–176.

Magnus, W. 1913. Die atypische Embryonalentwicklung der Podostomaceen. Flora **105:** 275–336.

Maheshwari, P. 1931. Contribution to the morphology of *Albizzia lebbek*. Jour. Indian Bot. Soc. **10:** 241–264.

———. 1949. The male gametophyte of angiosperms. Bot. Rev. **15:** 1–75.

——— and Wulff, H. D. 1937 Recent advances in microtechnic. I. Methods of studying the male gametophyte of angiosperms. Stain Technol. **12:** 61–70.

Mohrbutter, C. 1936. Embryologische Studien an Loganiaceen. Planta **26:** 64–80.

Naithani, S. P. 1937. Chromosome studies in *Hyacinthus orientalis* L. III. Reversal of sexual state in the anthers of *H. orientalis* L. var. Yellow Hammer. Ann. Bot. **1:** 369–377.

Nawaschin, S. G. 1909. Über dasselbständige Bewegungsvermögen des Spermakerns bei einigen Angiospermen. Österr. bot. Ztschr. **59:** 457–467.

———. 1910. Näheres über die Bildung der Spermakerne bei *Lilium martagon*. Ann. Jard. Bot. Buitenzorg, 3rd Suppl. **2:** 871–904.

——— and Finn, W. W. 1913. Zur Entwicklungsgeschichte der Chalazogamen, *Juglans regia*, und *Juglans nigra*. Mém. Acad. Imp. des Sci. St. Petersburg VIII, **31:** 1–59.

Němec, B. 1898. Über den Pollen der petaloiden Antheren von *Hyacinthus orientalis* L. Rozpravy Česke Akad. Prag II, 7(17).

Newman, I. V. 1934. Studies in the Australian acacias. IV. The life history of *Acacia baileyana* F.V.M. Part 2. Gametophytes, fertilisation, seed production and germination, and general conclusion. Proc. Linn. Soc. N. S. Wales **59:** 277–313.

Nietsch, H. 1941. Zur systematische Stellung von *Cyanastrum*. Österr. bot. Ztschr. **90:** 31–52.

Oehler, E. 1927. Entwicklungsgeschichtlich-cytologische Untersuchungen an einigen saprophytischen Gentianaceen. Planta **3:** 641–733.

O'Mara, J. 1933. Division of the generative nucleus in the pollen tube of *Lilium*. Bot. Gaz. **94:** 567–578.

Paetow, W. 1931. Embryologische Untersuchungen an Taccaceen, Meliaceen und Dilleniaceen. Planta **14:** 441–470.

Piech, K. 1928. Zytologische Studien an der Gattung *Scirpus.* Bul. Internatl. Acad. Polonaise Sci. et Lettr. 1928 (1/2): 1–43.

Poddubnaja-Arnoldi, V. A. 1933. Künstliche Kultur und zytologische Untersuchung des Pollenschlauches vom *Senecio platanifolius* Benth. Planta **19:** 299–304.

——. 1936. Beobachtungen über die Keimung des Pollens einiger Pflanzen auf künstlichen Nährboden. Planta **25:** 502–529.

Raghavan, T. S., *et al.* 1939. Division of the generative cell in *Impatiens balsamina* L. Cytologia **9:** 389–392.

Rosenberg, O. 1901. Über die Pollenbildung von *Zostera.* Meddel. Stockholma Högskolas Bot. Inst.: 1–21.

Ruhland, W., and Wetzel, K. 1924. Der Nachweis von Chloroplasten in den generativen Zellen von Pollenschläuchen. Ber. deutsch. bot. Gesell. **42:** 3–14.

Samuelsson, G. 1913. Studien über die Entwicklungsgeschichte einiger Bicornes-Typen. Svensk Bot. Tidskr. **7:** 97–188.

Schaffner, J. H. 1901. A contribution to the life history and cytology of *Erythronium.* Bot. Gaz. **31:** 369–387.

Schnarf, K. 1937. Studien über den Bau der Pollenkörner der Angiospermen. Planta **27:** 450–465.

——. 1939. Variation im Bau des Pollenkörnes der Angiospermen. Tab. Biol. Periodicae **27:** 72–89.

——. 1941. "Vergleichende Zytologie des Geschlechtsapparates des Kormophyten. Monographien zur vergleichenden Zytologie." Berlin.

Schürhoff, P. N. 1921. Über die Teilung des generativen Kernes vor der Keimung des Pollenkorns. Arch. f. Zellforsch. **15:** 145–159.

Shattuck, C. H. 1905. A morphological study of *Ulmus americana.* Bot. Gaz. **40:** 209–223.

Smith, C. M. 1929. Development of *Dionaea muscipula.* I. Flower and seed. Bot. Gaz. **87:** 508–530.

Stout, A. B. 1912. The individuality of the chromosomes and their serial arrangements in *Carex aquatilis.* Arch. f. Zellforsch. **9:** 114–140.

Stow, I. 1930. Experimental studies on the formation of embryo sac-like giant pollen grain in the anther of *Hyacinthus orientalis.* Cytologia **1:** 417–439.

——. 1934. On the female tendencies of the embryo sac-like giant pollen grain of *Hyacinthus orientalis.* Cytologia **5:** 88–108.

Strasburger, E. 1908. Chromosomenzahlen, Plasmastrukturen, Vererbungsträger und Reduktionsteilung. Jahrb. f. wiss. Bot. **45:** 477–570.

Suita, N. 1936. Studies on the male gametophyte in Angiosperms. I. Studies in the degenerating process of pollen tube nucleus, with special reference to Feulgen's reaction. Bot. and Zool. [Tokyo] **4:** 2033–2044.

——. 1937a. On the mature pollen grains in angiosperms. Bot. Mag. [Tokyo] **51:** 524–530.

——. 1937b. Studies on the male gametophyte in angiosperms. II. Differentiation and behavior of the vegetative and generative elements in the pollen grains of *Crinum*. Cytologia, Fujii Jubl. Vol., pp. 920–933.

Swamy, B. G. L. 1941. The development of the male gametes in *Cymbidium bicolor* Lindl. Proc. Indian Acad. Sci. Sect. B. **14**: 454–460.

———. 1949. Embryological studies in the Orchidaceae. I. Gametophytes. Amer. Midland Nat. **41**: 184–201.

Tanaka, N. 1940. Chromosome studies in Cyperaceae. VI. Pollen development and additional evidence for the compound chromosome in *Scirpus lacustris* L. Cytologia **10**: 348–362.

———. 1941. Chromosome studies in Cyperaceae. XII. Pollen development in five genera, with special reference to *Rhyncospora*. Bot. Mag. [Tokyo] **55**: 55–65.

Tischler, G. 1917. Pollenbiologische Studien. Ztschr. f. Bot. **9**: 417–488.

Trankowsky, D. A. 1931. Zytologische Beobachtungen über die Entwicklung der Pollenschläuche einiger Angiospermen. Planta **12**: 1–18.

Tschnernojarow, M. 1915. Les nouvelles données dans l'embryologie du *Myosurus minimus* L. Mém. Soc. Nat. Kiew **24**: 95–170.

Upcott, M. 1936. The mechanism of mitosis in the pollen-tube of *Tulipa*. Proc. Roy. Soc. London, Ser. B. **121**: 207–220.

Wefelscheid, G. 1911. "Über die Entwicklung der generativen Zelle im Pollenkorn der dikotylen Angiospermen." Diss. Bonn.

Weinzieher, S. 1914. Beiträge zur Entwicklungsgeschichte von *Xyris indica* L. Flora **106**: 393–432.

Welsford, E. J. 1914. The genesis of the male nuclei in *Lilium*. Ann. Bot. **28**: 265–270.

West, G. 1930. Cleistogamy in *Viola riviniana*, with especial reference to the cytological aspects. Ann. Bot. **44**: 87–109.

Witmer, S. W. 1937. Morphology and cytology of *Vallisneria spiralis* L. Amer. Midland Nat. **18**: 309–327.

Wulff, H. D. 1933. Beiträge zur Kenntnis des männlichen Gametophyten der Angiospermen. Planta **21**: 12–50.

———. 1934. Untersuchungen an Pollenkörnern und Pollenschläuchen von *Impatiens parviflora*. Ber. deutsch. bot. Gesell. **52**: 43–47.

———. 1939*a*. Die Pollenentwicklung der Juncaceen. Jahrb. f. wiss. Bot. **87**: 533–556.

———. 1939*b*. Die Entwicklung der Pollenkörner von *Triglochin palustris* L. und die verschiedenen Typen der Pollenkornentwicklung der Angiospermen. Jahrb. f. wiss. Bot. **88**: 141–168.

——— and Maheshwari, P. 1938. The male gametophyte of angiosperms (a critical review). Jour. Indian Bot. Soc. **17**: 117–140.

——— and Raghavan, T. S. 1937. Beobachtungen an Pollenschlauchkulturen von der Hydrophyllaceae *Nemophila insignis*. Planta **27**: 466–473.

Wunderlich, R. 1937. Zur vergleichenden Embryologie der Liliaceae-Scilloideae. Flora **32**: 48–90.

Wylie, R. B. 1904. The morphology of *Elodea canadensis*. Bot. Gaz. **37**: 1–22.

———. 1923. Sperms of *Vallisneria spiralis*. Bot. Gaz. **75**: 191–202.

CHAPTER 6

FERTILIZATION

In gymnosperms the pollen grains usually land directly on the nucellus, while in angiosperms they are deposited on the stigma. There are various agencies which serve to bring about this transfer of pollen from the anthers to the stigma, but since this is primarily an ecological subject and information on it is readily available else-where, it need not be dealt with here. It is sufficient to say that, in the condition in which they are discharged from the anther, the pollen grains show considerable resistance to environmental changes. Sometimes they retain their viability for several weeks, and with proper methods of storage this period can be prolonged still further (see Chap. 12).

Germination of Pollen. Exact information on the time taken by pollen to germinate on the stigma is available for only a few plants, but the following examples will illustrate the range that has been observed: 2 days in *Garrya elliptica* (Hallock, 1930), 3 hours in *Reseda* spp. (Eigsti, 1937); 2 hours in *Beta vulgaris* (Artschwager and Starrett, 1933); and 5 minutes in *Taraxacum kok-saghys* (Poddub-naja-Arnoldi and Dianowa, 1934), *Zea mays* (Randolph, 1936), and *Hordeum distichon* (Pope, 1937). In *Saccharum officinarum* (Artschwager *et al.*, 1929) and *Sorghum vulgare* (Artschwager and McGuire, 1949) germination takes place almost immediately.

The first step in germination is the expansion of the pollen grain by the absorption of liquid from the moist surface of the stigma and the protrusion of the intine through a germ pore. The small tubular structure which arises in this way then continues to elongate, mak-ing its way down the tissues of the stigma and style. Only the distal part of the tube has living cytoplasm, and as the nuclei pass forward callose plugs are left in the empty portions behind them.

Most pollen grains are monosiphonous, *i.e.*, only a single pollen tube emerges from each pollen grain; others, like those of the Mal-vaceae, Cucurbitaceae and Campanulaceae, are polysiphonous. In *Althaea rosea* 10 tubes, and in *Malva neglecta* even 14 tubes, are

181

known to come out from the same pollen grain (Stenar, 1925). Eventually, however, only one of them makes further progress. Sometimes the same pollen tube may divide into one or more branches. Such a condition seems to be frequent in the Amentiferae, where the branching tubes give the appearance of a ramifying fungous mycelium (see Finn, 1928*b*). In plants whose pollen grains are united into tetrads or into pollinia, several pollen tubes are produced at the same time (Fig. 107*A*, *B*).

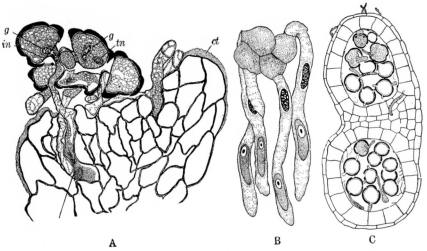

A   B   C

Fig. 107.   *Acacia baileyana*, pollinium germinating on stigma (*ct* = cuticle; *g* = generative cell; *tn* = tube nucleus; *in* = intine). (*After Newman, 1934.*)   *B, Cymbidium bicolor*, germination of pollen grains united in tetrads.   (*After Swamy, 1941.*) *C, Elatine triandra*, t.s. anther of cleistogamous flower, showing pollen grains germinating *in situ*. (*After Frisendahl, 1927.*)

The stigma is believed to play an important part in the germination of pollen, but in many plants germination can also be induced in a sugar solution of appropriate strength. Martin (1913) germinated the pollen of *Trifolium pratense* on hog's bladder moistened with distilled water and suggested that the only use of the stigma lies in controlling the water supply. Katz (1926) agreed with this view and said that the chief function of the stigmatic secretion is to protect the pollen as well as the stigma from desiccation. In her experiments the pollen germinated even on the cut surface of the style, provided the stigmatic secretion was applied to the stump and the latter was kept moist for some time.

Pollen grains may also germinate on other parts of the flower besides the stigma. In cleistogamous flowers (Frisendahl, 1927; Madge, 1929; West, 1930; Maheshwari and Singh, 1934) germination takes place within the anther loculi (Fig. 107*C*), and in *Aeginetia indica* (Juliano, 1935) even on the moist surface of the corolla tube. Frequently pollen grains germinate on a foreign stigma, *i.e.*, stigma of a different species (see Eigsti, 1937; Sanz, 1945). If fertilization takes place, it results in the formation of interspecific and intergeneric hybrids.

Course of Pollen Tube. After the tube has emerged from the pollen grain, it makes its way between the stigmatic papillae into the tissues of the style. The latter is extremely variable in length. In some plants it is so short that the stigma is described as sessile, while in *Zea mays* the so-called "silk" may attain a length of 50 cm.

Depending on the presence or absence of the transmitting tissue and on the extent of its development, styles have been classified into three main types called open, half-closed, and closed (Hanf, 1935). In the first type there is a wide stylar canal and the inner epidermis itself assumes the function of the nutrition and conduction of the pollen tube, as in the Papaveraceae, Aristolochiaceae, Ericaceae, and many monocotyledons. In the second type the canal is surrounded by a rudimentary transmitting tissue of two or three layers of glandular cells, as in several members of the Cactaceae. In the third or closed type, illustrated by *Datura* and *Gossypium*, there is no open channel but instead a solid core of elongated and richly protoplasmic cells through which the pollen tube grows downward in order to reach the ovary. Finally, there are other plants like *Salix, Acacia*, and many grasses in which the styles are solid but are not provided with any specialized transmitting tissue.

In open styles the pollen tube grows on the surface of the cells lining the stylar canal (often in the mucilage secreted by them); and in solid styles through the intercellular spaces between the cells of the transmitting tissue, enlarging the spaces by the hydrostatic pressure of its contents and secreting some enzymatic substances which bring about a dissolution of the middle lamellae. Only rarely does the pollen tube pass through the cells themselves.

After arriving at the top of the ovary, the tube may enter the ovule either through the micropyle or by some other route. The former is the usual condition and is known as porogamy, but even in plants ordinarily classed as porogamous there are several modifications.   To mention a few examples, in *Acacia* (Newman, 1934) the integuments are still below the apex of the nucellus at the time of fertilization so that a micropyle does not exist at this stage and in *Philadelphus, Utricularia, Vandellia,* and *Torenia* the embryo sac

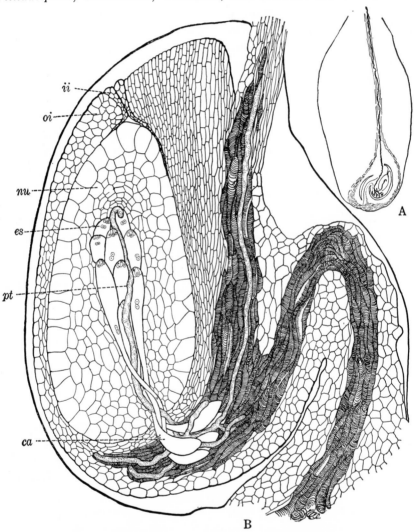

FIG. 108.   Course of pollen tube in ovule of *Casuarina equisetifolia. A,* optical longitudinal section of entire ovary; pollen tube is represented by heavy black line.   *B,* l.s. ovule reconstructed from several sections to show path of pollen tube. (*After Swamy, 1948.*)

protrudes out of the micropyle so that the pollen tube comes in direct contact with it. In several members of the Loranthaceae there is no integument and therefore nothing that can be called a micropyle. Here the embryo sacs undergo a remarkable elongation and meet the pollen tubes at some point in the stylar region (see also p. 143).

In some plants the pollen tube enters the ovule through the chalaza. This condition, known as chalazogamy (see page 17), was first reported in *Casuarina* (Treub, 1891) and soon afterwards

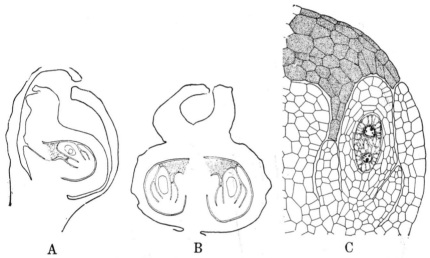

FIG. 109. Development of obturator in *Acalypha indica*. *A*, l.s. terminal flower of inflorescence, showing ovule at megaspore mother cell stage. Note beginning of formation of obturator (shaded). *B*, l.s. lateral flower at more advanced stage. *C*, ovule, enlarged to show hood-like obturator fitting over nucellus. (*After Maheshwari and Johri*, 1941.)

in several members of the Amentiferae. Nevertheless, it is not confined to them, being also known in *Rhus* (Grimm, 1912), *Circaeaster* (Junell, 1931), and a few other genera. Recent studies have, however, shown that even in such cases, where entry into the ovule is effected through the chalaza, the tube usually continues its growth over the surface of the embryo sac and penetrates it only after arriving near the egg apparatus. As examples may be mentioned *Ostrya carpinifolia* (Finn, 1936), *Juglans regia* (Nast, 1941), and *Casuarina equisetifolia* (Swamy, 1948) (Fig. 108).

In *Alchemilla* (Murbeck, 1901), *Cucurbita* (Longo, 1901; Kirkwood, 1906), and *Circaeaster* (Junell, 1931) the pollen tube enters through the funiculus or the integument. This is known as mesogamy.

Formerly considerable phylogenetic significance was attached to the route taken by the pollen tube during its entry into the ovule, but now this point is considered to be of physiological rather than phylogenetic importance, for we sometimes find considerable variation in this respect even in one and the same species. In *Brassica oleracea* (Thompson, 1933) the tube normally enters through the micropyle, but sometimes it may do so by way of the chalaza. In *Ulmus*, Shattuck (1905) speaks of its branching and apparently aimless wandering through the funiculus, the integuments, and occasionally the nucellus. In *Epilobium* (Werner, 1914; Täckholm, 1915) it may enter either through the micropyle, through the integuments, or by an intermediate route. In *Boerhaavia* (Maheshwari, 1929), although the tube actually enters through the micropyle, it first makes a horizontal crossing through the funiculus. In *Gossypium* (Gore, 1932) it often passes from the funiculus to the base of the ovule and then travels up along the wall of the latter to enter the micropyle.

An organ of special significance in facilitating the entry of the pollen tube into the ovule is the so-called obturator, to which reference had already been made by Hofmeister in the year 1849. Usually it is a swelling of the placenta which grows towards

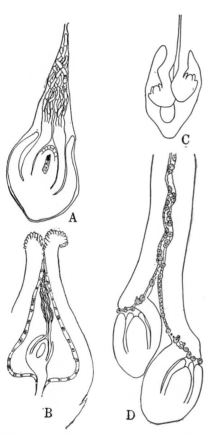

FIG. 110. Origin and structure of obturator in *Myriocarpa longipes* (A), *Leucosyke capitellata* (B), and *Quisqualis indica* (C, D). (*After Fagerlind 1944, 1941.*)

the micropyle and fits like a hood or canopy over the nucellus, serving as a sort of bridge for the pollen tube (Fig. 109). Often the cells of the obturator may be greatly elongated or may have a glandular appearance (Fig. 110C, D).

Some other structures having a different origin but serving the same function may also be included under the general term obturator. In the Thymelaeaceae (Fuchs, 1938) the cells belonging to the base of the stylar canal elongate and grow down as hairy

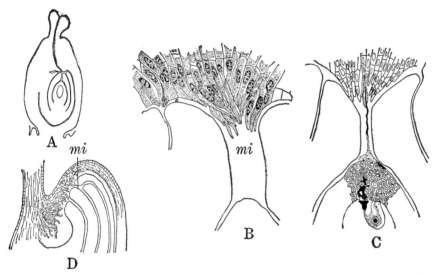

FIG. 111. Development of obturator in some members of Thymelaeaceae. *A, Daphne laureola,* l.s. pistil. *B,* same, part of ovary with cells of obturator protruding downward into micropyle. *C,* more advanced stage, showing path of pollen tube. *D, Passerina pectinata,* l.s. part of ovary, showing obturator (*mi* = micropyle). (*After Fuchs, 1938.*)

processes approaching the nucellus (Fig. 111). In *Pilea* (Fagerlind, 1944) a tuft of papillate cells extends from the base of the style to the apex of the ovule, coming in intimate contact with the latter. In *Myriocarpa* and *Leucosyke* (Fagerlind, 1944), on the other hand, it is the cells of the inner integument which elongate upward and penetrate into the stylar canal (Fig. 110A, B), forming what may be called an integumentary obturator.

Usually there are no special modifications in the cells lining the micropylar canal, but sometimes, as in *Berkheya* (Gelin, 1936),

Grevillea (Brough, 1933), and *Cynomorium* (Steindl, 1945), they become mucilaginous or glandular and seem to contribute to the nutrition of the pollen tube. In *Cardiospermum* (Kadry, 1946) not only the cells belonging to the inner integument but also those forming the apical portion of the nucellus give rise to a mucilaginous mass which facilitates the entry of the pollen tube. In plants with a many-layered nucellar tissue, like *Beta* (Artschwager and Starrett, 1933), those of its cells which are in continuity with the micropyle become elongated and richly protoplasmic and give an impression as though they were designed to lead the pollen tube through the path of least resistance.

It is of interest to note that even during its passage through the nucellus the pollen tube usually makes its way between the cells and not through them. Normally it causes but little disturbance in their position and they soon return to their original shape, but in a few families like the Lythraceae, Sonneratiaceae, Onagraceae, and Cucurbitaceae the tubes are so broad that they destroy the cells which lie in their way and cause a permanent break in the tissues.

Entry of Pollen Tube into Embryo Sac. After penetrating the wall of the embryo sac, the pollen tube may either pass between the egg and one synergid as in *Fagopyrum* (Mahony, 1935), or between the embryo sac wall and a synergid as in *Cardiospermum* (Kadry, 1946), or directly into a synergid as in *Oxalis* (Krupko, 1944), *Elodea* (Ernst-Schwarzenbach, 1945), and *Daphne* (Venkateswarlu, 1947). In *Viola* it not only enters a synergid but is said to force its way through the base of the latter (Madge, 1929).

As a rule only one synergid is destroyed by the impact of the pollen tube and the other remains intact until some time afterward, but in *Mimusops, Achras,* and *Bassia* (Murthy, 1941) both are destroyed and in *Phryma* (Cooper, 1941) and *Tropaeolum* (Walker, 1947) neither of them seems to be affected.

In some genera, such as *Tacca, Wormia* (Paetow, 1931), and *Nelumbo* (Ohga, 1937), the synergids degenerate even before the entry of the pollen tube, and in others like *Plumbago, Vogelia,* and *Plumbagella* (see Maheshwari, 1948) they are not formed at all. This seems to indicate that they are not essential for fertilization, and the view that they secrete substances which exercise a chemotactic influence over the pollen tube, or that they act as shock absorbers against its impact, does not rest on a sound basis (see also Dahlgren, 1938). In *Zauschneria latifolia* (Johansen, 1931*b*) pollen tubes were found to enter even those ovules whose embryo sacs had degenerated and virtually disappeared.

Detailed information regarding the exact manner of discharge of the male gametes is lacking. In *Crepis capillaris* (Gerassimova, 1933) and *Taraxacum kok-saghys* (Warmke, 1943) the tip of the

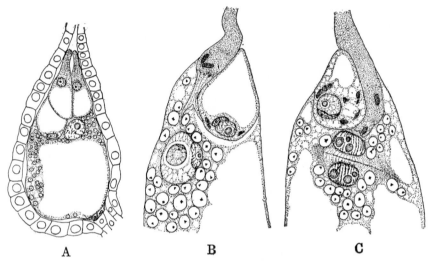

| A | B | C |

FIG. 112. Stages in fertilization in *Petunia*; globular bodies scattered inside embryo sac are starch grains. *A*, mature embryo sac surrounded by cells of integumentary tapetum. *B*, upper portion of embryo sac at time of double fertilization; note two branches of pollen tube, through which two male gametes have been discharged; just behind bifurcation are two X-bodies. *C*, upper portion of embryo sac, showing zygote and two endosperm nuclei with cell plate forming between them; X-bodies are still visible inside tip of pollen tube. (*After Cooper, 1946.*)

pollen tube becomes "wedged in" between the egg and the polar fusion nucleus, so that both the male gametes are discharged in close proximity to their mates. Fagerlind (1939) noted some embryo sacs of *Peperomia* in which the tip of the tube had divided into two short branches, one of which was directed toward the egg. Cooper (1940, 1941, 1946) refers to a similar bifurcation of the tip of the pollen tube in *Portulaca, Phryma,* and *Petunia* (Fig. 112), one branch becoming closely appressed to the egg and the other extending in the direction of the polar nuclei, and suggests that the two male gametes reach their destinations by way of these separate branches.   In *Coffea arabica* (Mendes, 1941) the pollen tube does not bifurcate but shows two subterminal openings through which the two male gametes are discharged into the cavity of the embryo sac.

Rate of growth of pollen tube.[1]   A considerable amount of information is available on the subject but most of the older records are rather vague and perhaps only rough estimates.   It must also be kept in mind that the rate of growth of the pollen tube is affected to an appreciable degree by the environmental conditions prevailing at the time of observation, and most of the existing data are therefore to be considered as approximate only.

In certain members of the Fagaceae and Betulaceae several months elapse between the time the pollen grains alight on the stigma and the time the pollen tube enters the embryo sac.   In some species of *Quercus* (Bağda, 1948) this period may be as long as 12 to 14 months.   In *Hamamelis virginiana* (Shoemaker, 1905) pollination occurs in late autumn, and at the beginning of winter the tips of the tubes reach near the base of the funiculus.   But here they "hibernate" for the rest of the winter and growth is resumed only in the spring.   Fertilization takes place in May, about 5 to 7 months after pollination.   In *Alnus glutinosa* and *Corylus avellana* (Benson, 1894) 3 to 4 months elapse between pollination and fertilization.   Since such long periods are also found in several gymnosperms, it is tempting to infer that this is a primitive feature, but long intervals are also known in the Orchidaceae where the ovules are not even formed until after pollination has taken place.   To mention a few examples, in *Paphiopedilum maudiae* (Duncan and Curtis, 1942b) approximately 19 to 20 weeks elapse between pollination and fertilization; in *P. villosum* (Duncan and Curtis, 1942b) the period is 14 weeks; in *Phalaenopsis pamala* (Duncan and Curtis, 1942a) and *Dendrobium annosum* (Pastrana and Santos, 1931) about 10 weeks; in *Cattleya* spp. (Duncan and Curtis, 1943) about 6 weeks; in *Cypripedium parviflorum* (Carlson, 1940) 26 to 33 days; in *C. pubescens* (Duncan and Curtis, 1942b) about 4 weeks; and in *Orchis maculatus* (Hagerup, 1944) about 2 weeks.

Fairly long intervals between pollination and fertilization are also known in plants belonging to other families.   In *Garrya elliptica*

[1] For a more detailed account of this topic, see Finn (1937a).

(Hallock, 1930) the pollen tube takes 17 days to arrive at the apex of the nucellus, and in *Carica papaya* (Foster, 1943) about 10 days; fertilization occurs a few days later. In *Colchicum autumnale* (Heimann-Winawer, 1919) there is an interval of about 10 to 11 days between pollination and fertilization, and in *Carya illinoensis* (McKay, 1947) about 4 to 7 days.

In most plants, however, the period ranges from 24 to 48 hours, and in some it is still shorter. In *Oryza sativa* (Juliano and Aldama, 1937), *Coffea arabica* (Mendes, 1941), and *Oxybaphus nyctagineus* (Cooper, 1949) fertilization takes place in about 12 to 14 hours after pollination, and in *Lactuca muralis* (Dahlgren, 1920) within 6 to 7 hours. In *L. sativa* (Jones, 1927, 1929) sperm nuclei have been seen in the embryo sac 3 hours after pollination and a couple of hours later most of the embryo sacs were already fertilized. In *Portulaca oleracea* (Cooper, 1940) the period between pollination and fertilization is 3 to 4 hours; in *Impatiens sultani* (Lebon, 1929) and *Hordeum distichon palmella* (Pope, 1937) pollen tubes arrive inside the embryo sac in less than an hour after pollination; and in *Parthenium argentatum* (Dianowa *et al.*, 1935) and *Crepis capillaris* (Gerassimova, 1933) fertilization is completed within 60 minutes after pollination. The shortest period on record is in *Taraxacum kok-saghys* (Poddubnaja-Arnoldi and Dianowa, 1934; Warmke, 1943), where fertilization occurs within 15 to 45 minutes after pollination.

Several computations have been made of the average hourly distance traversed by the pollen tube: 4 mm. in *Iris versicolor* (Sawyer, 1917), 6.25 mm. in *Zea mays* (Miller, 1919), 15 mm. in *Crepis capillaris* (Gerassimova, 1933), and 35 mm. in *Taraxacum kok-saghys* (Poddubnaja-Arnoldi and Dianowa, 1934). It is likely, however, that the actual rate of growth is still higher; for the path of the pollen tube from the stigma to the ovule is not like a straight line but is marked by many twists and convolutions.

Of the factors influencing the rate of growth, temperature is the most important. As early as 1861, Hofmeister had observed that in *Crocus vernus*, in warm moist air and bright sunshine, the pollen tubes can be seen in the micropyle within 24 hours after pollination, while in cooler and drier weather they take twice or thrice this time. Working on *Monotropa uniflora*, Shibata (1902) found that in the first week of May the pollen tubes took 10 days to reach the embryo sac, but in June only 6 days were necessary. He further observed that tube growth is adversely affected by abnormally low temperatures (8 to 10°C.) as well as abnormally high ones (above 31°C.) and he was able to lengthen or shorten the interval between pollination and fertilization merely by altering the experimental conditions. In plums (Dorsey, 1919) a low temperature (4.5 to 10.5°C.) renders fertilization uncertain because of a retardation of pollen tube growth.

The first detailed and direct study of the problem was made by Buchholz and Blakeslee (1927) who found that in *Datura stramonium* the rate of growth of the pollen tube steadily increased when the temperature was raised from 11 to 33°C. At 33°C. it was four and a half times that at 11°C.

Since then a somewhat similar range has been reported in several other plants. In *Lycopersicum esculentum* (Smith and Cochran, 1935) the maximum growth rate occurs at 21°C., gradually declining at both lower and higher temperatures. At 38°C. germination was extremely poor; 84 hours after pollination only 3.9 per cent of the pollen grains had germinated, none of the pollen tubes had grown more than 2 mm. long, and even these had become abnormally swollen and bulbous at the tips. In *Hordeum vulgare* var. *pallidum* (Pope, 1943) the optimum temperature is about 23°C. At this temperature the male gametes were found to reach the embryo sac in about 20 minutes after pollination, while at 5°C. 140 minutes were required for the attainment of this stage.

It may be concluded that according to present records (based mostly on observations made in temperate regions) pollen germination and tube growth are definitely inhibited at temperatures below 5°C., but occur freely above 10°C. and reach an optimum at about 25 to 30°C. Although the pollen grains themselves can withstand higher as well as lower temperatures and escape serious damage, such extremes are definitely harmful to the delicate tissues of the stigma and style. This may be the reason why many European vegetables fail to set seed in the tropics.

Another factor which markedly affects the rate of pollen tube growth is the degree of compatibility between the male gametophyte and the sporophytic tissues of the pistil. When their reciprocal relations are correct, the pollen tubes travel down the full length of the style and fertilization is accomplished before the formation of an abscission layer at the base of the flower. In incompatible matings, on the other hand, the tubes grow very slowly, if at all, and the flower withers away before they reach the embryo sac.

In *Brassica pekinensis*, which has been thoroughly studied by Stout (1931), the pollen tubes grow rapidly in cross-pollinated flowers. Self-pollinated flowers, on the other hand, exhibit the following incompatibility reactions: (1) low percentage of germination of pollen on "own" stigma, (2) coiling of pollen tubes on the stigmatic papillae, (3) feeble or limited growth of the tubes through the style, and (4) coiling of tips of the tubes in the ovary or ovules. In *Petunia violacea* (Yasuda, 1930) also the pollen tubes grow rapidly and reach the base of the pistil in about 36 hours after cross-pollination. In self-pollinated flowers, on the other hand, not only is the initial growth rate much lower, but also it continues to decrease and the tubes reach only about one-fifth of the length of the style, forming irregular swellings at their tips. In sugar solutions to which an extract of "own" stigma is added, the growth of the tubes is also extremely slow, but on the addition of extract from a different strain of the species the tubes grow normally. Anderson and Sax (1934) report that in *Tradescantia* the growth of the incompatible pollen tubes is much slower and the generative cell does not enter the tube even after 24 hours, while in compatible matings this takes place in only 40 minutes. In *Linaria reticulata* (Sears, 1937) compatible tubes reach the base of the style in less than 25 hours, while incompatible tubes grow only about one-fourth of the distance even in four days' time. In *Nemesia strumosa* (Sears, 1937) incompatible tubes grow at approximately the same rate as compatible ones through the first three-fourths or four-fifths of the style, but slow down rather suddenly and finally come to a stop at the base of the style. In *Trifolium repens* (Atwood, 1941) incompatible matings are characterized by two interference zones, one on the stigma and the other in the style. Germination of pollen is poor, and the few pollen tubes which happen to be formed seldom travel more than three-fourths of the way down the style. Those which do proceed further grow so slowly that the flowers wither and fall off before fertilization can take place.

An effect more or less similar to the above is seen in the so-called "illegitimate pollinations" between plants showing heterostyly. Working on *Fagopyrum esculentum*, Stevens (1912) found that in legitimate pollinations, fertilization takes place in 18 hours, but in illegitimate pollinations more than 72 hours are required and frequently fertilization fails altogether.[2]

A point of considerable interest is that while compatible pollen tubes grow faster at higher temperatures, the incompatible tubes show a further decline in their growth rate. This seems to indicate that incompatibility is probably due to a chemical reaction similar to an antigen-antibody reaction in animals, and that its speed, like that of all chemical reactions, is increased by a rise in temperature (Lewis, 1948).

Gametic Fusion. After the pollen tube has discharged its contents into the embryo sac, one male gamete fuses with the egg (syngamy) and the other with the two polar nuclei (triple fusion). Because of the technical difficulties encountered in studying the process, very few detailed accounts of it have appeared up to this time. The time between the beginning and the end of the gametic fusions is so short that one rarely succeeds in "catching" the material at the right stage. There is also an element of chance in obtaining proper median sections, for the embryo sac is usually large enough at this stage to run into several sections, and thick sections do not stain satisfactorily. Besides, even if the material has been properly selected and the desired stages are actually at hand, detailed observations may still prove difficult for the following reasons: (1) the pollen tube discharges a deeply staining material into the embryo sac which surrounds the egg and decreases visibility; (2) one or both of the synergids disorganize at this time and their contents become converted into a tenacious mucus-like material which stains densely; and (3) the vegetative nucleus (or its fragments) and the nuclei of the synergids "wander" into the upper part of the embryo sac and are liable to be confused with the male gametes.

In view of these difficulties it is not surprising that our knowledge of the events concerned with fertilization has not advanced very far beyond where it stood during the early part of this century. Several workers have confessed with a feeling of disappointment that, in spite of repeated efforts and the study of hundreds of ovules, they failed to find many of the critical stages in the process.

The present status of the subject may be dealt with in two parts: (1) form and structure of the male gametes, and (2) details of the

---

[2] For further information on this topic, see Ernst, 1936.

two fusions—one between the egg and the first male gamete, and the other between the polar nuclei and the second male gamete.

In form, the male gametes may be spherical as in *Erigeron* (Land, 1900), ellipsoidal as in *Levisticum* (Håkansson, 1923), rod-shaped as in *Urtica* (Strasburger, 1910), or vermiform as in *Lilium* (Guignard, 1899) and *Fritillaria* (Sax, 1916). Frequently they may change their shape after their discharge into the embryo sac. Nawaschin (1898) reported that in *Fritillaria* the sperms lose their worm-like form just before fertilization. In *Silphium* (Land, 1900), *Monotropa* (Shibata, 1902), *Taraxacum* (Poddubnaja-Arnoldi and Dianowa, 1934), *Lactuca* (Jones, 1927), and *Nicotiana* (Goodspeed, 1947) they are at first elongated or oval, but gradually become shorter and more spherical as they approach the female nuclei. In *Juglans* (Nawaschin, 1900), on the other hand, they are spherical in the beginning but become curved afterward. The male cells of *Vallisneria* (Wylie, 1923, 1941) are originally only slightly longer than broad (Fig. 113*A–D*) but become considerably elongated as the pollen tube enters the ovarian cavity (Fig. 113*E, F*). Finally they once again present a contracted appearance at the time of their discharge into the embryo sac (Fig. 113*G–J*). Gerassimova (1933) found that the changes undergone by the male gametes of *Crepis* are so rapid that it is difficult to follow them satisfactorily. Eventually the sperms become more or less band-shaped and appear to consist of two definite halves, folded along their entire length. Sometimes they roll up into a ball-shaped body, but the two longitudinal halves still remain distinguishable.

There are a few reports of differences in the size and shape of the two male nuclei discharged by a pollen tube. Guignard (1899) stated that in *Scilla nonscripta* the male nucleus destined to fertilize the egg is smaller than the one fusing with the polar nuclei, and Hoare (1934) has confirmed this although admitting that the size difference is not a constant feature. In *Lilium auratum* (Blackman and Welsford, 1913), *Iris versicolor* (Sawyer, 1917), *Fritillaria pudica* (Sax, 1916, 1918), *Trillium grandiflorum* (Nothnagel, 1918), *Acacia baileyana* (Newman, 1934), and *Camassia leichtlinii* (Smith, 1942) also, the male gamete entering the egg is said to be somewhat smaller than the one fusing with the polar nuclei and is sometimes also not so vermiform.

In some other plants the reverse condition has been reported.

Persidsky (1926) states that in *Orobanche cumana* the sperm nucleus fertilizing the egg is shaped like a hemisphere and is larger than the other, which has an oval outline. In *O. ramosa* (Finn and Rudenko, 1930) also, the sperm nucleus fusing with the egg is looser and more

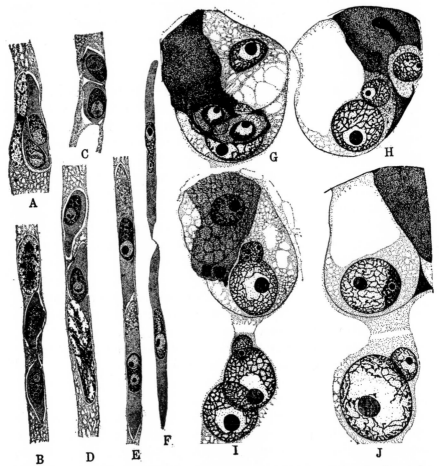

FIG. 113. Fertilization in *Vallisneria americana*. *A–D*, portions of pollen tubes from stylar region, showing male cells; note also vegetative nucleus in *A*, *B*, and *D*. *E,F*, elongated male cells from pollen tubes which have entered the ovarian chamber. *G*, upper part of embryo sac, showing egg, one synergid, two male cells, and a densely staining mass formed by tube and second synergid. *H*, first male nucleus lying tangent to the egg nucleus within the egg cell; nucleus of second male cell emerging from its sheath. *I*, nucleus of first sperm fusing with egg nucleus and second sperm nucleus touching the upper polar. Note the two X-bodies at the tip of the pollen tube. *J*, later stage, showing male and female nuclei in advanced stage of fusion, and second sperm nucleus in contact with secondary nucleus. (*After Wylie, 1923, 1941*.)

faintly staining than the other. In *Vallisneria* (Wylie, 1923) both nuclei are oval at the time of their discharge from the pollen tube but the second soon becomes spherical. Very recently Kadry (1946) has reported that in *Cardiospermum* the male nucleus fertilizing the egg is swollen and rounded in front but tapering behind, and that it is about four times as long as the other male nucleus, which is more or less spherical. In *Vinca minor* (Finn, 1928a) also, the sperm cells are unequal, one with a larger and the other with a shorter plasma tail, but it could not be determined which fuses with the egg and which with the polar nuclei.

Although slight differences in the size and shape of the two male gametes are possible, the few examples cited above do not seem adequate to justify any generalization. In the first place considerable care has to be taken to make sure that the observed differences are not due to the plane of sectioning. Stages in fertilization are infrequent, and in the same section one male gamete may be cut across its longer diameter and the other in a plane at right angles to it, so that the two appear to be of different sizes, although in fact they are quite similar. Further, the male gametes often change their form and, as Gerassimova (1933) has suggested, the reported size differences may well be due to a disparity in the rates of their transformation.

There has been a good deal of discussion about the mechanism of movement of the generative cell and the male gametes. It is well known that the antherozoids of the thallophytes, bryophytes, and pteridophytes are actively motile. Even among the gymnosperms, the Cycadales and Ginkgoales have ciliated sperms and their pollen tube serves merely as a haustorial organ. In the Coniferales, Gnetales, and angiosperms, on the other hand, cilia are absent and the pollen tube becomes the agent for the transport of the male gametes from the pollen chamber or the stigma to the embryo sac. Long ago, Strasburger (1884, 1900, 1908) put forth the view that the male gametes are carried passively by the streaming movements of the cytoplasm inside the pollen tube. On the other hand, Nawaschin (1898) and some other workers believed that the vermiform appearance of the male gametes, observed in several members of the Liliaceae and Compositae, is indicative of an independent power of movement. Studies on living pollen tubes (Wulff, 1933) seem to support Nawaschin's view. The cytoplasm in the tube shows several plasma strands running in opposite directions, while the male gametes move in the forward direction only. This would hardly be possible unless the male gametes have the power to move independently of the strands of cytoplasm.

Concerning the actual course of fusion of the gametic nuclei, only a few observers have described it in sufficient detail. The most careful account is that of Gerassimova (1933) on *Crepis capillaris*. At the time of its approach to the egg nucleus, the male nucleus has the appearance of a continuous thread rolled into a ball (Fig. 114*A*), which soon begins to unwind and spread out with its entire surface adjacent to the nuclear membrane of the egg (Fig. 114*B*). It then gradually "immerses" itself within the egg nucleus, although still remaining distinguishable for a long time (Fig. 114*C–F*). Meanwhile, a nucleolus arises from it "at first as a small, scarcely visible, weakly stained drop, which gradually increases in size" (Fig. 114*E, F*). At the same time the body of the sperm "becomes more porous and breaks up lengthwise, losing its continuity" (Fig. 114*G–H*). Very soon the male chromatin becomes indistinguishable from the female, and it is only the presence of the two nucleoli which serves to distinguish the fertilized from the unfertilized egg (Fig. 114*I–K*). Finally, however, the male nucleolus increases in size and fuses with the female nucleolus "thus closing the perceivable phenomena of sexual union of the nuclei" (Fig. 114*L*).

The fusion of the second sperm with the secondary nucleus takes place in very much the same way. Here also the sperm has the shape of a rolled thread, which gradually unwinds itself and comes in contact with the secondary nucleus all along its surface. This is followed by the immersion of the sperm into the secondary nucleus and the formation of a small nucleolus. Finally the two chromatins merge into each other, followed by a fusion of the nucleoli.

From the less frequent occurrence of stages in the fertilization of the secondary nucleus, Gerassimova concludes that triple fusion is accomplished more quickly than syngamy. She states that in triple fusion "the formation of the nucleolus takes place so rapidly that it is almost impossible to catch the beginning of the process" and that "although fertilization always begins first in the nucleus of the egg-cell, the stage of a complete fusion of the nuclei is often simultaneous and sometimes terminates even earlier in the nucleus of the endosperm." In several of her preparations she found that triple fusion had already ended (as judged by the fusion of the

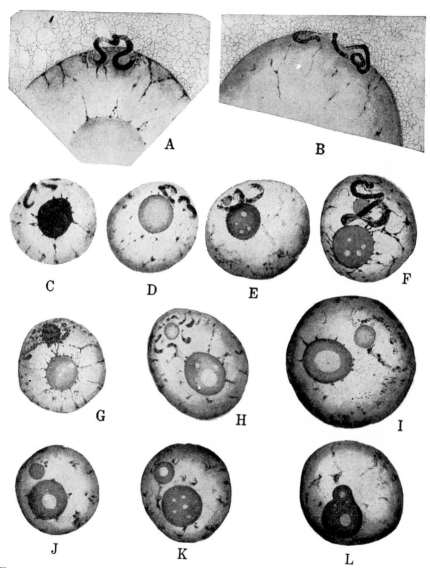

FIG. 114. Some stages in syngamy in *Crepis capillaris*. *A*, portion of egg nucleus with sperm lying on nuclear membrance. *B*, uncoiling of sperm nucleus, showing dual bead-like appearance at some places. *C*, *D*, entry of sperm nucleus inside nuclear membrane of egg. *E–I*, a gradual disintegration of the sperm thread and appearance of its nucleolus. *J*, *K*, intermingling of contents of male and female nuclei. *L*, later stage, showing fusion of the two nucleoli. (*After Gerassimova, 1933.*)

nucleoli), while inside the egg nucleus the male chromatin was still distinguishable from the female.[3]

In most plants gametic fusion takes place when the nuclei are in a resting condition, but there are exceptions. In *Lilium Martagon*, *L. auratum* (Welsford, 1914), *L. philadelphicum*, *L. longiflorum* (Weniger, 1918), *Fritillaria pudica* (Sax, 1918), and *Viola odorata* (Madge, 1929) the fusing nuclei are in prophase. In the cleistogamous flowers of *Viola* (Madge, 1929) the male nucleus is in a "spireme," and in *Malus* (Wanscher, 1939) "both gametes are in a spireme stage during their union." In *Triticum* (Sax, 1918) the first male nucleus and the nucleus of the egg were both found to be in the "spireme" stage, but the second male nucleus had already progressed into the early metaphase stage at the time of its fusion with the polar nuclei. According to some reports, fusion may also take place at a stage even before the male nuclei have recovered from their original telophasic condition. Nawaschin (1909) believed this to be the case in *Lilium martagon*, Frisendahl (1912) in *Myricaria germanica*, and Newman (1934) in *Acacia baileyana*. In *Scilla nonscripta*, according to Hoare (1934), the male nuclei formed after the division of the generative cell "never pass into a complete resting stage" but show a dense chromatin reticulum which is interpreted as "the previous early telophase."

Conflicting statements have been made regarding the presence or absence of a nucleolus in the male nuclei. In certain plants like *Cuscuta* (Finn, 1937*b*) and *Camassia* (Smith, 1942) no nucleolus has been seen. In *Orobanche* (Finn and Rudenko, 1930), *Crepis* (Gerassimova, 1933), *Malus* (Wanscher, 1939), and *Oxybaphus* (Cooper, 1949) a nucleolus was not distinguishable at the time of formation of the sperm cells but could be seen shortly before or during fertilization, and in *Taraxacum kok-saghys* (Warmke, 1943) it appeared only after fertilization. In *Viola riviniana* (West, 1930), on the other hand, the male nuclei always showed a distinct nucleolus, and the one entering into triple fusion is said to be represented almost entirely by its nucleolus. In *Orchis maculatus* (Hagerup, 1944) also, the male nuclei have one or more distinct nucleoli.

---

[3] In *Tacca* (Paetow, 1931) and *Jussieua* (Khan, 1942) syngamy is completed only after 16 to 32 endosperm nuclei have been formed. In *Oxybaphus nyctagineus* (Cooper, 1949), on the other hand, "nuclear fusion is completed in the zygote prior to that in the endosperm mother cell."

From the cytological as well as the genetical standpoint, it is of considerable interest to know whether the cytoplasm of the male gamete also enters the egg in addition to the nucleus. Finn (1925) considered it probable in *Asclepias*. Johri (1936*a*, *b*) in *Sagittaria graminea* and *Butomopsis lanceolata*, and Smith (1942) in *Camassia leichtlinii*, traced the male gametes as distinct cells up to the time of their discharge into the embryo sac, but were unable to follow the succeeding events in sufficient detail.

Wylie's (1923, 1941) work on *Vallisneria* is an important contribution to the subject. The male gametes of *V. americana* maintain their integrity as cells up to the time they approach the egg (Fig. 113*A–G*), and the several cases of physical contact observed between the first male *cell* and the egg strongly suggest their union as protoplasts rather than naked nuclei (Fig. 113*H*). Further, the fact that no residue of the first male cell could be seen on the surface of the zygote (as would be expected if only the naked nucleus entered the egg), while the same embryo sac clearly showed the cytoplasmic sheath left behind by the second male gamete, is cited in support of the view that the sperm fusing with the egg functions as a cell and the other as a naked nucleus.

Some other investigators have, however, denied any participation of the male cytoplasm in fertilization. Considering only the more recent literature, Gurgenova (1928), Gerassimova (1933), and Hoare (1934) mention having observed almost all stages of fertilization in *Orobanche* (= *Phelipaea*) *ramosa*, *Crepis capillaris*, and *Scilla nonscripta* but report only sperm nuclei. Madge (1929) saw male cells in the pollen tubes of *Viola odorata* but believed that the sheath is lost at the time of syngamy. Breslavetz (1930) studied *Melandrium album*, using mitochondrial fixatives, but failed to detect "even the thinnest plasma layer" around the sperm nuclei. In *Tulipa* (Botschanzeva, 1937) the male nuclei are said to slip out of their sheaths at the time of fertilization; and Trankowsky (1938) and Gershoy (1940) report the gradual disappearance of the male cytoplasm in the pollen tubes of *Drosera* and *Viola*. In a recent study of *Petunia*, Cooper (1946) also implies that the male gametes lose their sheaths at the time of fertilization.

It seems difficult to set aside all these observations as based on inadequate technique. Nevertheless, Finn and Rudenko (1930), in contradistinction to Gurgenova (1928), were able to see the cytoplasmic sheath around the male nuclei of *Orobanche*, although they could not follow it up to the time of fertilization. The inability of Breslavetz (1930) to find mitochondria and plastids around the male nuclei also cannot be considered as an absolute proof of the absence of the plasma layer; in fact her reference to certain lighter areas around the male nuclei is a fairly good indication of the presence of the male cytoplasm. Gershoy's observations, of which only a preliminary account has so far appeared, seem to be contradicted by those of West (1930).

In conclusion, it may be well to emphasize that until a few years ago the male gametes of angiosperms were usually considered to be naked nuclei. Recent studies on the subject leave no doubt, however, that the cytoplasmic sheath remains intact at least for the period during which the male gametes are in the pollen tube.[4] It would not be surprising, therefore, if with some further improvement in technique it may be possible in future to trace the fate of the male cytoplasm in a more precise manner than has been done up to this time. Finn (1935, 1940, 1941) has suggested that in order to decide the point with certainty the whole series of events should be studied in living material, but this seems to be impracticable with most plants, as the embryo sac is enclosed in several opaque layers which interfere with a direct and detailed observation of its contents.[5] The only alternative is to look for some suitable material in which (1) fertilization stages may be found abundantly, (2) the process does not take place too rapidly, and (3) the gametic cells not only are fairly large but also respond more favorably to our staining methods. In addition every effort must of course be made to develop new methods of fixing and staining which would be more suitable for a study of the contents of the embryo sac at the time of fertilization.

Multiple Fusions and Polyspermy. As is well known, usually only one pollen tube enters an ovule. Compton (1912) saw an ovule of *Lychnis* with two embryo sacs, each of which had been penetrated

---

[4] See also p. 168.

[5] In a few genera like *Torenia* and *Utricularia*, where the embryo sac protrudes out of the micropyle, it may be possible to make direct observations on living material. In certain others, like *Monotropa* and some members of the *Orchidaceae*, the seed coat is thin and transparent. No recent studies have, however, been made on the phenomenon of fertilization in any of these plants.

by a pollen tube. Another ovule with a single embryo sac had also received two pollen tubes, but only one of them had entered the sac, the other remaining behind in the nucellus. He concluded that there is a quantitative relation between embryo sacs and pollen tubes, two embryo sacs secreting enough chemotactic material to attract two pollen tubes, while one can attract only one tube.

Némec (1931) considered that there are mechanical contrivances which exclude other pollen tubes from entering an ovule after the first had done so. He found that in *Gagea lutea* the micropyle is originally in close contact with the glandular conducting tissue of the placenta, but that after a pollen tube has entered the micropyle, there is a slight elongation of the funiculus causing the ovule to retract from its original position and thus make it difficult for other tubes to gain entrance.

Beside the position effect noted by Némec, there must no doubt be some other factors also which bring about a similar result. In the pistils of *Phaseolus vulgaris* (Weinstein, 1926) there are many more pollen tubes than ovules, yet only one tube enters each ovule; the superfluous tubes grow down to the basal end of the ovary and eventually disintegrate. In *Scurrula atropurpurea*, Rauch (1936) frequently saw several pollen tubes attached to the wall of the embryo sac, but only one entered it, and as soon as this had been accomplished the wall of the sac seemed to become firmer and more resistant so as to exclude the others. Cooper (1938) states that in *Pisum sativum* he frequently saw two or more pollen tubes at the entrance to the micropyle, but only one actually entered it. More recently, Pope (1946) saw an ovule of *Hordeum* with one pollen tube inside the micropyle and four at its mouth, but how the embryo sac admitted the first and excluded the others could not be determined.

Although one pollen tube to an embryo sac may thus be considered as the usual condition, the entry of accessory tubes is not unknown. To quote a few examples, two pollen tubes have been recorded in *Elodea* (Wylie, 1904), *Ulmus* (Shattuck, 1905), *Juglans* (Langdon, 1934), *Xyris* (Weinzieher, 1914), *Oenothera* (Ishikawa, 1918), *Boerhaavia* (Maheshwari, 1929), *Beta* (Artschwager and Starrett, 1933), *Acacia* (Newman, 1934), *Fagopyrum* (Mahony, 1935), *Sagittaria* (Johri, 1936b), *Cephalanthera*, *Platanthera* (Hagerup, 1947).

and *Nicotiana* (Goodspeed, 1947); three in *Statice* (Dahlgren, 1916), *Gossypium* (Iyengar, 1938), and *Orchis* (Hagerup, 1944); and as many as five in *Juglans* (Nawaschin and Finn, 1913).

The entry of additional pollen tubes naturally results in the release of supernumerary male gametes inside the embryo sac. Rarely, one and the same pollen tube may also carry more than two sperms. This abnormality may originate either in the pollen grain or in the pollen tube. To mention a few examples, three sperms were sometimes seen in the pollen grains of *Cuscuta epithymum* (Fedortschuk, 1931) (Fig. 99C); and four in *Helosis cayennensis* (Umiker, 1920), *Vinca herbacea* (Finn, 1928a) (Fig. 99K), *Parthenium argentatum*, and *P. incanum* (Dianowa, Sosnovetz, and Steschina, 1935). Four sperms have also been seen in the pollen tubes of *Allium rotundum*, *A. zebdanense* (Weber, 1929), *Galanthus nivalis* (Trankowsky, 1931), *Crepis capillaris* (Gerassimova, 1933) (Fig. 117D), and *Polygonatum canaliculatum* (Eigsti, 1941) (Fig. 115C). Further, Gerassimova (1933) saw two, three, and even five pairs of sperms in the embryo sacs of *Crepis capillaris* and considers it probable that they originated through additional divisions of the original pair of sperms. Warmke (1943) saw eight sperms in an embryo sac of *Taraxacum koksaghys*, and in another there

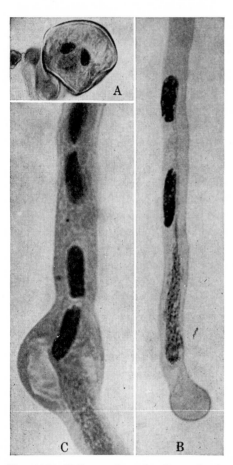

Fig. 115. Pollen grain and pollen tubes in *Polygonatum canaliculatum*. A, mature pollen grain, showing vegetative nucleus and two sperms. B, pollen tube, showing elongated vegetative nucleus and two sperms. C, portion of pollen tube, showing four sperms. (*After Eigsti, 1941.*)

were eight in addition to the two which took part in fertilization.

The presence of extra sperms inside the embryo sac, whether they are derived from one or more than one pollen tube, may result in two kinds of abnormalities. Either some of the supernumerary sperms enter the egg, resulting in a polyploid offspring, or more than one cell of the egg apparatus may be fertilized, resulting in multiple embryos. In *Monotropa hypopitys* (Strasburger, 1884), *Iris sibirica* (Dodel, 1891), and *Gagea lutea* (Némec, 1912), and in *Oenothera nutans* pollinated by *O. pycnocarpa* (Ishikawa, 1918), two sperms were sometimes observed to enter the egg. Michaelis and Dellinghausen (1942), who obtained a triploid plant from a cross between *Epilobium hirsutum* and *E. luteum*, considers it probable that it resulted from the entry of an *E. luteum* sperm into the egg after it had already been fertilized by an *E. hirsutum* sperm.

Fertilization of more than one cell of the egg apparatus has been reported in several plants[6] of which *Sagittaria graminea* (Johri, 1936b) and *Crepis capillaris* (Gerassimova, 1933) may be cited as examples. In *Sagittaria* fertilization usually occurs normally, one male gamete fusing with the egg and the other with the two polar nuclei. But the synergids often assume an egg-like appearance (Fig. 116A) and sometimes a second pollen tube enters the embryo sac, releasing two additional sperms (Fig. 116B). Although an actual fertilization of the synergids was not seen, the presence of two pollen tubes and three proembryos in the upper part of the embryo sac (Fig. 116E) leave no doubt that this may happen.

In *Crepis capillaris*, Gerassimova (1933) observed some embryo sacs with two to five eggs in addition to the two synergids (Fig. 117A). Usually only one of the eggs gives rise to an embryo (Fig. 117B) and the others eventually degenerate and disappear, but if a pollen tube carrying more than two sperms enters the embryo sac there is a possibility of the production of additional embryos.

---

[6] Tischler (1943) has recently given a complete list of such plants but in some cases the inference is based merely on the presence of a second or third embryo beside the zygotic embryo. It is now known that even unfertilized synergids can undergo a few divisions and sometimes develop into fully mature haploid embryos, or the zygotic embryo may itself give rise to additional embryos by a process of cleavage or budding (see Chaps. 9 and 10).

Figure 117C shows two fertilized eggs in division, one in prophase and the other in metaphase.

A couple of instances of fertilization of antipodal cells are also on

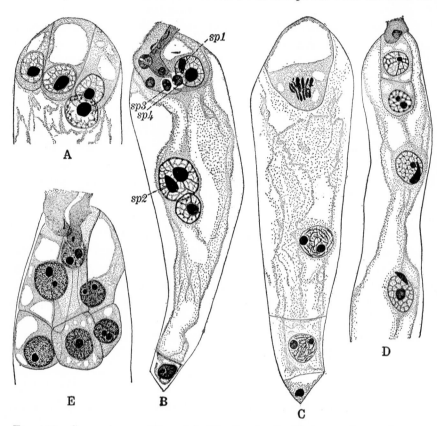

FIG. 116.   Some abnormalities of fertilization in *Sagittaria graminea*.   *A*, upper part of embryo sac, showing egg-like synergids, egg, and upper polar nucleus.   *B*, embryo sac, showing double fertilization (sp_1 = male gamete fusing with egg; sp_2 = male gamete fusing with polar nuclei); note second pollen tube with another pair of male gametes (sp_3, sp_4).   *C*, first division of primary endosperm nucleus completed; nucleus of zygote in metaphase.   *D*, part of fertilized embryo sac, showing two-celled proembryo, and two male gametes attached to two endosperm nuclei. *E*, three two-celled proembryos, two of which have probably arisen from fertilized synergids; note two pollen tubes.   (*After Johri, 1936a.*)

record.   Derschau (1918) reported the fusion of two sperms with an antipodal cell in *Nigella arvensis*, and judging from the statements of Shattuck (1905) and Ekdahl (1941) it seems probable that sometimes the fertilization of an antipodal cell may also occur in *Ulmus*.

Embryo sacs which have received more than two sperms may also show other abnormalities. Frisendahl (1912) noted that in *Myricaria germanica* each of the polar nuclei may sometimes fuse with a

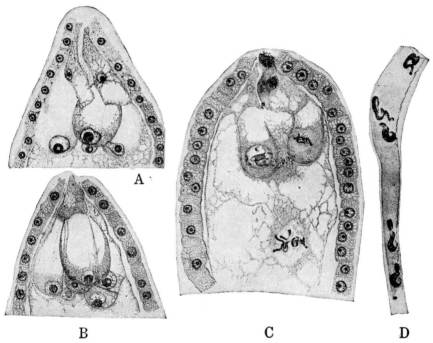

A

B   C   D

Fɪɢ. 117. Some abnormalities of fertilization in *Crepis capillaris*. *A*, upper part of embryo sac, showing four eggs and two synergids. *B*, four egg-like cells and two-celled embryo. *C*, supernumerary sperm near apex of embryo sac; two eggs, one in prophase and the other in metaphase, and two dividing endosperm nuclei. *D*, portion of pollen tube, showing two pairs of sperms and unidentified body at upper end which may be one of a third pair of sperms. (*After Gerassimova, 1933.*)

separate male nucleus.[7] In *Acacia baileyana*, Newman (1934) observed division figures of the primary endosperm nucleus showing $4n$, $7n$, and $8n$ chromosomes.[8] Since such embryo sacs seemed to have received more than one pollen tube, it is inferred that extra

[7] Since the upper polar nucleus in *Myricaria* is haploid and the lower triploid, some of the endosperm nuclei would be diploid $(n + n)$ and some tetraploid $(3n + n)$.

[8] Rarely he found only the haploid number of chromosomes, presumably due to an independent division of either a polar nucleus or a male nucleus.

sperms fused with the secondary nucleus. A different type of abnormality, reported sometimes, is that the triple fusion nucleus undergoes one or two divisions and then the male nuclei discharged from a second pollen tube fuse with some of the endosperm nuclei (Fig. 116*D*).

When two or more pollen tubes are discharged inside an embryo sac, it is also possible that the sperm fusing with the egg is derived from one tube and the one fusing with the secondary nucleus from another. This "heterofertilization" has not yet been cytologically demonstrated, but Sprague (1932), has inferred it in *Zea mays* on genetical grounds. In a study of the inheritance of scutellum color he found several kernels with white aleurone but a colored scutellum, and their progeny segregated for aleurone color in ratios similar to those obtained from hybrid kernels with colored aleurone. He therefore concludes that in such cases the egg and polar nuclei had been fertilized by sperms of unlike genotypes.

Single Fertilization.   Although double fertilization is the rule in angiosperms, the question arises whether development can proceed with only a single fertilization, *i.e.*, if there is syngamy without triple fusion or triple fusion without syngamy. Cooke and Shively (1904) stated that in *Epiphegus virginiana* endosperm formation begins before fertilization, and Anderson (1922) reported the same in *Martynia louisiana*. In *Ramondia nathaliae* and *R. serbica* (Glišić, 1924) syngamy occurs regularly, but triple fusion is said to be "facultative" and is frequently omitted. Wiger (1935) stated that in some members of the Buxaceae and Meliaceae, endosperm formation is entirely independent of fertilization.

` All these reports are, however, of a doubtful nature (see also Mauritzon, 1935). Without going into details it may be said that some of the above workers seem to have overlooked the pollen tube, and others mistook the unfused polar nuclei for the first pair of endosperm nuclei. It is only rarely that development can take place without triple fusion. Guignard (1921) reported a case in *Vincetoxicum nigrum* in which the zygote had divided several times while the polar nuclei were still lying unfused and the second male gamete had not yet been discharged from the pollen tube. More recently, Dahlgren (1930, 1939) has figured embryo sacs of *Mitella pentandra* and *Zostera marina* (Fig. 118) in which a several-celled embryo is associated with an undivided secondary nucleus, and

Johansen (1931*a*, *b*) has reported similar occurrences in *Taraxia ovata* and *Zauschneria latifolia*. Sooner or later, however, such embryos are likely to stop growth so that no viable seeds are produced.

The second of the two alternatives—*i.e.*, the occurrence of triple fusion without an accompaniment of syngamy—has been reported in several plants, but the ovules soon begin to degenerate. If seeds are formed, they are without embryos and therefore nonviable. Rarely, however, the unfertilized egg may develop into a haploid embryo. Such cases will be discussed in connection with apomixis (see Chap. 9).

Persistence and Possible Haustorial Function of Pollen Tube. Usually the pollen tube collapses soon after fertilization, and there is little evidence of it after the embryo has commenced its development. There are a few cases on record, however, in which it has been known to persist for longer periods. In *Galinsoga ciliata* (Popham, 1938) it is recognizable up to the seven-celled stage of the embryo, and in *Ulmus americana* (Shattuck, 1905) up to the 20-celled satge. In *Hicoria pecan*, according to Woodroof (1928), it persists for two to three weeks, and in one ovule he saw the dead end of the tube beside the fertilized egg even seven weeks after pollination.

Cook (1909) noted a very peculiar behavior of the pollen tube in *Passiflora adenophylla*. Although fertilization stages were frequent, in the majority of ovules the pollen tube did not discharge its contents but continued its growth within the embryo sac, becoming greatly twisted and tangled in the process. Its growth was sometimes so vigorous that all the contents of the sac, including the egg apparatus, were completely absorbed. A few years later, Cook (1924) noted a similar phenomenon in an ovule

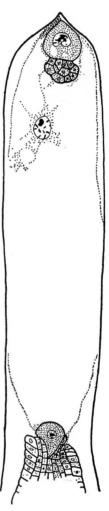

FIG. 118. L.s. embryo sac of *Zostera marina*, showing young embryo and undivided secondary nucleus. (*After Dahlgren, 1939.*)

of *Crotalaria sagittalis*. Cook regarded these as examples of parasitization of the male gametophyte on the female.

It has also been suggested that the pollen tube may sometimes serve as a haustorial organ, not for its own benefit but for that of the embryo sac or embryo. Longo (1903) believes this to be the case in *Cucurbita*. He found that owing to a cutinization of the walls of the nucellar epidermis and the formation of a suberized hypostase, the embryo sac becomes cut off from the usual sources of its food supply. The pollen tube is said to compensate for this deficiency. As it approaches the embryo sac, it expands into a large swelling or "bulla," which gives out a number of branches. One of these penetrates the embryo sac and effects fertilization, but the others ramify into the tissues of the nucellus and inner integument, absorbing food materials from the adjacent cells and transmitting them to the embryo.

A somewhat similar phenomenon has been reported in certain members of the Onagraceae (Werner, 1914; Täckholm, 1915). The pollen tube becomes greatly broadened in the micropyle[9] and often sends out branches into the outer integument and the nucellus, while the tip continues to grow toward the embryo sac, destroying the cells lying in its path. The tube is recognizable even when the embryo has attained a fairly large size, and it probably serves to absorb food materials from the surrounding tissues and transmit them to the embryo.

A broad and massive pollen tube has also been seen in *Carica papaya* (Foster, 1943). It persists for about eight weeks after fertilization and probably helps in conveying food materials to the embryo. In *Ottelia alismoides*, *Hydrilla verticillata* (Maheshwari and Johri, 1950), and *Oxybaphus nyctagineus* (Cooper, 1949) the pollen tube persists throughout the development of the seed. According to Cooper, it acts as a haustorium and transports nutritive materials from the secretory cells of the funiculus to the embryo.

---

[9] A broad and persistent pollen tube may sometimes be mistaken for a synergid haustorium or a micropylar extension of the embryo sac. Karsten (1891) reported that in *Sonneratia* the fertilized embryo sac bored a hole through the wall layers and came in direct contact with the nucellar epidermis, but Venkateswarlu (1937) and Mauritzon (1939) have shown that this is incorrect and that Karsten was actually looking at the pollen tube.

X-bodies. In his studies on fertilization Nawaschin observed certain densely staining structures either in the tip of the pollen tube or adjacent to it. Since their exact nature could not be determined, he called them X-bodies. They have been variously interpreted in different plants and by different authors. In *Adoxa* they are believed to be the nuclei of the disorganized synergids (Lagerberg, 1909); in *Crepis* as fragments of the vegetative nucleus (Gerassimova, 1933); in *Petunia* as the degenerated cytoplasmic sheaths of the male gametes (Cooper, 1946); and in *Beta* as supernumerary male nuclei in process of disintegration (Artschwager and Starrett, 1933). Some authors have also interpreted them as the nuclei of the adjacent nucellar cells, which become pushed into the embryo sac by the impact of the pollen tube. Tschernojarow (1926) states that in *Myosurus* they represent the remains of the degenerating megaspores and nucellar cells which lie over the embryo sac and are presumably carried into it at the time of entry of the pollen tube. In *Datura* (Satina and Blakeslee, 1935) there are two X-bodies, one said to be the nucleus of a disorganized synergid and the other the degenerating vegetative nucleus.

Wylie (1923) devoted special attention to the nature of the X-bodies in *Vallisneria* (Fig. 113*I*). Since the sperms enter the embryo sac as complete cells, he rules out the possibility of the X-bodies being the remains of their cytoplasmic sheaths. The sheaths were also seen intact in the "cystoids" or "tuber-like enlargements" formed by some pollen tubes which terminated in the ovarian chamber without reaching the ovules. The cystoids showed no X-bodies if the vegetative nucleus was still intact, but in those cases in which this was not visible they showed structures which were identical with X-bodies. It is therefore concluded by Wylie that, whatever their origin in other plants, the X-bodies of *Vallisneria* are nothing other than the decomposition products of the vegetative nucleus.

References

Anderson, E., and Sax, K. 1934. A cytological study of self-sterility in *Tradescantia*. Bot. Gaz. **95**: 609–621.

Anderson, F. 1922. The development of the flower and embryogeny of *Martynia louisiana*. Bul. Torrey Bot. Club **49**: 141–157.

Artschwager, E., Brandes, E. W., and Starrett, R. C. 1929. Development of flower and seed of some varieties of sugarcane. Jour. Agr. Res. **39:** 1–30.

—— and McGuire, R. C. 1949. Cytology of reproduction in *Sorghum vulgare.* Jour. Agr. Res. **78:** 659–673.

—— and Starrett, R. C. 1933. The time factor in fertilization and embryo development in sugar beet. Jour. Agr. Res. **47:** 823–843.

Atwood, S. S. 1941. Cytological basis for incompatibility in *Trifolium repens.* Amer. Jour. Bot. **28:** 551–557.

Bağda, H. 1948. Morphologische und biologische Untersuchungen über Valonea Eichen (*Quercus macrolepis* Ky.) im Haci-Kadin-Tal bei Ankara. Comm. Fac. Sci. de l'Univ. Ankara. **1:** 89–125.

Benson, M. 1894. Contribution to the embryology of the Amentiferae. I. Trans. Linn. Soc. London. III. Bot. **2:** 409–424.

Blackman, V. H., and Welsford, E. J. 1913. Fertilisation in *Lilium.* Ann. Bot. **27:** 111–114.

Botschanzeva, Z. P. 1937. Spermogenesis bei *Tulipa* una seine Erlerung zwecks Kariosystematik. Bul. Univ. Asie Centrale [Tashkent] **22:** 329–338.

Breslavetz, L. 1930. Spermatogenesis and fertilization process in some plants in connection with the question of heredity through the plasma. Proc. U.S.S.R. Cong. Genetics **2:** 181–186.

Brough, P. 1933. The life history of *Grevillea robusta* Cunn. Proc. Linn. Soc. N. S. Wales **58:** 33–73.

Buchholz, J. T., and Blakeslee, A. F. 1927. Pollen-tube growth at various temperatures. Amer. Jour. Bot. **14:** 358–369.

Carlson, M. C. 1940. Formation of the seed of *Cypripedium parviflorum.* Bot. Gaz. **102:** 295–301.

Compton, R. H. 1912. Note on a case of doubling of embryo sac, pollen tube and embryo. Ann. Bot. **26:** 243–244.

Cook, M. T. 1909. Notes on the embryo-sac of *Passiflora adenophylla.* Bul. Torrey Bot. Club **36:** 373–374.

——. 1924. Development of seed of *Crotalaria sagittalis.* Bot. Gaz. **77:** 440–445.

Cooke, E., and Shively, A. 1904. Observations on the structure and development of *Epiphegus virginiana.* Contrib. Bot. Lab. Univ. Pa. 1904, pp. 352–398.

Cooper, D. C. 1938. Embryology of *Pisum sativum.* Bot. Gaz. **100:** 123–132.

——. 1940. Macrosporogenesis and embryology of *Portulaca oleracea.* Amer. Jour. Bot. **27:** 326–330.

——. 1941. Macrosporogenesis and the development of the seed of *Phryma leptostachya.* Amer. Jour. Bot. **28:** 755–761.

——. 1946. Double fertilization in *Petunia.* Amer. Jour. Bot. **33:** 54–57.

——. 1949. Flower and seed development in *Oxybaphus nyctagineus.* Amer. Jour. Bot. **36:** 348–355.

Dahlgren, K. V. O. 1915. Über die Überwinterungsstadien der Pollensäcke und der Samenanlagen bei einigen Angiospermen. Svensk Bot. Tidskr. **9:** 1–12.

——. 1916. Zytologische und embryologische Studien über die Reihen Primulales und Plumbaginales. K. Svenska Vet.-Akad. Handl. **56**(4): 1–80.

——. 1920. Zur Embryologie der Kompositen mit besonderer Berücksichtigung der Endospermbildung. Ztschr. f. Bot. **12:** 481–516.

Dahlgren, K. V. O. 1930. Zur Embryologie der Saxifragoideen. Svensk Bot. Tidskr. **24:** 429–448.

——. 1938. Hakenbildungen bei Synergiden. Zweite Mitteilung. Svensk Bot. Tidskr. **52:** 221–237.

——. 1939. Endosperm- und Embryobildung bei *Zostera marina*. Bot. Notiser 1939, pp. 607–615.

Derschau, M. v. 1918. Über disperme Befruchtung der Antipoden von *Nigella arvensis*. Ber. deutsch. bot. Gesell. **36:** 260–262.

Dianowa, W. J., Sosnovetz, A. A., and Steschina, N. A. 1935. Vergleichende zytoembryologische Untersuchung der Varietäten vom *Parthenium argentatum* Gray und *P. incanum* Gray. Beihefte bot. Centbl. **53A:** 293–339.

Dodel, A. 1891. Beiträge zur Kenntnis der Befruchtungserscheinungen bei *Iris sibirica*. Festschr. f. Nägeli u. Kölliker, Zürich 1891.

Dorsey, M. J. 1919. A study of sterility in the plum. Genetics **4:** 417–488.

Duncan, R. E., and Curtis, J. T. 1942a. Intermittent growth of *Phalaenopsis*. A correlation of the growth phases of an orchid fruit with internal development. Bul. Torrey Bot. Club **69:** 167–183.

—— and ——. 1942b. Intermittent growth of fruits of *Cypripedium* and *Paphiopedilum*. A correlation of the growth of orchid fruits with their internal development. Bul. Torrey Bot. Club **69:** 353–359.

—— and ——. 1943. Growth of fruits in *Cattleya* and allied genera in the Orchidaceae. Bul. Torrey Bot. Club **70:** 104–119.

Eigsti, O. J. 1937. Pollen tube behavior in self-fertile and interspecific pollinated Resedaceae. Amer. Nat. **71:** 520–521.

——. 1941. The occurrence of a pollen tube with four sperms and two tube nuclei in *Polygonatum*. Proc. Okla. Acad. Sci. **21:** 134–136.

Ekdahl, I. 1941. Die Entwicklung von Embryosack und Embryo bei *Ulmus glabra* Huds. Svensk Bot. Tidskr. **35:** 143–156.

Ernst, A. 1936. Der heutige Stand der Heterostylieforschung. Proc. 6th Internatl. Bot. Cong. 35–53.

Ernst-Schwarzenbach, M. 1945. Kreuzungsversuche an Hydrocharitaceen. Arch. Julius Klaus-Stift. f. Vererbungsforsch **20:** 22–41.

Fagerlind, F. 1939. Die Entwicklung des Embryosackes bei *Peperomia pellucida*. Arkiv för. Bot. **29A:** 1–15.

——. 1941. Der Bau der Samenanlage und des Makrogametophyten bei *Quisqualis indica*. Bot. Notiser 1941, pp. 217–222.

——. 1944. Die Samenbildung und die Zytologie bei agamospermischen und sexuellen Arten von *Elatostema* und einigen nahestehenden Gattungen nebst Beleuchtung einiger damit zusammenhängender Probleme. K. Svenska Vet.-Akad. Handl. III **21**(4): 1–130.

Fedortschuk, W. 1931. Embryologische Untersuchung von *Cuscuta monogyna* Vahl. und *Cuscuta epithymum* L. Planta **14:** 94–111.

Finn, W. W. 1925. Male cells in angiosperms. I. Spermatogenesis and fertilization in *Asclepias cornutii*. Bot. Gaz. **80:** 1–25.

——. 1928a. Spermazellen bei *Vinca minor* und *V. herbacea*. Ber. deutsch. bot. Gesell. **46:** 235–246.

——. 1928b. Über den Pollenschlauch bei *Fagus sylvatica*. Nawaschin Festschr., pp. 63–66.

Finn, W. W. 1935. Einige Bemerkungen über den männlichen Gametophyten der Angiospermen. Ber. deutsch. bot. Gesell. **53:** 679–686.

———. 1936. Zur Entwicklungsgeschichte der Chalazogamen, *Ostrya carpinifolia* Scop. Jour. Inst. Bot. Acad. Sci. Ukraine **8:** 15–25.

———. 1937*a*. Entwicklungsgeschwindigkeit des männlichen Gametophyten bei den Angiospermen. Trav. Inst. Rech. Sci. Biol., Univ. Kiew 1937, pp. 71–86.

———. 1937*b*. Vergleichende Embryologie und Karyologie einiger *Cuscuta*-Arten. Jour. Inst. Bot. Acad. Sci. Ukraine **20**(28): 77–96.

———. 1940. Spermazellen bei Angiospermen. Jour. Bot. de l'U.R.S.S. **26:** 155–175.

———. 1941. Männlichen Gameten bei Angiospermen. Compt. Rend. (Dok.) Acad. des Sci. U.R.S.S. **30:** 451–458.

——— and Rudenko, T. 1930. Spermatogenesis und Befruchtung bei einigen Orobanchaceae. Bul. Jard. Bot. de Kieff **11:** 69–82.

Foster, L. T. 1943. Morphological and cytological studies on *Carica papaya*. Bot. Gaz. **105:** 116–126.

Frisendahl, A. 1912. Cytologische und Entwicklungsgeschichtliche Studien an *Myricaria germanica* Desv. K. Svenska Vet.-Akad. Handl. **48**(7): 1–62.

———. 1927. Über die Entwicklung chasmogamer und kleistogamer Blüten bei der Gattung *Elatine*. Acta Hort. Gothoburg **3:** 99–142.

Fuchs, A. 1936. Untersuchungen über den männlichen Gametophyten von *Elaeagnus angustifolia*. Österr. bot. Ztschr. **85:** 1–16.

———. 1938. Beiträge zur Embryologie der Thymelaeaceae. Österr. bot. Ztschr. **87:** 1–41.

Gelin, O. E. V. 1936. Zur Embryologie und Zytologie von *Berkheya bergiana* Söderb. und *B. aldami* Hook. f. Svensk Bot. Tidskr. **30:** 324–328.

Gerassimova, H. 1933. Fertilization in *Crepis capillaris*. Cellule **42:** 103–148.

Gershoy, A. 1940. The male gametophyte in some species of violets. Amer. Jour. Bot. **27:** 4s.

Glišić, Lj. 1924. "Development of the X-generation and embryo in *Ramondia*." Diss. Belgrade.

Goodspeed, T. H. 1947. Maturation of the gametes and fertilization in *Nicotiana*. Madroño **9:** 110–120.

Gore, U. R. 1932. The development of the female gametophyte and embryo in cotton. Amer. Jour. Bot. **19:** 795–807.

Grimm, J. 1912. Entwicklungsgeschichtliche Untersuchungen an *Rhus* und *Coriaria*. Flora **104:** 309–334.

Guignard, L. 1899. Sur les antherozoides et la double copulation sexuelle chez les végétaux angiospermes. Compt. Rend. Acad. des Sci. Paris **128:** 864–871.

———. 1921. La fécondation et la polyembryonie chez les *Vincetoxicum*. Mém. Acad. Sci. Inst. France II, **57:** 1–25.

Gurgenova, M. 1928. Fertilization in *Phelipaea ramosa*. Nawaschin Festschr., pp. 157–168.

Hagerup, O. 1944. On fertilisation, polyploidy and haploidy in *Orchis maculatus* L. Dansk Bot. Arkiv. **11**(5): 1–26.

Hagerup, O. 1947. The spontaneous formation of haploid, polyploid, and aneuploid embryos in some orchids. K. Danske Vidensk. Selsk., Biol. Meddel. **20**(9): 1–22.

Håkansson, A. 1923. Studien über die Entwicklungsgeschichte der Umbelliferen. Lunds Univ. Årsskr. N.F. Avd. II, **18**: 1–120.

Hallock, F. A. 1930. The relationship of *Garrya*. The development of the flower and seeds of *Garrya* and its bearing on the phylogenetic position of the genus. Ann. Bot. **44**: 771–812.

Hanf, M. 1935. Vergleichende und entwicklungsgeschichtliche Untersuchungen über Morphologie und Anatomie der Griffel und Griffeläste. Beihefte bot. Centbl. **54A**: 99–141.

Heimann-Winawer, P. 1919. Beiträge zur Embryologie von *Colchicum autumnale* L. Arb. Inst. allg. Bot. Pflanzenphysiol., Univ. Zürich **21**.

Hoare, G. 1934. Gametogenesis and fertilization in *Scilla nonscripta*. Cellule **42**: 269–292.

Hofmeister, W. 1849. "Die Entstehung des Embryo der Phanerogamen." Leipzig.

———. 1861. Neue Beiträge zur Kenntnis der Embryobildung der Phanerogamen. II. Monokotyledonen. Abh. Königl. Sächs. Ges. Wiss. **7**: 629–760.

Ishikawa, M. 1918. Studies on the embryo sac and fertilization in *Oenothera*. Ann. Bot. **32**: 279–317.

Iyengar, N. K. 1938. Pollen-tube studies in *Gossypium*. Jour. Genet. **37**: 69–106.

Johansen, D. A. 1931*a*. Studies on the morphology of the Onagraceae. III. *Taraxia ovata* (Nutt.) Small. Ann. Bot. **45**: 111–124.

———. 1931*b*. Studies on the morphology of the Onagraceae. V. *Zauschneria latifolia*, typical of a genus characterised by irregular embryology. Ann. N. Y. Acad. Sci. **33**: 1–26.

Johri, B. M. 1936*a*. Studies in the family Alismaceae. IV. *Alisma plantago* L.; *A. plantago-aquatica* L.; and *Sagittaria graminea* Mich. Proc. Indian Acad. Sci. Sect. B. **4**: 128–138.

———. 1936*b*. The life history of *Butomopsis lanceolata* Kunth. Proc. Indian Acad. Sci. Sect. B. **4**: 139–162.

Jones, H. A. 1927. Pollination and life history studies of lettuce (*Lactuca sativa*). Hilgardia **2**: 425–442.

———. 1929. Pollination and life history studies of lettuce (*Lactuca sativa*). Proc. Internatl. Cong. Plant Sci., Ithaca N. Y. **2**: 1045–1049.

Juliano, J. B. 1935. Anatomy and morphology of the Bunga, *Aeginetia indica* L. Philippine Jour. Sci. **56**: 405–451.

——— and Aldama, M. J. 1937. Morphology of *Oryza sativa* L. Philippine Agr. **26**: 1–134.

Junell, S. 1931. Die Entwicklungsgeschichte von *Circaeaster agrestis*. Svensk Bot. Tidskr. **25**: 238–270.

Kadry, A. E. R. 1946. Embryology of *Cardiospermum halicacabum* L. Svensk Bot. Tidskr. **40**: 111–126.

Karsten, G. 1891. Über die Mangrove-Vegetation im malayischen Archipel. Biblioth. Bot. **22**.

Katz, E.   1926.   Über die Funktion der Narbe bei der Keimung des Pollens. Flora **120:** 243–273.

Khan, R.   1942.   A contribution to the embryology of *Jussieua repens* L.   Jour. Indian Bot. Soc. **21:** 267–282.

Kirkwood, J. E.   1906.   The pollen tube in some of the Cucurbitaceae.   Bul. Torrey Bot. Club **33:** 327–342.

Krupko, S.   1944.   On the sterility of *Oxalis cernua* in the Mediterranean.   Przyroda 1944, pp. 1–32.

Lagerberg, T.   1909.   Studien über die Entwicklungsgeschichte und systematische Stellung von *Adoxa moschatellina* L.   K. Svenska Vet.-Akad. Handl. **44**(4): 1–86.

Land, W. J. G.   1900.   Double fertilization in Compositae.   Bot. Gaz. **30:** 252–260.

Langdon, L. M.   1934.   Embryogeny of *Carya* and *Juglans*, a comparative study. Bot. Gaz. **96:** 93–117.

Lebon, E.   1929.   Sur la formation de l'albumen chez *Impatiens sultani*.   Compt. Rend. Soc. de Biol. Paris **101:** 1168–1170.

Lewis, D.   1948.   Pollen-tubes, incompatibility and osmotic pressure in plants. School Sci. Rev. **108:** 206–212.

Longo, B.   1901.   La mesogamia nella commune zucca (*Cucurbita pepo* L.).   Rend. R. Accad. Lincei Roma V. **10:** 168–172.

――――.   1903.   La nutrizione dell'embrione delle *Cucurbita* operate per mezzo del tubetto pollinico.   Ann. di Bot. **1:** 71–74.

Madge, M.   1929.   Spermatogenesis and fertilisation in the cleistogamous flowers of *Viola odorata* var. *praecox*.   Ann. Bot. **43:** 545–577.

Maheshwari, P.   1929.   Contributions to the morphology of *Boerhaavia diffusa*. I. Jour. Indian Bot. Soc. **8:** 219–234.

――――.   1948.   The angiosperm embryo sac.   Bot. Rev. **14:** 1–56.

――――   1949.   The male gametophyte of angiosperms.   Bot. Rev. **15:** 1–75.

―――― and Johri, B. M.   1941.   The embryo sac of *Acalypha indica* L.   Beihefte bot. Centbl. **61A:** 125–136.

―――― and ――――.   1950.   The occurrence of persistent pollen tubes in *Hydrilla*, *Ottelia* and *Boerhaavia*, together with a discussion of the possible significance of this phenomenom in the life history of angiosperms.   Jour. Indian Bot. Soc. **29:** 47–51.

―――― and Singh, Bahadur.   1934.   A preliminary note on the morphology of the aerial and underground flowers of *Commelina benghalensis* Linn.   Current Sci. [India] **3:** 158–160.

Mahony, K. L.   1935.   Morphological and cytological studies on *Fagopyrum esculentum*.   Amer. Jour. Bot. **22:** 460–475.

Martin, J. N.   1913.   The physiology of pollen of *Trifolium pratense*.   Bot. Gaz. **56:** 112–126.

Mauritzon, J.   1935.   Kritik von J. Wigers Abhandlung "Embryological studies on the families Buxaceae, Meliaceae, Simarubaceae and Burseraceae."   Bot. Notiser 1935, pp. 490–502.

――――.   1939.   Contributions to the embryology of the orders Rosales and Myrtales.   Lunds Univ. Årsskr. N.F. Avd. II, **35:** 1–120.

McKay, J. W. 1947. Embryology of pecan. Jour. Agr. Res. **74:** 263–283.

Mendes, A. J. T. 1941. Cytological observations in *Coffea*. VI. Embryo and endosperm development in *Coffea arabica* L. Amer. Jour. Bot. **28:** 784–789.

Michaelis, P., and Dellinghausen, M. v. 1942. Über reziprok verschiedene Sippenbastarde bei *Epilobium hirsutum*. IV. Weitere Untersuchungen über die genetischen Grundlagen der extrem stark gestörten Bastarde der *E. hirsutum*-Sippe. Jenaische Ztschr. f. Vererbungslehre **80** (3): 373–429.

Miller, E. C. 1919. Development of the pistillate spikelet and fertilization in *Zea mays* L. Jour. Agr. Res. **18:** 255–266.

Murbeck, S. 1901. Über das Verhalten des Pollenschlauches bei *Alchemilla arvensis* und das Wesen der Chalazogamie. Lunds Univ. Årsskr. N. F. Avd. II, **9:** 1–46.

Murthy, S. N. 1941. Morphological studies on the Sapotaceae. I. Embryology of *Bassia latifolia* Roxb. and related genera. Jour. Mysore Univ. Sect. B. **2:** 67–80.

Nast, C. G. 1941. The embryogeny and seedling morphology of *Juglans regia*. L. Lilloa **6:** 163–205.

Nawaschin, S. G. 1898. Resultate einer Revision der Befruchtungsvorgänge bei *Lilium martagon* und *Fritillaria tenella*. Bul. Acad. Imp. des Sci. St. Petersburg **9:** 377–382.

——. 1900. Über die Befruchtungsvorgänge bei einigen Dicotyledonen. Ber. deutsch. bot. Gesell. **18:** 224–230.

——. 1909. Über dasselbständige Bewegungsvermögen des Spermakerns bei einigen Angiospermen. Österr. bot. Ztschr. **59:** 457–467.

—— and Finn, W. W. 1913. Zur Entwicklungsgeschichte der Chalazogamen, *Juglans regia* und *Juglans nigra*. Mém. Acad. Imp. des Sci. St. Petersburg VIII, **31:** 1–59.

Némec, B. 1912. Über die Befruchtung bei *Gagea*. Bul. Internatl. Acad. Sci. Bohême **17**.

——. 1931. Fecundation in *Gagea lutea*. Preslia **10:** 104–110.

Newman, I. V. 1934. Studies in the Australian acacias. IV. The life history of *Acacia baileyana* F.V.M. Part 2. Gametophytes, fertilization, seed production and germination, and general conclusions. Proc. Linn. Soc. N. S. Wales **59:** 277–313.

Nothnagel, M. 1918. Fecundation and formation of the primary endosperm nucleus in certain Liliaceae. Bot. Gaz. **66:** 141–161.

Ohga, I. 1937. On the fertilization of *Nelumbo nucifera*. Cytologia, Fujii Jubl. Vol., pp. 1033–1035.

Paetow, W. 1931. Embryologische Untersuchungen an Taccaceen, Meliaceen und Dilleniaceen. Planta **14:** 441–470.

Pastrana, M. D., and Santos, J. K. 1931. A contribution on the life history of *Dendrobium anosmum* Lindley. Nat. and Appl. Sci. Bul., Philippines Univ. **1:** 133–144.

Persidsky, D. 1926. Zur Embryologie der *Orobanche cumana* Wall. und der *O. ramosa* L. Bul. Jard. Bot. de Kieff **4:** 6–10.

Poddubnaja-Arnoldi, V. A. and Dianowa, V. 1934. Eine zytoembryologische Untersuchung einiger Arten der Gattung *Taraxacum*. Planta **23:** 19–46.

Pope, M. N. 1937. The time factor in pollen tube growth and fertilization in barley. Jour. Agr. Res. **54:** 525–529.

———. 1943. The temperature factor in fertilization and growth of barley. Jour. Agr. Res. **66:** 389–402.

———. 1946. The course of the pollen tube in cultivated barley. Jour. Amer. Soc. Agron. **38:** 432–440.

Popham, R. A. 1938. A contribution to the life history of *Galinsoga ciliata*. Bot. Gaz. **97:** 543–555.

Randolph, L. F. 1936. Developmental morphology of the caryopsis in maize. Jour. Agr. Res. **53:** 881–916.

Rauch, K. V. 1936. Cytologisch-embryologische Untersuchungen an *Scurrula atropurpurea* Dans. und *Dendrophthoe pentandra* Miq. Ber. schweiz. bot. Gesell. **45:** 5–61.

Sanz, C. 1945. Pollen-tube growth in intergeneric pollinations on *Datura stramonium*. Proc. Natl. Acad. Sci. **31:** 361–367.

Satina, S., and Blakeslee, A. F. 1935. Fertilization in the incompatible cross *Datura stramonium* × *D. metel*. Bul. Torrey. Bot. Club **62:** 301–312.

Sawyer, M. L. 1917. Pollen tubes and spermatogenesis in *Iris*. Bot. Gaz. **64:** 159–164.

Sax, K. 1916. Fertilization in *Fritillaria pudica*. Bul. Torrey Bot. Club **43:** 505–522.

———. 1918. The behavior of the chromosomes in fertilization. Genetics **3:** 309–327.

Sears, E. R. 1937. Cytological phenomena connected with self-sterility in flowering plants. Genetics **22:** 130–181.

Shattuck, C. H. 1905. A morphological study of *Ulmus americana*. Bot. Gaz. **40:** 209–223.

Shibata, K. 1902. Die Doppelbefruchtung bei *Monotropa uniflora*. Flora **90:** 61–66.

Shoemaker, D. N. 1905. On the development of *Hamamelis virginiana*. Bot. Gaz. **39:** 245–266.

Smith, F. H. 1942. Development of the gametophytes and fertilization in *Camassia*. Amer. Jour. Bot. **29:** 657–663.

Smith, O., and Cochran, H. L. 1935. Effect of temperature on pollen germination and tube growth in tomato. Cornell Univ. Agr. Expt. Sta. Mem. **175:** 1–11.

Souèges, E. C. R. 1910. Recherches sur l'embryogénie des Ranunculacées-Clematidées. I. L'embryon. Bul. Soc. Bot. de France **57:** 242–250, 266–275.

Sprague, G. F. 1932. The nature and extent of hetero-fertilization in maize. Genetics **17:** 358–368.

Steindl, F. 1945. Beitrag zur Pollen- und Embryobildung bei *Cynomorium coccineum* L. Arch. Julius Klaus-Stift. f. Vererbungsforsch. **20:** 342–355.

Stenar, H. 1925. "Embryologische Studien. I. Zur Embryologie der Columniferen. II. Die Embryologie der Amaryllideen." Diss. Uppsala.

Stevens, N. 1912. Observations on heterostylous plants. Bot. Gaz. **53:** 277–308.

Stout, A. B. 1931. Pollen-tube behavior in *Brassica pekinensis* with reference to self-incompatibility in fertilization. Amer. Jour. Bot. **18**: 686–695.

Strasburger, E. 1884. "Neuere Untersuchungen über den Befruchtungsvorgang bei den Phanerogamen als Grundlage für eine Theorie der Zeugung." Jena.

————. 1900. Einige Bemerkungen zur Frage nach der doppelten Befruchtung bei Angiospermen. Bot. Ztg. **58**: 293–316.

————. 1908. Chromosomenzahlen, Plasmastrukturen, Vererbungsträger und Reduktionsteilung. Jahrb. f. wiss. Bot. **45**: 477–570.

————. 1910. Sexuelle und apogame Fortpflanzung bei der Urticaceen. Jahrb. f. wiss. Bot. **47**: 245–288.

Swamy, B. G. L. 1941. The development of the male gametes in *Cymbidium bicolor* Lindl. Proc. Indian Acad. Sci. Sect. B. **14**: 454–460.

————. 1948. A contribution to the life history of *Casuarina*. Proc. Amer. Acad. Arts and Sci. **77**: 1–32.

Täckholm, G. 1915. Beobachtungen über die Samenentwicklung einiger Onagraceen. Svensk Bot. Tidskr. **9**: 294–361.

Thompson, R. C. 1933. A morphological study of flower and seed development in cabbage. Jour. Agr. Res. **47**: 215–232.

Tischler, G. 1943. "Allgemeine Pflanzenkaryologie." Vol. II. Berlin.

Trankowsky, D. A. 1931. Zytologische Beobachtungen über die Entwicklung der Pollenschläuche einiger Angiospermen. Planta **12**: 1–18.

————. 1938. La spermogenèse et la fécondation chez la Drosère (*Drosera*). Bul. Soc. Nat. de Moscou, Sect. Biol. **47**: 104–112.

Treub, M. 1891. Sur les Casuarinées et leur place dans le système naturel. Ann. Jard. Bot. Buitenzorg **10**: 145–231.

Tschernojarow, M. W. 1926. Befruchtungserscheinungen bei *Myosurus minimus*. Österr. bot. Ztschr. **75**: 197–206.

Umiker, O. 1920. "Entwicklungsgeschichtlich-zytologische Untersuchungen an *Helosis guayensis* Rich." Diss. Zürich.

Venkateswarlu, J. 1937. A contribution to the embryology of Sonneratiaceae. Proc. Indian Acad. Sci. Sect. B. **5**: 206–223.

————. 1947. Embryological studies in the Thymelaeaceae. II. *Daphne cannabina* Wall. and *Wikstroemia canescens* Meissn. Jour. Indian Bot. Soc. **26**: 13–39.

Walker, R. I. 1947. Megasporogenesis and embryo development in *Tropaeolum majus* L. Bul. Torrey Bot. Club **74**: 240–249.

Wanscher, J. H. 1939. Contribution to the cytology and life history of apple and pear. Roy. Vet. and Agr. Coll. Copenhagen, Yearbook 1939, pp. 21–70.

Warmke, H. E. 1943. Macrosporogenesis, fertilization, and early embryology of *Taraxacum kok-saghys*. Bul. Torrey Bot. Club **70**: 164–173.

Weber, E. 1929. Entwicklungsgeschichtliche Untersuchungen über die Gattung *Allium*. Bot. Arch. **25**: 1–44.

Weinstein, A. J. 1926. Cytological studies on *Phaseolus vulgaris*. Amer. Jour. Bot. **13**: 248–263.

Weinzieher, S. 1914. Beiträge zur Entwicklungsgeschichte von *Xyris indica* L. Flora **106:** 393–432.

Welsford, E. J. 1914. The genesis of the male nuclei in *Lilium*. Ann. Bot. **28:** 265–270.

Weniger, W. 1918. Fertilization in *Lilium*. Bot. Gaz. **66:** 259–268.

Werner, E. 1914. Zur Ökologie atypischer Samenanlagen. Beihefte bot. Centbl. **32:** 1–14.

West, G. 1930. Cleistogamy in *Viola riviniana*, with especial reference to the cytological aspects. Ann. Bot. **44:** 87–109.

Wiger, J. 1935. "Embryological Studies on the Families Buxaceae, Meliaceae, Simarubaceae and Burseraceae." Diss. Lund.

Woodroof, N. C. 1928. Development of the embryo sac and young embryo in *Hicoria pecan*. Amer. Jour. Bot. **15:** 416–421.

Wulff, H. D. 1933. Beiträge zur Kenntnis des männlichen Gametophyten der Angiospermen. Planta **21:** 12–50.

Wylie, R. B. 1904. The morphology of *Elodea canadensis*. Bot. Gaz. **37:** 1–22.

———. 1923. Sperms of *Vallisneria spiralis*. Bot. Gaz. **75:** 191–202.

———. 1941. Some aspects of fertilization in *Vallisneria*. Amer. Jour. Bot. **28:** 169–174.

Yasuda, S. 1930. Physiological researches. VIII. On the self-fertilizing ability of flowers in buds of self-incompatible plants. Bot. Mag. [Tokyo] **44:** 678–687.

CHAPTER 7

THE ENDOSPERM[1]

The endosperm is important because it is the main source of food for the embryo. In gymnosperms it is haploid and forms a continuation of the female gametophyte. In angiosperms, on the other hand, it is a new structure formed in most cases as the result of a fusion of the two polar nuclei and one of the male gametes. Since all three of the fusing nuclei are usually haploid, the endosperm contains the triploid number of chromosomes (Fig. 119).[1a]

Endosperm formation is suppressed in two families, the Orchidaceae and Podostemonaceae.[2] In the former, triple fusion is usually completed, but the fusion product either degenerates immediately or undergoes only one or two divisions (Fig. 120). Only in *Calopogon* (Pace, 1909), *Vanilla* (Swamy, 1947), and *Cephalanthera* (Hagerup, 1947) a few free nuclei are produced, but even these soon degenerate and disappear. In the Podostemonaceae there is formed in the nucellus a large cavity or pseudoembryo sac (Fig. 67*C*,*F*) into which the embryo is pushed down by the elongation of the suspensor. The pseudoembryo sac seems to serve as a kind of substitute for the endosperm, although it has an entirely different origin.

Types of Endosperm Formation. There are three general modes of endosperm formation. In the Nuclear type, the first division and usually several of the following ones are unaccompanied by wall formation (Fig. 121). The nuclei may either remain free or in later stages they may become separated by walls. In the Cellular type, the first and most of the subsequent divisions are accompanied by wall formation, so that the sac becomes divided into several chambers, some of which may contain more than one nucleus (Figs. 127, 132). The third or Helobial type (so called because of its frequent occurrence in the order Helobiales) is intermediate between the

---

[1] For more detailed information on this topic see Brink and Cooper (1947).

[1a] The exceptions to this condition are discussed in Chap. 13.

[2] In *Crinum latifolium* also, according to Tomita (1931), embryo development is often completed without endosperm formation.

Nuclear and the Cellular types.   Here the first division is followed by a transverse wall resulting in a micropylar and a chalazal chamber.   Subsequent divisions are usually free nuclear and may take place in both chambers, but as a rule the main body of the endosperm is formed by the micropylar chamber only (Fig. 139).

Nuclear Endosperm.   Usually at least the first few divisions are synchronous, but in later stages some of the nuclei may be seen in the prophase stage, others in metaphase, and still others in anaphase or telophase.[3] Thus the number of endosperm nuclei may not always be a multiple of two.   As divisions progress, the nuclei become pushed more and more towards the periphery, so that the center is occupied by a large vacuole.   Often the nuclei are especially aggregated at the micropylar and chalazal ends of the sac and form only a thin layer at the sides.   An interesting condition has been reported in *Musa errans* (Juliano and Alcala, 1933), where some of the endosperm nuclei divide more actively than others, forming isolated groups or "nodules."   They become invested with a distinct cytoplasmic wall and extend into the center of the embryo sac, developing as separate endosperm masses (Fig. 122).   Similar nodules and vesicles have been seen in a few other plants, but their further fate and function have not been clarified.   In *Isomeris arborea* (Billings, 1937) they are said to give rise to embryos, but this deserves confirmation.

Fig. 119.   Embryo sac of *Crepis capillaris,* showing diploid chromosome complement $(2n = 6)$ in cells of embryo and triploid chromosome complement $(3n = 9)$ in cells of endosperm.   (*After Gerassimova, 1933.*)

Frequently the endosperm nuclei in the chalazal part of the embryo sac have been

[3] Nuclei in different stages of division are not indiscriminately scattered, however.   They often show a remarkable gradation, presumably due to the influence of some kind of slowly diffusing hormonal substance (see Dixon, 1946).

observed to be larger than those in the micropylar part.[4] This may
be due to an actual growth in their size as in *Colutea* (Némec, 1910),
Ranunculus (Schürhoff, 1915), and some members of the Cistaceae
(Chiarugi, 1925), or to a fusion of adjacent nuclei as in *Primula*

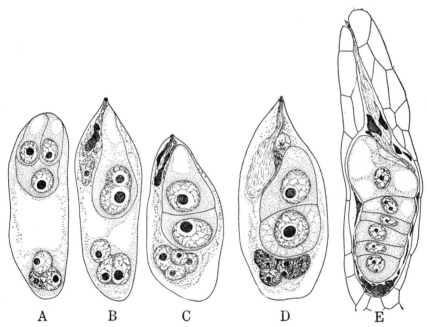

Fig. 120. Endosperm in orchids. *A, Corallorhiza maculata,* six-nucleate embryo
sac; micropylar polar nucleus has migrated to the base of the sac. *B,* a stage in
fertilization, showing one male nucleus fusing with the egg nucleus and the second
male nucleus still in micropylar part of embryo sac. *C,* embryo sac, showing the
young proembryo and the second male nucleus fusing with the other free nuclei in
sac. *D, Bletia shepherdii,* young proembryo and triple fusion nucleus. *E,* same,
later stage of proembryo accompanied by degeneration of endosperm nucleus.
(*After Sharp, 1912.*)

(Dahlgren, 1916), *Tilia* (Stenar, 1925), *Malus* (Wanscher, 1939),
and some members of the Compositae (Poddubnaja-Arnoldi, 1931).[5]
    An especially interesting case of an increase in size of the endo-
sperm nuclei has recently been described in *Echinocystis macrocarpa*

---

    [4] Rarely, as in *Fagraea* (Mohrbutter, 1936), the reverse happens and the micro-
pylar nuclei are the larger.
    [5] Although fusions may take place during the free nuclear stage, they are more
abundant after wall formation has taken place and the endosperm has become
chambered into several multinucleate protoplasts.

(Scott, 1944). At first the nuclei measure 7 to 10 microns in diameter and have one to three nucleoli, but in later stages they become 150 to 200 microns in diameter and their nucleoli present a great variation in size, shape, and number. The following patterns

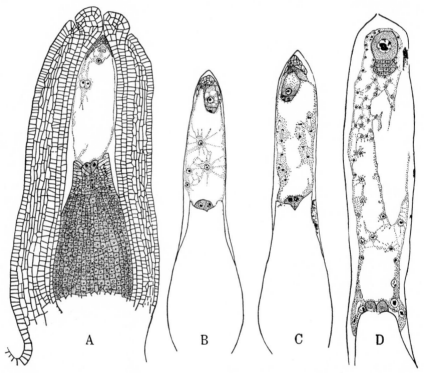

FIG. 121. Endosperm formation in *Zostera marina*. *A*, l.s. ovule, showing mature embryo sac. *B*, two-celled embryo and four-nucleate endosperm; note persisting antipodal cells. *C*, *D*, more advanced stages in endosperm formation; note larger size of nuclei in lower part of endosperm. (*After Dahlgren, 1939.*)

were observed: (1) the nucleus has several nucleoli, all of a small size (Fig. 123*A*); (2) some of the nucleoli are small, and others are of a medium size (Fig. 123*B*); and (3) most of the nucleoli are small, but one to three are of a very large size and these may have a spherical, elliptical, or highly erratic outline (Fig. 123*C*, *D*). In later stages the largest nucleoli become subdivided into irregular segments, as if in readiness to break up into pieces (Fig. 123*E*). Since an increased number of nucleoli in a nucleus is generally considered to be an index of chromosome duplication, it seems likely that the abnormalities described above are due to a high degree of polyploidy in the endosperm.

There are occasional reports of atypical or irregular divisions of the endosperm nuclei. In *Zauschneria latifolia* (Johansen, 1931*b*), a member of the Onagraceae, the endo-sperm nuclei lying close to the embryo divide amitotically. In another member of the same family, *Anogra pallida* (Johansen, 1931*c*), the unfertilized polar nucleus is said to undergo repeated amitotic divisions to form more than a hundred nuclei of various sizes. There are also other records of amitotic divisions in the endosperm, but most statements of this kind are far from dependable.[6] To mention two examples, Longo (1909) failed to find any mitoses in the endosperm of *Ficus carica* and

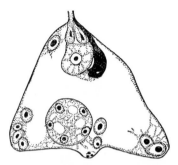

Fig. 122. Embryo sac of *Musa errans*, showing free nuclear endosperm and vesicle containing five endosperm nuclei. (*After Juliano and Alcala, 1933.*)

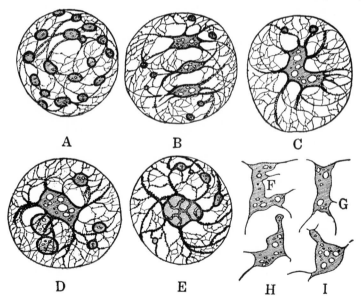

A   B   C

D   E   F   G   H   I

Fig. 123. *Echinocystis macrocarpa*, endosperm nuclei, showing peculiar behavior of nucleoli. Only the nucleolus is shown in *F–I*. (*After Scott, 1944.*)

[6] Appearances formerly accepted as evidences of amitosis are now considered to be the results of deranged mitoses or of nuclear fusions.

concluded that the division took place by fragmentation, but Condit (1932) demonstrated the presence of mitotic figures in both *F. carica* and *F. palmata*. Similarly Langdon's (1934) statement that in *Juglans* a period of free nuclear divisions lasting for 4 to 5 days is "characterized by the total absence of achromatic figures, suggesting an amitotic division of the nuclei at this time" has been contradicted by Nast (1935, 1941).

The number of free nuclear divisions varies in different plants. In *Primula* (Dahlgren, 1916), *Malva* (Stenar, 1925), *Cochlospermum* (Schnarf, 1931), *Brexia* (Mauritzon, 1933), *Mangifera* (Maheshwari, 1934), *Juglans* (Nast, 1935), *Malus* (Wanscher, 1939),[7] *Jussieua* (Khan, 1942), and *Citrus* (Bacchi, 1943) several hundred endosperm nuclei may be seen lining the wall of the embryo sac. In some genera, *e.g.*, *Lopezia* (Täckholm, 1915), *Stenosiphon* (Johansen, 1931*a*), *Cardiospermum* (Kadry, 1946), *Tropaeolum* (Walker, 1947), and *Melastoma* (Subramanyam, 1948) wall formation does not take place at all. In others like *Asclepias* (Frye, 1902), *Rafflesia* (Ernst and Schmid, 1913), *Leiphaimos*, *Cotylanthera* (Oehler, 1927), *Calotropis* (Sabet, 1931), *Xeranthemum* (Poddubnaja-Arnoldi, 1931), and *Crepis* (Gerassimova, 1933) it occurs at a very early stage when only 8 or 16 nuclei have been formed, and in *Coffea* (Mendes, 1941) at the 4-nucleate stage.

When wall formation occurs, it is usually by the laying down of cell plates which progress from the periphery of the sac towards the center or from its apex towards the base. Less commonly, wall formation may take place simultaneously in all parts of the sac as in *Tacca* (Paetow, 1931), or it may start from the base toward the apex as in *Elatine* (Frisendahl, 1927), *Cimicifuga* (Earle, 1938), and *Carya* (McKay, 1947). Very little is known, however, about the exact origin of the partition walls.[8] In *Asclepias* (Frye, 1902), *Calotropis* (Sabet, 1931), *Ficus* (Condit, 1932), and *Gossypium* (Gore, 1932) minute vacuoles appear in the areas between the nuclei, and it seems that partitioning of the embryo sac takes place by a process of "indentation." In some other plants the formation of cell plates is preceded by the appearance of secondary spindle fibers between the nuclei (Jungers, 1931). Whatever the precise mode of cell formation, eventually either the entire embryo sac is

---

[7] Between two and three thousand nuclei have been counted in some varieties of *Malus*.

[8] The difficulty in ascertaining the precise mechanism of wall formation is no doubt due to the rapidity of the event and the poor fixation obtained at this stage.

filled with cells; or there are one or two peripheral layers of cells and the rest of the endosperm remains in the free nuclear state; or cell formation is restricted only to the micropylar part of the sac. Sometimes all three types occur in one and the same family, *e.g.*, the Caryophyllaceae (Rocén, 1927). Not infrequently several nuclei become enclosed in a cell where they may subsequently fuse to form a single nucleus; or an originally uninucleate cell may become multinucleate by divisions of its nucleus. Such variations are so common that it is unnecessary to cite specific examples.

Special mention must be made of the haustorial structures met with in some members of the Proteaceae (Kausik, 1938*a,b*, 1942). Here most of the endosperm nuclei are distributed in the upper portion of the embryo sac. Cell formation is restricted to this region, while the lower portion of the sac remains free nuclear. In *Macadamia ternifolia* (Fig. 124*A–C*) this part forms several prominent lobes or diverticulae which invade the nutritive tissue at the chalazal end of the ovule and thus function as haustoria. It is only in later stages, when the food material in the chalazal cells is completely used up, that the activity of these haustorial lobes comes to an end.

In another member of the Proteaceae, *Grevillea robusta* (Fig. 124*D–G*), the lower coenocytic part of the endosperm grows in the form of a coiled and tubular worm-like structure, which has been aptly designated as the "vermiform appendage." It serves as a haustorium of a very aggressive type whose coils invade the cells of the chalaza and bring about their virtual dissolution. Later, the appendage becomes partitioned into several large chambers which undergo further subdivisions into smaller units, so that the cells formed in this way constitute a kind of secondary endosperm tissue. The reason why the vermiform appendage had been missed by earlier workers is that they used only sections, which fail to give any clear or complete picture of this organ, while Kausik used both sections and whole mounts and was therefore able to give a very thorough account of its development and organization. Using a similar technique, Anantaswamy Rau (1950) has found that in *Cassia tora* wall formation takes place only in the micropylar part of the embryo sac. The chalazal part forms a narrow tube with dense cytoplasm and many free nuclei. The lower part of the tube becomes irregularly coiled and twisted to form a very efficient haustorium.

The lateral haustoria or "diverticulae" mentioned on page 144

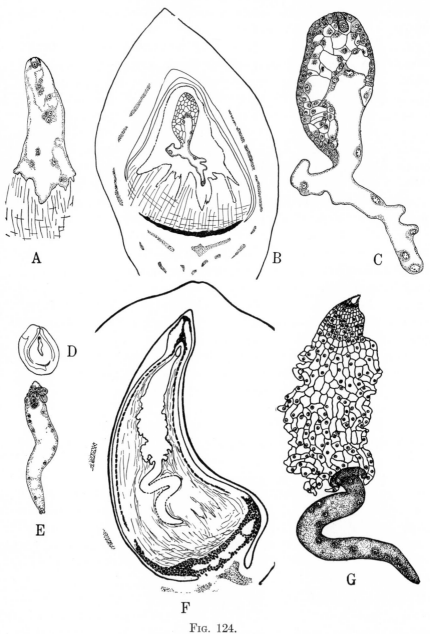

A   B   C

D

E   F   G

Fig. 124.

often show increased activity in postfertilization stages. In *Agrostemma* (Fig. 125) the primary endosperm nucleus, originally situated just below the zygote, enters the base of the diverticulum and divides to form two daughter nuclei, one remaining in the embryo sac and giving rise to the bulk of the endosperm and the other passing into the diverticulum. Similar diverticulae are seen in several other members of the Caryophyllaceae, but the time of their appearance is not the same. In *Gypsophila* the outgrowth originates even before fertilization; in *Saponaria*, after the second nuclear division in the endosperm; and in *Melandrium*, at a still later stage (Rocén, 1927).

Cellular Endosperm. In the Cellular type the division of the primary endosperm nucleus is followed immediately by a chambering of the sac. The first wall is usually transverse but sometimes vertical or oblique, and in a few cases the plane of division is not constant. On the basis of the orientation of the walls following the first two or three divisions, this type of endosperm has been classified into several subtypes (see Schnarf, 1929). For our purpose, however, it will suffice to refer to a few concrete examples in order to illustrate the range of variation that has been reported.

Adoxa (Lagerberg, 1909) is a well-known instance in which the first as well as the second division of the endosperm mother cell is vertical, resulting in the formation of four large cylindrical cells, all similar to one another (Fig. 126*A–B*). The third division is transverse and results in eight cells arranged in two tiers (Fig. 126*C*). The fourth division is also transverse but further divisions are irregular.

A similar orientation of the first wall is known in *Scabiosa* (Doll, 1927) and *Circaeaster* (Junell, 1931). In *Peperomia* (Johnson, 1900), *Centranthus* (Asplund, 1920) (Fig. 126*D*), and *Helosis* (Fagerlind, 1938) also, the first wall is longitudinal but sometimes it may be

FIG. 124. Stages in development of endosperm in *Macadamia ternifolia* (*A–C*) and *Grevillea robusta* (*D–G*). *A*, *Macadamia*, embryo sac showing free endosperm nuclei; lower end of sac is invading nutritive tissue in chalaza. *B*, l.s. young seed showing embryo sac with upper cellular endosperm and lower free nuclear endosperm. *C*, embryo sac from *B*, enlarged to show details of endosperm; two-celled proembryo is seen at upper end of sac. *D*, *Grevillea*, l.s. ovule (diagrammatic). *E*, embryo sac from *D*, enlarged to show young embryo and free nuclear endosperm. *F*, l.s. young seed, showing "vermiform appendage" formed from basal part of endosperm. *G*, whole mount of endosperm, showing vermiform appendage. (*After Kausik 1938a,b.*)

oblique, and in *Senecio* (Afzelius, 1924) there is no constancy about its orientation. Frequently it is longitudinal, but it may also be transverse or oblique.

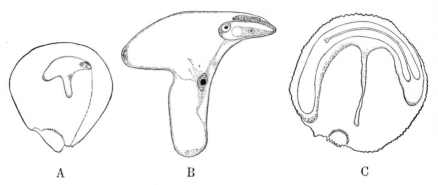

A   B   C

FIG. 125. Formation of lateral haustorium or diverticulum in embryo sac of *Agrostemma githago*. *A*, l.s. ovule, showing early stage in formation of diverticulum. *B*, enlarged view of embryo sac from *A*. *C*, l.s. nearly mature seed, showing large embryo and persisting diverticulum. (*After Rocén, 1927.*)

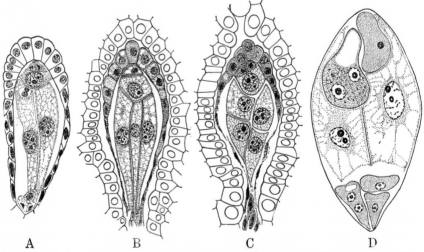

A   B   C   D

FIG. 126. Early stages in development of endosperm in *Adoxa moschatellina* (*A–C*) and *Centranthus macrosiphon* (*D*). In both cases, the first wall is vertical. (*A–C, after Lagerberg, 1909; D, after Asplund, 1920.*)

Except in the few plants cited above, the first division of the endosperm mother cell is generally transverse. In the Anonaceae, Aristolochiaceae, Sarraceniaceae, Gentianaceae, Boraginaceae (see

Schnarf, 1929), and Marcgraviaceae (Mauritzon, 1939) the second division, and sometimes the third also, is transverse, resulting in a row of four or more cells (Fig. 127). More commonly, however, the second division is vertical, and subsequent walls are laid down in variable planes.

Of special interest are several members of the Sympetalae and of a few families belonging to the Archichlamydeae and the Mono-cotyledons, in which there is a differentiation of prominent endo-sperm haustoria. The haustoria may arise at the chalazal end, or

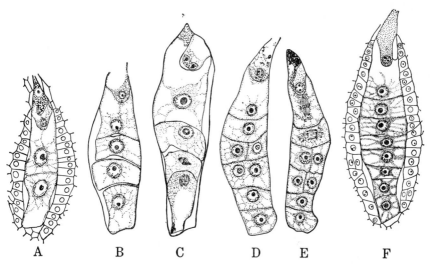

A	B	C	D	E	F

Fig. 127. Development of endosperm in *Villarsia reniformis.* *A*, two-celled stage. *B,C*, four-celled stage. *D–F*, eight-celled stage. (*After Stolt, 1921.*)

at the micropylar end, or at both. Taking the simplest forms first, in the Nymphaeaceae and Araceae the primary chalazal cell formed after the first division of the endosperm mother cell undergoes no further divisions and functions directly as a haustorium. A whole mount of the endosperm of *Peltandra* (Goldberg, 1941), belonging to the Araceae, shows several strands of streaming cytoplasm trav-ersing the large vacuole of this cell. Its nucleus becomes lobed and hypertrophied, and the nucleolus breaks down into a number of highly vacuolated fragments.

A similar large chalazal cell is seen in *Thesium* (Schulle, 1933; Rutishauser, 1937) and *Balanophora* (Zweifel, 1939). The first division of the primary endosperm nucleus, which lies in the vicinity of the zygote, results in the formation of a small micropylar and a considerably larger chalazal chamber. Further divisions take place in the micropylar chamber only (Fig. 128*A*,*B*). In *Balanophora*, where the sequence has been followed in greater detail, the micropylar chamber (Fig. 128*C*) divides vertically to form two adjoining cells enveloping the zygote (Fig. 128*D*). The second and third divisions are transverse and result in four and eight cells respectively (Fig. 128*E*,*F*). The following divisions are less regular, but the young embryo soon becomes surrounded by a number of small endosperm cells. Later, owing to a further increase in the number of endosperm cells and their enlargement, the large chalazal haustorium becomes squeezed and crushed.

A very well developed and aggressive micropylar haustorium occurs in *Impatiens* (Dahlgren, 1934*b*). The first division of the primary endosperm nucleus gives rise to two chambers (Fig. 129*A*). The micropylar chamber, which is the smaller, divides transversely into three cells (Fig. 129*B*). The uppermost of these, containing the zygote, forms a giant haustorium whose branching arms extend as far as the funiculus (Fig. 129*C–F*). The next gives rise to a group of cells which lie in close proximity to the young embryo. The third, in which the divisions are not accompanied by wall formation, fuses with the large chalazal chamber, which also contains only free nuclei. Eventually cell formation takes place here also, but some rounded masses of plasma, often containing several nuclei, seem to become detached from the wall of the embryo sac and swim as "free plasma balls" in the liquid below the cotyledons.

Passing now to plants in which both micropylar and chalazal haustoria are formed, we may first refer to the family Acanthaceae, several members of which have been studied by Mauritzon (1934). In *Ruellia* and most other genera the first division of the primary endosperm nucleus cuts off a small chalazal haustorium with dense cytoplasm, in which there are two nuclear divisions resulting in four free nuclei (Fig. 130*B*). The micropylar cell divides transversely to give rise to two daughter cells, of which the upper becomes binucleate and forms the micropylar haustorium (Fig. 130*C*). The central cell, which is the largest, forms a sac-like outgrowth in which there are several free nuclear divisions (Fig. 130*D–G*). A large vacuole appears in the center of the cell, and the nuclei become distributed in the peripheral layer of cytoplasm, with a stronger

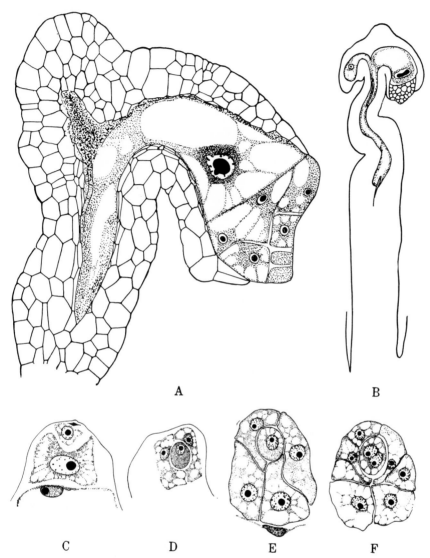

A   B

C   D   E   F

Fɪɢ. 128. Some stages in development of endosperm in *Thesium montanum* (*A,B*)
and *Balanophora abbreviata* (*C–F*). *A, Thesium;* l.s. ovule, showing cell formation
in primary micropylar chamber, while chalazal chamber remains undivided and
forms large haustorium. *B,* l.s. central placenta, showing extent of growth of
chalazal haustorium; somewhat diagrammatic and drawn at a much lower magnification than *A.* (*After Schulle, 1933.*) *C, Balanophora;* upper part of embryo
sac, showing micropylar endosperm chamber with zygote, and a portion of chalazal
endosperm chamber. *D–F,* same, showing cell formation in micropylar endosperm
chamber, while large chalazal chamber (not shown in figures) remains undivided.
(*After Zweifel, 1939.*)

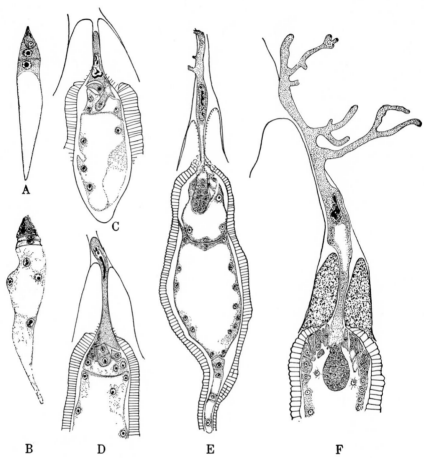

A   B   C   D   E   F

Fig. 129.   Development of endosperm in *Impatiens roylei*.   *A*, first division of endosperm mother cell, resulting in formation of small micropylar and large chalazal chambers.   *B*, more advanced stage, showing large chalazal chamber and three cells formed by transverse divisions of micropylar chamber.   *C*, uppermost cell of micropylar chamber has grown into micropyle; zygote nucleus in division.   *D*, haustorium has penetrated beyond tip of inner integument.   Note two-celled embryo and laying down of walls in second endosperm cell from above.   *E*, further growth of micropylar haustorium.   *F*, upper part of ovule, showing hypha-like ramifications of haustorium and their penetration into tissues of funiculus.   (*After Dahlgren, 1934b.*)

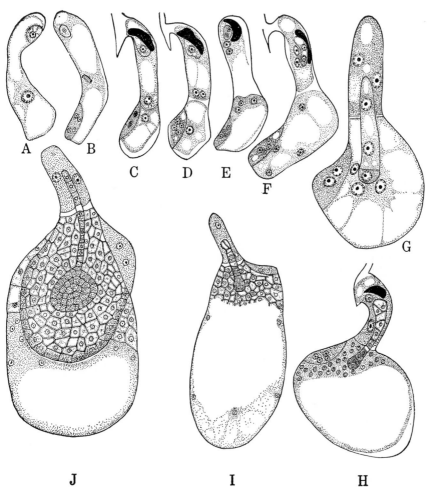

FIG. 130. Development of endosperm in *Ruellia*. *A, R. solitaria*, embryo sac showing fertilized egg and primary endosperm nucleus. *B*, same, later stage, showing delimitation of chalazal haustorium. *C,D, R. squarrosa*, micropylar haustorium, chalazal haustorium, and central endosperm chamber. *E,F, R. solitaria*, increase in number of free nuclei in central chamber. *G, R. pulcherrima*, similar stage. *H, R. decaisniana*, micropylar and chalazal haustoria and central endosperm chamber with many free nuclei. *I, R. solitaria*, more advanced stage, showing beginning of wall formation in upper part of central chamber. *J, R. pulcherrima*, central chamber consisting of upper cellular and lower free nuclear portion. (*After Mauritzon, 1934.*)

accumulation of them in the region adjacent to the embryo and the two haustoria (Fig. 130*H*). Cell formation commences only after 64 or more nuclei have been produced and is confined to the upper part, the lower still remaining free nuclear (Fig. 130*I*). In later stages, therefore, the endosperm shows four distinct regions: micropylar haustorium, chalazal haustorium, cellular endosperm, and free nuclear endosperm (Fig. 130*J*). This last, which Mauritzon calls the "basal apparatus," seems to be an intermediary for con-

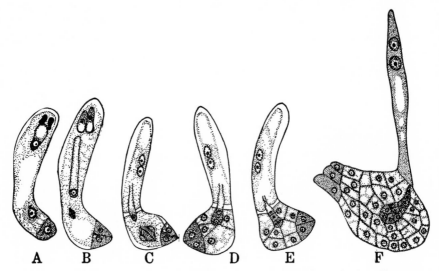

F<small>IG</small>. 131.   Development of endosperm in *Crossandra nilotica*.   *A*, first division of endosperm mother cell.   *B*, chalazal chamber divided vertically into two cells. *C*, delimitation of central chamber from micropylar and chalazal haustorium.   *D,E*, cell divisions in central chamber.   *F*, more advanced stage, showing binucleate micropylar haustorium, central chamber with cellular endosperm and embryo, and four-celled chalazal haustorium.   (*After Mauritzon, 1934.*)

veying food materials from the integument to the cellular portion of the endosperm.   An interesting point to be noted is that owing to the continued curvature of the embryo sac, the micropylar and chalazal haustoria come to lie in close proximity to each other.

Most genera of the family are essentially similar to *Ruellia*, but a somewhat different condition prevails in *Crossandra* (Fig. 131), where the divisions in the chalazal haustorium as well as the central chamber are accompanied by wall formation.   The former undergoes two vertical divisions to form four cells.   In the central chamber also the first two divisions are vertical, but these are followed by further divisions in varying planes, resulting in a small mass of endosperm tissue surrounding the embryo. In *Crossandra*, therefore, the endosperm consists of only three regions: the micropylar haustorium, the chalazal haustorium, and the central endosperm tissue. The genus *Acanthus* is more or less similar. *Thunbergia*, which seems to differ in several respects from both *Ruellia* and *Crossandra*, needs further study and will not be discussed here.

The genus *Nemophila*, belonging to the Hydrophyllaceae, presents an interesting mode of development. Of the two approximately equal cells formed by the first division of the endosperm mother cell, the lower functions directly as the chalazal haustorium (Fig. 132*A*). The upper divides transversely to give rise to a central cell, which is responsible for the origin of the main body of the endosperm, and a terminal cell, which serves as the micropylar haustorium (Fig. 132*B*). Cell divisions are confined to the central cell only, the first wall being transverse and the others more or less irregular (Fig. 132*C–F*). The chalazal haustorium sometimes gives out a prominent lateral branch (Fig. 132*D*) which grows toward the funiculus and penetrates it so as to come in direct contact with the starchy cells of the placenta. In one species, *N. aurita*, the micropylar haustorium, as well as the chalazal one, becomes large and aggressive. Fig. 132*G*, *H*, reconstructed from several sections, shows the central ball-shaped mass of endosperm and conspicuous haustoria.

Well-developed micropylar and chalazal haustoria also occur in the Lobeliaceae (Hewitt, 1939; Subramanyam, 1949). In *Lobelia amoena* (Hewitt, 1939) the first division of the endosperm mother cell is transverse and the second is vertical (Fig. 133*A,B*). Each of the four cells now divides transversely, resulting in four tiers of two cells each, *i.e.*, eight cells in all (Fig. 133*C*). The two cells of the micropylar tier do not divide again but extend around the zygote, forcing their way into the micropyle and forming a large haustorium; the two cells of the chalazal tier grow downward into the basal end of the ovule, forming a large chalazal haustorium; and the middle tiers give rise to the main body of the endosperm (Fig. 133*D,E*). Cross sections of the haustoria, both micropylar and chalazal, show their two-celled nature quite clearly.

An essentially similar mode of development occurs in *Utricularia coerulea* (Kausik, 1938c) (Fig. 134*A–C*). The first division of the

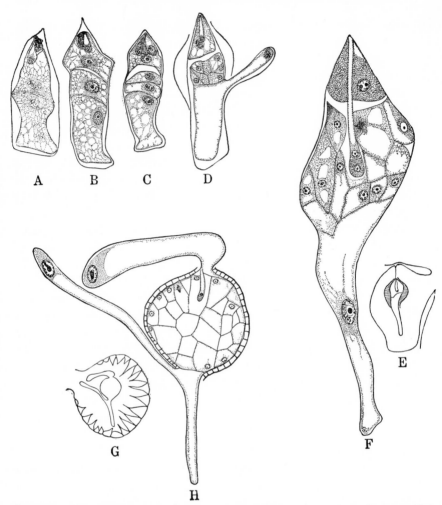

FIG. 132. Development of endosperm in *Nemophila*. *A, N. insignis*; two-celled endosperm. *B*, three-celled stage. *C*, four-celled stage resulting from transverse division of middle cell. *D*, more advanced stage, showing small mass of cells formed by divisions of two central cells; chalazal haustorium has given out a lateral branch. *E*, l.s. ovule, diagrammatic. *F*, embryo sac from *E*, magnified to show two-celled embryo, micropylar and chalazal haustoria, and central mass of endosperm cells. *G, N. aurita*, diagram of l.s. ovule. *H*, embryo sac of *G*, magnified to show aggressive micropylar and chalazal haustoria and central globular mass of endosperm cells. (*After Svensson, 1925.*)

endosperm mother cell is transverse, resulting in the formation of the two primary chambers, micropylar and chalazal. The second is vertical, but in both chambers the walls are incomplete and do not extend to the two poles of the embryo sac. The third division is

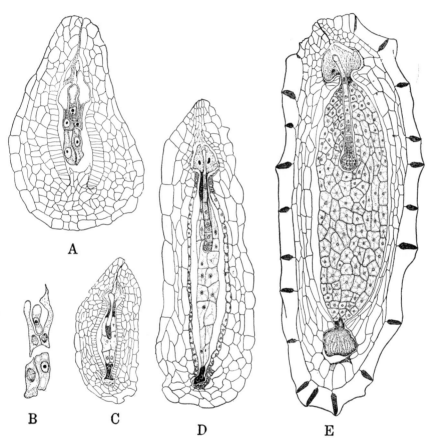

A

B   C

D   E

FIG. 133. Development of endosperm in *Lobelia amoena*. *A*, l.s. ovule, showing four-celled stage of endosperm. *B*, transverse division in some of the endosperm cells. *C*, laying down of micropylar and chalazal haustoria. *D,E*, more advanced stages, showing multiplication of cells of endosperm, the enlarging haustoria, and the developing embryo. (*After Hewitt, 1939.*)

transverse and takes place simultaneously in both the upper and the lower chambers. Thus the embryo sac now consists of a central portion of four cells, two contributed by the upper and two by the lower primary chamber, and two terminal portions with two nuclei

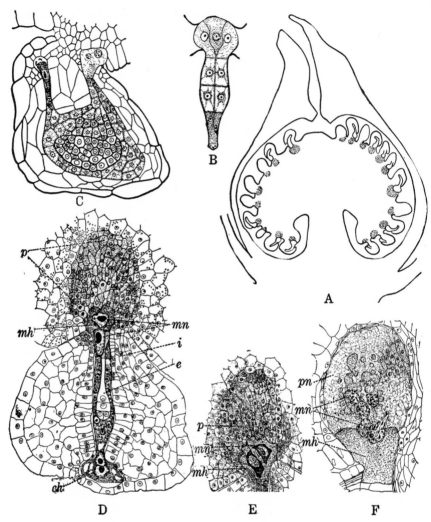

FIG. 134.   Endosperm formation in *Utricularia*.   *A, U. coerulea*; l.s. ovary, showing relation of ovules to the swollen placenta.   *B*, embryo sac showing sequence of wall formation in endosperm, resulting in a delimitation of the micropylar and chalazal haustoria.   *C*, l.s. seed, showing embryo and remnants of haustoria.   (*After Kausik, 1938c.*)   *D, U. vulgaris americana*; l.s. ovule, showing the embryo *e*, micropylar haustorium *mh*, nuclei of micropylar haustorium *mn*, chalazal haustorium *ch*, integument *i*, and placental tissue *p*.   *E*, invasion of placental tissue *p* by micropylar haustorium *mh*; note the two large nuclei *mn* of the micropylar haustorium.   *F*, more advanced stage, showing disappearance of cell walls of placental tissue and scattering of placental nuclei *pn*.   The more densely staining nuclei *mn* belong to micropylar haustorium *mh*.   (*After Wylie and Yocom, 1923.*)

each.   In subsequent stages only the four central cells divide further and give rise to the body of the endosperm, while the terminal cells remain undivided and take up a haustorial function.

An interesting feature, described in special detail in *Utricularia vulgaris americana* (Wylie and Yocom, 1923), is that, because of the disappearance of the nucellar epidermis and the protrusion of the embryo sac through the micropyle, the micropylar haustorium comes to lie in direct contact with the nutritive tissue of the placenta (Fig. 134*D*, *E*).   The walls of the placental cells frequently break down, so that their nuclei become scattered in a common mass of cytoplasm along with the nuclei of the haustorium.   The placental nuclei enlarge, and some of them fuse to form "tuber-like" structures many times their normal size.   The nuclei of the haustorium, which are usually still larger and more chromatic, become lobed and bud out into separate masses.   "These with the placental nuclei lying in the fluids of the haustorium offer a most peculiar assemblage of nuclear structures" (Fig. 134*F*).   The chalazal haustorium, although less massive, also digests its way through the intervening cells and ultimately comes in contact with the cells of the epidermis, which become perceptibly weakened at this point.

The occurrence of endosperm haustoria, both micropylar and chalazal, is also a universal feature of the Scrophulariaceae.   A widely distributed mode of development is illustrated by *Lathraea* (Glišić, 1932) (Fig. 135).   Of the two primary endosperm chambers, the chalazal functions directly as a haustorium after undergoing one nuclear division.   The micropylar divides vertically and then transversely to give rise to two tiers of two cells each.   Of these, the uppermost tier gives rise to two binucleate haustorial cells which later fuse to form a single tetranucleate structure, and the lower gives rise to the endosperm proper.

There are several variations of this scheme, which have been described by Krishna Iyengar (1937, 1939, 1940, 1941, 1942) in recent publications.   Although the chalazal haustorium usually comprises a single binucleate cell, in certain plants like *Celsia*, *Isoplexis*, and *Verbascum* it is tetranucleate, while *Vandellia*, *Sopubia*, and *Alonsoa* (Fig. 136*D*) have two uninucleate prongs which may later fuse to form a single binucleate cell.   The micropylar haustorium is differentiated somewhat later, but it is more aggressive and persists for a longer time.   In some plants there are four uninucleate cells, which may remain as such as in *Alonsoa* (Fig. 136), *Isoplexis*,

Celsia, and *Ilysanthes*, or fuse to form a common tetranucleate structure as in *Vandellia* and *Torenia*. In a few plants like *Pedicularis* the haustorium is tetranucleate from the commencement.

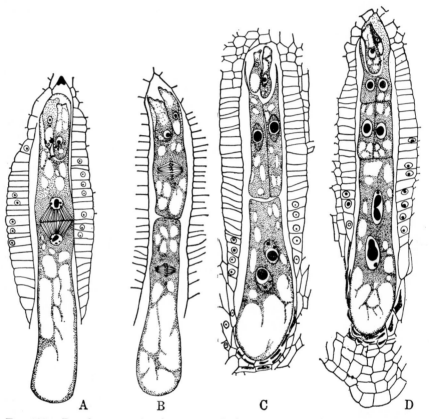

FIG. 135.   Development of endosperm in *Lathraea squamaria*.   *A*, first division of endosperm mother cell.   *B*, nuclear division in both endosperm cells.   *C*, division completed; basal cell binucleate and upper cell partitioned by longitudinal wall. *D*, basal cell forms large haustorium; transverse division in upper cells to form two-celled micropylar haustorium and two central cells, which are destined to give rise to main body of endosperm.   (*After Glišić, 1932.*)

In *Centranthera* neither the micropylar nor the chalazal haustorium is very active, but there are formed instead some secondary haustoria from the endosperm cells just beneath the micropylar haustorium (Fig. 137).   Similar secondary haustoria are seen in *Veronica*, but here they arise from the chalazal region of the haustorium.

In a few plants, well-developed and aggressive haustoria of all three kinds—micropylar, chalazal, and secondary—occur together and form a very efficient absorptive system. An interesting case of

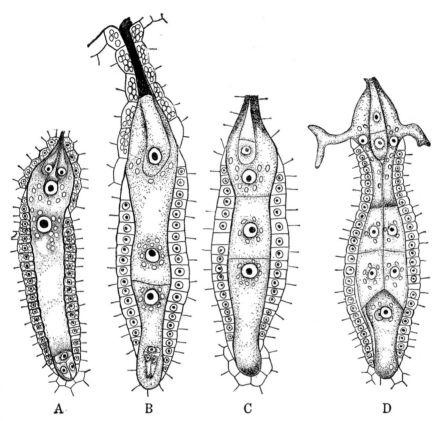

A   B   C   D

Fig. 136. Development of the endosperm in *Alonsoa*. Small globules lying around nuclei are starch grains. *A*, mature embryo sac. *B*, first division of endosperm mother cell. *C*, transverse division in micropylar chamber resulting in a three-celled stage. *D*, more advanced stage, showing four-celled micropylar haustorium (only two cells are seen in section), two-celled chalazal haustorium (one of the cells is lying over the other), and central cells destined to give rise to endosperm proper. (*After Krishna Iyengar, 1937*.)

this kind has been described by Rosén (1940) in *Globularia vulgaris*, belonging to the allied family Globulariaceae. The micropylar haustorium consists of two to four separate cells but they soon unite to form a single entity. This composite structure often grows out of the micropyle, and its hypha-like ramifications extend along the outer surface of the funiculus and placenta, later penetrating even the wall of the ovary.   The chalazal haustorium also branches

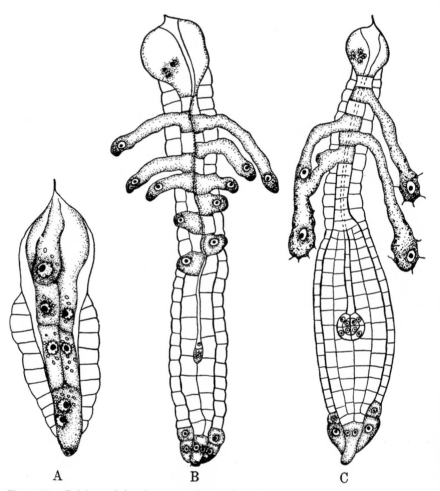

A   B   C

FIG. 137.   Origin and development of secondary haustoria in *Centranthera hispida.* Primary haustoria, both micropylar and chalazal, are very weakly developed in this plant.   (*After Krishna Iyengar, 1942.*)

profusely and "sucks" the contents of the integumentary cells, destroying their walls and causing the formation of large lacunae. In addition, the endosperm cells lying nearest to the chalazal haustorium also increase in size and send out secondary haustoria, so that the entire tissue of the chalaza and the integument becomes riddled by a number of haustorial processes.

A very peculiar mode of development, which seems to bear no relation to any of the others, occurs in several members of the Loranthoideae (Treub, 1885; Rauch, 1936; Schaeppi and Steindl, 1942; Singh, 1950; Johri and Maheshwari 1950; Maheshwari and Singh, 1950). Here the primary endosperm nucleus migrates to the chalazal end of the extremely long and tubular embryo sac. The exact sequence of divisions has not been traced, but eventually the whole of the comparatively broad lower portion of the embryo sac becomes cellular. Cell formation gradually extends upward to the point at which the embryo sac protrudes out of the ovary into the style (Fig. 138). Frequently the development of the endosperm and embryo is initiated in several embryo sacs. Since these lie close to one another, the separating walls between them get dissolved and their endosperms fuse to form a single composite tissue. Sometimes, the boundaries between the individual embryo sacs are still distinguishable at their upper ends, although their basal portions have already fused and show several embryos surrounded by a common mass of endosperm.

Helobial Endosperm. The Helobial type of endosperm is intermediate between the Nuclear and the Cellular. The first division of the primary endosperm nucleus results in the partition of the embryo sac into two chambers, of which the micropylar is usually much larger than the chalazal. Several free nuclear divisions take place in the former, but in the latter either the nucleus remains undivided or undergoes only a small number of divisions. Earlier workers often mistook the chalazal chamber for a hypertrophied antipodal cell.

Eremurus (Stenar, 1928a) may be cited as an example of a typical Helobial endosperm. The first division of the primary endosperm nucleus results in the formation of two chambers, a large micropylar and a small chalazal (Fig. 139A). Free nuclear divisions occur in both but are more rapid in the micropylar chamber (Fig. 139B–D). Thus, when there are four nuclei in the chalazal chamber, the micropylar has eight; when there are eight in the chalazal, the micropylar has 16; and when there are 30 to 32 nuclei in the chalazal chamber, the micropylar has a considerably larger number. In older ovules the chalazal chamber becomes depleted of its cytoplasm and begins

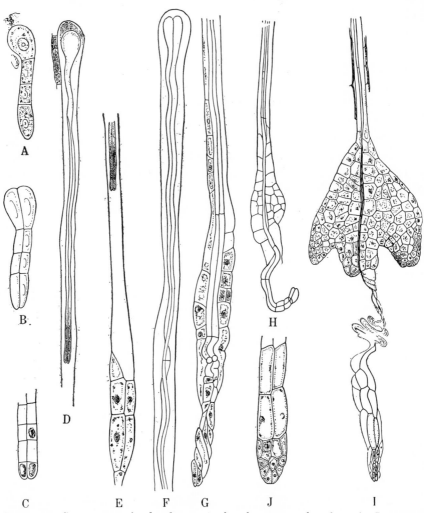

FIG. 138. Some stages in development of endosperm and embryo in *Loranthus sphaerocarpus* Bl. *A,B*, young proembryos of same age viewed from two different sides. *C*, lower end of young proembryo. *D*, upper part of embryo sac, showing elongated proembryo. *E*, lower part of same embryo sac, showing early stage in endosperm formation. *F,G*, upper and lower halves of embryo sac, showing embryo and endosperm. *H*, embryo beginning to penetrate through endosperm. *I*, same, more advanced stage. *J*, terminal part of embryo, shown at a somewhat higher magnification. (*After Treub, 1885.*)

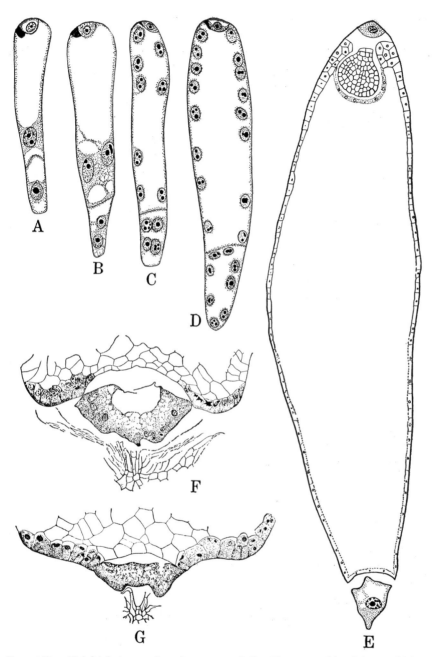

Fig. 139. Helobial type of endosperm. *A–D, Eremurus himalaicus.* (*After Stenar, 1928a*) *E, Scheuchzeria palustris.* (*After Stenar, 1935.*) *F, G, Muscari racemosum.* (*After Wunderlich, 1937.*) In *Scheuchzeria* the chalazal chamber is uninucleate, while in *Muscari* it becomes multinucleate; *Eremurus* is intermediate.

to show signs of degeneration.   Finally, when cell formation takes place in the micropylar chamber, the chalazal is almost crushed and shows only a few disorganized nuclei.

Other plants may show a fewer or a larger number of divisions in the chalazal chamber.   In *Scheuchzeria* (Stenar, 1935) it gradually enlarges and becomes highly vacuolated, but the nucleus does not undergo any division (Fig. 139*E*).   An essentially similar condition occurs in *Echinodorus* (Dahlgren, 1934*a*), *Vallisneria* (Witmer, 1937), and *Enalus* (Kausik, 1940).   In *Bulbine* (Stenar, 1928*a*) and *Sagittaria* (Dahlgren, 1934*a*) there is one division, resulting in two daughter nuclei; and in *Asphodelus* (Stenar, 1928*a*) and *Limnophyton* (Johri, 1935) there are two divisions resulting in four nuclei.   On the other hand, *Hypoxis* (Stenar,[8a] 1925), *Ornithogalum* (Schnarf, 1928*a*), *Dianella* (Schnarf and Wunderlich, 1939), and *Zephyranthes* (Swamy, 1946*a*) show a much larger number of nuclei in the chalazal chamber.   In *Muscari racemosum* (Wunderlich, 1937) (Fig. 139*F*) the chalazal chamber has 64 nuclei at the time when wall formation commences in the micropylar.   Yet another division takes place, resulting in the formation of approximately 128 nuclei, which are imbedded in a dense mass of cytoplasm.   After this stage the nuclei begin to degenerate, but the outline of the chalazal chamber remains recognizable for a long time (Fig. 139*G*).

In some plants the divisions in the chalazal chamber are accompanied by wall formation and result in a small mass of cells which is quite conspicuous for a time.   As examples may be mentioned *Saxifraga granulata* (Juel, 1907), *Boykinia occidentalis*, *Mitella diphylla* (Dahlgren, 1930) (Fig. 140), and *Lyonothamnus floribundus* (Juliano, 1931*a*).   Or, the first few divisions may be free nuclear, and wall formation may occur at a slightly later stage, as in *Heloniopsis breviscapa* (Ono, 1928) and *Tofieldia japonica* (Ono, 1929).   In *Narthecium asiaticum* (Ono, 1929) the free nuclear divisions are followed by a transverse segmentation of the chalazal chamber into a few large multinucleate cells.

In *Ixiolirion montanum* (Stenar, 1925) the primary endosperm nucleus comes to lie laterally, although the antipodal cells, which

[8a] The recent work of De Vos (1948, 1949) shows that in *Hypoxis* (= *Ianthe*) the endosperm does not follow the same type of development in all species.   Some species such as *I. schlechteri* come under the Helobial type, while others like *I. alba*, *I. aquatica* and *I. minuta* come under the Nuclear type.

are large and conspicuous, remain in their usual position in the basal part of the embryo sac. Two endosperm chambers are formed after the first division, but the chalazal is situated toward one side rather than directly over the antipodal cells (Fig. 141C). For a time free nuclear divisions take place in both chambers. Later cell formation occurs in the micropylar chamber, while the chalazal one degenerates.

Svensson (1925) has reported that in *Echium plantagineum*, a member of the Boraginaceae, the first division wall in the embryo sac is oblique, separating a small lateral chamber from a large central chamber. The lateral chamber, which has denser cytoplasm, divides first and gives rise to two cells which later show several hypertrophied nuclei (Fig. 141D–F). The central chamber is more vacuolate, and the divisions are all free nuclear, wall formation taking place at a much later stage.

In *Anthericum ramosum* (Stenar, 1928b; Schnarf, 1928b) the chalazal chamber is cut off in its usual position just above the small and ephemeral antipodals, but the embryo sac soon gives out a lateral outgrowth which advances toward the funicular side of the ovule and becomes an extremely conspicuous structure (Fig. 141A,B).

Fig. 140. Embryo sac of *Mitella diphylla*, showing cell formation in chalazal endosperm chamber. (*After Dahlgren, 1930.*)

More remarkable still are the lateral haustoria of *Monochoria*, a member of the Pontederiaceae (Ono, 1928; Juliano, 1931b). The early stages are similar to those in other plants having a typical Helobial endosperm (Fig. 142G,H). The chalazal chamber remains small and has only about half a dozen nuclei or less. But the micropylar chamber shows active nuclear divisions and soon gives rise to two tubular outgrowths (one on each side of the chalazal chamber) which grow downward and invade the tissues of the chalaza (Fig. 142*I–L*). Subsequently the main body of the chamber also elongates and fuses with the two haustoria to form a continuous mass of endosperm cells with the chalazal chamber still recognizable at the base (Fig. 142*A–F*).

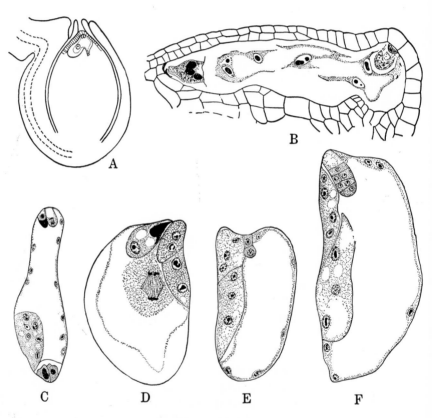

FIG. 141. Modifications of Helobial endosperm as illustrated by *Anthericum ramosum, Ixolirion montanum,* and *Echium plantagineum*. *A, Anthericum,* l.s. ovule showing mature embryo sac; secondary nucleus lies in diverticulum. *B,* same, l.s. nucellus, showing further development of diverticulum and formation of endosperm of Helobial type. (*After Schnarf, 1928b.*) *C, Ixolirion,* embryo sac, showing laterally situated chalazal chamber; only two of the antipodal cells are seen in section. (*After Stenar, 1925.*) *D, Echium,* embryo sac, showing laterally placed chalazal chamber consisting of two binucleate cells. *E,F,* more advanced stages, showing formation of several free nuclei in "central" as well as "lateral" chambers. (*After Svensson, 1925.*)

An interesting deviation, which is of a very different nature from those described above, occurs in *Hyoscyamus niger* (Svensson, 1926). Here the first division of the primary endosperm nucleus takes place in the vicinity of the egg, so that the chalazal chamber is the larger. In the micropylar chamber either four to eight free nuclei are produced before cell formation takes place, or at first there are two longitudinal walls and then some irregular divisions resulting in a small mass of cells. In the chalazal chamber there are repeated

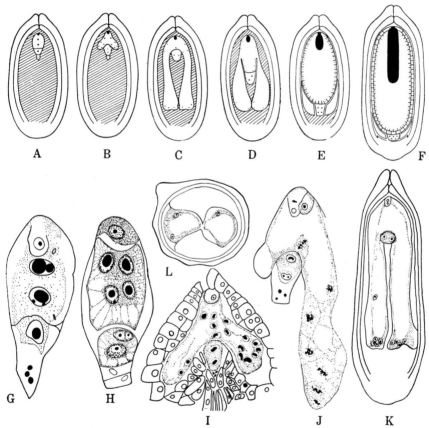

Fig. 142. Development of endosperm in *Monochoria.* *A–F,* diagrams showing stages in development of endosperm. *G, M. vaginalis;* chalazal chamber is uninucleate and micropylar is binucleate. (*After Ono, 1928.*) *H,* more advanced stage, showing four nuclei in micropylar chamber and two in chalazal. (*After Juliano, 1931b.*) *I, M. korasakowii;* initiation of lateral haustoria from micropylar chamber. *J, M. vaginalis,* haustorium visible on one side only. *K, M. korsakowii,* haustoria in advanced stage of development. *L,* cross section of ovule, passing through haustoria. (*After Ono, 1928.*)

free nuclear divisions, resulting in a number of nuclei distributed in the peripheral layer of cytoplasm.   Eventually cell formation occurs here also and it becomes virtually impossible to distinguish the two portions of the endosperm, one derived from the micropylar and the other from the chalazal chamber.

Relationships between Different Types of Endosperm.   We are still in the dark regarding the phylogenetic sequence of the evolution of the various types of endosperm.   There are no doubt transitional forms which interconnect the Nuclear, Helobial, and Cellular types so that the classification is one of convenience rather than of absolute accuracy, but whether the series is to be read from the Nuclear toward the Cellular type or vice versa is not clear.

In a discussion of some of the transitional forms, reference may first be made to *Hypericum* (Stenar, 1938).   The initial divisions of the primary endosperm nucleus are free nuclear (Fig. 143*A–C*), but at the eight-nucleate stage the two uppermost nuclei come to lie in a dense mass of cytoplasm adjacent to the zygote (Fig. 143*D*). Following the next division, four nuclei are seen in the micropylar part of the embryo sac, 11 are distributed in the peripheral layer of cytoplasm, and one becomes delimited in a dense mass of cytoplasm at the chalazal end (Fig. 143*E*).   With further divisions, the endosperm may be said to comprise three more or less distinct regions— micropylar, chalazal, and central.   The first two have a denser cytoplasm and seem to be separated from the third, which has a large central vacuole, by thin plasma membranes (Fig. 143*F–I*). At about the octant stage of the embryo, the distinction between the micropylar and the central portions becomes less sharp, and eventually the two merge into one another.   The chalazal portion, however, forms a coenocytic "cyst," whose upper surface "seems to become hardened and delimited from the rest of the embryo sac" (Swamy, 1946*b*).   At this stage the endosperm of *Hypericum* may, therefore, be mistaken for one of the Helobial type (Palm, 1922), although the developmental studies made by Stenar and Swamy leave no doubt that it is Nuclear.   It does illustrate, however, a kind of transition between the Nuclear and the Helobial types.

Lappula echinata, a member of the Boraginaceae, also shows a condition which may be regarded as intermediate between the Nuclear and the Cellular type.   As reported by Svensson (1923) the first division of the primary endosperm nucleus is followed by the formation of a vertical wall, but since most of the cytoplasm of the embryo sac is aggregated in its micropylar part and the chalazal is occupied by a large vacuole, the wall ends blindly, reaching down to the upper margin of the vacuole only. The next wall also, which is vertical but at right angles to the first, ends similarly and results

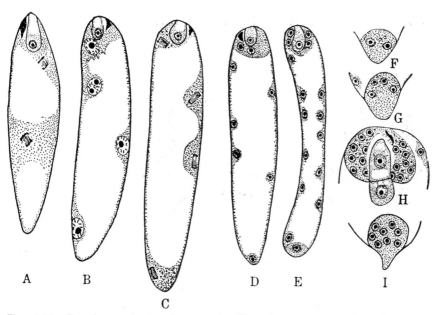

A   B   C   D   E   I

Fig. 143. Development of endosperm in *Hypericum acutum*. *A*, embryo sac showing fertilized egg and endosperm nuclei in division. *B*, embryo sac with four endosperm nuclei. *C*, same, all four nuclei dividing. *D*, eight-nucleate stage of endosperm; two of the nuclei are at upper end and one at lower end of embryo sac. *E*, 16-nucleate stage showing four nuclei at upper end, one at chalazal, and the rest irregularly distributed in middle. *F,G*, chalazal end of embryo sac showing two and four endosperm nuclei respectively. *H*, micropylar part of embryo sac, showing two-celled embryo surrounded by mass of 16 endosperm nuclei; endosperm nucleus on right belongs to central portion. *I*, chalazal part of embryo sac of same age, showing mass of eight endosperm nuclei. (*After Stenar, 1938.*)

in the formation of four cells, all open toward the base. In the following divisions some of the daughter nuclei remain free and pass into the cytoplasmic layer lining the vacuole, while others divide with the accompaniment of walls. Eventually, therefore, the upper part of the embryo sac shows Cellular endosperm and the lower shows Nuclear endosperm.

Some botanists have attempted to relate the occurrence of the Nuclear or the Cellular endosperm to the spatial conditions (*Raumverhältnisse*) in the embryo sac.   According to them, long and narrow embryo sacs generally have a Cellular endosperm, while broad and short embryo sacs have a Nuclear endosperm.   This difference is attributed to the fact that in broad embryo sacs the phragmoplast is unable to form a complete partition across the embryo sac and

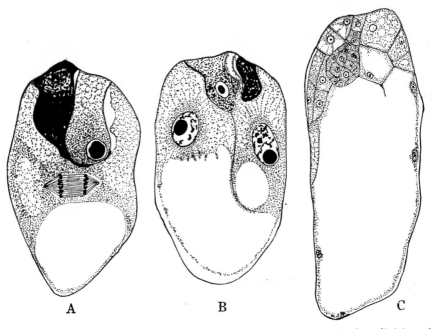

A   B   C

FIG. 144.   Development of endosperm in *Lappula echinata*.   *A,B*, first division of primary endosperm nucleus; partition wall ends blindly, without reaching down to base of embryo sac.   *C*, more advanced stage, showing cell formation in upper part and free nuclei in lower.   (*After Svensson, 1925.*)

soon disappears.   While such an explanation may seem plausible at first sight, it fails to take account of those cases in which the first wall is longitudinal and bisects the embryo sac from pole to pole (Fig. 126*A*), nor can it apply to others in which the Nuclear as well as the Cellular types are both found in the same species and sometimes even in the same ovary (see Svensson, 1925; Sabet, 1931).

V. S. Rao (1938) suggested a correlation between the type of endosperm and the rate of growth of the embryo.   According to his survey, those plants in which growth and differentiation of the embryo take place rapidly have a free nuclear endosperm. Others, in which the growth is slow or the mature seed contains only an undifferentiated embryo, have a Cellular endosperm or show cell formation at a very early stage. Numerous examples can, however, be cited in which there is no such correlation. In *Impatiens*, cited by Rao in support of this theory, the endosperm is not Nuclear as stated by him but Cellular (Dahlgren, 1934*b*).

Finally the question arises as to which of the two types, the Nuclear or the Cellular, is the more primitive and which is the more advanced, but to this we have no definite answer. Coulter and Chamberlain (1903) suggest that the Cellular type is the more primitive, since "even when the endosperm begins with free nuclear division, a rudimentary cell-plate often appears, suggesting derivation from an endosperm in which nuclear division was followed by cell-formation." Schürhoff (1926), Ono (1928), and Glišić (1928) have supported this view. Most other authors, however, consider the reverse derivation, *i.e.*, from the Nuclear to the Cellular type, to be the more plausible (Schnarf, 1929). However, this is still a debatable question, since both types occur side by side in the most primitive orders (*e.g.*, Ranales) as well as the most advanced (*e.g.*, Campanulales).[8b] Further, in the Rubiaceae and Orchidaceae also, which are generally admitted to be among the most highly evolved families, we have a free nuclear endosperm.

Histology of the Endosperm. The cells of the endosperm are usually isodiametric and store large quantities of food materials whose exact nature and proportions vary from one plant to another. As a rule the walls are thin and devoid of pits, but when hemicellulose is the chief food reserve they are greatly thickened and pitted. In such cases they may be more or less homogeneous as in *Phytelephas*, or show a distinct stratification as in *Fritillaria*. The pit canals are sometimes very long and their mouths dilated in a trumpet-shaped manner. Worthy of note also are the plasmodesma strands so clearly seen in the endosperm cells of several plants (Jungers, 1930).

In the grasses and some other plants, the peripheral layer of the endosperm functions like a cambium and produces on its inside a series of thin-walled cells which become packed with starch. As the seed approaches maturity, the outermost layer ceases to divide,

[8b] See in this connection De Vos (1948, 1949) and Stenar (1950).

its cells become filled with aleurone grains, and the walls become slightly thickened.[9]

There is much uncertainty regarding the possible function of this "aleurone layer." According to Haberlandt (1914), its chief function is not that of storage but the secretion of diastase and other enzymes so that the food materials stored in the endosperm may be made available to the embryo in a soluble form. Arber (1934) mentions experiments in which isolated fragments of the aleurone layer were placed on damp filter paper and then covered with a mixture of starch and water. As a control, a similar mixture of starch and water was laid upon damp filter paper without any aleurone layer. After 24 hours the starch grains of the control experiment were still intact while those kept on the aleurone layer had been corroded and were about to fall into pieces.

A different kind of differentiation of the outer layers of the endosperm is seen in *Circaeaster* (Junell, 1931). Here the integument is completely used up during the maturation of the seed, and the peripheral cells of the endosperm become suberized to form a protective layer. In *Crinum* (Tomita, 1931; Merry, 1937), where the ovule is naked (see page 63) and the endosperm ruptures the thin pericarp so as to become completely exposed to the air, the suberization is still more marked, and on being wounded the cells react like a phellogen by undergoing tangential divisions and forming additional layers of cells.

In the Annonaceae, Myristicaceae, and some members of the Palmaceae and Rubiaceae, there is a "ruminate" endosperm. It is said to arise as the result of invaginations of the outer tissues, which penetrate deeper and deeper and eventually appear as dark wavy bands in the mature seeds.[10] In *Psychotria*, recently studied by Fagerlind (1937), it seems that the rumination is not a passive phenomenon but is due to the activity of the endosperm itself, which grows out and fills the ridges arising in the integument in postfertilization stages.

Several workers (see Arber, 1934) have commented on the peculiar

[9] In some plants like *Oryza* (Juliano and Aldama, 1937) there are two or three layers of aleurone cells.

[10] In most books the invaginations are said to be derived from the perisperm, but this needs to be verified by careful developmental studies. As stated in Chap. 3, the nucellus is often so ephemeral that there is no perisperm in postfertilization stages.

appearance of the nuclei in the cells of the endosperm. In the earlier stages of development they appear to be in full activity and their nucleoli are clearly visible, but with the gradual deposition of starch in the cells the nucleoli disappear and the nuclei become "deformed and squeezed out into networks of varying degrees of coarseness" (Brenchley, 1912). Eventually they become completely disorganized or reduced to "amorphous lumps" and in the mature seed even their remains can be made out only with the greatest difficulty. In two recent studies dealing with the endosperm of *Agropyrum*[11] and *Triticum*, Alexandrov and Alexandrova (1938) have confirmed this degeneration of the nuclei and discussed its implications in some detail. According to them, the disorganization of the nuclei occurs first and the deformation follows later, owing to the pressure exerted on them by the surrounding starch grains. They state that "cells with dying nuclei may continue to live for some time," but the coordination between the activities of the cytoplasm and plastids is disturbed. Further, "in fully ripe grains the endosperm represents a physiologically dead tissue." Its death is no disadvantage, however, for the embryo is supposed to be able to secure the food materials necessary for its growth and further development, more easily from a dead rather than a living tissue, and the "dying off of the nuclei in the endosperm cells promotes filling of the grain."

Regarding the final fate of the endosperm, in some plants (*Ricinus, Phoenix, Triticum*, etc.) it forms a permanent storage tissue which persists until the germination of the seed, while in others (*Cucurbita, Pisum, Arachis*, etc.) it is used up by the growing embryo and is no longer seen in the mature seed.[12] Of special interest is *Symplocarpus* (Rosendahl, 1909) in which the embryo "devours" not only the endosperm but also the two integuments, so that it ultimately lies naked inside the wall of the ovary. An even more extreme case is that of *Melocanna bambusioides* (Stapf, 1904), a member of the Bambuseae, in which the embryo dissolves even the ovary wall so that it lies completely naked at maturity.[13]

[11] In this case the place of the degenerated endosperm nuclei is eventually taken by druses of calcium oxalate, one in each cell.

[12] Many seeds, described in taxonomic literature as "exalbuminous," do have small amounts of endosperm. Others, described as "albuminous," may have little or no endosperm but a perisperm derived from the nucellus.

[13] In *Cyanastrum* (Fries, 1919; Nietsch, 1941) the nucellus and endosperm dis-

Xenia. In concluding this discussion of the development and organization of the endosperm, it seems desirable to call attention to the phenomenon known as xenia. This term was coined by Focke (1881) to denote the immediate or direct effect of pollen on the character of the seed or fruit. In practice it is now limited to the appearance of the endosperm only, and the effect, if any, on the somatic tissues lying outside the endosperm has begun to be designated as metaxenia.

To cite an example of xenia, it is well known that certain races of *Zea mays* have yellow (dominant) endosperm, while others have a white (recessive) endosperm. If pollen from the yellow endosperm race is placed on the stigmas of the white endosperm race, one might expect to obtain a hybrid embryo which would show the dominant character of the yellow endosperm when it grows into a mature plant and fruits in the following season. Actually, however, the yellow color appears in the endosperm of the same ovule.

This was very puzzling at first but the explanation became quite evident after Nawaschin's (1898) discovery of double fertilization. Briefly, if a white variety (yy) is pollinated with pollen from a yellow variety (YY), one of the male gametes (Y) unites with the egg (y) and produces a hybrid embryo (Yy) which will behave as a heterozygote for yellow endosperm in the next generation. The second male gamete (Y) unites with the two polar nuclei (y, y) and produces the primary endosperm nucleus (Yyy). Since the latter has a factor for yellowness, the endosperm will naturally show the color, although the ovule belongs to the white parent. In the reciprocal cross, *i.e.*, when pollen from a white-grained variety (yy) is used on a yellow-grained variety (YY), the grains are not white like those of the pollen parent, but yellow like those of the ovule parent. Here xenia would seem to be absent, but this is merely due to the fact that yellowness is dominant over whiteness and therefore the male gamete with a factor for whiteness has no effect on the color. It is thus evident that the same mechanism operates in all cases, but owing to dominance xenia appears only in certain plants and

---

appear during the development of the seed, but the cells in the chalazal part of the ovule, lying just above the vascular bundle, divide actively and form a very prominent tissue which, although loose and possessed of many air spaces, soon becomes filled with fat and starch and serves as a substitute for the endosperm. Fries, who gave it the name "chalazosperm," suggests that it may also function as a sort of food body designed to facilitate the distribution of the seed by animals.

not in others. Indeed, these effects are now so clearly understood that there is hardly any reason for continuing to refer to them by the obscure and somewhat confusing term xenia.

More difficult to interpret is the so-called metaxenia, *i.e.*, the effect of pollen on the maternal structures (seed coat or pericarp) lying outside the embryo sac. The most important work in this connection is that of Swingle (1928) who finds that in the date palm (*Phoenix dactylifera*) the time of maturity of the fruits as well as their size can be made to vary according to the type of pollen used in fertilization.[14] Regarding the nature of the mechanism which enables this to take place, he suggests that possibly the embryo or endosperm or both secrete hormones, or substances analogous to them, which diffuse out into the wall of the seed and fruit and exert a specific influence on them, varying according to the particular male parent used in the cross.

Although it is not inconceivable that pollen may sometimes exercise such an influence on the tissues of the ovary and consequently on the shape, color, or flavor of the fruit, it seems that other factors should also be taken into consideration before arriving at such a conclusion. Differences in size and shape of fruits may also be caused by the number, state of maturity, and genetic constitution of the seeds which develop inside them. To mention a single example, in certain apples self-pollination gives seedless or nearly seedless fruits which are ribbed towards the apex and have a greater height than breadth. On the other hand, the fruits formed after cross-pollination have many seeds, their shape is much more symmetrical, the height and breadth are almost equal, and the ribbing is scarcely noticeable (Crane and Lawrence, 1947). It must, therefore, be concluded that while Swingle's explanation may be correct, we do not yet have a sufficiently extensive or critical set of observations to afford a clear insight into the matter.

Mosaic Endosperm. A very interesting condition, occasionally encountered in some plants, is the lack of uniformity in the tissues of the endosperm. In *Zea mays*, patches of two different colors have sometimes been observed, forming a sort of irregular mosaic pattern, or part of the endosperm is starchy and part is sugary. Webber (1900), who observed an intermingling of red and white color in *Zea mays*, proposed an ingenious explanation to account for

[14] Similar reports have also been made for a few other plants (see Harrison, 1931; Nebel, 1936; Schreiner and Duffield, 1942).

it. To quote his words, "It is not improbable that in some cases the second sperm nucleus enters the embryo sac, but fails to unite with the two polar nuclei. In such cases it may be able to form a spindle and divide separately, the unfecundated embryo sac nucleus formed by the union of the two polar nuclei also dividing separately. If this occurs, there would then be formed in the protoplasm of the embryo sac, nuclei of two distinct characters, one group from the division of the embryo-sac nucleus and the other from the division of the sperm nucleus." Since the nuclei become interspersed during the free nuclear stage of the endosperm, such a hypothesis would account for the occurrence of variegated kernels. Yet another possibility which suggested itself to Webber was that the second sperm nucleus may fuse with only one of the two polar nuclei and that "after their fusion takes place the other nucleus is repelled and develops independently." As in the preceding case, there would thus arise two groups of nuclei—one from a fertilized polar nucleus containing both maternal and paternal elements, the other from an unfertilized polar nucleus containing only the maternal elements.

None of Webber's postulates has found adequate microscopic support up to this time. It is pertinent, however, to call attention to three reports which bear upon this subject.

In a study of *Petunia*, Ferguson (1927) claimed that endosperm formation is initiated independently of fertilization and that the pollen tube discharges its contents into the embryo sac only *after* the two- or four-celled stage of the endosperm. One sperm nucleus then fuses with the egg and the other with the nucleus of the uppermost of the endosperm cells. Consequently the endosperm tissue derived from this cell is triploid and the rest is diploid. She claimed to have counted 21 chromosomes in the micropylar cells of the endosperm and 14 in the chalazal cells.

Bhaduri (1933) reported a similar condition in a strain of *Lycopersicum esculentum*. Here also the polar fusion nucleus is said to divide before fertilization. Two cells result, a small micropylar and a large chalazal. After the discharge of the pollen tube one sperm fertilizes the egg and the other fuses with the nucleus of the micropylar endosperm cell.

The third report concerns *Acorus calamus* (Buell, 1938), in which the pollen tube is said to enter the embryo sac only after the secondary nucleus has divided to form two chambers, a large micropylar and a small chalazal. "Syngamy takes place normally but there is an indication that the second sperm fuses with the nucleus in the micropylar chamber." The endosperm formed by the chalazal chamber would therefore be diploid and that formed by the micropylar chamber would be triploid.

While the peculiar behavior reported by Ferguson, Bhaduri, and Buell would easily account for the presence of an endosperm made up of two different genetical constitutions, none of these reports seems to be dependable. Levan (1937) has shown that what Ferguson believed to be the unopened pollen tube in *Petunia* was really the fertilized egg. He demonstrated that double fertilization takes place in a perfectly normal fashion, and that all the cells of the endosperm, whether micropylar or chalazal, have the normal triploid number of chromosomes. Cooper (1946) has confirmed this, and with this complete refutation of Ferguson's work it seems likely that similar misinterpretations were made by Bhaduri and Buell.

In conclusion it may be stated that although it is possible that sometimes only one of the polar nuclei is fertilized while the other divides independently, this has not so far been cytologically demonstrated. At the same time Webber's first hypothesis of a series of independent divisions of the second male nucleus also seems improbable (cf. East, 1913). More likely, endosperm nuclei with deviating chromosome numbers arise because of disturbed mitoses. The most reasonable explanation for mosaic endosperms would, therefore, lie either in an aberrant behavior of the chromosomes or possibly in somatic mutations (cf. Clark and Copeland, 1940).

References

Afzelius, K. 1924. Embryologische und zytologische Studien in *Senecio* und verwandte Gattungen. Acta Horti Bergiani **8:** 123–219.

Alexandrov, V. G., and Alexandrova, O. G. 1938. On the endosperm nucleus and its role in the filling and ripening of the grains of cereals. Compt. Rend. (Dok.) Acad. des Sci. U.R.S.S. **20:** 613–616.

Anantaswamy Rau, M. 1950. Endosperm in *Cassia tora* Linn. Nature (London) **165:** 157.

Arber, A. 1934. "The Gramineae." Cambridge University Press.

Asplund, E. 1920. Studien über die Entwicklungsgeschichte der Blüten einiger Valerianaceen. K. Svenska Vet.-Akad. Handl. **61**(3): 1–66.

Bacchi, O. 1943. Cytological observations in *Citrus*. III. Megasporogenesis, fertilization, and polyembryony. Bot. Gaz. **105:** 221–225.

Bhaduri, P. N. 1933. A note on the "new type of fertilization" in plants. Current Sci. [India] **2:** 95.

Billings, F. H. 1937. Some new features in the reproductive cytology of angiosperms, illustrated by *Isomeris arborea*. New Phytol. **36:** 301–326.

Brenchley, W. E. 1912. The development of the grain of barley. Ann. Bot. **26:** 903–928.

Brink, R. A., and Cooper, D. C. 1947. The endosperm in seed development. Bot. Rev. **13:** 423–541.

Buell, M. F. 1938. Embryogeny of *Acorus calamus*. Bot. Gaz. **99:** 556–568.

Chiarugi, A. 1925. Embriologia delle Cistaceae. Nuovo Gior. Bot. Ital. N.S. **32:** 223–316.

Clark, F. J., and Copeland, F. C. 1940. Chromosome aberrations in the endosperm of maize. Amer. Jour. Bot. **27:** 247–251.

Condit, I. J. 1932. The structure and development of flowers in *Ficus carica* L. Hilgardia **6:** 443–481.

Cooper, D. C. 1946. Double fertilization in *Petunia*. Amer. Jour. Bot. **33:** 54–57.

Coulter, J. M., and Chamberlain, C. J. 1903. "Morphology of Angiosperms." New York.

Crane, M. B., and Lawrence, W. J. C. 1947. "The Genetics of Garden Plants." London.

Dahlgren, K. V. O. 1916. Zytologische und embryologische Studien über die Reihen Primulales und Plumbaginales. K. Svenska Vet.-Akad. Handl. **56**(4): 1–80.

———. 1930. Zur Embryologie der Saxifragoideen. Svensk Bot. Tidskr. **24:** 429–448.

———. 1934a. Die Embryosackentwicklung von *Echinodorus macrophyllus* und *Sagittaria sagittifolia*. Planta **21:** 602–612.

———. 1934b. Die Embryologie von *Impatiens roylei*. Svensk Bot. Tidskr. **28:** 103–125.

———. 1939. Endosperm- und Embryobildung bei *Zostera marina*. Bot. Notiser 1939, pp. 607–615.

De Vos, M. P. 1948. The development of the ovule and seed in the Hypoxideae. I. *Ianthe* Salisb. Jour. South Afri. Bot. **14:** 159–169.

———. 1949. The development of the ovule and seed in the Hypoxideae. II. The genera *Pauridia* Harv. and *Forbesia* Ecklon. Jour. South Afri. Bot. **15**.

Dixon, H. H. 1946. Evidence for a mitotic hormone: observations on the mitoses of the embryo-sac of *Fritillaria imperialis*. Sci. Proc. Roy. Dublin Soc. **24:** 119–124.

Doll, W. 1927. Beiträge zur Kenntnis der Dipsaceen und Dipsaceen-ähnlicher Pflanzen. Bot. Arch. **17:** 107–146.

Earle, T. T. 1938. Embryology of certain Ranales. Bot. Gaz. **100:** 257–275.

East, E. M. 1913. Xenia and the endosperm of angiosperms. Bot. Gaz. **56:** 217–224.

Ernst, A., and Schmid, E. 1913. Über Blüte und Frucht von *Rafflesia*. Ann. Jard. Bot. Buitenzorg II, **12:** 1–58.

Fagerlind, F. 1937. Embryologische, zytologische und bestäubungsexperimentelle Studien in der Familie Rubiaceae nebst Bemerkungen über einige Polyploiditätsprobleme. Acta Horti Bergiani **11:** 195–470.

Fagerlind, F. 1938. Bau und Entwicklung der floralen Organe von *Helosis cayennensis.* Svensk. Bot. Tidskr. **32:** 139–159.

Ferguson, M. C. 1927. A cytological and genetical study of *Petunia.* I. Bul. Torrey Bot. Club **54:** 657–664.

Focke, W. O. 1881. "Die Pflanzenmischlinge, ein Beitrag zur Biologie der Gewächse." Berlin.

Fries, Th. C. E. 1919. Der Samenbau bei *Cyanastrum* Oliv. Svensk Bot. Tidskr. **13:** 295–304.

Frisendahl, A. 1927. Über die Entwicklung chasmogamer und kleistogamer Blüten bei der Gattung *Elatine.* Acta Hort. Gothoburg. **3:** 99–142.

Frye, T. C. 1902. A morphological study of certain Asclepiadaceae. Bot. Gaz. **34:** 389–413.

Gerassimova, H. 1933. Fertilization in *Crepis capillaris.* Cellule **42:** 103–148.

Glišić, Lj. 1928. Development of the female gametophyte and endosperm in *Haberlea rhodopensis* Friv. Bul. Inst. Jard. Bot. Univ. Belgrade **1:** 1–13.

———. 1932. Zur Entwicklungsgeschichte von *Lathraea squamaria* L. Bul. Inst. Jard. Bot. Univ. Belgrade **2:** 20–56.

Goldberg, B. 1941. Life history of *Peltandra virginica.* Bot. Gaz. **102:** 641–662.

Gore, U. R. 1932. The development of the female gametophyte and embryo in cotton. Amer. Jour. Bot. **19:** 795–807.

Haberlandt, G. 1914. "Physiological Plant Anatomy." Engl. Transl. London.

Hagerup, O. 1947. The spontaneous formation of haploid, polyploid, and aneuploid embryos in some orchids. K. Danske Vidensk. Selsk., Biol. Meddel. **20:** 1–22.

Harrison, G. J. 1931. Metaxenia in cotton. Jour. Agr. Res. **42:** 521–544.

Hewitt, W. C. 1939. Seed development of *Lobelia amoena.* Jour. Elisha Mitchell Sci. Soc. **55:** 63–82.

Johansen, D. A. 1931*a.* Studies on the morphology of the Onagraceae. IV. *Stenosiphon linifolium.* Bul. Torrey Bot. Club **57:** 315–326.

———. 1931*b.* Studies on the morphology of the Onagraceae. V. *Zauschneria latifolia,* typical of a genus characterized by irregular embryology. Ann. N. Y. Acad. Sci. **33:** 1–26.

———. 1931*c.* Studies on the morphology of the Onagraceae. VI. *Anogra pallida.* Amer. Jour. Bot. **18:** 854–863.

Johnson, D. S. 1900. On the endosperm and embryo of *Peperomia pellucida.* Bot. Gaz. **80:** 1–11.

Johri, B. M. 1935. Studies in the family Alismaceae. I. *Limnophyton obtusifolium* Miq. Jour. Indian Bot. Soc. **14:** 49–66.

———. and Maheshwari, P. 1950. The development of the embryo sac, embryo and endosperm in *Helixanthera ligustrina* (Wall.) Dans. (In press.)

Juel, H. O. 1907. Studien über die Entwicklungsgeschichte von *Saxifraga granulata.* Nova Acta R. Soc. Sci. Uppsal. *IV,* **1**(9): 1–41.

Juliano, J. B. 1931*a.* Floral morphology of *Lyonothamnus floribundus.* Bot. Gaz. **91:** 426–438.

———. 1931*b.* Morphological study of the flower of *Monochoria vaginalis* (Burn f.) Presl. Philippine Agr. **20:** 177–186.

Juliano, J. B. and Alcala, P. E.   1933.   Floral morphology of *Musa errans* (Blanco) Teodoro var. *Botoan* Teodoro.   Philippine Agr. **22:** 91–126.

——— and Aldama, M. J.   1937.   Morphology of *Oryza sativa* L.   Philippine Agr. **26:** 1–134.

Junell. S.   1931.   Die Entwicklungsgeschichte von *Circaeaster agrestis*.   Svensk Bot. Tidskr. **25:** 238–270.

Jungers, V.   1930.   Recherches sur les plasmodesmes chez les végétaux.   I. Cellule **40:** 1–82.

———.   1931.   Figures caryocinétiques et cloisonnement du protoplasme dans l'endosperme d'*Iris*.   Cellule **40:** 293–354.

Kadry, A. E. R.   1946.   Embryology of *Cardiospermum halicacabum* L.   Svensk Bot. Tidskr. **40:** 111–126.

Kausik, S. B.   1938a.   Studies in the Proteaceae.   I. Cytology and floral morphology of *Grevillea robusta* Cunn.   Ann. Bot. N.S. **2:** 899–910.

———.   1938b.   Studies in the Proteaceae.   II. Floral anatomy and morphology of *Macadamia ternifolia* F. Muell.   Proc. Indian Acad. Sci. Sect. B. **8:** 45–62.

———.   1938c.   Pollen development and seed formation in *Utricularia coerulea* L.   Beihefte bot. Centbl. **58A:** 365–378.

———.   1940.   A contribution to the embryology of *Enalus acoroides* (L. fil.) Steud.   Proc. Indian Acad. Sci. Sect. B. **11:** 83–99.

———.   1942.   Studies in the Proteaceae.   VII. The endosperm of *Grevillea robusta* Cunn. with special reference to the structure and development of the vermiform appendage.   Proc. Indian Acad. Sci. Sect. B. **16:** 121–140.

Khan, R.   1942.   A contribution to the embryology of *Jussieua repens* Linn.   Jour. Indian Bot. Soc. **21:** 267–282.

Krishna Iyengar, C. V.   1937.   Development of embryo-sac and endosperm-haustoria in some members of the Scrophularineae.   I. An account of *Sopubia delphinifolia* G. Don. and *Alonsoa* sp.   Jour. Indian Bot. Soc. **16:** 99–109.

———.   1939.   Development of the embryo sac and endosperm haustoria in some members of Scrophularineae.   II. *Isoplexis canariensis* Lindl. and *Celsia coromandeliana* Vahl.   Jour. Indian Bot. Soc. **18:** 13–20.

———.   1940.   Development of the embryo sac and endosperm haustoria in some members of the Scrophularineae.   IV. *Vandellia hirsuta* Ham. and *V. scabra* Benth.   Jour. Indian Bot. Soc. **18:** 179–189.

———.   1941.   Development of the embryo sac and endosperm haustoria in *Torenia cordifolia* Roxb. and *T. hirsuta* Benth.   Proc. Natl. Inst. Sci. India **7:** 61–71.

———.   1942.   Development of seed and its nutritional mechanism in Scrophulariaceae.   I. *Rhamphicarpa longiflora* Benth., *Centranthera hispida* Br., and *Pedicularis zeylanica* Benth.   Proc. Natl. Inst. Sci. India **8:** 249–261.

Lagerberg, T.   1909.   Studien über die Entwicklungsgeschichte und systematischen Stellung von *Adoxa moschatellina* L.   K. Svenska Vet.-Akad. Handl. **44**(4): 1–86.

Langdon, L. M.   1934.   Embryogeny of *Carya* and *Juglans*, a comparative study.   Bot. Gaz. **96:** 93–117.

Levan, A.   1937.   Eine erbliche Anomalie der Samenanlage bei *Petunia*.   Bot. Notiser. 1937, pp. 35–55.

Longo, B. 1909. Osservazioni e ricerche sul *Ficus carica*. Ann. di Bot. 7: 235–256.

Maheshwari, P. 1934. The Indian mango. Current Sci. [India] 3: 97–98.

—— and Singh, Bahadur. 1950. The embryology of *Macrosolen cochinchinensis* Van Tieghem. (In press.)

Mauritzon, J. 1933. "Studien über die Embryologie der Familien Crassulaceae und Saxifragaceae." Diss. Lund.

——. 1934. Die Endosperm- und Embryoentwicklung einiger Acanthaceen. Lunds Univ. Årsskr. N.F. Avd. II, 30(5): 1–42.

——. 1939. Über die Embryologie von *Marcgravia*. Bot. Notiser 1939, pp. 249–255.

McKay, J. W. 1947. Embryology of pecan. Jour. Agr. Res. 74: 263–283.

Mendes, A. J. T. 1941. Cytological observations in *Coffea*. VI. Embryo and endosperm development in *Coffea arabica* L. Amer. Jour. Bot. 28: 784–789.

Merry, J. 1937. Formation of periderm in the endosperm of *Crinum asiaticum*. Papers Mich. Acad. Sci., Arts, and Letters 22: 159–164.

Mohrbutter, C. 1936. Embryologische Studien an Loganiaceen. Planta 26: 64–80.

Nast, C. G. 1935. Morphological development of the fruit of *Juglans regia*. Hilgardia 9: 345–381.

——. 1941. The embryogeny and seedling morphology of *Juglans regia* L. Lilloa 6: 163–205.

Nawaschin, S. 1898. Resultate einer Revision der Befruchtungsvorgänge bei *Lilium martagon* und *Fritillaria tenella*. Bull. Acad. Imp. des Sci. St. Petersburg 9(4): 377–382.

Nebel, B. R. 1936. Metaxenia in apples. Jour. Hered. 27: 345–349.

Némec, B. 1910. "Das Problem der Befruchtungsvorgänge und andere zytologischen Fragen." Berlin.

Nietsch, H. 1941. Zur systematischen Stellung von *Cyanastrum*. Österr. Bot. Ztschr. 90: 31–52.

Oehler, E. 1927. Entwicklungsgeschichtlich-cytologische Untersuchungen an einigen saprophytischen Gentianaceen. Planta 3: 641–733.

Ono, T. 1928. Embryologische Studien an einigen Pontederiaceen. Sci. Rpt. Tôhoku Imp. Univ. IV. Biol. 3: 405–415.

——. 1929. Embryologie der Liliaceae, mit besonderer Rücksicht auf die Endospermbildung. I. Melanthioideae und Aletroideae. Sci. Rpt. Tôhoku Imp. Univ. IV. Biol. 4: 381–393.

Pace, L. 1909. The gametophytes of *Calopogon*. Bot. Gaz. 48: 126–137.

Paetow, W. 1931. Embryologische Untersuchungen an Taccaceen, Meliaceen und Dilleniaceen. Planta 14: 441–470.

Palm, B. 1922. Das Endosperm von *Hypericum*. Svensk Bot. Tidskr. 16: 60–68.

Poddubnaja-Arnoldi, W. 1931. Ein Versuch der Anwendung der embryologischen Methode bei der Lösung einiger systematischer Fragen. Beihefte. bot. Centbl. 48B: 141–237.

Rao, V. S. 1938. The correlation between embryo type and endosperm type. Ann. Bot. N.S. 2: 535–536.

Rauch, K. V. 1936. Cytologisch-embryologische Untersuchungen an *Scurrula atropurpurea* Dans. und *Dendrophthoe pentandra* Miq. Ber. schweiz. bot. Gesell. **45**: 5–61.

Rocén, T. 1927. "Zur Embryologie der Centrospermen." Diss. Uppsala.

Rosén, W. 1940. Notes on the embryology of *Globularia vulgaris* L. Bot. Notiser 1940, pp. 253–261.

Rosendahl, C. O. 1909. Embryo sac development and embryology of *Symplocarpus foetidus*. Minn. Bot. Studies **4**: 1–9.

Rutishauser, A. 1937. Entwicklungsgeschichtliche Untersuchungen an *Thesium rostratum*. Mitt. naturf. Gesell. Schaffhausen **13**: 25–47.

Sabet, Y. S. 1931. Development of the embryo sac in *Calotropis procera*, with special reference to endosperm formation. Ann. Bot. **45**: 503–518.

Schaeppi, H., and Steindl, F. 1942. Blütenmorphologische und embryologische Untersuchungen an Loranthoideen. Vrtljschr. naturf. Gesell. Zürich **87**: 301–372.

Schnarf, K. 1928a. Über die Endospermentwicklung bei *Ornithogalum*. Österr. bot. Ztschr. **77**: 173–177.

———. 1928b. Über das Embryosackhaustorium bei *Anthericum*. Österr. bot. Ztschr. **77**: 287–291.

———. 1929. "Embryologie der Angiospermen." Berlin.

———. 1931. Ein Beitrag zur Kenntnis der Samenentwicklung der Gattung *Cochlospermum*. Österr. bot. Ztschr. **80**: 45–50.

——— and Wunderlich, R. 1939. Zur vergleichenden Embryologie der Liliaceae-Asphodeloideae. Flora **33**: 297–327.

Schreiner, E. J., and Duffield, J. W. 1942. Metaxenia in an oak species cross. Jour. Hered. **33**: 97–98.

Schulle, H. 1933. Zur Entwicklungsgeschichte von *Thesium montanum* Ehrh. Flora **27**: 140–184.

Schürhoff, P. N. 1915. Amitosen von Riesenkernen im Endosperm von *Ranunculus acer*. Jahrb. f. wiss. Bot. **55**: 499–519.

———. 1926. "Die Zytologie der Blütenpflanzen." Stuttgart.

Scott, F. M. 1944. Cytology and microchemistry of nuclei in developing seed of *Echinocystis macrocarpa*. Bot. Gaz. **105**: 329–338.

Sharp, L. W. 1912. The orchid embryo sac. Bot. Gaz. **54**: 373–335.

Singh, Bahadur. 1950. The embryology of *Dendrophthoe falcata* (Linn. fil.) Ettingshausen. Proc. 37th. Indian Sci. Cong. Bot. Sect.

Stapf, O. 1904. On the fruit of *Melocanna bambusoides* Trin., an endospermless, viviparous genus of Bambuseae. Trans. Linn. Soc. London II Bot., **6**: 401.

Stenar, H. 1925. "Embryologische Studien I and II. I. Zur Embryologie der Columniferen. II. Die Embryologie der Amaryllideen." Diss. Uppsala.

———. 1928a. Zur Embryologie der Asphodeline-Gruppe. Ein Beitrag zur systematischen Stellung der Gattungen *Bulbine* und *Paradisea*. Svensk Bot. Tidskr. **22**: 145–159.

———. 1928b. Zur Embryologie der *Veratrum*- und *Anthericum*-Gruppe. Bot. Notiser 1928, pp. 357–378.

———. 1935. Embryologische Beobachtungen über *Scheuchzeria palustris* L. Bot. Notiser 1935, pp. 78–86.

Stenar, H. 1938. Das Endosperm bei *Hypericum acutum* Moench. Bot. Notiser 1938, pp. 515–527.

——. 1950. Studien über das Endosperm bei *Galtonia candicans* (Bak.) Decne und anderen Scilloideen. Acta Horti Bergiani **15**: 169–184.

Stolt, K. A. H. 1921. Zur Embryologie der Gentianaceen und Menyanthaceen. K. Svenska Vet.-Akad. Handl. **61**(14): 1–56.

Subramanyam, K. 1948. An embryological study of *Melastoma malabathricum*. Jour. Indian Bot. Soc. **27**: 1–9.

——. 1949. An embryological study of *Lobelia pyramidalis* Wall., with special reference to the mechanism of nutrition of the embryo in the family Lobeliaceae. New Phytol.: **48**: 365–374.

Svensson, H. G. 1923. Om endospermet hos *Lappula*. Svensk. Bot. Tidskr. **17**: 387–388.

——. 1925. "Zur Embryologie der Hydrophyllaceen, Borraginaceen und Heliotropiaceen." Diss. Uppsala.

——. 1926. Zytologische-embryologische Solanaceenstudien I. Über die Samenentwicklung von *Hyoscyamus niger* L. Svensk Bot. Tidskr. **20**: 420–434.

Swamy, B. G. 1946a. Development of endosperm in *Zephyranthes andersonii* Baker. Proc. Natl. Inst. Sci. India **12**: 187–190.

——. 1946b. Endosperm in *Hypericum mysorense* Heyne. Ann. Bot. N.S. **9**: 165–169.

——. 1947. On the life history of *Vanilla planifolia*. Bot. Gaz. **108**: 449–456.

Swingle, W. T. 1928. Metaxenia in the date palm. Jour. Hered. **19**: 257–268.

Täckholm, G. 1915. Beobachtungen über die Samenentwicklung einiger Onagraceen. Svensk Bot. Tidskr. **9**: 294–361.

Tomita, K. 1931. Über die Entwicklung des nackten Embryos von *Crinum latifolium* L. Sci. Rpt. Tôhoku Imp. Univ. IV. Biol. **6**: 163–169.

Treub, M. 1885. Observations sur les Loranthacées. I. Developpement dans les sacs embryonnaires dans le *Loranthus sphaerocarpus*. II. Embryogénie du *Loranthus sphaerocarpus*. Ann. Jard. Bot. Buitenzorg **2**: 54–76.

Walker, R. I. 1947. Megasporogenesis and embryo development in *Tropaeolum majus* L. Bul. Torrey Bot. Club **74**: 240–249.

Wanscher, J. H. 1939. Contribution to the cytology and life history of apple and pear. Roy. Vet. and Agr. Coll. Copenhagen Yearbook 1939, pp. 21–70.

Webber, H. J. 1900. Xenia, or the immediate effect of pollen in maize. U.S. Dept. Agr. Div. Veg. Path. and Physiol. Bul. **22**.

Witmer, S. W. 1937. Morphology and cytology of *Vallisneria spiralis* L. Amer. Midland Nat. **18**: 309–327.

Wunderlich, R. 1937. Zur vergleichenden Embryologie der Liliaceae-Scilloideae. Flora **32**: 48–90.

Wylie, R. B., and Yocom, A. E. 1923. The endosperm of *Utricularia*. Univ. Iowa Studies Nat. Hist. **10**(2): 3–18.

Zweifel, R. 1939. "Cytologisch-embryologische Untersuchungen an *Balanophora abbreviata* Blume und *B. indica* Wall." Diss. Zürich.

CHAPTER 8

THE EMBRYO[1]

After syngamy the zygote undergoes a period of rest during which the large vacuoles originally present in the upper part of the cell gradually disappear and the cytoplasm assumes a fairly homogeneous appearance. Vacuoles may appear once again when the cell begins to grow in preparation for the first division, but these are more or less uniformly distributed and are not restricted to any special portion.

The resting period of the zygote varies with different species and is to some extent dependent on environmental conditions. In general the primary endosperm nucleus divides first and the zygote divides shortly afterwards. In *Theobroma cacao* (Cheesman, 1927) the primary endosperm nucleus divides 4 to 5 days after fertilization and the zygote 14 to 15 days after fertilization. In the fertile banana "Rodoe Clamp" (White, 1928), *Carya illinoensis* (McKay, 1947), and *Epidendrum prismatocarpum* (Swamy, 1948) the zygote remains undivided for about 6 weeks, and in *Viscum album* (Pisek, 1923) for about 8 weeks after fertilization. In *Colchicum autumnale* (Heiman-Winawer, 1919) fertilization takes place in autumn and endosperm nuclei are formed soon after, but the zygote remains dormant for a period of 4 to 5 months during the winter.

The shortest resting periods occur in the Compositae and Gramineae. In *Crepis capillaris* (Gerassimova, 1933), for example, the primary endosperm nucleus undergoes its first division within 4 to 7 hours after pollination and its second division 1 to 3 hours later, while the first division of the zygote takes place 5 to 10 hours after pollination. In *Oryza sativa* (Noguchi, 1929) the first division of the zygote occurs about 6 hours after fertilization and 18 hours later the embryo consists of four to seven cells. After 4 days it begins to differentiate into the various body regions and in 10 days it is completely mature.

The data on *Hordeum distichon palmella* (Pope, 1937) give the

[1] For a detailed treatment of the various modes of embryonal development met with in the angiosperms, reference should be made to Souèges (1934*a*, 1937*a*, 1934–1939).

sequence of events from the time of pollination to the first division of the zygote. These data are given in the accompanying table. In some plants the first division of the zygote and that of the primary endosperm nucleus occur at approximately the same time. As examples may be cited *Alisma, Damasonium* (Dahlgren, 1928),

Hordeum distichon palmella

Time elapsed after pollination	Growth of pollen tube	Development of embryo	Development of endosperm
5 min..........	Pollen germinated		
10 min..........	Male gametes inside pollen tube		
45 min..........	Entry of pollen tube into embryo sac	One male gamete in contact with egg	Other male gamete in contact with polar nuclei
5 hr..........		Male nucleus forming a sector of the egg nucleus	Male nucleus and polar nuclei in process of fusion
6 hr..........		Male sector of zygote nucleus becoming more and more diffuse	First division of primary endosperm nucleus
10 hr..........			Second division of primary endosperm nucleus
13 hr..........		Prophase of first division of zygote	Four endosperm nuclei
15 hr..........		First division of zygote nearing completion	Eight endosperm nuclei

Cuscuta (Smith, 1934), *Echinodorus* (Dahlgren, 1934) and *Taraxacum kok-saghys* (Cooper and Brink, 1949). Less frequently the zygote may divide before the primary endosperm nucleus as in *Cynomorium* (Steindl, 1945), *Restio* (Borwein *et al.*, 1949), and some species of *Allium* (Weber, 1929). In any case eventually the development of the endosperm proceeds at a quicker rate and surpasses that of the embryo.[2]

[2] *Oxybaphus nyctagineus* (Cooper, 1949) is an exception to this. At first nuclear divisions in the endosperm keep pace with cell divisions in the embryo, but after

The second table summarizes the time relations of the divisions in the embryo and endosperm of *Taraxacum kok-saghys* (Poddubnaja-Arnoldi and Dianowa, 1934), where at least for the first few days both develop more or less concurrently and neither has any appreciable advantage over the other.

In all cases the first division of the zygote is followed by wall formation. This is in sharp contrast with the condition in the

Taraxacum kok-saghys

Time elapsed after pollination	Pollen tube growth	Development of embryo	Development of endosperm
15 min............	Entry of pollen tube into embryo sac		
45 min...........	Discharge of pollen tube and approach of male gametes toward egg and secondary nucleus		
1 hr., 15 min.....		Syngamy	Triple fusion
3 hr., 50 min.....			First division of primary endosperm nucleus
5 hr.............		First division of zygote	
6 hr., 15 min.		Two-celled proembryo	Two-nucleate endosperm
8 hr., 15 min.		Four-celled embryo	Four-nucleate endosperm
24 hr., 45 min....		Several-celled proembryo	Multicellular endosperm

gymnosperms, where the first few divisions are almost always free nuclear. The only reported instance of a free nuclear embryo in

the 64-nucleate stage the embryo becomes more aggressive and mitoses occur more slowly in the endosperm.

Pope (1943) suggests that the extra number of chromosomes and genes in the primary endosperm nucleus may be a factor contributing to the more rapid growth of the endosperm as compared with that of the embryo. This is an interesting suggestion, but even in the Onagraceae, where the zygote and the primary endosperm nucleus have the same genetic constitution, the development of the endosperm proceeds at a much quicker rate.

angiosperms is that of *Moringa oleifera*, in which Rutgers (1923) claimed that wall formation commenced only after the 16-nucleate stage. Puri (1941) has shown, however, that the free nuclear embryo of Rutgers was really a micropylar accumulation of endosperm nuclei, while the real embryo, which is formed quite normally, was entirely overlooked by him.[3]

In the earlier stages of development there are no fundamental differences between the embryos of the dicotyledons and those of the monocotyledons. However, since the mature embryos are so markedly different in the two groups, they will be treated separately in the following account.

DICOTYLEDONS

Except in a very few species, which will be considered later, the first division of the zygote is almost always followed by the laying down of a transverse wall. Of the two cells thus formed, the one which lies towards the interior of the embryo sac is called the terminal cell and the other the basal cell. In the next stage the terminal cell may divide transversely or longitudinally. The basal cell usually undergoes a transverse division, but in some plants it remains undivided and becomes hypertrophied to form a large vesicular structure.

The French embryologist Souèges, who is the chief authority on the development of the embryo in angiosperms, considers the mode of origin of the four-celled proembryo and the contribution made by each of these cells to the body regions of the mature embryo as the most important aids in a classification of the embryonal types. Following him, Schnarf (1929) and Johansen (1945) have recognized five principal types of embryos among the dicotyledons. These may be distinguished from one another as follows:

I. The terminal cell of the two-celled proembryo divides by a longitudinal wall—

(i) The basal cell plays only a minor part or none in the subsequent development of the embryo......Crucifer type[4]

[3] The free nuclear divisions of the zygote reported in *Ficus* (Tischler, 1913) and *Ruta* (Cappaletti, 1929) are in the nature of abnormalities which need not be considered here.

[4] Johansen (1945) prefers the term "Onagrad type" as the embryo of the Onagraceae is simpler and more typical than that of *Capsella* (Cruciferae), usually described in textbooks.

(ii) The basal and terminal cells both contribute to the development of the embryo.............Asterad type

II. The terminal cell of the two-celled proembryo divides by a transverse wall—

    1. The basal cell plays only a minor part or none in the subsequent development of the embryo—

        (i) The basal cell usually forms a suspensor of two or more cells...............................Solanad type

        (ii) The basal cell undergoes no further division, and the suspensor, if present, is always derived from the terminal cell.............................Caryophyllad type

    2. The basal and terminal cells both contribute to the development of the embryo.................Chenopodiad type

Crucifer Type. As mentioned in Chap. 1, the embryo of *Capsella bursa-pastoris* was among the first to receive detailed attention. Subsequent to the classical researches of Hanstein (1870) and Famintzin (1879), Souèges (1914, 1919) has made a still more thorough study of its embryogeny. The first division of the zygote is transverse resulting in a basal cell cb and a terminal cell ca (Fig. 145A,B). The former divides transversely and the latter divides longitudinally, resulting in a $\perp$-shaped proembryo composed of four cells (Fig. 145C–E). Each of the two terminal cells now divides by a vertical wall lying at right angles to the first, so as to result in a quadrant stage (Fig. 145J). The quadrant cells in turn become partitioned by a transverse wall, so as to form octants (Fig. 145K, L). Of these the lower four are destined to give rise to the stem tip and cotyledons and the upper four to the hypocotyl. All the eight cells divide periclinally (Fig. 145M,N). The outer derivatives form the dermatogen, while the inner ones undergo further divisions to give rise to the periblem and plerome initials (Fig. 145 O–Q).

Meanwhile, the two upper cells, ci and cm, of the four-celled proembryo (Fig. 145D) divide to form a row of 6 to 10 suspensor cells (Fig. 145F–K) of which the uppermost cell v becomes swollen and vesicular and probably serves a haustorial function. The lowest cell h functions as the "hypophysis" (Fig. 145N). Although at first similar in shape to the other cells of the suspensor, it soon becomes somewhat rounded at the lower end and divides transversely to form two daughter cells (Fig. 145O), each of which undergoes two divisions by walls which are oriented at right angles to one another. Of the resulting eight cells, the lower four form the initials of the root cortex and the upper four give rise to the root cap and the root epidermis.

At the same time further divisions take place in the embryo proper, especially at two points in the lower tier which are destined to form the cotyledons. At this stage the embryo appears more or

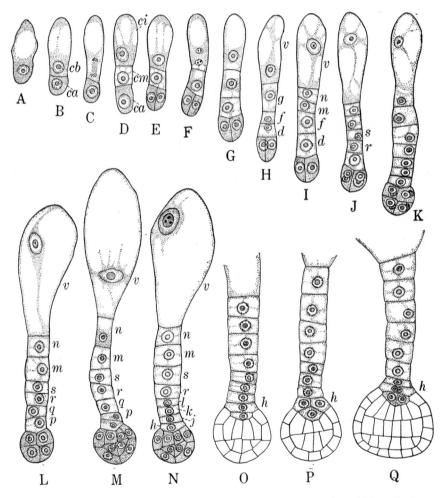

Fig. 145. Development of embryo in *Capsella bursa-pastoris*. (*After Souèges, 1914, 1919.*)

less cordate in longitudinal section (Fig. 146*A*,*B*).   The hypocotyl as well as the cotyledons soon elongate in size, mostly by transverse divisions of their cells (Fig. 146*C*,*D*).   During further development the ovule becomes curved like a horseshoe and the growing cotyledons also conform to this shape for spatial reasons (Fig. 146*E*,*F*).

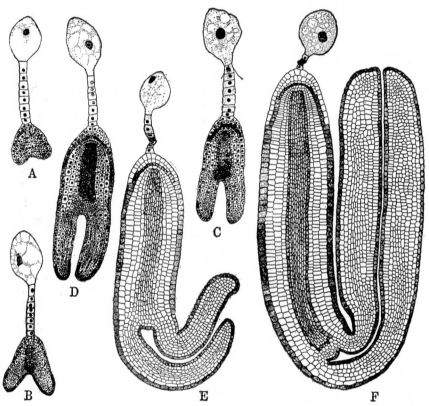

Fig. 146. Older stages in development of embryo of *Capsella bursa-pastoris*. (*After Schaffner, 1906*.)

Although *Capsella* has been used for over fifty years to illustrate the embryogeny of the dicotyledons, the embryos of the Onagraceae are of a simpler and more uniform type and *Ludwigia palustris* (Souèges, 1935*a*) may be used as an illustration.   The first division of the zygote is transverse (Fig. 147*A*) after which the terminal cell *ca* divides longitudinally to form two juxtaposed cells and the basal cell *cb* divides transversely to form the two cells *ci* and *m* (Fig.

147*B*). This is the four-celled stage of the proembryo. At the third cell generation, the two cells of the tier *ca* divide by a vertical wall, at right angles to the first, to give rise to the quadrant stage (Fig. 147*C*). The quadrants *q* divide transversely to produce a group of eight cells called the octants (*l* and *l'*) and *ci* gives rise to the two suspensor cells *n* and *n'* (Fig. 147*D,E*). The wall in the middle cell *m*, which functions as the hypophysis, is curved and joined on both sides to the transverse wall which originally separated *ca* from *cb*, and now separates the tiers *l'* and *m* (Fig. 147*F*).

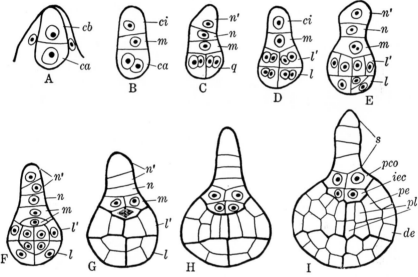

Fig. 147. Development of embryo in *Ludwigia palustris*. (*After Souèges, 1935a.*)

Of the two daughter cells formed from *m*, the lower, which is lenticular in shape, gives rise to the initials of the root tip while the upper gives rise to the root cap. The cells of the tier *l* and *l'* give rise to the cotyledons and the stem tip. Figure 147*G–I* shows some of the stages in the differentiation of the dermatogen *de*, periblem *pe*, plerome *pl*, the cells *pco* which are destined to form the root cap, and the cells *iec*, which are destined to form the root cortex.

Asterad Type. *Lactuca sativa* (Jones, 1927) may be used as an illustration of the Asterad type which has been based on the studies of Carano (1915) and Souèges (1920*c*) on various members of the Compositae. The four-celled proembryo consists of two juxtaposed cells derived from the terminal cell ca and two superposed cells ci and m derived from the basal cell cb (Fig. 148A–C). In the following stage, each of the four cells divides again so that the terminal tier now comprises the quadrant cells q, the middle tier comprises the two juxtaposed cells at m, and ci divides transversely to form the daughter cells n and n' (Fig. 148D). Thus the upper three tiers of this stage owe their origin to the basal cell cb, and the lowest tier of four cells to the terminal cell ca of the two-celled proembryo. The four cells of the tier q divide to form the octant stage, the walls segmenting the quadrant cells being oriented more or less diagonally; the two cells of the tier m undergo a vertical division to give rise to four cells lying directly above the octants; n also divides by a vertical wall; and n' divides by a transverse wall to form o and p

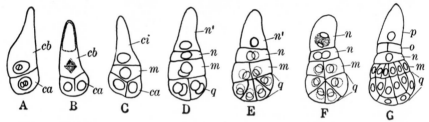

Fig. 148.   Development of embryo in *Lactuca sativa*.   (*After Jones, 1927*.)

(Fig. 148E–G). At the same time tangential walls are laid down in the tiers q and m to cut off an outer layer of dermatogen cells from the inner cells which undergo further divisions to give rise to the periblem and plerome (Fig. 148G). Regarding further development, the cell p gives rise to a suspensor consisting of a variable number of cells; o to the root cap and dermatogen of the root; n to the remaining part of the root tip; m to the hypocotyledonary region; and q to the cotyledons and stem tip.

Geum urbanum (Souèges, 1923b) offers a significant variation from the above scheme in the early demarcation of a special cell called the epiphysis initial.[5] After the two-celled stage (Fig. 149A) the first wall in ca is markedly oblique, resulting in two unequal cells a and b (Fig. 149B–C). Of these, a divides to cut off a wedge-shaped cell e, which is called the epiphysis (Fig. 149D,E). At the same time the middle cell m divides vertically and ci divides transversely, so that there are now four tiers of cells in all, designated as q, m, n,

[5] For further information on the epiphysis, see Souèges (1934b).

and n', lying directly above the epiphysis initial e (Fig. 149F). Of these, q gives rise to the cotyledonary region, m to the hypocotyl, n or one of its derivatives to the hypophysis and a part of the suspensor, and n' to the greater portion of the suspensor. Some of the stages in development are shown in Fig. 149G–L.

An epiphysis initial has also been reported in *Fragaria* and *Viola* (Souèges, 1935b, 1937c). The former is essentially similar to *Geum*, but the latter shows some differences in that the derivatives

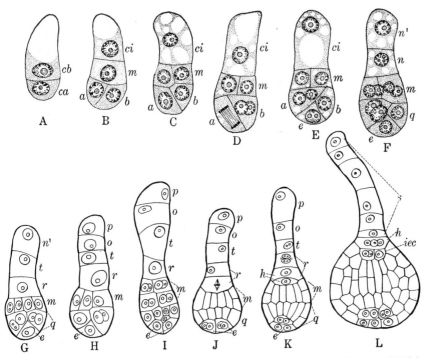

Fig. 149. Development of embryo in *Geum urbanum*. (*After Souèges, 1923b*.)

of the tier q, lying just above the epiphysis, produce not only the cotyledonary region but also the lower portion of the hypocotyl, while the tier m contributes to the upper portion of the hypocotyl and the root. A suspensor is virtually absent, as the uppermost tier ci is devoted to the formation of the root cap.

Solanad Type. Souèges (1920b, 1922) and Bhaduri (1936) have studied a number of species of the Solanaceae, of which *Nicotiana* may be described here as an example. The first division of the zygote is transverse (Fig. 150*A,B*). The terminal cell *ca* and the basal cell *cb* both divide transversely to give rise to a four-celled proembryo (Fig. 150*C–F*). The four tiers may be designated from below upward as *l, l', m,* and *ci*. Now *l* and *l'* divide by vertical

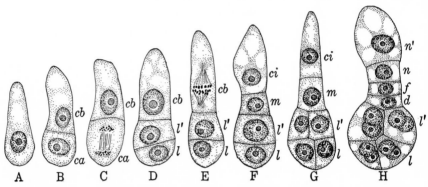

FIG. 150.   Development of embryo in *Nicotiana*.   (*After Souèges, 1922.*)

walls oriented at right angles to each other to give rise to octants, while *m* and *ci* divide transversely to produce *d, f, n,* and *n'* (Fig. 150 *G–H*). By subsequent divisions the tier *l* gives rise to the cotyledonary portion, *l'* to the hypocotyl and to the periblem and

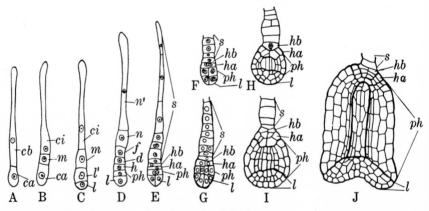

FIG. 151.   Development of embryo in *Lobelia amoena*.   (*After Hewitt, 1939.*)

plerome of the root, and *d* to the root tip.   The remaining cells *f, n,* and *n'* produce the suspensor.

Hewitt (1939) has recently given a very full account of the embryogeny of *Lobelia amoena*, which also belongs to the Solanad type.

After the two-celled stage (Fig. 151A) the basal cell cb divides transversely to produce ci and m (Fig. 151B) and the terminal cell divides to produce l and l' (Fig. 151C). Following this four-celled stage, m and ci divide to produce the cells $d, f, n,$ and n' (Fig. 151D), each of which may divide again, resulting in a suspensor which is about 8 to 12 cells long. At the same time the cell l' segments into ph and h (Fig. 151D) after which l and ph divide by longitudinal walls oriented at right angles to each other, and h divides by a transverse wall. Two juxtaposed cells are thus produced from l and ph and two superposed cells (ha and hb) from h (Fig. 151E). The embryo proper (excluding the suspensor cells) now consists of four tiers, $l,$ $ph, ha,$ and hb. In l and ph the next division is vertical and in a plane at right angles to the first division. At the same time ha also divides by a vertical wall, resulting in two tiers of four cells each at l and ph, one tier of two cells at ha, and one of a single cell hb (Fig. 151F). In the cells of the apical tier l, the next division walls are diagonal, followed by periclinal divisions which cut off the dermatogen. The cells of the tier ph divide periclinally; the outer cells form the dermatogen, and the inner undergo further longitudinal divisions to form the periblem and plerome initials of the stem (Fig. 151G). The two cells of the tier ha give rise to a single semicircular layer of cells which contributes to the periblem, the dermatogen, and a part of the root cap (Fig. 151H–J). The cell hb divides only at a comparatively late stage, at first by a transverse wall and then by a vertical wall in each of the daughter cells. The upper derivatives form a part of the root cap, which is supplemented on all sides by a cell from the tier ha and in some cases by extra cells cut off from the dermatogen of tier ph. A peculiarity of the suspensor is the widening and vertical divisions of two or three of its cells lying just above the embryo proper (Fig. 151H).

In *Sherardia* (Souèges, 1925), a member of the Rubiaceae, the four-celled proembryo arises in the same way as in *Nicotiana* and *Lobelia*. The first division in the cells l and l' (Fig. 152A) may be either transverse or vertical, but m and ci always divide transversely (Fig. 152B). The eight-celled stage may thus comprise six, seven (Fig. 152D), or eight (Fig. 152C) tiers of cells. Normally the derivatives of l form the cotyledonary region and those of l' form the hypocotyl; m and ci give rise to a massive suspensor, which is filamentous towards the apical end but is composed of a number of large vesicular cells at the basal end (Fig. 152E–G). Presumably the last cell of the suspensor functions as a hypophysis and contributes to a portion of the root tip.

Chenopodiad Type. *Chenopodium bonus-henricus* (Souèges, 1920*a*) is similar to *Nicotiana* in having a four-celled proembryo

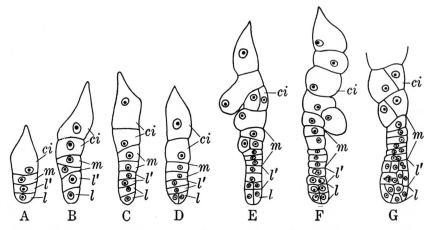

Fig. 152.   Development of embryo in *Sherardia arvensis.* (*After Souèges, 1925.*)

consisting of the cells *l*, *l'*, *m*, and *ci* arising by a transverse division of *ca* and *cb* (Fig. 153*A–C*). During the course of further development *l*, *l'*, and *m* become segmented into four cells each by the

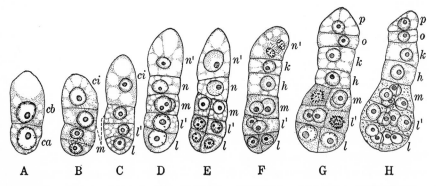

Fig. 153.   Development of embryo in *Chenopodium bonus-henricus.* (*After Souèges, 1920a.*)

laying down of two vertical walls oriented at right angles to each other, while *ci* divides transversely to form *n* and *n'* and then the four cells *h*, *k*, *o*, and *p* (Fig. 153*D–H*). During further development the tier l gives rise to the cotyledons, l' to the lower part of the hypocotyl, and m to the upper part of the hypocotyl. The cells originating from ci form the suspensor except the last cell h, which functions as the hypophysis and contributes to the root tip.

Beta vulgaris (Artschwager and Starrett, 1933), which is also a member of the Chenopodiaceae, is similar to *Chenopodium* except for a few minor details. Following the four-celled stage (Fig. 154A), each cell of the proembryo divides again. The cell l always divides by a vertical wall (Fig. 154B–D); l' may divide either transversely (Fig. 154C) or vertically (Fig. 154B,D), the latter being the more frequent condition; m may also divide either transversely (Fig. 154B–E) or vertically (Fig. 154F); and ci divides transversely (Fig.

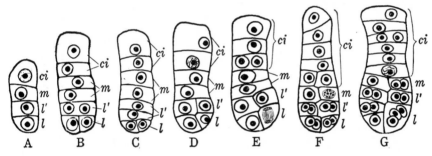

Fig. 154. Development of embryo in *Beta vulgaris*. (*After Artschwager and Starrett, 1933.*)

154B,C). Thus, depending on the direction of the partition walls in l' and m the eight-celled embryo may comprise five, six (Fig. 154D), or seven tiers (Fig. 154E). During the next division, which gives rise to the 16-celled stage, the walls are so arranged as to produce about eight tiers of cells (Fig. 154F). The authors emphasize that no strict law governs the sequence of cell divisions, although "a certain balance seems to be maintained so that the final product is remarkably uniform."

The four-celled proembryo of *Myosotis hispida* (Souèges, 1923a) also originates in the same way as that of *Chenopodium* and *Beta*, but the cell l divides by two oblique walls so as to form a wedge-shaped epiphysis initial e as in *Geum*, already described under the Asterad type (Fig. 155 A–C). The epiphysis gives rise to the stem tip, while the other cells produced by the tier l produce the cotyledons. The tiers l' and m form the hypocotyl; and ci gives rise to the daughter cells n and n', of which the former functions as a hypophysis and gives rise to the root cap and periblem initials of the root, and the latter gives rise to a short suspensor (Fig. 155D,E).

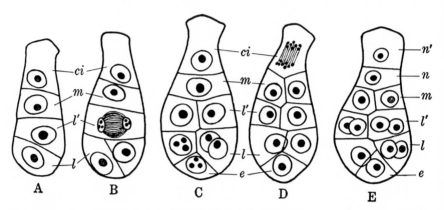

FIG. 155.   Development of embryo in *Myosotis hispida*.   (*After Souèges, 1923a.*)

Caryophyllad Type.   The embryo of *Sagina procumbens* (Souèges, 1924a), which is the most typical of all the forms described under the Caryophyllad type, is characterized by the fact that here the basal cell cb remains undivided and forms a large vesicular struc-

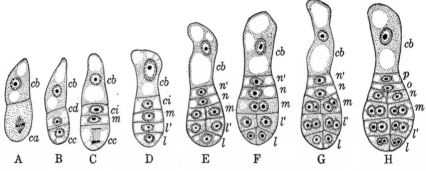

FIG. 156.   Development of embryo in *Sagina procumbens*.   (*After Souèges, 1924a.*)

ture which does not take any further part in the development of the embryo.   The terminal cell ca undergoes transverse divisions to form a row of four cells designated as ci, m, l', and l (Fig. 156A–D). Of these, each of the three lower cells divides by a vertical wall and the upper cell ci divides by a transverse wall (Fig. 156E,F).   The embryo now comprises five tiers (excluding cb), namely n', n, m, l', and l. The next division is also vertical (at right angles to the first) in l, l', and m, and results in the formation of three quadrants; n also divides by a vertical wall; and n' divides by a transverse wall to give rise to o and p (Fig. 156G,H). Of the six tiers formed in this way, l is destined to give rise to the stem tip, l' to the cotyledons, m to the hypocotyl, n to the root cap, and o and p to a short suspensor which abuts on the large cell cb.

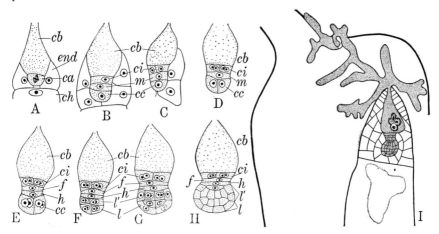

FIG. 157. *A–H*, development of embryo in *Sedum acre*; cells marked *end* belong to endosperm and *ch* is the chalazal haustorium. (*After Souèges, 1927.*) *I*, l.s. portion of ovule, showing haustorial processes formed from basal cell of proembryo. (*After Mauritzon, 1933.*)

Sedum acre (Souèges, 1927, 1936d) resembles *Sagina* in having a large and undivided basal cell (cb), but in other respects the development shows some differences. The terminal cell ca, which is small and lenticular, divides transversely into two superposed cells, of which the upper again divides transversely (Fig. 157A,B). Of the resulting four cells, cc undergoes two vertical divisions to form quadrants (Fig. 157D,E) and then a transverse division to form octants (Fig. 157F); m divides transversely into two flattened cells h and f, the former of which constitutes the hypophysis (Fig. 157E); ci becomes partitioned by vertical walls to form four juxtaposed cells which do not divide again but become greatly flattened and form a short suspensor (Fig. 157$C–H$); cb forms an aggressive haustorium whose branches penetrate the seed coat (Fig. 157I).

During further development, l gives rise to the cotyledons and stem tip, l' to the hypocotyl, h to the root tip, f and ci to the suspensor.

Saxifraga granulata (Souèges, 1936a) shows a variation in that here the basal cell cb undergoes a few divisions to produce four to eight large cells which form part of the suspensor. The terminal cell ca first divides transversely to produce the two cells cc and cd (Fig. 158A), of which the latter divides into two daughter cells m and ci (Fig. 158B). Of the resulting cells, ci divides vertically into two juxtaposed cells which contribute to the middle portion of the suspensor; and m divides transversely into f and d (Fig. 158D,E)

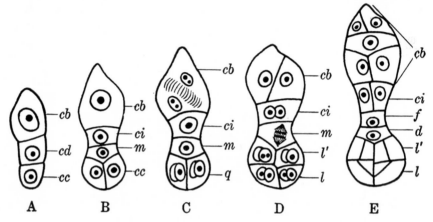

Fig. 158.   Development of embryo in *Saxifraga granulata*.   (*After Souèges, 1936a*.)

the former contributing to the suspensor and the latter functioning as the hypophysis. Meanwhile the cell cc undergoes two vertical divisions (Fig. 158B,C) and one transverse division (Fig. 158D) to give rise to the tiers l and l', which eventually produce the cotyledonary and hypocotyledonary portions of the embryo.

The embryo of *Androsaemum officinale* (Souèges, 1936b), belonging to the family Hypericaceae, also deserves mention here. In this case the terminal as well as the basal cell of the two-celled proembryo divides transversely to give rise to a quartet of four superposed cells (Fig. 159A,B). Of these the lowest cell cc divides vertically into two juxtaposed cells (Fig. 159C), each of which undergoes another vertical division to form the quadrant stage (Fig. 159D) and then a transverse division to give rise to the octants $l–l'$

(Fig. 159E). The cell cd, sister to cc, divides into two superposed cells m and ci (Fig. 159C) of which the former again segments into d and f (Fig. 159D). Subsequently l and l' produce the cotyledonary and hypocotyledonary parts of the embryo; d becomes differentiated as the hypophysis; and the cells f, ci, and cb contribute to the formation of a filamentous suspensor. Occasionally a few vertical divisions may also take place in the suspensor, but these are sporadic and of no importance.

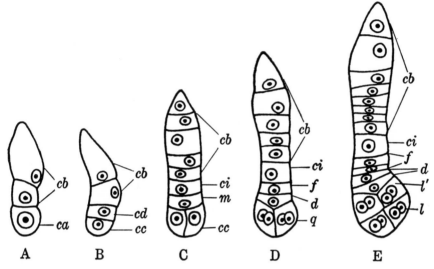

Fig. 159. Development of embryo in *Androsaemum officinale*. (*Redrawn after Souèges, 1936b.*)

The embryogeny of *Drosera rotundifolia* (Souèges, 1936c) is peculiar in that it shows points of resemblance with three or four different types of embryonal development. The basal cell cb undergoes only one or two divisions to give rise to a short suspensor. The terminal cell ca divides transversely into two superposed cells cc and cd (Fig. 160A–C). The former again divides transversely to form two cells l and l' (Fig. 160D) both of which become vertically partitioned to form first quadrants (Fig. 160E) and then octants (Fig. 160F). Meanwhile, cd also undergoes a transverse division into two superposed cells h and h', both of which become partitioned by vertical walls (Fig. 160E,F). Regarding the further fate of these

tiers, l gives rise to the cotyledonary region, l' to the hypocotyledonary region, h to the initials of the root periblem, and h' to the
root cap (Fig. 160*G–K*).

Comparing the development of the embryo of *Drosera* with the
types previously described, it is clear that the filamentous form of
the proembryo corresponds with that in the Solanad type (Fig. 150);
the behavior of the tiers h and h' corresponds with that of the tiers
m and n in the Asterad type (Fig. 148); and the disposition of the

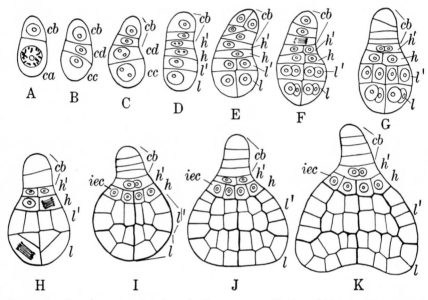

FIG. 160.   Development of embryo in *Drosera rotundifolia*.   (*After Souèges, 1936c.*)

quadrants resembles that under the Solanad and Chenopodiad
types (Fig. 153).   However, the greatest resemblance is with the
Caryophyllad type (Fig. 156) as in both cases the embryo is produced almost entirely from the terminal cell of the proembryonal
quartet, while the basal cell *cb* of the two-celled stage takes practically no part in further development.

MONOCOTYLEDONS

As already mentioned there is no essential difference between the
monocotyledons and the dicotyledons regarding the early cell divisions of the proembryo.   However, since the mature embryo is so

different in the two groups, a few illustrative examples are described below to show the range of variation in the monocotyledons.

Luzula forsteri (Souèges, 1923c), a member of the family Juncaceae, is characterized by a very simple type of embryogeny. The terminal cell ca of the two-celled proembryo divides by a longitudinal wall to produce two juxtaposed cells (Fig. 161A,B), and a little later the basal cell cb divides by a transverse wall to produce the two cells ci and m (Fig. 161C). In the next stage the two cells of the tier ca undergo another vertical division, at right angles to the first, to give rise to the quadrants q; cell m also divides by a longitudinal

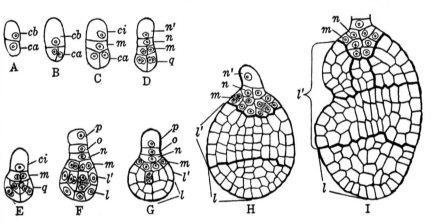

FIG. 161. Development of embryo in *Luzula forsteri*. (*Redrawn after Souèges, 1923c.*)

wall to give rise to two juxtaposed cells; and ci divides transversely to form two cells n and n' (Fig. 161D). By further divisions the quadrants become partitioned into two portions l and l', of which l gives rise to the lower part of the single cotyledon and l' to its upper part and to the hypocotyl and plumule. Of the remaining tiers, m gives rise to the periblem and part of the root cap; n to the remaining part of the root cap; and n' to the short suspensor. An important point, worthy of note in the embryogeny of *Luzula*, is the extremely precocious differentiation of the epidermal initials, which are cut off immediately after the quadrant stage (Fig. 161E), although in other angiosperms this occurs only after the octants have been formed.

The embryogeny of *Muscari comosum* (Souèges, 1932), a representative of the family Liliaceae, may be described next. As in *Luzula*, the basal cell *cb* divides transversely and the terminal cell *ca* divides longitudinally (Fig. 162*A,B*). In the next stage, the two cells at *ca* and the middle cell *m* divide longitudinally, while the upper cell *ci* divides transversely into *n* and *n'* (Fig. 162*C*). Of the eight cells formed in this way, *n'* divides to give rise to *o* and *p*; *n* divides vertically; the two juxtaposed cells of the tier *m* also divide vertically, although in a somewhat irregular fashion, to produce four cells; and the quadrants at *q* divide by diagonal walls to produce the octants (Fig. 162*D,E*). Finally, the tier *q* gives rise to the cotyledon, *m* to the hypocotyl and stem tip, *n* to the initials of the root, *o* to the root cap, and *p* to the suspensor (Fig. 162*F,G*).

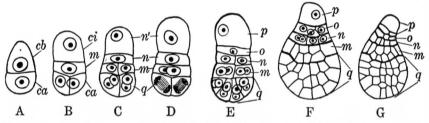

FIG. 162.   Development of embryo in *Muscari comosum*.   (*After Souèges, 1932.*)

The proembryo of *Sagittaria* (Souèges, 1931) is similar in some respects to that of *Sagina* (Fig. 156) described under the dicotyledons. The zygote divides transversely into the terminal cell *ca* and the basal cell *cb* (Fig. 163*A*). The basal cell, which is the larger, does not divide again but becomes transformed directly into a large vesicular structure.[6] The terminal cell undergoes a transverse division to form the two cells *c* and *d* (Fig. 163*B,C*). Of these, the lower cell *c* divides vertically to form a pair of juxtaposed cells, and the middle cell *d* divides transversely into *m* and *ci* (Fig. 163*D*). In the next stage the two cells at *c* undergo another vertical division to form quadrants, *m* also divides vertically, and *ci* divides transversely (Fig. 163*E,F*). The quadrant cells at *c* now divide transversely to give rise to octants (*l*, *l'*), the two juxtaposed cells at *m* become vertically partitioned to give rise to four cells, and the two daughter cells of *ci* divide to form the cells *n*, *o*, *h*, and *s* (Fig. 163*F–H*). With further cell divisions and growth the tiers *l* and *l'* become trans-

----

[6] A similar large basal cell occurs in almost all members of the Helobiales and has recently been reported in *Lloydia* (Bianchi, 1946) belonging to the Liliaceae.

formed into the single cotyledon, m gives rise to the stem tip, n to the root tip, o to the periblem and a part of the root cap, h to the uppermost layer of the root cap, and s to the suspensor composed of three to six superposed cells.

The embryo of the Gramineae is so different from that of most monocotyledons that it merits separate attention. In *Poa annua* (Souèges, 1924b), which is the most thoroughly investigated species, the first division of the zygote is transverse and results in the formation of two cells ca and cb (Fig. 164A). The next division is transverse in the basal cell and vertical in the terminal cell (Fig. 164B,C).

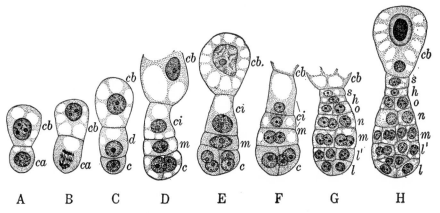

A   B   C   D   E   F   G   H

FIG. 163. Development of embryo in *Sagittaria sagittifolia*. (*After Souèges, 1931.*)

Of the four cells thus formed, the two at the lower end undergo a further longitudinal division, resulting in the quadrant stage (Fig. 164D); and each of the quadrant cells in turn becomes partitioned by a more or less transverse wall to give rise to the two tiers l and l' (Fig. 164E). At the same time the upper cell ci divides transversely to form n and n', followed by a vertical division in m and n and a transverse division in n'. As further development proceeds, the tiers l and l' give rise to the scutellum and part of the coleoptile; m gives rise to the remaining part of the coleoptile cl–cl', the stem tip pv, and the periblem and plerome of the root tip; n to the root cap, coleorrhiza, and epiblast eb^{ca}; and o and p, daughter cells of n', to the hypoblast and the suspensor (Fig. 164F–I). The most conspicuous part of the grass embryo is the scutellum.

[ca] This is a small scale-like structure lying opposite to the scutellum (see p. 429).

Much has been written on its morphological nature. Arber (1934) considers that the scutellum and coleoptile jointly constitute the cotyledon, the coleoptile representing the cotyledonary sheath. Others contend that the coleoptile is the true cotyledon and that the scutellum is a lateral outgrowth of the young axis. Avery (1930), who has made a thorough study of the comparative anatomy and morphology of the embryos and seedlings of maize, oat, and wheat, interprets the scutellum as the cotyledon; the coleoptile as the second leaf; and the elongated structure between the cotyledon

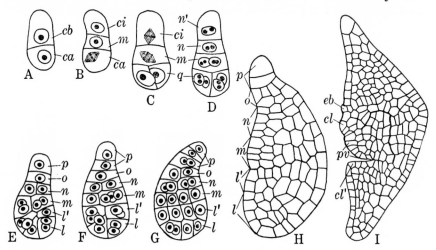

Fig. 164.   Development of embryo in *Poa annua*.   (*Redrawn after Souèges, 1924b.*)

and the coleoptile, sometimes called the "mesocotyl," as the first internode.

It is to be noted that, on the side which is in contact with the endosperm, the cells of the scutellum frequently elongate to form finger-like processes, which project into the endosperm and probably serve for the absorption of food from the latter.

MODIFICATIONS OF SUSPENSOR

In the above account of the principal types of embryonal development in the dicotyledons and monocotyledons, the main emphasis was on the embryo proper and little attention was paid to the suspensor. This is because in the majority of angiosperms the suspensor has no special function except that of pushing the embryo into the endosperm, where it is surrounded by cells containing abundant food materials. Especially striking examples of an elongated proembryo are seen in the long and narrow embryo sacs of the Sympetalae and have been fully described and illustrated in *Haberlea* (Glišić, 1928), *Gratiola* (Glišić, 1933), *Utricularia* (Kausik, 1938), and several other plants. In later stages the narrow basal portion of the proembryonal tube becomes crushed and obliterated, while the broader terminal portion, which is destined to give rise to the embryo proper, becomes favorably placed in the central mass of endosperm. In *Salvia splendens* (Carlson and Stuart, 1936) not only does the proembryonal filament elongate downward into the endosperm but it also protrudes in the opposite direction, so that a portion of it comes to lie inside the endosperm haustorium produced at its micropylar end.

In several plants the suspensor cells show a pronounced increase in size or give rise to prominent haustorial structures which penetrate between the cells of the endosperm and encroach upon the surrounding tissues of the ovule. The range of variation in this respect may be illustrated by referring to a few families and genera which are of special interest from this point of view.

Guignard (1882) gave a very detailed account of the modifications of the suspensor in the Leguminosae. In several members of the subfamily Mimosaceae and of the tribe Hedysareae, a suspensor is virtually absent and the proembryo forms a spherical or ovoid mass of cells without any differentiation. *Soja, Amphicarpaea*, and *Trifolium* have a rudimentary suspensor consisting of three or four cells. In *Pisum* and *Orobus*, which have a suspensor consisting of two pairs of cells arranged in a crosswise fashion, the two micropylar cells are elongated but the next two are more or less spherical; all four of the cells are multinucleate (Fig. 165*E,F*). In *Cicer* (Fig. 165*G*) and *Lupinus* (Fig. 165*A–C*) the suspensor is much longer. In *L. pilosus* (Fig. 165*A*) some of the cells become detached from one another and lie free in the micropylar part of the embryo sac. In *Ononis* (Fig. 165*I*) the suspensor consists of a filament of large and conspicuous cells which are packed with food materials. In *Medicago* and *Trigonella* it is more massive, and *Phaseolus* (Fig. 165*D*) is similar except that here the distinction between the cells of the suspensor and embryo proper is not very sharp. Finally, in

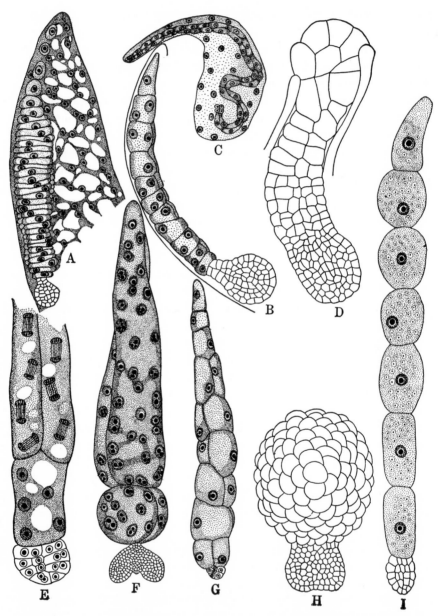

FIG. 165. Modifications of suspensor in Leguminosae. *A, Lupinus pilosus,* l.s. upper part of embryo sac; suspensor consists of a row of several large flattened cells, of which a few at upper end have become isolated. *B, L. luteus;* most of suspensor cells are binucleate. *C, L. subcarnosus;* greatly elongated suspensor, composed of

Cytisus (Fig. 165*H*) the suspensor cells are large and spherical and appear like a bunch of grapes.

During recent years more detailed accounts have appeared of the embryogeny of the Leguminosae,[7] of which *Pisum sativum* (Cooper, 1938) may be referred to very briefly. The zygote divides transversely into two cells, of which the basal divides vertically to form two suspensor cells and the other divides transversely to form a middle cell and a terminal cell (Fig. 166*A–D*). The nuclei of the two basal cells now divide without wall formation and the middle cell becomes vertically partitioned by a wall placed at right angles to that separating the two basal cells. At the same time the terminal cell divides by an oblique wall (Fig. 166*F,G*). Hereafter the basal cells undergo much elongation and their nuclei as well as those of the middle or subbasal cells undergo a series of free nuclear divisions (Fig. 166*H–J*). Eventually the basal cells have as many as 64 nuclei and the subbasal cells have 32 nuclei each. A longitudinal section of the ovule cut at this stage shows a free nuclear endosperm, a globular embryo, and the four multinucleate suspensor cells (Fig. 166*K*).

The suspensor haustoria of some members of the Rubiaceae have been well known since the days of Hofmeister (1858). Lloyd (1902) and Souèges (1925) gave further details of their origin and structure. At first the suspensor is merely a filament of cells, but later the micropylar cells send out lateral protrusions which penetrate into the endosperm and swell at their distal ends (Fig. 167). Lloyd was so impressed by their appearance that he remarked: "The function of the suspensor in these forms is therefore not alone to bring the embryo into favorable position with relation to the food supply in a mechanical sense, but to act as a temporary embryonic root." Fagerlind's (1937) work seems to indicate, however, that the sus-

[7] See especially Souèges (1946*c–g*; 1947*a, b*; 1948).

about 20 pairs of cells; outside embryo are nuclei of endosperm. *D, Phaseolus multiflorus*; large massive suspensor, whose cells grade imperceptibly into those of embryo proper. *E,F, Pisum sativum* and *Orobus angustifolius*; suspensor composed of large multinucleate cells. *G, Cicer arietinum*, biseriate suspensor. *H, Cytisus laburnum*; suspensor appearing like bunch of grapes; embryo showing initiation of two cotyledons. *I, Ononis fruticosa*, suspensor composed of a row of seven large cells, each with a single prominent nucleus and many starch grains. (*After Guignard, 1882.*)

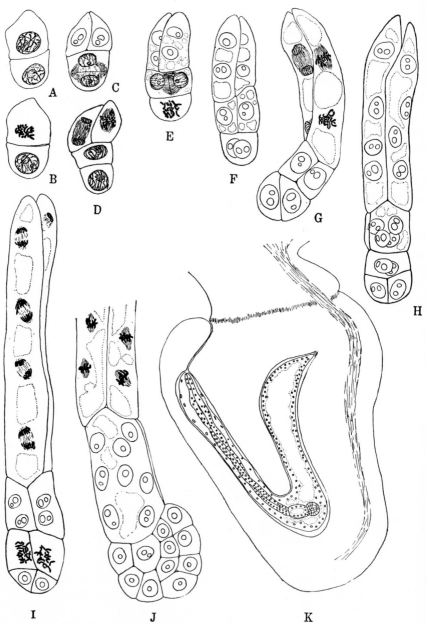

Fig. 166. Development of suspensor in *Pisum sativum*. (*After Cooper, 1938.*)

pensor cells soon lose their connection with the main body of this organ and occur merely as islands within the endosperm. Further, sometimes they degenerate even before the connection is lost, and if this be so, they naturally cannot function effectively as absorbing organs.

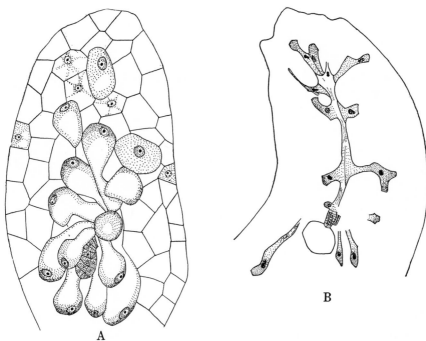

A B

FIG. 167. Suspensor haustoria of *Asperula*. *A*, young embryo with prominent suspensor haustoria; the surrounding cells belong to endosperm. *B*, older stage, showing extreme development of haustoria. (*After Lloyd, 1902.*)

The suspensor haustoria of the Halorrhagidaceae bear a remarkable resemblance to synergids (Fig. 168*A–G*). Stolt (1928) and Souèges (1940) have shown that in *Myriophyllum* the two-celled proembryo consists of a large basal cell and a much smaller terminal cell. The former divides longitudinally to form two daughter cells, which enlarge to such an extent as to occupy the entire space in the micropylar part of the embryo sac. They remain distinguishable even up to the time of differentiation of the cotyledons.

Three members of the family Fumariaceae are also of much interest in this connection. In *Hypecoum* (Souèges, 1943*a*,*b*) the basal cell *cb* does not divide but becomes greatly swollen and vesicular. The terminal cell *ca* divides diagonally into two unequal cells, of which the larger cell *cd* becomes swollen like the basal cell. These two haustorial cells, *cb* and *cd*, persist for a long time and appear like synergids (Fig. 169*A–F*).

In *Corydalis* (Souèges, 1946*a,b*) the basal cell *cb* undergoes a number of free nuclear divisions and becomes multinucleate. The terminal cell *ca* divides transversely to form a short filament, whose upper cells (*cd* and *cf*) become large and multinucleate and contribute to the suspensor. Only the apical cell takes part in the development of the embryo proper (Fig. 169*G–L*).

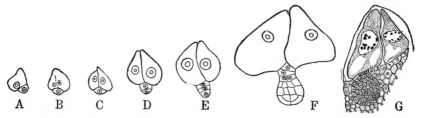

Fig. 168. Synergid-like suspensor cells of *Myriophyllum alterniflorum*. (*A–F*, after Souèges, 19/0; *G*, after Stolt, 1928.)

In the third genus *Fumaria* (Souèges, 1941*a,b*) the nuclear divisions in *cb* are accompanied by wall formation. All the derivatives of this cell, as well as the upper derivatives of *ca*, give rise to the suspensor, the embryo proper being produced only from the lower derivatives of *ca*. Thus, approximately three-fourths of the zygote is given to the production of the suspensor (Fig. 169*M–R*).

Since the publication of Treub's (1879) classical paper on the embryogeny of the orchids there have been several other investigations on the family, among which those of Stenar (1937, 1940) and Swamy (1942*a,b*, 1943, 1946, 1948, 1949) deserve special mention. It is noteworthy that while some genera like *Epipactis*, *Listera*, and *Zeuxine* completely lack a suspensor, others show a remarkable variation in the form and organization of this organ, which may be illustrated by the following examples. In *Spathoglottis*, *Goodyera*, and *Achroanthes* the basal cell of the proembryo enlarges and sometimes grows out of the micropyle. In *Gymnadenia*, *Phajus*, *Epidendrum*, and *Habenaria* it divides to form a filament of cells which may frequently become very long and twisted and grow out as far as

the placenta.   The suspensor cells of *Eulophea* (Fig. 195) form long
fluffy structures which extend in various directions, piercing the cells of
the inner integument and coming in contact with those of the outer

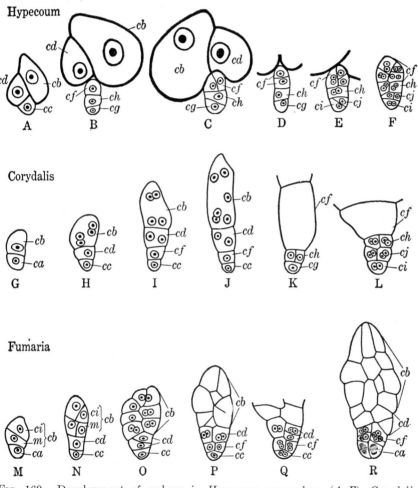

FIG. 169.   Development of embryo in *Hypecoum procumbens* (A–F), *Corydalis lutea* (G–L), and *Fumaria officinalis* (M–R).   (*After Souèges, 1943a,b; 1946a,b; 1941a,b.*)

one.   In *Phalaenopsis* the suspensor cells send outgrowths both
above and below, the former protruding out of the micropyle and
the latter surrounding the embryo.   In *Stanhopea* the spherical
proembryo consists of 10 to 12 cells, only one of which gives rise to

the embryo proper, while the rest grow out into long tubes, some pushing their way between the cells of the integuments and others extending into the micropyle.

A reference has already been made to the well-developed suspensor haustoria of the Crassulaceae (Mauritzon, 1933) (Fig. 157*I*). Sometimes their branching is so profuse that it is hardly possible to get a correct idea of it from the study of single sections. In some species of *Sedum* and *Pistoria* the haustorial processes pierce the integuments and even extend outside the ovule.

Walker (1947) has recently given a detailed account of the origin of the massive haustoria of *Tropaeolum majus*. Here the basal cells of the proembryo divide more actively than the other cells. Such of the cells of this mass as lie on the side away from the funiculus give rise to a long haustorial process which pierces the micropylar part of the integument and finally enters the pericarp. Slightly later, a second protuberance arises from those cells of the mass which lie on the side nearest the funiculus. This, the placental haustorium, grows through the integument and funiculus and reaches up to the point of entry of the vascular bundle of the raphe.

Perhaps the longest suspensors in angiosperms occur in the Loranthaceae. As mentioned on page 143, in several genera of this family the embryo sacs grow up into the style, and after fertilization there is a remarkable elongation of the two-rowed suspensor, pushing the terminal cells of the proembryo into the ovary.

UNCLASSIFIED OR ABNORMAL EMBRYOS

Although there are several plants whose embryos do not conform to any of the types described previously, only a few need be mentioned here.

In all the angiosperms described so far, the first division of the zygote is transverse, but Treub (1885) reported long ago that in *Macrosolen cochinchinensis* the first wall in the zygote is not transverse but vertical. Since then a vertical or nearly vertical division has also been described in several other members of the family, *viz.*, *Korthalsella* (Rutishauser, 1935), *Scurrula*, *Dendrophthoe*, (Rauch, 1936; Singh, 1950) (Fig. 170), *Lepeostegeres*, *Amyema*, *Helixanthera*, and *Taxillus* (Schaeppi and Steindl, 1942). In *Balanophora* (Zweifel, 1939) the first as well as the second division is vertical and this is probably also true of the third (Fig. 171). In

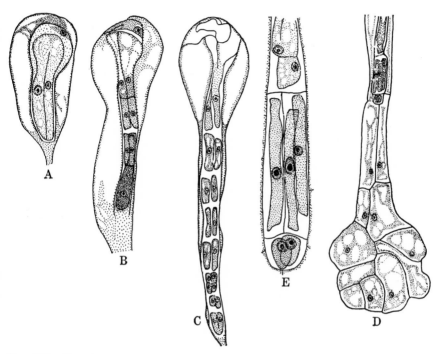

FIG. 170. Development of embryo of *Scurrula atropurpurea*. *A*, first division of zygote. *B,C*, formation of biseriate proembryo; in *B*, the two terminal cells of proembryo happen to overlap each other. *D*, proembryo penetrating inside endosperm. *E*, enlarged view of terminal portion of proembryo of approximately same age as *D*; note beginning of differentiation between cells of suspensor and those of embryo proper. (*After Rauch, 1936.*)

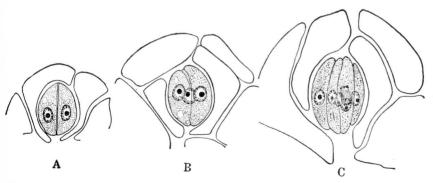

FIG. 171. Early stages in development of embryo of *Balanophora abbreviata*. *A*, two-celled embryo formed by vertical division of zygote. *B,C*, more advanced stages. (*After Zweifel, 1939.*)

Leitneria (Pfeiffer, 1912) and *Sassafras* (Coy, 1928) the condition is variable, and the first wall may be either transverse or longitudinal.

In *Scabiosa succisa*, which has been described in detail by Souèges (1937b), the first wall in the zygote is diagonal, dividing it into two somewhat unequal cells, *a* and *b* (Fig. 172A). The former corresponds to the terminal and the latter to the basal cell of the two-celled stage. In the next division each cell is partitioned more or less transversely, producing the daughter cells *c*, *d*, *e*, and *f* (Fig. 172B). The following divisions do not follow any definite sequence (Fig. 172C–E), but derivatives of *c* and *e* give rise to the cotyledonary zone, *d* and the lower part of *f* give rise to the hypocotyledonary

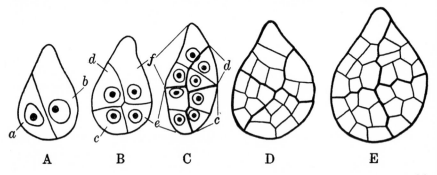

A   B   C   D   E

FIG. 172.   Development of embryo of *Scabiosa succisa*.   (*After Souèges, 1937b.*)

region, and the upper part of *f* to the root cap and a poorly differentiated suspensor. The dermatogen is differentiated at an early stage, but the periblem and plerome are distinguishable only after the appearance of the cotyledons.

A well-differentiated suspensor is also lacking in *Cimicifuga* (Earle, 1938). Here the first division of the zygote is transverse. The basal cell, which is considerably larger, divides vertically, and the terminal divides obliquely. Further divisions are slow and irregular and the proembryo soon becomes a club-shaped mass, about ten cells long and two to four cells broad. There is no clear line of demarcation between the suspensor and the embryo, and the cells of the former are distinguishable only by their position and vacuolated cytoplasm.

In several members of the Gramineae also there is no regular

pattern of cell divisions in the development of the embryo. The
two-celled stage consists of a small lenticular terminal cell and a
much larger basal cell (Fig. 173*A*). The terminal cell may divide
vertically (Fig. 173*C*) or obliquely (Fig. 173*B*), and sometimes the
first oblique wall is followed by another wall of the same type,
resulting in a kind of apical cell (Fig. 173*D*). The following divi-

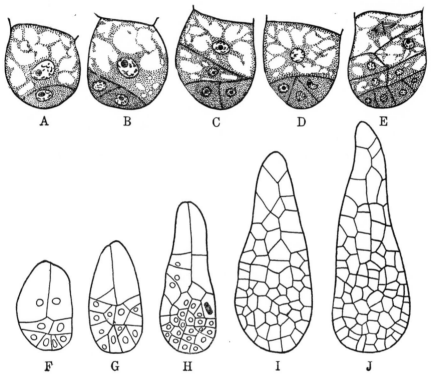

Fig. 173. Development of embryo of *Zea mays*. (*After Randolph, 1936.*)

sions are quite irregular (Fig. 173*E*). Further growth is limited
chiefly to the terminal region, and only a few cell divisions occur in
the basal or suspensor region (Fig. 173*F–J*).

Carya glabra, Juglans mandshurica (Langdon, 1934), and *J. nigra*
(Nast, 1941) are similar in that the first division wall may be horizontal or slightly oblique. The terminal cell does not form any
quadrants but divides by two oblique walls and then by a transverse
wall to form a group of six cells. The cells on the sides give rise to

the cotyledons and those in the center to the stem tip, offering some resemblance in this respect to *Geum* (Fig. 149) and *Myosotis* (Fig. 155), which have already been described.

Attention may finally be called to the fact that although Souèges lays much emphasis both on the constancy in the destiny of the cells of the four-celled proembryo and on their significance in indicating relationships between different families and genera, his conclusions have not been supported by other workers. For example, Borthwick (1931) points out that in *Daucus* each cell of the four-celled proembryo does not always give rise to the same part of the mature embryo. Bhaduri (1936) also states that "the method of origin of the different parts of the mature embryo varies in different and sometimes even in the same species of Solanaceae."

UNORGANIZED AND REDUCED EMBRYOS

Whatever their mode of origin and development, as a rule all embryos become differentiated at maturity into three main parts, *viz.*, root tip, stem tip, and cotyledons (or cotyledon). In some plants, however, the embryo remains small and rudimentary even until the shedding stage of the seed. This condition is especially prevalent in the families Balanophoraceae, Rafflesiaceae, Gentianaceae, Pirolaceae, Orobanchaceae, Burmanniaceae, and Orchidaceae, and appears to be associated in some degree with a parasitic or saprophytic mode of life.

In the Orchidaceae the embryo is almost always a simple or ovoid mass of cells in which even the differentiation of the primary layers takes place only after the seeds have been shed. Swamy (1949) recognizes two fundamental types of development. In the first type (Fig. 174*A–O*), which is the more frequent, the zygote divides by a transverse wall to form two cells, of which the basal again divides transversely so as to result in a proembryo of three cells. The upper cell adjacent to the wall of the embryo sac frequently gives rise to one or more suspensor haustoria, which become very prominent and aggressive structures in some species. The terminal cell divides vertically to form two daughter cells, which by further divisions give rise to the greater part of the embryo, the rest being contributed by the middle cell. In the second type of development (Fig. 174*P–U*), which has been reported only in a few genera like *Cymbidium, Eulophia, Geodorum*, and *Stanhopea*, the zygote may divide by either a transverse or an oblique wall. Further divisions, which do not follow any definite pattern, give rise to a mass of five to ten cells, some of which begin to enlarge enormously and assume a haustorial function. One or two cells divide transversely to form

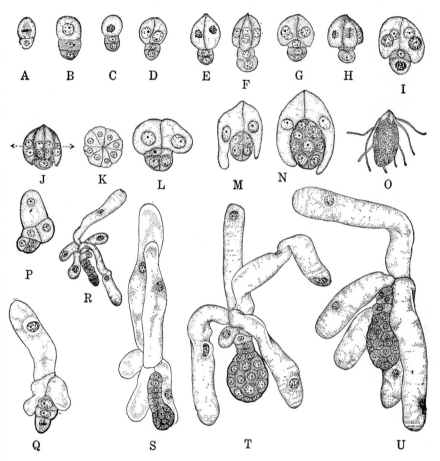

FIG. 174. Development of embryo in *Vanda parviflora* (*A–O*) and *Cymbidium bicolor* (*P–U*). *A*, *Vanda*, two-celled proembryo with basal cell dividing. *B*, three-celled proembryo. *C*, same, upper cell dividing. *D*, vertical division of primary suspensor cell. *E–J*, development of eight-celled suspensor by three vertical divisions of primary suspensor cell. *K*, optical t.s. through suspensor region of a stage similar to *J*. *L–N*, stages in elongation of suspensor cells. *O*, mature embryo with remnants of suspensor haustoria. *P–R*, *Cymbidium*, early stages in development of embryo. *S–U*, later stages, showing maximum elongation of suspensor cells. (*After Swamy, 1942a,b.*)

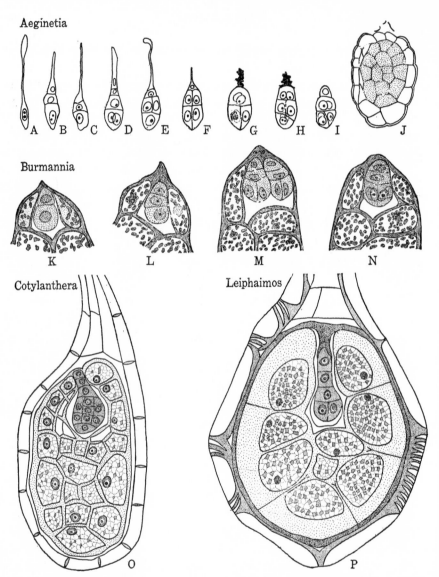

FIG. 175. Some stages in development of embryos of *Aeginetia indica* (*A–J*), *Burmannia coelestis* (*K–N*), *Cotylanthera tenuis* (*O*), and *Leiphaimos spectabilis* (*P*). *A–I*, *Aeginetia*, stages in development of proembryo. *J*, l.s. nearly mature seed (seed coat not included), showing spherical embryo (shaded cells) surrounded by endosperm. (*After Juliano, 1935.*) *K–N*, *Burmannia*, l.s. upper part of seed, showing endosperm and embryo; of the two embryos seen in *M*, one is probably derived from a synergid. (*After Ernst and Bernard, 1912.*) *O*, *Cotylanthera*, l.s. seed showing embryo, endosperm, and seed coat. *P*, *Leiphaimos*, l.s. seed showing five-celled embryo surrounded by thick-walled cells of endosperm and seed coat. (*After Oehler, 1927.*)

304

a filament of variable length whose lower portion gives rise to the embryo proper.

Ernst and Schmid (1913) report that in *Rafflesia patma* the terminal cell of the two-celled proembryo undergoes a transverse division to form two cells, each of which divides longitudinally. At the same time the basal cell divides vertically. At this stage the proembryo enters into a period of rest although cell divisions continue to take place in the endosperm. When development is resumed, only one or two more divisions take place in the embryo.

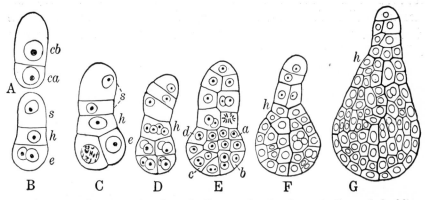

FIG. 176. Development of embryo in *Ranunculus ficaria* up to time of shedding of seed. (*After Souèges, 1913.*)

In *Aeginetia indica*, a member of the Orobanchaceae (Juliano, 1935), the zygote remains dormant for a considerable time after endosperm formation has commenced. The first two divisions are transverse, resulting in a short filament (Fig. 175A–C). The narrow suspensor cells soon become crushed and disorganized, and the two terminal cells divide to give rise to a small globose embryo without any differentiation into a radicle, plumule, or cotyledons (Fig. 175D–I). Figure 175J shows a longitudinal section of the mature seed with the spherical embryo surrounded by a layer of endosperm cells.

Embryos of an extremely reduced type are also known in the Burmanniaceae (Ernst and Bernard, 1912). In *Burmannia coelestis* (Fig. 175K–N) the basal cell of the two-celled embryo divides by a transverse wall and the terminal cell divides by two vertical walls to produce a quadrant. Development seems to be arrested at this six-celled stage.

Four saprophytic members of the Gentianaceae, studied by Oehler (1927) are also of much interest in this connection. In *Voyriella parviflora* the first division of the zygote takes place when the endosperm is composed of 10 to 12 cells. A filamentous proembryo of six or seven cells is formed. Of these, the three or four terminal cells divide further to give rise to a mass of 16 to 24 cells. *Cotylanthera tenuis* (Fig. 175*O*) and *Voyria coerulea* are similar but somewhat more reduced. They have a suspensor of three or four cells and an embryonal portion consisting of about a dozen cells. The most reduced of the four is *Leiphaimos spectabilis* in which only the terminal cell of the four-celled embryo divides again, so that at the shedding stage of the seed the embryo consists of no more than five cells arranged in four tiers (Fig. 175*P*).

Reduced embryos without the usual organization into a radicle, plumule, and cotyledons have also been described in *Ranunculus ficaria* (Souèges, 1913) (Fig. 176), *Corydalis cava* (Hegelmaier, 1878), and a few other plants, although these are not characterized by a parasitic or saprophytic habit.

References

Arber, A. 1934. "The Gramineae." Cambridge University Press.

Artschwager, E., and Starrett, R. C. 1933. The time factor in fertilization and embryo development in the sugar beet. Jour. Agr. Res. **47:** 823–843.

Avery, G. S., Jr. 1930. Comparative anatomy and morphology of embryos and seedlings of maize, oats and wheat. Bot. Gaz. **89:** 1–39.

Bhaduri, P. N. 1936. Studies in the embryology of the Solanaceae. I. Bot. Gaz. **98:** 283–295.

Bianchi, R. 1946. Untersuchungen über die Fortpflanzungsverhältnisse von *Gagea fistulosa* (Ram.) und *Lloydia serotina* (Rchb.). Diss. Zürich.

Borthwick, R. A. 1931. Development of the macrogametophyte and embryo of *Daucus carota*. Bot. Gaz. **92:** 23–44.

Borwein, B., Coetsee, M. L., and Krupko, S. 1949. Development of the embryo sac of *Restio dodii* and *Elegia racemosa*. Jour. South Afri. Bot. **15:** 1–11.

Cappaletti, C. 1929. Sterilita di origine micotica nella *Ruta patavina* L. Ann. di Bot. **18:** 145–166.

Carano, E. 1915. Ricerche sull'embriogenesi delle Asteraceae. Ann. di Bot. **13:** 251–301.

Carlson, E. M., and Stuart, B. C. 1936. Development of spores and gametophytes in certain New World species of *Salvia*. New Phytol. **35:** 65–81.

Cheesman, E. E. 1927. Fertilization and embryogeny in *Theobroma cacao* L. Ann. Bot. **41:** 107–126.

Cooper, D. C. 1938. Embryology of *Pisum sativum*. Bot. Gaz. **100**: 123–132.

———. 1949. Flower and seed development in *Oxybaphus nyctagineus*. Amer. Jour. Bot. **36**: 348–355.

——— and Brink, R. A. 1949. The endosperm-embryo relationship in an autonomous apomict, *Taraxacum officinale*. Bot. Gaz. **111**: 139–152.

Coy, G. V. 1928. Morphology of *Sassafras* in relation to phylogeny of angiosperms. Bot. Gaz. **86**: 149–171.

Dahlgren, K. V. O. 1928. Die Embryologie einiger Alismataceae. Svensk Bot. Tidskr. **22**: 1–17.

———. 1934. Die Embryosackentwicklung von *Echinodorus macrophyllus* und *Sagittaria sagittifolia*. Planta **21**: 602–612.

Earle, T. T. 1938. Embryology of certain Ranales. Bot. Gaz. **100**: 257–275.

Ernst, A., and Bernard, Ch. 1912. Entwicklungsgeschichte des Embryosackes und des Embryos von *Burmannia candida* Engl. und *B. championii* Thw. Ann. Jard. Bot. Buitenzorg II, **10**: 161–188.

——— and Schmid, E. 1913. Über Blüte und Frucht von *Rafflesia*. Ann. Jard. Bot. Buitenzorg II, **12**: 1–58.

Fagerlind, F. 1937. Embryologische, zytologische und bestäubungsexperimentelle Studien in der Familie Rubiaceae nebst Bemerkungen über einige Polyploiditätsprobleme. Acta Horti Bergiani **11**: 195–470.

Famintzin, A. 1879. Embryologische Studien. Mém. Acad. Imp. des Sci. St. Petersburg VII, **26**(10).

Gerassimova, H. 1933. Fertilization in *Crepis capillaris*. Cellule **42**: 103–148.

Glišić, Lj. 1928. Development of the female gametophyte and endosperm in *Haberlea rhodopensis* Friv. Bull. Inst. Jard. Bot. Univ. Belgrade **1**(1): 1–13.

———. 1933. Zur Entwicklungsgeschichte von *Gratiola officinalis* L. Bull. Inst. Jard. Bot. Univ. Belgrade **2**: 129–152.

Guignard, L. 1882. "Recherches anatomiques et physiologiques sur des légumineuses." Diss. Paris.

Hanstein, J. 1870. Entwicklungsgeschichte der Keime der Monokotyle und Dikotyle. Bot. Abhandl. Bonn. **1**: 1–112.

Hegelmaier, F. 1878. "Vergleichende Untersuchungen über die Entwicklung dikotyledoner Keime mit Berücksichtigung der pseudo-monokotyledonen." Stuttgart.

Heimann-Winawer, P. 1919. Beiträge zur Embryologie von *Colchicum autumnale* L. Arb. Inst. allg. Bot. Pflanzenphysiol., Univ. Zürich **21**.

Hewitt, W. C. 1939. Seed development of *Lobelia amoena*. Jour. Elisha Mitchell Sci. Soc. **55**: 63–82.

Hofmeister, W. 1858. Neuere Beobachtungen über Embryobildung der Phanerogamen. Jahrb. f. wiss. Bot. **1**: 82–186.

Johansen, D. A. 1945. A critical survey of the present status of plant embryology. Bot. Rev. **11**: 87–107.

Jones, H. A. 1927. Pollination and life history studies of lettuce (*Lactuca sativa*). Hilgardia **2**: 425–442.

Juliano, J. B.   1935.   Anatomy and morphology of the Bunga, *Aeginetia indica* L.   Philippine Jour. Sci. **56**: 405–451.

Kausik, S. B.   1938.   Pollen development and seed formation in *Utricularia coerulea* L.   Beihefte bot. Centbl. **58A**: 365–378.

Langdon, L. M.   1934.   Embryogeny of *Carya* and *Juglans*, a comparative study.   Bot. Gaz. **96**: 93–117.

Lloyd, F. E.   1902.   The comparative morphology of the Rubiaceae.   Mem. Torrey Bot. Club **8**: 1–112.

Mauritzon, J.   1933.   Studien über die Embryologie der Familien Crassulaceae und Saxifragaceae.   Diss. Lund.

McKay, J. W.   1947.   Embryology of pecan.   Jour. Agr. Res. **74**: 263–283.

Nast, C. G.   1941.   The embryogeny and seedling morphology of *Juglans regia* L.   Lilloa **6**: 163–205.

Noguchi, Y.   1929.   Zur Kenntnis der Befruchtung und Kornbildung bei den Reispflanzen.   Jap. Jour. Bot. **4**: 385–403.

Oehler, E.   1927.   Entwicklungsgeschichtlich-cytologische Untersuchungen an einigen saprophytischen Gentianaceen.   Planta **3**: 641–733.

Pfeiffer, W. M.   1912.   The morphology of *Leitneria floridana*.   Bot. Gaz. **53**: 189–203.

Pisek, A.   1923.   Chromosomenverhältnisse, Reduktionsteilung und Revision der Keimentwicklung der Mistel (*Viscum album*).   Jahrb. f. wiss. Bot. **62**: 1–19.

Poddubnaja-Arnoldi, V., and Dianowa, V.   1934.   Eine zytoembryologische Untersuchung einiger Arten der Gattung *Taraxacum*.   Planta **23**: 19–46.

Pope, M. N.   1937.   The time factor in pollen tube growth and fertilization in barley.   Jour. Agr. Res. **54**: 525–529.

———.   1943.   The temperature factor in fertilization and growth of the barley ovule.   Jour. Agr. Res. **66**: 389–402.

Puri, V.   1941.   Life history of *Moringa oleifera* Lamk.   Jour. Indian Bot. Soc. **20**: 263–284.

Randolph, W. M.   1936.   Developmental morphology of the caryopsis in maize.   Jour. Agri. Res. **53**: 881–916.

Rauch, K. V.   1936.   Cytologisch-embryologische Untersuchungen an *Scurrula atropurpurea* Dans. and *Dendrophthoe pentandra* Miq.   Ber. schweiz. bot. Gesell. **45**: 5–61.

Rutgers, F. L.   1923.   Embryo sac and embryo of *Moringa oleifera*. The female gametophyte of angiosperms.   Ann. Jard. Bot. Buitenzorg **33**: 1–66.

Rutishauser, A.   1935.   Entwicklungsgeschichtliche und zytologische Untersuchungen an *Korthalsella dacrydii* (Ridl.) Danser.   Ber. schweiz. bot. Gesell. **44**: 389–436.

Schaeppi, H., and Steindl, F.   1942.   Blütenmorphologische und embryologische Untersuchungen an Loranthoideen.   Vrtljschr. naturf. Gesell. Zürich **87**: 301–372.

Schaffner, M.   1906.   The embryology of the shepherd's purse.   Ohio Nat. **7**: 1–8.

Schnarf, K.   1929.   "Embryologie der Angiospermen."   Berlin.

Singh, Bahadur.   1950.   The embryology of *Dendrophthoe falcata* (Linn. fil.) Ettingshausen.   Proc. 37th Indian Sci. Cong. Bot. Sect.

Smith, B. E.   1934.   A taxonomic and morphological study of the genus *Cuscuta*, dodders, in North Carolina.   Jour. Elisha Mitchell Sci. Soc. **50:** 283–302.

Souèges, E. C. R.   1913.   Recherches sur l'embryogénie des Renonculacées. Renonculées (*Ficaria ranunculoides* Roth).   II. L'embryon.   Bul. Soc. Bot. de France **60:** 237–243, 283–289.

———.   1914.   Nouvelle recherches sur le développement de l'embryon chez les Crucifères.   Ann. Sci. Nat. IX. Bot. **19:** 311–339.

———.   1919.   Les premières divisions de l'oeuf et les différenciations du suspenseur chez le *Capsella bursa-pastoris*.   Ann. Sci. Nat. X. Bot. **1:** 1–28.

———.   1920*a*.   Développement de l'embryon chez le *Chenopodium bonus-henricus* L.   Bul. Soc. Bot. de France **67:** 233–257.

———.   1920*b*.   Embryogénie des Solanacées.   Développement de l'embryon chez les *Nicotiana*.   Compt. Rend. Acad. Sci. Paris **170:** 1125–1127.

———.   1920*c*.   Embryogénie des Composées. I. Les premiers stades du développement de l'embryon chez le *Senecio vulgaris* L. II.   Les derniers stades du développement de l'embryon chez le *Senecio vulgaris* L.   Compt. Rend. Acad. des Sci. Paris **171:** 254–256; 356–357.

———.   1922.   Recherches sur l'embryogénie des Solanacees.   Bul. Soc. Bot. de France **69:** 163–178, 236–241, 352–365, 555–585.

———.   1923*a*.   Développement de l'embryon chez le *Myosotis hispida* Schlecht. Bul. Soc. Bot. de France **70:** 385–401.

———.   1923*b*.   Développement de l'embryon chez le *Geum urbanum* L.   Bul. Soc. Bot. de France **70:** 645–660.

———.   1923*c*.   Embryogénie des Joncacées.   Développement de l'embryon chez le *Luzula forsteri* DC.   Compt. Rend. Acad. des Sci. Paris **177:** 705–708.

———.   1924*a*.   Développement de l'embryon chez le *Sagina procumbens*. L. Bul. Soc. Bot. de France **71:** 590–614.

———.   1924*b*.   Embryogénie des Graminées.   Développement de l'embryon chez le *Poa annua* L.   Compt. Rend. Acad. des Sci. Paris **178:** 1307–1310.

———.   1925.   Développement de l'embryon chez le *Sherardia arvensis* L.   Bul. Soc. Bot. de France **72:** 546–565.

———.   1927.   Développement de l'embryon chez le *Sedum acre* L.   Bul. Soc. Bot. de France **74:** 234–251.

———.   1931.   L'embryon chez le *Sagittaria sagittifolia* L.   Le cône végétatif de la tige et l'extrémite radiculaire chez le monocotylédones.   Ann. Sci. Nat. X. Bot. **13:** 353–402.

———.   1932.   Recherches sur l'embryogénie des Liliacées (*Muscari comosum* L.). Bul. Soc. Bot. de France **79:** 11–23.

———.   1934a.   "Titres et travaux scientifiques."   Saint-Dizier.

———.   1934*b*.   L'hypophyse et l'épiphyse; les problèmes d'histogenèse qui leur sont liés. I and II.   Bul. Soc. Bot. de France **81:** 737–758.

———.   1934–1939.   "Exposés d'embryologie et de morphologie végétales." Vols. I–X.   Paris.

———.   1935*a*.   Embryogénie des Oenothéracées.   Les principaux termes du développement de l'embryon chez le *Ludwigia palustris* Elliott.   Compt. Rend. Acad. des Sci. Paris **200:** 1626.

Souèges, E. C. R.   1935*b*.   Observations embryologiques sur quelques *Fragaria* de culture. Bul. Soc. Bot. de France **82:** 458–461.

———.   1936*a*.   Embryogénie des Saxifragacées.   Développement de l'embryon chez le *Saxifraga granulata* L.   Compt. Rend. Acad. des Sci. Paris **202:** 240–242.

———.   1936*b*.   Embryogénie des Hypericacées.   Développement de l'embryon chez l'*Androsaemum officinale* All.   Compt. Rend. Acad. des Sci. Paris **202:** 679–681.

———.   1936*c*.   Embryogénie des Droseracées.   Développement de l'embryon chez le *Drosera rotundifolia* L.   Compt. Rend. Acad. des Sci. Paris **202:** 1457–1459.

———.   1936*d*.   Modifications au tableau récapitulatif des lois du développement chez *Sedum acre* L.   Bul. Soc. Bot. de France **83:** 13–18.

———.   1937*a*.   "Titres et travaux scientifiques.   Deuxième notice (1934–1937)." Saint-Dizier.

———.   1937*b*.   Embryogénie des Dipsacacées.   Développement de l'embryon chez le *Scabiosa succisa* L.   Compt. Rend. Acad. des Sci. Paris **204:** 292–294.

———.   1937*c*.   Embryogénie des Violacées.   Développement de l'embryon chez le *Viola tricolor* L.   Compt. Rend. Acad. des Sci. Paris **205:** 169–171.

———.   1940.   Embryogénie des Haloragacées.   Développement de l'embryon he le *Myriophyllum alterniflorum* DC.   Compt. Rend. Acad. des Sci. Paris **211:** 185–187.

———.   1941*a*.   Embryogénie des Fumariacées.   L'origine du corps de l'embryon chez le *Fumaria officinalis* L.   Compt. Rend. Acad. des Sci. Paris **213:** 528–530.

———.   1941*b*.   Embryogénie des Fumariacées.   La différenciation des régions fondamentales du corps chez le *Fumaria officinalis* L.   Compt. Rend. Acad. des Sci. Paris **213:** 699–702.

———.   1943*a*.   Embryogénie des Fumariacées.   L'origine et les premières divisions de la cellule embryonnaire proprement dite chez l'*Hypecoum procumbens* L.   Compt. Rend. Acad. des Sci. Paris **216:** 310–311.

———.   1943*b*.   Embryogénie des Fumariacées.   Le différenciation des régions fondamentales du corps chez l'*Hypecoum procumbens* L.   Compt. Rend. Acad. des Sci. Paris **216:** 354–356.

———.   1946*a*.   Embryogénie des Fumariacées.   Développement de l'embryon chez le *Corydalis lutea* DC.   Compt. Rend. Acad. des Sci. Paris **222:** 161–163.

———.   1946*b*.   Embryogénie des Fumariacées.   La différenciations des régions fondamentales du corps chez le *Corydalis lutea* DC.   Compt. Rend. Acad. des Sci. Paris **222:** 253–255.

———.   1946*c*.   Embryogénie des Papilionacées.   Développement de l'embryon chez *Melilotus arvensis* Vallr.   Compt. Rend. Acad. des Sci. Paris **222:** 1361–1363.

———.   1946*d*.   Embryogénie des Papilionacées.   Développement de l'embryon chez l'*Orobus vernus* L. (=*Lathyrus vernus* Bernh.).   Compt. Rend. Acad. des Sci. Paris **223:** 60–62

Souègues, E. C. R. 1946e. Embryogénie des Papilionacées. Développement de l'embryon chez le *Vicia sepium* L. Compt. Rend. Acad. des Sci. Paris **223:** 389–391.

———. 1946f. Embryogénie des Papilionacées. Développement de l'embryon chez l'*Orobus tuberosus* L. (=*Lathyrus macrorrhizus* Wimm.). Compt. Rend. Acad. des Sci. Paris **223:** 493–495.

———. 1946g. Embryogénie des Papilionacées. Développement de l'embryon chez l'*Ervum hirsutum* L. (=*Vicia hirsuta* S. F. Gray). Compt. Rend. Acad. des Sci. Paris **223:** 838–840.

———. 1947a. Embryogénie des Papilionacées. Développement de l'embryon chez le *Genista tinctoria* L. Compt. Rend. Acad. des Sci. Paris **224:** 79–81.

———. 1947b. Embryogénie des Papilionacées. Développement de l'embryon chez le *Sarothamnus scoparius* Koch. (=*Cytisus scoparius* Link.). Compt. Rend. Acad. des Sci. Paris **225:** 776–778.

———. 1948. Embryogénie des Papilionacées. Développement de l'embryon chez le *Vicia faba* L. (= *Faba vulgaris* Moench). Compt. Rend. Acad. des Sci. Paris **226:** 2101–2103.

Steindl, F. 1945. Bietrag zur Pollen- und Embryobildung bei *Cynomorium coccineum* L. Arch. Julius Klaus-Stift. f. Vererbungsforsch. **20:** 342–355.

Stenar, H. 1937. Om *Achroanthes monophyllos* (L.) Greene, dess geografiska utbredning och embryologi. Heimbygdas Tidskr., Felskr. Erik Modin 1937/1938, pp. 177–221.

———. 1940. Biologiska och embryologiska notiser rörande *Calypso bulbosa* (L.) Oakes. Jämten Heimbyg las Förlag, Östersund 1940, pp. 184–189.

Stolt, K. A. H. 1928. Die Embryologie von *Myriophyllum alterniflorum* DC. Svensk Bot. Tidskr. **22:** 305–319.

Swamy, B. G. L. 1942a. Female gametophyte and embryogeny in *Cymbidium bicolor* Lindl. Proc. Indian Acad. Sci. Sect. B **15:** 194–201.

———. 1942b. Morphological studies in three species of *Vanda*. Current Sci. [India] **11:** 285.

———. 1943. Gametogenesis and embryogeny of *Eulophea epidendraea* Fischer. Proc. Natl. Inst. Sci. India **9:** 59–65.

———. 1946. The embryology of *Zeuxine sulcata* Lindl. New Phytol. **45:** 132–136.

———. 1948. The embryology of *Epidendrum prisma!ocarpum*. Bul. Torrey Bot. Club **75:** 245–249.

———. 1949. Embryological studies in the Orchidaceae. II. Embryogeny. Amer. Midland Nat. **41:** 202–232.

Tischler, G. 1913. Über die Entwicklung der Samenanlagen in parthenocarpen Angiospermenfrüchten. Jahrb. f. wiss. Bot. **52:** 1–84.

Treub, M. 1879. Notes sur l'embryogénie des quelques Orchidées. Natuurk. Verh. Koninkl. Akad. Amsterdam **19:** 1–50.

———. 1885. Observations sur les Loranthacées. I. Développement dans les sacs embryonnaires dans le *Loranthus sphaerocarpus*. II. Embryogénie du *Loranthus sphaerocarpus*. Ann. Jard. Bot. Buitenzorg **2:** 54–76.

Walker, R. I. 1947. Megasporogenesis and embryo development in *Tropaeolum majus* L. Bul. Torrey Bot. Club **74:** 279–282.

Weber, E.   1929.   Entwicklungsgeschichtliche Untersuchungen über die Gattung
Allium.   Bot. Arch. **25:** 1–44.

White, P. R.   1928.   Studies on the banana: an investigation of the floral morphology and cytology of certain types of the genus *Musa* L.   Zeitschr. f. Zellforsch.
u. mikros. Anat. **7:** 673–733.

Zweifel, R.   1939.   "Cytologisch-embryologische Untersuchungen an *Balanophora
abbreviata* Blume und *B. indica* Wall.   Diss. Zürich.

CHAPTER 9

APOMIXIS[1]

Apomixis may be defined (Winkler, 1908, 1934) as the substitution for sexual reproduction (amphimixis) of an asexual process which does not involve any nuclear fusion. For the sake of convenience it may be subdivided into four classes. In the first, or nonrecurrent apomixis, the megaspore mother cell undergoes the usual meiotic divisions and a haploid embryo sac is formed. The new embryo may then arise either from the egg (haploid parthenogenesis) or from some other cell of the gametophyte (haploid apogamy). Since the plants produced by this method contain only a single set of chromosomes, they are usually sterile, and the process is not repeated from one generation to another.

In the second or recurrent type of apomixis, the embryo sac may arise either from a cell of the archesporium (generative apospory)[2] or from some other part of the nucellus (somatic apospory). There is no reduction in the number of chromosomes, and all the nuclei of the embryo sac are diploid. The embryo may arise either from the egg (diploid parthenogenesis) or from some other cell of the gametophyte (diploid apogamy).

In the third type, whatever the method by which the embryo sac is formed and whether it is haploid or diploid, the embryos do not arise from the cells of the gametophyte but from those of the nucellus or the integument. This is called adventive embryony or sporophytic budding.[3] Here we have no alternation of generations, as the diploid tissues of the parent sporophyte directly give rise to the new embryo.

In the fourth type the flowers are replaced by bulbils or other vegetative propagules which frequently germinate while still on

[1] For a more detailed treatment of apomixis, see Gustafsson (1946, 1947 *a, b*).

[2] Some authors (see Gustafsson, 1946) call it "diplospory."

[3] Winkler (1934) regards this as only a special form of vegetative propagation, but, as Gustafsson (1946) points out, the morphological and physiological characters of adventive embryos do not support this view.

the plant. But since this is merely a form of vegetative reproduction, it will not be considered in the present account.

NONRECURRENT APOMIXIS

The development of a haploid cell of the gametophyte into the embryo is a comparatively infrequent occurrence, and as mentioned before, the plants arising in this way are sterile. Several years ago, Kusano (1915) and Haberlandt (1922) observed mitoses in the unfertilized egg cells of *Gastrodia* and *Oenothera*, but the development was found to stop at a very early stage. Fully developed haploid plants, first found in *Datura* (Blakeslee *et al.*, 1922), have now been recorded in several genera[4] but their exact origin remains obscure except in a very few cases.

For the first critical account of the origin of haploid embryos, we are indebted to C. A. Jørgensen (1928). He treated 90 flowers of *Solanum nigrum* with the pollen of *S. luteum*, resulting in 43 fruits with 70 seeds. From these arose 35 *S. nigrum* seedlings of which seven turned out to be haploid.[5] A developmental study showed that the pollen of *S. luteum* readily germinated on the stigmas of *S. nigrum* and the pollen tubes reached the embryo sacs in the normal way. One of the sperms also entered the egg but failed to fuse with the female nucleus and soon degenerated. Its presence sufficed, however, to stimulate the haploid egg to develop parthenogenetically and give rise to an embryo (Fig. 177).

In some species of *Lilium* (Cooper, 1943), in *Bergenia delavayi* (Lebègue, 1949) and in *Erythraea centaurium* (Crété, 1949), one of the synergids may divide in a small number of the ovules. Twin embryos are thus produced, one diploid and the other haploid (Fig. 178). However, in most cases of this kind the synergid embryo usually degenerates at an early stage, and only the zygotic embryo is seen in the mature seed.

In some recent studies of *Orchis maculata*, *Epipactis latifolia*, *Platanthera chlorantha*, *Cephalanthera damasonium*, and *Listera ovata*, Hagerup (1944, 1945, 1947) found a number of haploid embryos. He observed that while some ovules received more than one pollen tube (Fig. 179), others received none at all, or the tube arrived too

---

[4] For detailed references see Kostoff (1941).

[5] The remaining seedlings were diploid and are believed to have arisen by a process of endoduplication or nuclear division without cell formation, followed by a fusion of the spindles in the next division.

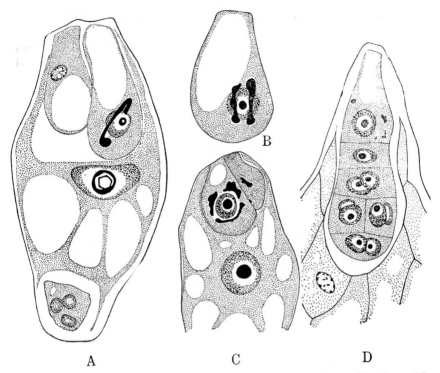

A   C   D

FIG. 177. Origin of haploid embryos in *Solanum nigrum* after pollination with *S. luteum*. *A*, mature embryo sac of *S. nigrum*, showing egg, secondary nucleus, one synergid, and the antipodals. Note sperm nucleus inside egg. *B*, egg with two sperm nuclei. *C*, upper part of embryo sac, showing disintegrating sperm nucleus inside egg. *D*, young embryo and part of endosperm. (*After Jørgensen, 1928.*)

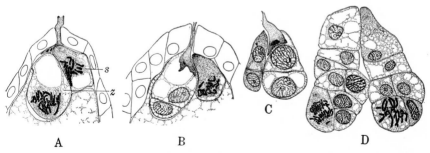

A   B   C   D

FIG. 178. Development of synergid embryos in *Lilium martagon*. *A*, apical portion of ovule, showing first division of zygote and synergid. *B*, two-celled zygotic proembryo; division of synergid not yet completed. *C*, twin proembryos; smaller proembryo, on left, has arisen from a synergid. *D*, more advanced stage; proembryo on right has arisen from an unfertilized synergid and is haploid; proembryo on left has arisen from fertilized egg and is diploid. (*After Cooper, 1943.*)

late to be able to effect fertilization. Under the two last-named conditions, the unfertilized egg was frequently found to divide and give rise to a haploid embryo ("facultative parthenogenesis") (Fig. 180).[6] In *Orchis, Listera,* and *Platanthera* instances of a different nature were also noted, in which the egg was fertilized and gave rise to a normal embryo, but simultaneously an unfertilized synergid also began to develop, so that two embryos were formed, one diploid

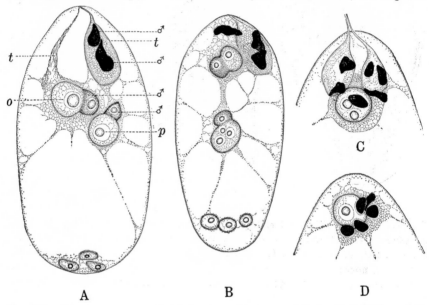

FIG. 179. Supernumerary pollen tubes in embryo sacs of *Epipactis latifolia*. *A,B,* double fertilization, showing one sperm nucleus fusing with egg and the other with secondary nucleus; note presence of second undischarged pollen tube. *C,* micropylar part of embryo sac, showing two pollen tubes. *D,* micropylar part of another embryo sac, showing five sperm nuclei in proximity to egg. (*After Hagerup, 1945.*)

and the other haploid. Further, in one ovule of *Orchis* in which the pollen tube had not yet entered the embryo sac, the egg as well as one of the synergids had begun to divide, thus indicating the possibility of a production of twin haploid embryos (Fig. 181*C*).[7]

[6] In some embryo sacs of another orchid, *Spiranthes australis*, the pollen tube was found to have entered the embryo sac but the male gametes were still undischarged, while embryo formation had already commenced (Maheshwari and Narayanaswami, 1950).

[7] Rarely the egg cell of *Orchis* was found to receive two sperms (Fig. 181*A*) and give rise to a triploid embryo (Fig. 181*B*), or both the egg and one synergid were fertilized to give rise to twin diploid embryos (Fig. 181*D*).

Three cases of androgenic haploids, in which the male nucleus alone is concerned in the development, are also on record, but no developmental studies have been made and the evidence is entirely genetical. Kostoff (1929) pollinated *Nicotiana tabacum* var. *macrophylla*, having 72 chromosomes, with *N. langsdorffii*, having 18 chromosomes. Out of about 1000 seedlings resulting from this

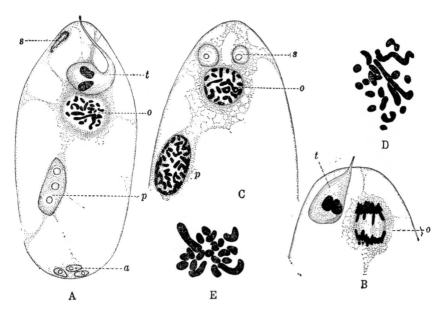

FIG. 180. Haploid parthenogenesis in *Epipactis latifolia* (s = synergid; o = egg; t = pollen tube; p = secondary nucleus). *A,B*, embryo sacs showing division of haploid egg; pollen tube t is still undischarged. *C*, embryo sac has not received any pollen tube, but egg and secondary nucleus are ready to divide. *D,E*, metaphases in first division of haploid egg, showing 20 chromosomes. (*After Hagerup, 1945.*)

cross, one reached maturity. This showed none of the characters of *N. tabacum* but strongly resembled a dwarf *N. langsdorffii*. The number of chromosomes turned out to be 9, strongly suggesting its origin from a male gamete of *N. langsdorffii*.

In the same year Clausen and Lammerts (1929) reported a parallel case in *N. tabacum*. They crossed *N. digluta* ♀, an allohexaploid having 72 chromosomes, with *N. tabacum* ♂, having 48 chromosomes, and obtained a plant with 24 chromosomes. This plant agreed morphologically and cytologically with other haploid *tabacum* plants and is therefore believed to have arisen from a male gamete of *N. tabacum.*

The third androgenic haploid was reported in *Crepis* by Gerassimova (1936). She castrated the flowers of plants of *C. tectorum* having certain dominant characters and treated them with X-rays. They were then crossed with plants of the same species having recessive characters. One haploid plant of the recessive type was

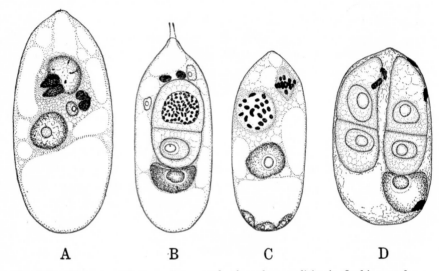

| A | B | C | D |

FIG. 181. Presence of twin embryos and other abnormalities in *Orchis maculatus.* *A*, four male nuclei in embryo sac; two of these are in close contact with the egg, suggesting the possibility of both fusing with it. Note also secondary nucleus and nucleus of a displaced synergid (?). *B*, embryo sac has received two pollen tubes; presence of 60 chromosomes (*n* = 20) in embryo seems to indicate that egg nucleus had fused with two male nuclei. *C*, unfertilized embryo sac, showing division of haploid egg and a synergid. *D*, embryo sac with twin embryos. (*After Hagerup, 1944.*)

obtained. It is believed that the X-ray treatment killed the egg nucleus and the haploid embryo arose from the sperm nucleus only.

Summing up, haploid embryos may result in various ways. The first and most important source is the unfertilized egg. Failure of fertilization may be due to any of the following causes: (1) absence of a pollen tube, (2) inability of the tube to discharge its contents, (3) an insufficient attraction between the male and female nuclei, (4) an early degeneration of the sperms, and (5) a discordance in the time of maturation of the egg and the entrance of the male gametes. It is also possible that there may be two embryo sacs in the same ovule. The egg of one of these may be fertilized and give rise to a normal diploid embryo, while that of the neighboring sac is stimulated to develop without fertilization. A second source of origin of haploid embryos may be some cell of the embryo sac other than the egg. Usually this is a synergid, but rarely even antipodal cells may give rise to embryos. The third possibility is the origin of the embryo from a male gamete. This may be due either to a degeneration of the egg nucleus, so that the male nucleus alone is left to function, or to failure of pollen tube to open, so that one or both of the male gametes begin to develop *in situ*.

RECURRENT APOMIXIS

In the second or recurrent type of apomixis the embryo sac is diploid and may arise either from a cell of the archesporium or from some other cell of the nucellus. The distinction between the two forms, known as generative and somatic apospory, is somewhat artificial, as it is frequently difficult to say whether the cell in question belongs to the archesporial tissue or to the "somatic" tissues of the nucellus.

Since there is no reduction in the chromosome number, the first division of the initial cell is mitotic, semiheterotypic, or pseudo-homotypic. The mitotic division requires no explanation except that in apomictic plants there is a retardation of the prophase and the resting nucleus shows an intense hydration of the chromosomes. They do not exhibit either the pairing or the marked contraction characteristic of meiosis, and at anaphase the two halves of each chromosome move apart to the poles (Fig. 182*M–R*). The semiheterotypic division begins like a meiotic prophase,[8] but a normal metaphase plate is not organized; instead the chromosomes are widely scattered on the spindle. In the anaphase there are numerous laggards, and eventually a nuclear membrane is laid down in such a manner as to incorporate the entire chromosome complement within a single "restitution nucleus" (Fig. 182*A–G*). This nucleus is somewhat dumbbell-shaped in the beginning, but it soon becomes

[8] A pairing of the chromosomes and the occurrence of "bivalent-like formations" have been noticed in some cases of semiheterotypic division, but chiasmata are rare or absent (see Gustafsson, 1946).

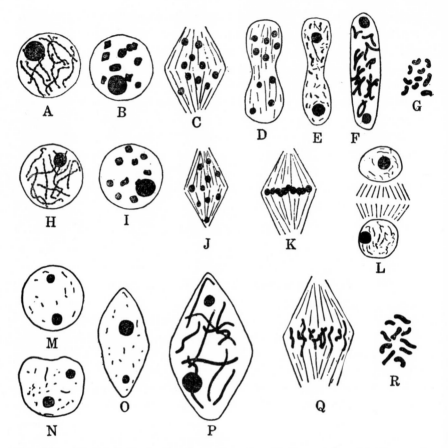

Fig. 182.   Diagrams illustrating formation of restitution nucleus (A–G); pseudo-homotypic division (H–L); and somatic division (M–R) in megaspore mother cells of apomictic angiosperms.   A, nucleus of megaspore mother cell in prophase; note absence of pairing.   B, diakinesis.   C, semiheterotypic metaphase.   D,E, formation of nuclear membrane enclosing all the chromosomes.   F, fully formed restitution nucleus.   G, homotypic metaphase.   H, nucleus of megaspore mother cell in prophase.   I–L, stages in formation of daughter nuclei by pseudohomotypic division.   M–R, somatic division of nucleus of megaspore mother cell.   (After Gustafsson, 1935.)

rounded and the following divisions are entirely mitotic.   In the pseudohomotypic division the chromosomes are short, thick, and contracted, as in meiosis, but do not show any pairing.   In the beginning of the metaphase the univalents are scattered over the spindle, but gradually they arrange themselves in an equatorial plate and undergo the usual longitudinal splitting, followed by a separation of the daughter chromosomes (Fig. 182*H–L*).

Generative apospory. Holmgren (1919) has made a very detailed study of the embryology of several species of the genus *Eupatorium*. Some species are entirely normal and reproduce sexually, but *E.*

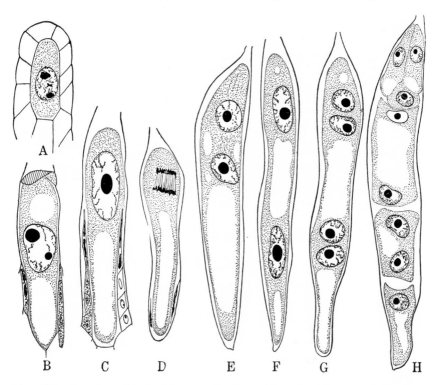

FIG. 183. Development of embryo sac in *Eupatorium glandulosum*. *A–C*, megaspore mother cell. *D*, nucleus of megaspore mother cell in division. *E,F*, two-nucleate embryo sacs. *G*, four-nucleate embryo sac. *H*, eight-nucleate embryo sac. (*After Holmgren, 1919.*)

glandulosum, which is a triploid, is apomictic (Fig. 183). Here the division of the megaspore mother cell differs little from a somatic mitosis except in the fact that the cell elongates considerably, demolishing the nucellar epidermis and becoming vacuolate even before it is ready to divide. There is no synapsis or pairing of chromosomes. Three nuclear divisions take place, to give rise to an eight-nucleate embryo sac with two or three antipodal cells which may

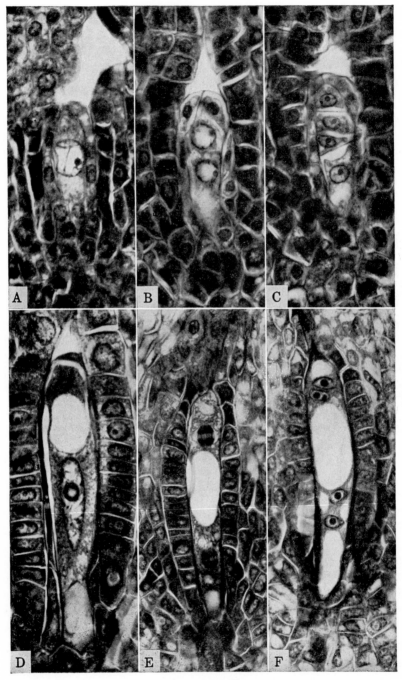

FIG. 184 A-F.

undergo a further division with or without the formation of a cell wall. The embryo arises from the unfertilized but diploid egg cell.

An essentially similar condition occurs in the guayule, *Parthenium argentatum* (Esau, 1946). This species comprises two races, one with 36 chromosomes and the other with 72. The former is mainly sexual and the latter mainly apomictic. Since the condition is not absolutely fixed, the apomixis may be regarded as facultative. In the 36-chromosome race there is usually an orderly sequence of events in megasporogenesis (Fig. 184*A–C*) and gametophyte development. Megaspore mother cells are seen in various phases of meiosis, megaspore tetrads are abundant, and uninucleate embryo sacs are associated with the crushed remnants of the nonfunctioning megaspores. Views of pollen tubes in embryo sacs, followed by syngamy and triple fusion, are common in artificially pollinated flowers, and the development of the embryo and endosperm is closely correlated. In the 72-chromosome plants, on the other hand, there is no orderly sequence of stages in the development of the embryo sac (Fig. 184*D–F*). Young stages tend to persist in fairly large ovules; megaspore mother cells enlarge, become vacuolate, and directly assume the characteristics of uninucleate embryo sacs without the intervention of the dyad and tetrad stages; embryo and endosperm show little correlation in their development; and frequently even unpollinated flowers give rise to embryos. Nevertheless pollination is highly beneficial or even necessary for the continued development of the endosperm without which the embryo does not grow to maturity.

A good example of a semiheterotypic division, followed by the formation of a restitution nucleus, is seen in *Ixeris* (Okabe, 1932), also belonging to the family Compositae. The basic chromosome number in this genus is 7. Species with the diploid number ($2n = 14$) reproduce normally by the sexual method, but *I. dentata*, which

---

Fig. 184. Some stages in development of embryo sac in 36-chromosome and 72-chromosome races of *Parthenium argentatum*. *A*, 36-chromosome race; megaspore mother cell. *B*, dyad formation. *C*, tetrad of megaspores. *D*, 72-chromosome race; megaspore mother cell elongating and functioning directly as diploid spore. Note vacuolation of its cytoplasm and disorganization of the nucellar epidermis, accompanied by a differentiation of the integumentary tapetum. *E*, binucleate embryo sac with both nuclei in division. *F*, four-nucleate embryo sac. (*After Esau, 1946.*)

is a triploid ($2n = 21$), is an apomict (Fig. 185).   During the division of the megaspore mother cell there is no evidence of any pairing of the chromosomes.   Even at anaphase the chromosomes are

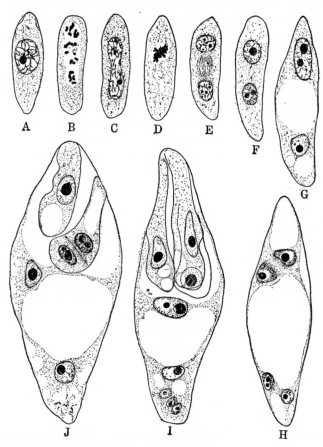

Fig. 185.   Development of unreduced embryo sac in *Ixeris dentata*.   *A*, prophase of first division of megaspore mother cell.   *B*, later stage, showing 21 univalent chromosomes.   *C*, restitution nucleus.   *D*, metaphase.   *E*, telophase.   *F,G*, two-nucleate embryo sacs.   *H*, four-nucleate embryo sac.   *I*, mature embryo sac. *J*, later stage, showing two-celled proembryo.   (*After Okabe, 1932.*)

irregularly scattered on the spindle, and instead of forming two separate groups they become enclosed in a common nuclear membrane, forming a restitution nucleus which contains the unreduced chromosome number.   Further divisions are entirely mitotic and lead to the formation of an eight-nucleate embryo sac, organized in the usual manner.

The diploid species of the genus *Taraxacum* go through the usual meiotic divisions and tetrad formation, followed by syngamy, but the polyploid species show a semiheterotypic division and dyad formation, followed by the development of an unreduced egg cell into the embryo (Osawa, 1913; Sears, 1922; Poddubnaja-Arnoldi and Dianowa, 1934; Gustafsson, 1935; Fagerlind, 1947a). Usually it is the chalazal dyad cell which functions (Fig. 186), but in *T. laevigatum* (Sears, 1922) it is frequently the upper.

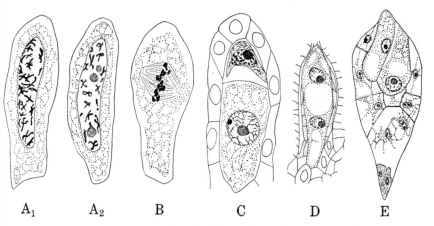

A_1 A_2 B   C   D   E

FIG. 186. Development of unreduced embryo sac in *Taraxacum albidum*. A_1, A_2, consecutive sections of megaspore mother cell. *B*, megaspore mother cell in division. *C*, formation of dyad cells, of which the lower functions and gives rise to embryo sac. *D*, two-nucleate embryo sac. *E*, mature embryo sac, showing endosperm formation. (*After Osawa, 1913.*)

In *Erigeron* some species are sexual, others partially apomictic, and still others almost entirely apomictic. In *E. annuus* (Fagerlind, 1947b), which belongs to the third category, a restitution nucleus is formed during the first meiotic division. This divides without wall formation to give rise to the mature embryo sac, which is usually eight-nucleate. Ordinarily the development of the embryo and endosperm go hand in hand (Holmgren, 1919), but sometimes the endosperm may lag behind, so that occasionally a many-celled embryo is associated with an undivided endosperm nucleus (Tahara, 1921).

Bergman (1941) has recently reported a considerable range of

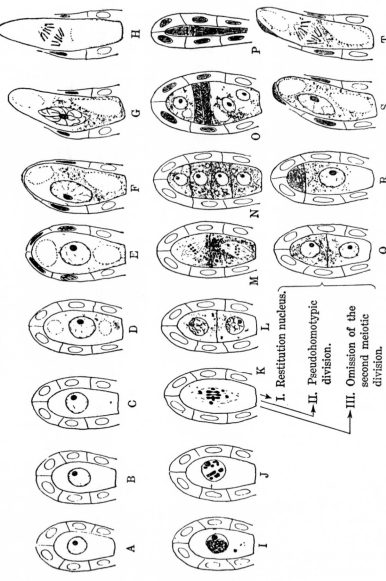

FIG. 187. Diagrams showing different types of division of megaspore mother cell in apomictic species of *Hieracium*. (*A–H*), mitotic type. *I–P*, meiotic type which is, however, followed by degeneration of all the products of meiosis. *Q–T*, meiotic type followed by formation of dyad cells either through production of restitution nucleus, or through pseudohomotypic divisions as though an initof second meiotic disi-

I. Restitution nucleus.

II. Pseudohomotypic division.

III. Omission of the second meiotic division.

variation in several species of the genus *Hieracium*, subgenus *Archieracium*. In some cases the division is of the mitotic type and the megaspore mother cell develops directly into the embryo sac (Fig. 187*A–H*). In others both the meiotic divisions take place but several chromosomes remain unpaired, resulting in disturbances in tetrad formation and consequent sterility (Fig. 187*I–P*). In still other cases there is a production of unreduced dyad cells (Fig. 187*Q–T*) either by the formation of a restitution nucleus or by a pseudohomotypic division. Rarely, the first meiotic division takes place in the usual way, but this is followed by a prolonged inter-kinetic stage in which the chromosomes divide longitudinally so that the diploid number is restored. In all three cases one of the dyad cells functions and gives rise to the embryo sac.

Somatic Apospory. Rosenberg (1907) described the occurrence of somatic apospory in three species of the genus *Hieracium* (subgenus *Pilosella*), viz., *H. excellens* (Fig. 188*A–E*), *H. flagellare* (Fig. 188*F–H*), and *H. aurantiacum*. The megaspore mother cell goes through the usual meiotic divisions, but at just about this stage a somatic cell situated in the chalazal region begins to enlarge and becomes vacuolated. This cell gradually increases in volume, encroaching upon the megaspores and finally crushing them. The aposporic embryo sac, arising from it, has the unreduced chromosome number and is able to function without fertilization. In *H. excellens* the normal and reduced embryo sac, as well as the aposporic and unreduced embryo sac, sometimes develops simultaneously but this is rare in the other two species.[9] *H. aurantiacum* is peculiar in that the aposporic embryo sac usually originates from a cell of the nucellar epidermis.

Aposporic embryo sacs have also been reported in several other genera like *Malus* (Dermen, 1936), *Crepis* (Stebbins and Jenkins, 1939), *Hypericum* (Noack, 1939), *Ranunculus* (Häfliger, 1943), and *Poa* (Håkansson, 1943; Nielsen, 1945, 1946). The cell giving rise to the embryo sac may belong either to the integument or to some part of the nucellar epidermis. In every case, however, the development is characterized by two common features—an increase in the

[9] As remarked by Rosenberg, it is because of this combination of typical as well as unreduced embryo sacs that *H. excellens* can give rise to hybrids in spite of being an apomict.

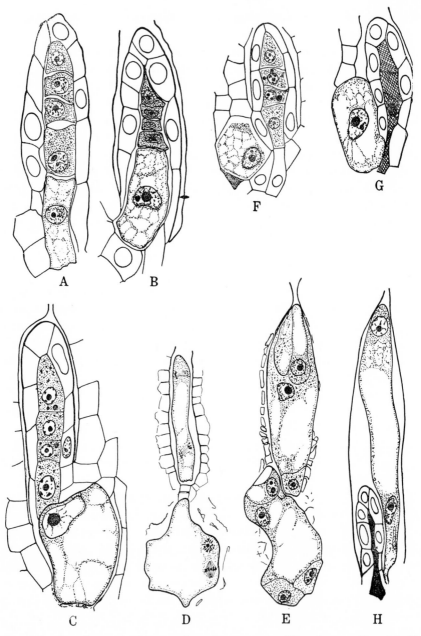

FIG. 188.   Development of aposporic embryo sacs in *Hieracium excellens* (*A–E*)
and *H. flagellare* (*F–H*).   *A*, nucellus, showing tetrad of megaspores; note enlargement of cell lying just below chalazal megaspore.   *B*, megaspore tetrad in process

size of the cell and a vacuolation of its cytoplasm, both taking place prior to nuclear division.

Unclassified Cases. In several plants it is difficult to draw a sharp distinction between generative and somatic apospory. *Atraphaxis frutescens* (Edman, 1931) may be cited as an example of this kind. Here we have a multicellular archesporium. Usually only one or two of its cells, those which have a more central position, take the characters of megaspore mother cells, while the rest undergo a series of mitotic divisions. The true mother cells or their derivatives soon degenerate. The aposporic embryo sacs arise from either of the following sources: (1) the derivatives of the potentially sporogenous cells lying close to the megaspore mother cell and greatly resembling it in appearance (Fig. 189), or (2) the purely somatic cells of the chalaza (Fig. 190).

In *Antennaria alpina* and some other species of this genus (Juel, 1900; Stebbins, 1932; Bergman, 1941) the megaspore mother cell may divide meiotically or mitotically. In the first or meiotic type, the chromosomes become greatly contracted and lie scattered over the spindle in a disorderly fashion. The separation of the daughter chromosomes takes place irregularly, so that although the number is reduced it is not exactly halved and several univalents are left out altogether. The next division may result in a tetrad of four megaspores, but more often five, six, or even seven cells may be formed. The gametophytes arising from them are functionless and soon degenerate. In the second or mitotic type, the dividing cell grows vigorously and attains a large size even before the onset of the prophase. There is no reduction in the number of chromosomes and the embryo sacs derived in this way are diploid and functional.

In *Alchemilla arvensis* (Murbeck, 1901; Böös, 1924) the megaspore mother cell enters a meiotic prophase, but the nucleus soon degenerates. Meanwhile, the surrounding cells, which are potentially sporogenous, undergo a number of mitotic divisions resulting in a few parietal cells and two to six axial cells, which may divide either

---

of degeneration; chalazal cell showing increase in size and vacuolation. *C*, megaspore tetrad and large nucellar cell destined to give rise to embryo sac. *D*, normal and aposporic embryo sacs growing simultaneously. *E*, two fully developed embryo sacs; lower is probably of aposporic origin. *F–H*, some stages in development of aposporic embryo sac; note progressive degeneration of megaspore tetrad. (*After Rosenberg, 1907.*)

meiotically or mitotically. The reduced embryo sacs must be fertilized before they can give rise to embryos. The unreduced embryo sacs, on the other hand, can function without fertilization.

Fagerlind (1944) has recently made a detailed study of some species belonging to the genus *Elatostema*. In *E. acuminatum* the

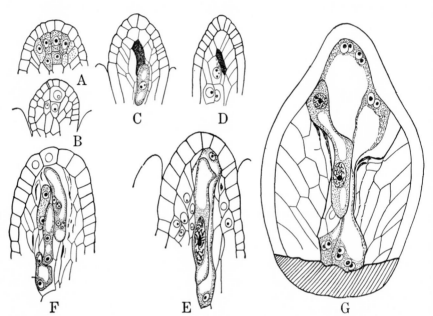

Fɪɢ. 189. Development of aposporic embryo sacs in *Atraphaxis frutescens* (striped portion in ovule represents hypostase). *A,B,* l.s. nucellus, showing archesporial tissue. *C,D,* degeneration of cells belonging to primary archesporial tissue and appearance of secondary archesporium. *E,* a two-nucleate haploid embryo sac accompanied by uninucleate diploid embryo sac. *F,* young aposporic embryo sacs. *G,* nucellus, showing three embryo sacs—one diploid and two-nucleate, another haploid and four-nucleate, and the third haploid and eight-nucleate. (*After Edman, 1931.*)

megaspore mother cell enters into a meiotic prophase, but because of the occurrence of certain irregularities the derivative cells are nonviable and soon degenerate. The adjacent cells of the nucellus divide mitotically to give rise to unreduced embryo sacs (somatic apospory), but these also usually degenerate, resulting in consider-able sterility. In *E. eurhynchum* there is little or no tendency towards meiosis but several unreduced embryo sacs arise by mitotic divisions in the central cells of the archesporium (generative apospory). The same condition also occurs in *E. machaerophyllum* except that here the division may be mitotic or pseudohomotypic, or there may be a semiheterotypic division followed by the formation of a restitution nucleus.

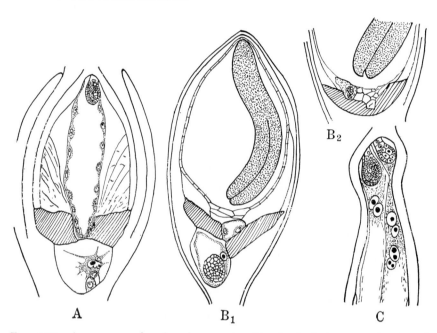

FIG. 190. Apospory and polyembryony in *Atraphaxis frutescens*. *A*, normal embryo sac with embryo and endosperm; additional aposporic embryo sac at chalazal end showing inverted polarity. *B₁B₂*, consecutive sections of ovule showing well-developed embryo in upper embryo sac and aborted embryos in chalazal region. *C*, twin embryo sacs—one on left with two overlapping embryos, that on right with one embryo. (*After Edman, 1931.*)

In some species of *Potentilla* (Rutishauser, 1943) there is a multicellular archesporium without any well-marked distinction between the axial and the lateral cells of the sporogenous tissue. Embryo sacs may arise either from such cells by ordinary mitotic division as in *P. verna* (generative apospory), or from the chalazal cells of the nucellus as in *P. canescens*, *P. praecox*, and *P. argentea* (somatic apospory). Håkansson (1946) has confirmed this in *P. argentea* and also reported the occurrence of aposporic embryo sacs in *P. crantzii*. In the latter it is the nucellar cells adjacent to the archesporium which give rise to embryo sacs.

Organization of Aposporic Embryo Sacs. By whichever method the aposporic embryo sac may arise (*i.e.*, by generative or by somatic apospory), it is usually eight-nucleate. Sometimes fewer than eight nuclei occur as in *Ochna serrulata* (Chiarugi and Francini, 1930) and *Atraphaxis frutescens* (Edman, 1931), or more than eight as in *Elatostema eurrhynchum* (Fagerlind, 1944), but these are occasional deviations without any special significance. A more common feature is the disturbed polarity and lack of proper organization of the various elements of the embryo sac. Frequently the egg and synergids are indistinguishable from one another, and sometimes there are more than two polar nuclei, while the remaining elements of the embryo sac remain undifferentiated. In *Atraphaxis* (Edman, 1931) some embryo sacs were found to lack an egg apparatus and some the antipodal cells; occasionally both egg apparatus and antipodal cells were found to be absent and all the nuclei were aggregated in the center. However, such embryo sacs are probably functionless.

Not only the number but also the behavior of the polar nuclei is extremely variable. In *Zephyranthes texana* (Pace, 1913) the two polar nuclei fuse with a male nucleus to give rise to a pentaploid endosperm, while the embryo is formed by the unfertilized but diploid egg cell. In the apomictic forms of *Chondrilla* (Poddubnaja-Arnoldi, 1933), *Taraxacum* (Poddubnaja-Arnoldi and Dianowa, 1934), *Ranunculus* (Häfliger, 1943), and *Elatostema* there is no triple fusion and the endosperm is tetraploid. In *Antennaria alpina* (Juel, 1900) and *Alchemilla arvensis* (Murbeck, 1901) the polar nuclei are said to divide independently and the endosperm is diploid. In *Eupatorium glandulosum* (Holmgren, 1919) and *Ixeris dentata* (Okabe, 1932) the condition is variable and the endosperm may be diploid or tetraploid. In *Balanophora globosa*, according to Ernst (1913), the lower polar nucleus degenerates and only the upper forms the endosperm.

Development of Embryo in Aposporic Embryo Sacs. Theoretically the new sporophyte may arise from any cell or nucleus of the diploid embryo sac, but usually it is only the egg which is capable of such development (diploid parthenogenesis). Sometimes one or

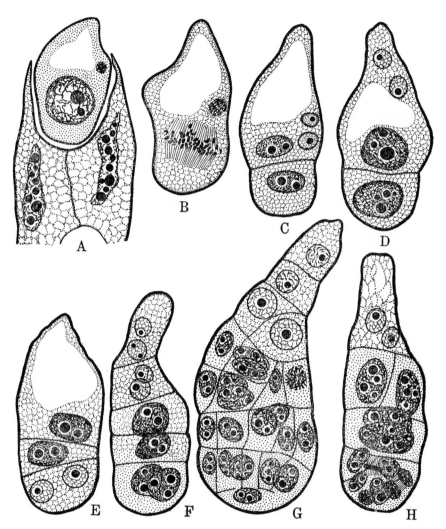

Fig. 191. Semigamy in *Rudbeckia speciosa*. *A*, part of embryo sac, showing two-celled endosperm and egg containing male and female nuclei. *B*, egg, showing division of both male and female nuclei. *C,D*, two-celled proembryos; two small nuclei in basal cell have arisen by division of sperm nucleus. *E*, three-celled proembryo showing nuclei derived from sperm in terminal cell. *F–H*, more advanced stages; nuclei derived from sperm occupy variable positions in proembryo. (*After Battaglia, 1947.*)

both of the synergids, and less frequently the antipodal cells, may give rise to embryos (diploid apogamy). In some plants such development takes place without the stimulus of pollination (autonomous apomixis) and may begin even in the bud stage. More commonly, however, the stimulus of pollination is essential and even triple fusion occurs more or less regularly. This condition is called pseudogamy.[10]

There are a few reports of embryos arising from the cells or nuclei of the endosperm. Rosenberg (1907), Schnarf (1919), and Gentscheff (1937) reported such an occurrence in some species of *Hieracium*. However, in a later paper Rosenberg (1930) withdrew this interpretation. He now thinks that here several aposporic embryo sacs develop in the same ovule and fuse with one another so that the boundaries between them get lost, and the embryos, although really arising from the egg cells of the different embryo sacs, become included in a common mass of endosperm tissue. The reports of Billings (1937) and of Jeffrey and Haertl (1939) about the origin of endosperm embryos in *Isomeris* and *Trillium* are also open to criticism.[11] To date there is, therefore, no established case of the origin of embryos from the endosperm.

Mention must finally be made of the peculiar phenomenon called "semigamy" which has been discovered very recently by Battaglia (1946, 1947). Here a sperm nucleus enters the diploid egg cell but does not fuse with its nucleus and divides independently to form a few daughter nuclei. Embryonal chimaeras are thus produced in which most of the cells and nuclei are diploid but a few are haploid. The endosperm, however, is pentaploid, being formed as the result of a fertilization of the secondary nucleus by one male nucleus. So far this condition has been reported only in two species of *Rudbeckia*, *R. laciniata* and *R. speciosa* (Fig. 191), but it is possible that it occurs in other apomicts and has been overlooked.

ADVENTIVE EMBRYONY

In adventive embryony there is no alternation of generations and the embryos originate from the diploid cells of the ovule lying out-

---

[10] For a more detailed discussion of pseudogamy, see Häfliger (1943) and Fagerlind (1946).

[11] Swamy (1948), who has recently studied the development of the embryo and endosperm in *Trillium undulatum*, refutes the occurrence of endosperm embryos in this species but states that adventive embryony is frequent.

side the embryo sac and belonging either to the nucellus or the integument. A common feature of the process is that the cells concerned in such development become richly protoplasmic and actively divide to form small groups of cells, which eventually push their way into the embryo sac and grow further to form true embryos. Frequently the zygotic embryo also develops at the same time and is distinguishable from the adventive embryos only by the somewhat lateral position and lack of a suspensor in the latter.

A favorite and frequently quoted instance of adventive embryony is that of *Citrus* (Strasburger, 1878; Osawa, 1912; Webber and Batchelor, 1943), (Fig. 192) in which four or five embryos are com-

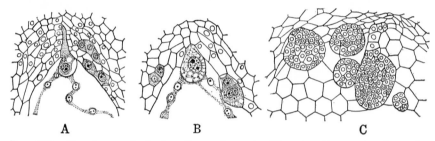

A   B   C

FIG. 192. Development of adventive embryos in *Citrus trifoliata*. *A*, micropylar portion of embryo sac, showing fertilized egg, pollen tube, and endosperm nuclei; some of the nucellar cells have enlarged and show prominent nucleus and dense cytoplasm. *B*, same, more advanced stage. *C*, upper part of embryo sac, showing several embryos lying in endosperm; only zygotic embryo has suspensor. (*After Osawa, 1912.*)

mon and sometimes as many as 13 viable embryos can be found in the same seed. Among other examples may be cited *Euphorbia dulcis* (Carano, 1926), *Sarcococca ilicifolia* (Wiger, 1930), *Eugenia* spp. (Tiwary, 1926; Pijl, 1934), *Capparis frondosa* (Mauritzon, 1934), *Mangifera indica* (Juliano, 1937), and *Hiptage madablota* (Subba Rao, 1940). The chief variation in development concerns the place of origin of the embryos. Whenever the nucellus is intact, the adventive embryos originate from the nucellar cells, but when it becomes disorganized the cells of the integument may take over this function. Also, sometimes a single cell may become the progenitor of an embryo, while on other occasions it is a small group of cells.

An especially interesting type of adventive embryony occurs in the Scandinavian forms of the orchid *Nigritella nigra* (Afzelius,

1928, 1932).[12]   As in other members of the family, the nucellus is reduced to a single layer of cells surrounding the megaspore mother cell (Fig. 193*A*).   The latter gives rise to three or four daughter cells of which the chalazal functions and proceeds to form the embryo sac (Fig. 193*B–E*).   Its development becomes arrested at the four-nucleate stage, but meanwhile one or two cells of the nucellar epidermis show a considerable increase in size and begin dividing to give rise to adventive embryos which are very close to the apex of

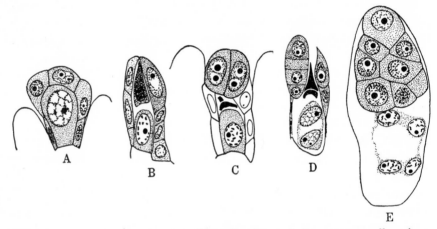

FIG. 193.   Adventive embryony in *Nigritella nigra*.   *A*, l.s. young nucellus, showing megaspore mother cell.   *B*, older stage, showing micropylar dyad cell in course of degeneration.   *C*, functioning megaspore with remains of degenerating megaspores; note enlargement of two cells of nucellar epidermis.   *D*, two-nucleate embryo sac with young adventive embryos arising from cells of nucellar epidermis. *E*, large nucellar embryo lying at apex of four-nucleate embryo sac.   (*After Afzelius, 1928.*)

the embryo sac and are enclosed by the integuments (Fig. 193*B–E*). *Zeuxine sulcata* (Swamy, 1946) is very similar except that here, owing to disturbed meiosis, there is no regular megaspore formation and if any embryo sacs are produced they abort at a very early stage.   As in *Nigritella*, the cells of the nucellar epidermis possess a remarkable capacity for growth and differentiation.   One or two of them elongate considerably to give rise to filamentous proembryos (often four-celled and therefore looking like megaspore

[12] It is interesting to note that those forms of this species which occur in the Alps show normal sexual reproduction (see Gustafsson, 1947*a*).

tetrads) which may undergo a secondary increase in number by further proliferation, budding, or cleavage.

Adventive embryony may be completely autonomous, *i.e.*, independent of pollination and fertilization, or it may be induced by one or both of these factors. The former condition prevails in *Alchornea ilicifolia* (Strasburger, 1878), *Euphorbia dulcis* (Carano, 1926), and *Sarcococca pruniformis* (Wiger, 1930). In *Nigritella nigra* (Afzelius, 1928) also, neither pollination nor fertilization are essential, but the occurrence of pollen tubes in the ovary seems to accelerate the tendency towards the production of adventive embryos. In most other plants, either pollination, or pollination followed by fertilization, is an important factor in stimulating the development of adventive embryos, although their exact roles have not been properly elucidated. In the orchid *Zygopetalum mackayi* (Süssenguth, 1923) unpollinated flowers were found to degenerate and fall off shortly after blooming, but on treating the stigmas with pollen from *Oncidium* the adventive embryos developed to maturity and viable seeds were formed. Here the foreign pollen, although quite incapable of effecting fertilization, exercised some kind of a chemical influence which affected the growth of the embryos in a favorable manner. *Eugenia jambos* (Pijl, 1934) seems to illustrate the next step, for in this plant the adventive embryos may originate quite independently of pollination but do not attain their full development unless fertilization has taken place. In most varieties of *Citrus* also (see Webber and Batchelor, 1943) fertilization is considered necessary for the maturation of the adventive embryos, and a similar condition occurs in the "carabao" mango (Juliano, 1937).

In all cases of adventive embryony there is a formation of the endosperm, whether it originates as the result of triple fusion or without it. The only exception is *Opuntia aurantiaca* (Archibald, 1939). Here the egg, synergids, and antipodals are said to degenerate, and later also the polar nuclei, so that an endosperm is not formed at all and the whole embryo sac is reduced to an irregular darkly staining cavity.[13] The nucellar tissue becomes more massive, however, and certain cells lying below the nucellar cap and bordering on the cavity of the embryo sac enlarge and become

[13] It should be noted, however, that Ganong (1898), who found nucellar embryony in another species—*O. vulgaris*—records normal fertilization and the formation of an "abundant endosperm."

rounded. Their walls become thickened and each cell undergoes two divisions at right angles to each other to form a four-celled proembryo. With further divisions the proembryo increases in size and finally ruptures the wall of the parent cell and enters into the cavity of the sac. Several other embryos are formed similarly but owing to mutual competition only one or two reach maturity.

An interesting feature, which has often been commented on, is that although the adventive embryos have precisely the same germinal constitution as sporophytic buds, their developmental behavior is quite different. A sporophytic bud, whether terminal or axillary, directly proceeds to the formation of a stem, leaves, and flowers, while the adventive embryo recapitulates in a very striking manner the morphological features of true seedlings, *viz.*, presence of cotyledons, radicle, plumule, epicotyl, and hypocotyl. In *Citrus*, sporophytic buds produce virtually thornless plants, but the nucellar embryos produce plants which are thorny, like the zygotic seedlings with which they are associated.[14]

Swingle (1927) suggested that this extraordinary recapitulation of a stage in ontogeny, already undergone by the generation which produces the nucellar embryos, is probably due to some powerful morphogenetic influence exercised upon the embryos by the "magic bath" of the embryo sac. However, we have no knowledge so far of the true nature of these influences, and it would be interesting to know how the nucellar embryos would behave if they are removed from the ovule at a comparatively early stage of development and grown in artificial media.

REFERENCES

Afzelius, K. 1928. Die Embryobildung bei *Nigritella nigra*. Svensk Bot. Tidskr. **22:** 82–91.

———. 1932. Zur Kenntnis der Fortpflanzungsverhältnisse und Chromosomenzahlen bei *Nigritella nigra*. Svensk. Bot. Tidskr. **26:** 365–369.

Archibald, E. E. A. 1939. The development of the ovule and seed of jointed cactus (*Opuntia aurantiaca* Lindley). South African Jour. Sci. **36:** 195–211.

Battaglia, E. 1946. Ricerche cariologiche e embriologiche sul genere *Rudbeckia* (Asteraceae). VIII. Semigamia in *Rudbeckia laciniata* L. Nuovo Gior. Bot. Ital. N.S. **53:** 483–511.

[14] It has also been noted (see Cook, 1938; Hodgson and Cameron, 1938; Frost, 1938) that *Citrus* clones continually propagated by cuttings eventually become weak and sterile. Horticulturists rejuvenate the clone by using nucellar seedlings, as the plants obtained from them show greater vigor and a more upright growth than those obtained from cuttings.

Battaglia, E. 1947. Ricerche cariologiche e embriologiche sul genere *Rudbeckia* (Asteraceae). XI. Semigamia in *Rudbeckia speciosa* Wender. Nuovo Gior. Bot. Ital. N.S. **54:** 1–29.

Bergman, B. 1937. Eine neue apomiktische *Antennaria*. Svensk Bot. Tidskr. **36:** 429–443.

———. 1941. Studies on the embryo sac mother cell and its development in *Hieracium* subg. *Archieracium*. Svensk Bot. Tidskr. **35:** 1–42.

Billings, F. H. 1937. Some new features in the reproductive cytology of angiosperms, illustrated by *Isomeris arborea*. New Phytol. **36:** 301–326.

Blakeslee, A. F., Belling, J., Franham, M. E., and Bergner, A. D. 1922. A haploid mutant in the Jimson weed, *Datura stramonium*. Science **55:** 646–647.

Böös, G. 1924. Neue embryologische Studien über *Alchemilla arvensis* (L.) Scop. Bot. Notiser 1924, pp. 209–250.

Carano, E. 1926. Ulteriori osservazioni su *Euphorbia dulcis* L. in rapporto col suo comportamento apomittico. Ann. di Bot. **17:** 50–79.

Chiarugi, A., and Francini, E. 1930. Apomissia in *Ochna serrulata* Walp. Nuovo Gior. Bot. Ital. N.S. **37:** 1–250.

Clausen, R. E., and Lammerts, W. E. 1929. Interspecific hybridization in *Nicotiana*. X. Haploid and diploid merogony. Amer. Nat. **63:** 279–322.

Cook, R. 1938. A note on embryo rejuvenation. Jour. Hered. **29:** 419–422.

Cooper, D. C. 1943. Haploid-diploid twin embryos in *Lilium* and *Nicotiana*. Amer. Jour. Bot. **30:** 408–413.

Crété, P. 1949. Un cas de polyembryonie chez une Gentianacee, l'*Erythraea centaurium* Pers. Bull. Soc. Bot. de France **96:** 113–115.

Dermen, H. 1936. Aposporic parthenogenesis in a triploid apple, *Malus hupehensis*. Jour. Arnold Arboretum **17:** 90–105.

Edman, G. 1931. Apomeiosis und Apomixis bei *Atraphaxis frutescens* C. Koch. Acta Horti Bergiani **11:** 13–66.

Ernst, A. 1913. Zur Kenntnis von Parthenogenesis und Apogamie bei Angiospermen. Verh. schweiz. naturf. Ges. II, **96:** 1–13.

Esau, K. 1946. Morphology of reproduction in guayule and certain other species of *Parthenium*. Hilgardia **17:** 61–101.

Fagerlind, F. 1944. Die Samenbildung und die Zytologie bei agamospermischen und sexuellen Arten von *Elatostema* und einigen nahestehenden Gattungen nebst Beleuchtung einiger damit zusammenhängender Probleme. K. Svenska Vet.-Akad. Handl. III, **21**(4): 1–130.

———. 1946. Sporogenesis, Embryosackentwicklung und pseudogame Samenbildung bei *Rudbeckia laciniata* L. Acta Horti Bergiani **14:** 39–90.

———. 1947a. Makrosporogenese und Embryosackbildung bei agamospermischen *Taraxacum*-Biotypen. Svensk Bot. Tidskr. **41:** 365–390.

———. 1947b. Macrogametophyte formation in two agamospermous *Erigeron* species. Acta Horti Bergiani **14:** 221–247.

Frost, H. B. 1938. Nucellar embryony and juvenile characters in clonal varieties of *Citrus*. Jour. Hered. **29:** 423–432.

Ganong, W. F. 1898. Upon polyembryony and its morphology in *Opuntia vulgaris*. Bot. Gaz. **25:** 221–228.

Gentscheff, G. 1937. Zytologische und embryologische Studien über einige *Hieracium*-Arten. Planta **27**: 165–195.

Gerassimova, H. 1936. Experimentell erhaltene haploide Pflanze von *Crepis tectorum* L. Planta **25**: 696–702.

Gustafsson, A. 1935. Studies on the mechanism of parthenogenesis. Hereditas **21**: 1–112.

———. 1946. Apomixis in higher plants. I. The mechanism of apomixis. Lunds Univ. Årsskr. N.F. Avd. II, **42**(3): 1–67.

———. 1947a. Apomixis in higher plants. II. The causal agent of apomixis. Lunds Univ. Årsskr. N.F. Avd. II, **43**(2): 71–179.

———. 1947b. Apomixis in higher plants. III. Biotype and species formation. Lunds Univ. Årsskr. N.F. Avd. II, **43**(12): 183–370.

Haberlandt, G. 1922. Über Zellteilungshormone und ihre Beziehungen zur Wundheilung, Befruchtung, Parthenogenesis und Adventivembryonie. Biol. Zentbl. **42**: 145–172.

Häfliger, E. 1943. Zytologisch-embryologische Untersuchungen pseudogamer Ranunkulen der Auricomus Gruppe. Ber. schweiz. bot. Gesell. **53**: 317–382.

Hagerup, O. 1944. On fertilization, polyploidy and haploidy in *Orchis maculatus* L. Dansk Bot. Arkiv. **11**(5): 1–26.

———. 1945. Facultative parthenogenesis and haploidy in *Epipactis latifolia*. K. Danske Vidensk. Selsk., Biol. Meddel. **19**(11): 1–13.

———. 1947. The spontaneous formation of haploid, polyploid and aneuploid embryos in some orchids. K. Danske Vidensk. Selsk., Biol. Meddel. **20**(9): 1–22.

Håkansson, A. 1943. Die Entwicklung des Embryosacks und die Befruchtung bei *Poa alpina*. Hereditas **29**: 25–61.

———. 1946. Untersuchungen über die Embryologie einiger *Potentilla*-Formen. Lunds Univ. Årsskr. N.F. Avd. II, **42**(5): 1–70.

Hodgson, R. W., and Cameron, S. H. 1938. Effects of reproduction by nucellar embryony on clonal characteristics in *Citrus*. Jour. Hered. **29**: 417–419.

Holmgren, J. 1919. Zytologische Studien über die Fortpflanzung bei den Gattungen *Erigeron* und *Eupatorium*. K. Svenska Vet.-Akad. Handl. **59**(7): 1–118.

Jeffrey, E. C., and Haertl, E. J. 1939. Apomixis in *Trillium*. Cellule **48**: 79–88.

Jørgensen, C. A. 1928. The experimental formation of heteroploid plants in the genus *Solanum*. Jour. Genet. **19**: 133–211.

Juel, H. O. 1900. Vergleichende Untersuchungen über typische und parthenogenetische Fortpflanzung bei der Gattung *Antennaria*. K. Svenska Vet.-Akad. Handl. **33**(5): 1–59.

Juliano, J. B. 1934. Origin of embryos in the strawberry mango. Philippine Jour. Sci. **54**: 553–556.

———. 1937. Embryos of carabao mango, *Mangifera indica* L. Philippine Agr. **25**: 749–760.

Kostoff, D. 1929. An androgenic *Nicotiana* haploid. Ztschr. f. Zellforsch. u. Mikros. Anat. **9**: 640–642.

Kostoff, D. 1941. The problem of haploidy (cytogenetic studies on *Nicotiana* haploids and their bearings to some other cytogenetic problems). Bibl. Genetica **13**: 1–148.

Kuhn, E. 1930. Pseudogamie und Androgenesis bei Pflanzen. Züchter **2**: 124–136.

Kusano, S. 1915. Experimental studies on the embryonal development in an angiosperm. Jour. Col. Agr. Tokyo Imp. Univ. **6**: 7–120.

Lebègue, A. 1949. Embryologie des Saxifragacées. Polyembryonie chez le *Bergenia delavayi* Engl. Bull. Soc. Bot. de France **96**: 38–39.

Maheshwari, P., and Narayanaswami, S. 1950. Parthenogenetic development of the egg in *Spiranthes australis* Lindl. (In press.)

Mauritzon, J. 1934. Die Embryologie einiger Capparidaceen sowie von *Tovaria pendula*. Arkiv. för Bot. **26A** 1–14.

Murbeck, S. 1901. Parthenogenetische Embryobildung in der Gattung *Alchemilla*. Lunds Univ. Årsskr. N.F. Avd. II, **36**(7): 1–41.

Nielsen, E. L. 1945. Cytology and breeding behavior of selected plants of *Poa pratensis*. Bot. Gaz. **106**: 357–382.

———. 1946. The origin of multiple macrogametophytes in *Poa pratensis*. Bot. Gaz. **108**: 41–50.

Noack, K. 1939. Über *Hypericum*-Kreuzungen. VI. Fortpflanzungs-verhältnisse und Bastarde von *Hypericum perforatum* L. Ztschr. f. Inductive Abstam. u. Vererbungsleshre **76**: 569–601.

Okabe, S. 1932. Parthenogenesis bei *Ixeris dentata*. Bot. Mag. [Tokyo] **46**: 518–532.

Osawa, I. 1912. Cytological and experimental studies in *Citrus*. Jour. Col. Agr. Imp. Univ. Tokyo **4**: 83–116.

———. 1913. Studies on the cytology of some species of *Taraxacum*. Arch. f. Zellforsch. **10**: 450–469.

Pace, L. 1913. Apogamy in *Atamosco*. Bot. Gaz. **56**: 376–394.

Pijl, L. v. 1934. Über die Polyembryonie bei *Eugenia*. Rec. des Trav. Bot. Néerland. **31**: 113–187.

Poddubnaja-Arnoldi, V. 1933. Geschlechtliche und ungeschlechtliche Fortpflanzung bei einigen *Chondrilla* Arten. Planta **19**: 46–86.

——— and Dianowa, V. 1934. Eine zytoembryologische Untersuchung einiger Arten der Gattung *Taraxacum*. Planta **23**: 19–46.

Rosenberg, O. 1907. Cytological studies on the apogamy in Hieracium. Bot. Tidskr. **28**: 143–170.

———. 1930. Apogamie und Parthenogenesis bei Pflanzen (From Baur, E., and Hartman, M. "Handbuch der Vererbungswissenschaft." Berlin, **12**: 1–66).

Rutishauser, A. 1943. Über die Entwicklungsgeschichte pseudogamer Potentillen. Arch. Julius Klaus-Stift. f. Vererbungsforsch. **18**: 687–691.

Schnarf, K. 1919. Beobachtungen über die Endospermentwicklung von *Hieracium aurantiacum*. Sitzber. Akad. der Wiss. math. natur. Wien. Kl. I, **128**: 1–17.

Sears, P. B. 1922. Variation in cytology and gross morphology of *Taraxacum*. Bot. Gaz. **73:** 308–326.

Stebbins, G. L. 1932. Cytology of Antennaria. II. Parthenogenetic species. Bot. Gaz. **94:** 322–344.

———— and Jenkins, J. A. 1939. Aposporic development in the North American species of *Crepis*. Genetica **21:** 1–34.

Strasburger, E. 1878. Über Polyembryonie. Jenaische Ztschr. f. Naturw. **12:** 647–670.

Subba Rao, A. M. 1940. Studies in the Malpighiaceae. I. Embryo sac development and embryogeny in the genera *Hiptage, Banisteria* and *Stigmatophyllum*. Jour. Indian Bot. Soc. **18:** 145–156.

Süssenguth, K. 1923. Über Pseudogamie bei *Zygopetalum mackayi* Hook. Ber. deutsch. bot. Gesell. **41:** 16–23.

Swamy, B. G. L. 1946. The embryology of *Zeuxine sulcata* Lindl. New Phytol. **45:** 132–136.

————. 1948. Post-fertilization development of *Trillium undulatum*. Cellule **52:** 7–14.

Swingle, W. T. 1927. Seed production in sterile *Citrus* hybrids—its scientific explanation and practical significance. Mem. Hort. Soc. N. Y. **3:** 19–21.

Tahara, M. 1921. Cytologische Untersuchungen an einigen Compositen. Jour. Col. Sci. Imp. Univ. Tokyo **43**(7): 1–53.

Tiwary, N. K. 1926. On the occurrence of polyembryony in the genus *Eugenia*. Jour. Indian Bot. Soc. **5:** 124–136.

Webber, H. J., and Batchelor, L. D. 1943. "The Citrus Industry." Vol. I. Berkeley.

Wiger, J. 1930. Ein neuer Fall von autonomer Nuzellarembryonie. Bot. Notiser 1930, pp. 368–370.

Winkler, H. 1908. "Über Parthenogenesis und Apogamie im Pflanzenreiche." Jena.

————. 1934. "Fortpflanzung der Gewächse." VII. Apomixis (In Handwörterbuch der Naturwissenschaft," 2d. ed. Jena. Vol. 4, pp. 451–461).

CHAPTER 10

POLYEMBRYONY

The phenomenon of polyembryony,[1] *i.e.*, the occurrence of more than one embryo in a seed, has attracted much attention ever since its initial discovery in the orange by Leeuwenhoek (1719). Ernst (1918) and Schnarf (1929), who have reviewed the older literature, classify it into two types—"true" and "false"—depending on whether the embryos arise in the same embryo sac or in different embryo sacs in the ovule. This classification, although useful, is open to some objections. It has been pointed out that while those cases in which two or more embryos are formed as a consequence of the development of aposporic embryo sacs are here classed under the "false" type, others showing adventive embryos—which also originate from tissues outside the embryo sac—are classed as "true." To obviate this difficulty, Gustafsson (1946) has proposed that the term false polyembryony should be restricted to those cases only in which two or more nucelli, each with its own embryo sac, fuse at an early stage. All others are included under true polyembryony. Since the first is only a teratological condition, we may confine our attention to true polyembryony only.

Cleavage Polyembryony. The simplest method of an increase in the number of embryos is a cleavage of the zygote or proembryo into two or more units. Although common in gymnosperms, its occurrence is only sporadic in the angiosperms. Jeffrey (1895) gave a detailed account of cleavage polyembryony in *Erythronium americanum* (Fig. 194). After fertilization the synergids degenerate and disappear, and the zygote divides to form a small group of cells, which do not show any definite order or arrangement. This group continues to increase in volume, and outgrowths arise at its lower end which eventually function as independent embryos. The production of two or three embryos from such an "embryogenic mass"

[1] For more detailed treatments of this topic see Webber (1940), Gustafsson (1946), and Maheshwari (1950).

343

was found to be a common feature, but sometimes as many as four were distinguishable.

Following Jeffrey's discovery, which has been confirmed by Guérin (1930) for another species of *Erythronium*, a similar proliferation of the embryonic cells was reported in *Tulipa gesneriana* (Ernst, 1901) and *Limnocharis emarginata* (Hall, 1902). In the latter the first division of the zygote is transverse and results in the formation of a large basal cell and a small terminal cell. As a rule, the former increases in size without undergoing any further divisions. In some cases, however, it "divides and subdivides to form an embryogenic mass" from which several embryos bud forth as

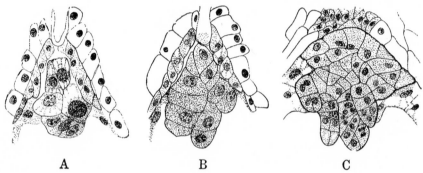

A   B   C

Fig. 194.   Cleavage polyembryony in *Erythronium americanum*.   *A*, Upper part of embryo sac, showing the "embryogenic mass" formed from zygote. *B,C*, proliferation of embryogenic mass to give rise to embryos. (*After Jeffrey, 1895.*)

in *Erythronium*.   No older stages were seen, however, and it could not be ascertained whether these embryos grow to full maturity.

Most other cases of cleavage polyembryony reported since then have been in the nature of abnormalities.   Cook (1902) noted an embryo sac of *Nymphaea advena* showing twin embryos which he considered to have originated by the "splitting of a very young embryo."   Later, the same author (1924) observed one instance of two embryos, and another of four, at the micropylar end of the embryo sac of *Crotalaria sagittalis*.   Since the synergids are quite ephemeral in this plant, these embryos are believed to have arisen by a splitting of the single zygotic embryo.   Samuelsson (1913) also reported a similar splitting of the proembryo in *Empetrum nigrum*, Guignard (1922) in *Vincetoxicum nigrum*, and Johansen (1931) in *Zauschneria latifolia*.   In *Lobelia syphilitica* (Crété, 1938) frequently one and sometimes two additional embryos develop at the expense of the suspensor. In *Nicotiana rustica* Cooper (1943) noted an ovule with two embryos of which the smaller had apparently arisen as an outgrowth from the apex of the primary embryo. Kausik and Subramanyam (1946) figure an embryo sac of *Isotoma longiflora* in which an additional embryo seems to have budded out from a suspensor cell.[1a]

It is only in the family Orchidaceae that cleavage polyembryony seems to be of more frequent occurrence. In *Eulophia epidendraea*,

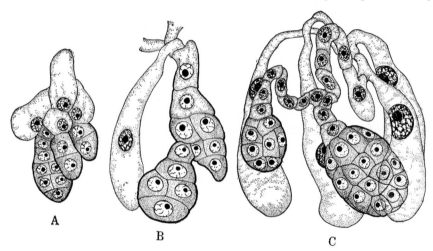

A   B   C

FIG. 195. Polyembryony in *Eulophia epidendraea;* drawings made from whole mounts of ovules. *A*, zygote has given rise to group of cells, three of which have divided to form independent embryos. *B*, "bud" arising from right side of embryo. *C*, two embryos presumed to have arisen by splitting of a single embryo; large vacuolate cells belong to suspensor. (*After Swamy, 1943.*)

which may be cited as an example, Swamy (1943) records the following variations: (1) the zygote divides irregularly to form a mass of cells, of which those lying towards the chalazal end grow simultaneously and give rise to multiple embryos (Fig. 195*A*); (2) the filamentous proembryo becomes branched and each of the branches grows into an embryo (Fig. 195*C*); (3) the proembryo gives out small buds or outgrowths which may themselves function as embryos (Fig. 195*B*).

[1a] It may be noted that some of the above-mentioned examples of cleavage polyembryony may equally well be interpreted as cases of an intimate juxtaposition of two embryos (see Fagerlind, 1944). For some reason, this possibility has not been taken into account by most workers.

Origin of Embryos from Cells of the Embryo Sac Other than the Egg. Besides the zygotic embryo produced from the egg, embryos may also be produced from other parts of the embryo sac. The most common source is the synergids which frequently become egg-like and may be fertilized by sperms from an additional pollen tube (Fig. 116E) or develop without fertilization (Fig. 178). Several cases of both kinds are known and have already been discussed in Chaps. 6 and 9.

Production of embryos from antipodal cells is much rarer. Shattuck (1905) noted that the antipodal cells of *Ulmus americana* often present an egg-like appearance and in some cases he actually found embryos in this position. Ekdahl (1941) has confirmed this in *U. glabra* (Fig. 196A–C), and Modilewski (1931), Mauritzon (1933), and Fagerlind (1944) have figured similar cases in *Allium odorum*, (Fig. 196D), *Sedum fabaria*, and *Elatostema sinuatum eusinuatum* (Fig. 196E). The further fate of these antipodal embryos has not been determined, however, and it is not known whether they are viable. It is to be noted that the egg-like antipodal cells which have been recorded in some other plants like *Plumbagella* (Dahlgren, 1916) and *Rudbeckia* (Maheshwari and Srinivasan, 1944) have not been observed to give rise to embryos. Nor have the laterally situated egg-like cells of *Penaea* (Stephens, 1909), *Plumbago* (Dahlgren, 1937), *Vogelia* (Mathur and Khan, 1941), and *Acalypha* (Maheshwari and Johri, 1941) ever shown such a behavior.

Embryos Arising from Cells outside Embryo Sac. The development of embryos from the cells of the nucellus and integument has already been considered in Chap. 9. *Citrus, Eugenia,* and *Mangifera* are well-known examples of this type of polyembryony. The embryos, although initiated outside the embryo sac, subsequently come to lie inside it and are nourished by the endosperm (Fig. 192).

Recent work indicates that the occurrence of adventive embryony may not be a constant feature of all the individuals of a species. Swamy (1948) has found that the orchid *Spiranthes cernua* comprises three races. The first shows normal sexual reproduction and a single zygotic embryo is produced in each seed. In the second race, which is apomictic, the male and female gametophytes are both functionless. Fertilization does not occur but the cells of the inner layer of the inner integument give rise to adventive embryos of which two to six may mature in a seed. In the third race, which is of an intermediate type, some ovules of an ovary follow the course outlined for the first race and others for the apomictic race.

Embryos Originating from Other Embryo Sacs in the Ovule. As mentioned in the introductory paragraph, the polyembryonate

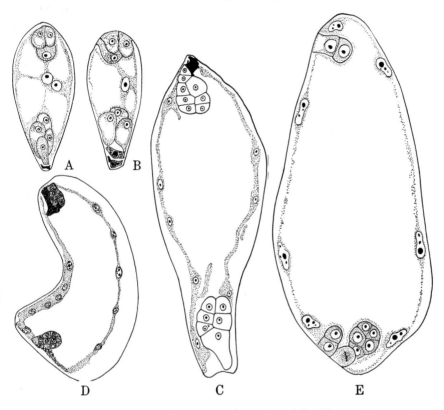

FIG. 196. Origin of embryos from antipodal cells. *A,B, Ulmus glabra;* embryo sacs with egg-like antipodal cells. *C, U. glabra,* embryo sac, showing zygotic embryo at micropylar end and antipodal embryo at chalazal end. (*After Ekdahl, 1941.*) *D, Allium odorum;* embryo sac, showing two embryos, one derived from egg and the other from antipodal cell. (*After Modilewski, 1931.*) *E, Elatostema sinuatum eusinuatum;* embryo sac with three antipodal embryos, of which one is several-celled, another two-celled, and the third undergoing first division; note egg embryo at upper end. (*After Fagerlind, 1944.*)

condition is sometimes due to the occurrence of multiple embryo sacs within the ovule. These may arise (1) either from the derivatives of the same megaspore mother cell, or (2) from two or more megaspore mother cells, or (3) from nucellar cells (apospory).

Bacchi (1943) sometimes found more than one embryo sac in an ovule of *Citrus* resulting in two zygotic embryos, and Nielsen (1946) has recorded the same in *Poa pratensis*.[2]

A Few Special Cases. In some plants multiple embryos are produced by the simultaneous operation of more than one of the methods named above. One of the most interesting of them is *Allium odorum*. Many years ago, Tretjakow (1895) and Hegelmaier (1897) recorded the occurrence of synergid and antipodal embryos in as many as one-third to one-half of the ovules of this species. Later, Haberlandt (1923, 1925) reported that even in castrated flowers there is an increase in the size of the ovules, accompanied by the production of embryos from several sources—egg, synergids, antipodals, and the cells of the inner integument. He found the diploid number of chromosomes in all the embryos. Modilewski (1925, 1930, 1931), who made a further study of the plant, found that it forms two kinds of embryo sacs, some haploid and others diploid. In the diploid embryo sacs only the polar nuclei are fertilized, resulting in a pentaploid endosperm; embryos arise from the unfertilized but diploid egg and antipodal cells. In haploid embryo sacs, on the other hand, viable embryos are formed only after fertilization. In conclusion, four possibilities are mentioned:

1. In a haploid and normally fertilized embryo sac, embryos may begin to develop from all cells of the embryo sac and even from the adjacent integumentary cells, but only the zygotic embryo survives so that the mature seeds contain a single embryo.

2. Embryos may also begin to form from one or more cells of the haploid and unfertilized embryo sac, but owing to the lack of an endosperm, which can arise only after triple fusion, their growth is soon arrested and they become nonviable.

3. In a diploid but unfertilized embryo sac, any of its cells (also the cells of the inner integument) may begin to form an embryo, but eventually they all degenerate owing to the absence of an endosperm.

4. In diploid embryo sacs, in which the secondary nucleus is fertilized, endosperm formation proceeds actively and all the cells of the sac are capable of giving rise to embryos, but only the egg embryo usually attains maturity.

[2] Species of the genus *Poa* show other abnormalities also, for which a reference may be made to the works of Tinney (1940), Engelbert (1941), Åkerberg (1939, 1943), and Håkansson (1943, 1944).

Woodworth (1930) has called attention to the frequent occurrence of polyembryonate seeds in *Alnus rugosa*. Meiosis was found to be disturbed and only 2 to 3 per cent of the pollen grains were viable. Pollen tubes were not observed, and bagged catkins produced perfectly normal and viable seeds, similar to those obtained from unbagged catkins. Embryo sac formation was not preceded by meiosis, and more than 50 per cent of the seeds showed diploid egg embryos at the micropylar end of the ovule. A few seeds had an embryo oriented in the opposite direction, suggesting its origin from an antipodal cell. One ovule showed three embryos at the micropylar end, two of which are believed to have originated from synergids and the third from the egg. Nucellar embryony was frequent. Some of the embryos were found sunken in the endosperm and are believed to have originated from the cells of the latter. Several ovules showed more than one embryo sac, each giving rise to one or more embryos. From the occurrence of four to seven cotyledonary buds on certain embryos, it further appeared that originally separate embryos could sometimes fuse to form a composite structure.

Woodworth's work, although of much interest, lacks the early stages in embryonal development, and therefore some of his conclusions about the origin of the polyembryonate condition need confirmation. In particular, his inference that endosperm cells may also give rise to embryos must be regarded as very doubtful (see page 334).

In *Atraphaxis frutescens*, Edman (1931) has described some interesting cases of polyembryony. Haploid embryo sacs are produced only rarely and must be fertilized before they can give rise to embryos. More often, meiosis fails and the embryo sacs are therefore diploid. Frequently two or more occur in the same ovule, and each of them may produce an embryo. Figure 190C shows two embryo sacs lying side by side, the left with two overlapping embryos and the right with one embryo at the micropylar end. Figure 190A shows a different condition, in which the second embryo sac has arisen from a chalazal cell and is inversely oriented in relation to the normal embryo sac. A similar but more advanced condition is seen in Fig. 190B_1,B_2, where a well-developed and nearly mature embryo is present in the upper embryo sac, but the chalazal embryo sacs and embryos failed to keep pace and are in the process of obliteration. In addition, embryos of nucellar and apogamous origin are also found in *Atraphaxis*.   Of the two embryos seen in the embryo sac on the left in Fig. 190*C*, one has obviously originated from a synergid.

Fagerlind's (1944) recent study of some apomictic species of *Elatostema* has also revealed some interesting features of a similar nature.   Briefly, the polyembryonate condition is due to one or more of the following causes: (1) the occurrence of multiple embryo

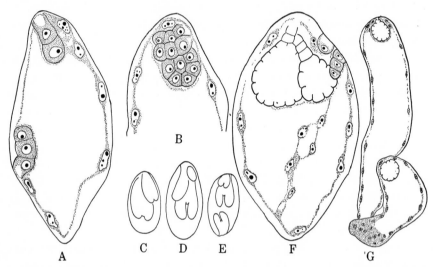

Fig. 197.   Polyembryony in *Elatostema*.   *A, E. eurhynchum;* embryo sac with two embryos, one arising laterally.   *B,* upper part of embryo sac, showing three embryos, two of which are lying somewhat horizontally.   *C,D,* older ovules, show- ing two embryos.   *E,* ovule, showing two embryos at micropylar and one at chalazal end.   *F, E. acuminatum;* compound embryo sac formed by fusion of two sacs. Embryo sac on left shows two well-developed embryos, and that on right shows two smaller embryos.   *G, E. pedunculosum;* two adjacent embryo sacs, each with normally developed embryo at micropylar end.   *(After Fagerlind, 1944.)*

sacs in the same ovule (Fig. 197*G*), (2) the formation of embryos from synergids and antipodal cells (Fig. 197*B–E*), and (3) nucellar budding (Fig. 197*F*).   Sometimes the separating wall between two embryo sacs dissolves so that they form a common cavity (Fig. 197*F*), and if adjacent embryos come in close contact they may fuse to form masses of tissue which defy analysis in later stages.

Twins and Triplets.   When multiple seedlings arise in a species in such a low frequency that it is not practicable to make a develop- mental study of the embryogeny, there is a good deal of speculation about their origin. Of special interest are the diploid-diploid, haploid-diploid, diploid-triploid, and haploid-triploid twins.[3]

Considering the diploid-diploid twins first, Randolph (1936) saw two embryos lying parallel to each other in some kernels of *Zea mays*, and the twin plants resulting from such kernels were found to be genetically identical even in heterozygous stocks. He also saw occasional seedlings with two plumules and a single radicle. Skovsted (1939) reported twins in *Trifolium pratense*, with both members having a chromosome fragment, and in *Medicago sativa*, with both having an extra chromosome. In all these cases the seedlings are interpreted as having originated by the cleavage of a single embryo. While this is probably true, it must be noted that cytologically similar diploid seedlings may also arise in other ways, the most frequent source being the fertilization of more than one cell of the embryo sac.[4] Diploid-diploid twins may also arise from embryos produced in two separate embryo sacs in an ovule or by nucellar budding. Also, it is possible that sometimes a haploid cell of the embryo sac may give rise to a diploid embryo by a process of "endoduplication" of the chromosomes. A monozygotic origin may, therefore, be assumed only when the seedlings are completely identical in all essential respects.[5]

Haploid-diploid twins were reported by Kappert (1933) in *Linum usitatissimum*, and by Ramiah et al. (1933, 1935) in *Oryza sativa*. Subsequently, they have been recorded in several other plants, viz., *Triticum durum* (Kihara, 1936), *Solanum tuberosum*, *Phleum pratense* (Müntzing, 1937), *Triticum vulgare* (Kasparayan, 1938), *Secale cereale* (Kostoff, 1939), *Capsicum annuum* (Christensen and Bamford, 1943), *Dactylis glomerata* (Müntzing, 1943), and *Gossypium barbadense* (Harland, 1936; Webber, 1938; Skovsted, 1939; Silow and Stephens, 1944). Kappert (1933) explained his twins of *Linum* on the basis that the diploid member of the complex was derived from the fertilized egg and the haploid member from an unfertilized cell of the same embryo sac. Ramiah et al. (1933) also

---

[3] See in this connection Webber's (1940) review of "polyembryony."

[4] Except in bi- and tetrasporic embryo sacs, all the nuclei of an embryo sac are genetically identical.

[5] Identical seedlings may also arise if the egg and one synergid are fertilized by the two male gametes discharged from the same pollen tube. Possibilities of such an occurrence seem to be indicated in some orchids (Hagerup, 1947).

made the same interpretation but later (1935) considered it more probable that the development of more than one embryo sac within an ovule could also account for the origin of the twins. Harland (1936) agreed with this view, adding that the fertilization of the egg in one embryo sac might stimulate a parthenogenetic development of the egg in the second and adjacent embryo sac. The remaining authors mentioned above fall in line with one or the other of these explanations. Briefly then, in a case of haploid-diploid seedlings, the haploid member is derived from an unfertilized cell belonging either to the same embryo sac or to an adjacent embryo sac.

Diploid-triploid twins have been reported in *Triticum vulgare* (Yamamoto, 1936), *Secale cereale* (Kostoff, 1939), and a few other plants (see especially Skovsted, 1939). According to Kostoff and Yamamoto, the triploids observed by them arose from a part of the endosperm, but this is merely a supposition without any positive evidence in its favor. It is more likely that the triploid embryo originated by the fertilization of an unreduced (aposporic) embryo sac or by the fusion of a cell of a haploid embryo sac with two male gametes or one unreduced male gamete.

Haploid-triploid seedlings are of comparatively rarer occurrence. Nissen (1937) recorded one such case in *Phleum*. It is probable that the haploid member arose from an unfertilized cell of the embryo sac and the triploid member by one of the methods mentioned in the preceding paragraph.

While these are the probable ways in which twins and triplets arise, it is often impossible to be sure of the exact origin of the aberrant member or members of the combination, and it is unsafe to make any categorical statements without taking all the possibilities into consideration.

A particularly careful cytogenetic study of the multiple seedlings of *Asparagus officinale* has recently been made by Randall and Rick (1945). Of 405 multiple seedlings, 97 per cent were twins, 11 were triplets, and one was a quadruplet. Diploids ($2n = 20$) were the most frequent, but a few showed other chromosome numbers: 30 (triploid), 21 (trisomic), 10 (haploid), and 40 (tetraploid). In haploid-diploid pairs the haploid member was always much smaller than its diploid partner, but aside from this combination the degree of difference in size seldom gave any clue to the chromosome number or the origin of the polyembryonate condition.

The authors critically analyze the possible origins of the multiple seedlings from a study of their chromosome numbers, stem color, and distribution of sexes, and conclude that about one-fourth of the diploid-diploid twin seedlings must have originated by a process of cleavage polyembryony. The remaining three-fourths are believed to have arisen from two cells belonging either to the same embryo sac or to two embryo sacs in an ovule. In addition a number of "conjoined" twins were found, which showed varying degrees of attachment to each other but were capable of developing into independent plants. To explain their origin the following alternatives are envisaged: (1) a partial fusion of two adjacent embryos, and (2) an incomplete cleavage of one embryo. From the complete identity in chromosome number and genetic characters between the members of the conjoined type, it is concluded, however, that they originated by an incomplete cleavage of a single initial embryo.

Conclusion. It may be said that polyembryony, although fairly widespread in angiosperms, is much less common in them than it is in the gymnosperms. The reason for this is that in the latter there are several archegonia, but in the former there is only one cell in the ovule (the egg) which is normally capable of giving rise to an embryo. Sometimes, however, the proembryo may become separated into two or more portions (cleavage polyembryony), or more than one cell of the embryo sac may develop into an embryo. Less frequently there may be two or more embryo sacs in an ovule, each of which may give rise to embryos. A fourth source of polyembryony is the "budding" or proliferation of the cells of the nucellus or integument (adventive embryony). The adventive embryos are diploid and similar to one another as well as to the plant from which they arise. Embryos produced by the cleavage of a single zygote are also identical in all essential respects. Embryos arising from two or more cells of one or separate embryo sacs may, however, have the same or different chromosome numbers. Even when developmental stages in embryogeny are not available, it is possible in some cases to infer the mode of origin of the polyembryonate condition on genetical evidence.

REFERENCES

Åkerberg, E. 1939. Apomictic and sexual seed formation in *Poa pratensis*. Hereditas **25**: 359–370.

――――. 1943. Further studies of the embryo and endosperm development in *Poa pratensis*. Hereditas **29**: 199–201.

Bacchi, O. 1943. Cytological observations in *Citrus*. III. Megasporogenesis, fertilization, and polyembryony. Bot. Gaz. **105:** 221–225.

Christensen, H. M., and Bamford, R. 1943. Haploids in twin seedlings of pepper. Jour. Hered. **34:** 99–104.

Cook, M. T. 1902. Development of the embryo sac and embryo of *Castalia odorata* and *Nymphaea advena*. Bul. Torrey Bot. Club **29:** 211–220.

———. 1924. Development of seed of *Crotalaria sagittalis*. Bot. Gaz. **77:** 440–445.

Cooper, D. C. 1943. Haploid-diploid twin embryos in *Lilium* and *Nicotiana*. Amer. Jour. Bot. **30:** 408–413.

Crété, P. 1938. La polyembryonie chez le *Lobelia syphilitica* L. Bull. Soc. Bot. de France **85:** 580–583.

Dahlgren, K. V. O. 1916. Zytologische und embryologische Studien über die Reihen Primulales und Plumbaginales. K. Svenska Vet.-Akad. Handl. **56**(4): 1–80.

———. 1937. Die Entwicklung des Embryosackes bei *Plumbago zeylanica*. Bot. Notiser 1937, pp. 487–498.

Edman, G. 1931. Apomeiosis und Apomixis bei *Atraphaxis frutescens* C. Koch. Acta Horti Bergiani **11:** 13–66.

Ekdahl, I. 1941. Die Entwicklung von Embryosack und Embryo bei *Ulmus glabra* Huds. Svensk Bot. Tidskr. **35:** 143–156.

Engelbert, V. 1941. The development of twin embryo sacs, embryos and endosperm in *Poa arctica* R. Br. Canad. Jour. Res., Sect. C., Bot. Sci. **19:** 135–144.

Ernst, A. 1901. Beiträge zur Kenntnis der Entwicklung des Embryosackes und des Embryos (Polyembryonie) von *Tulipa gesneriana* L. Flora **88:** 37–77.

———. 1918. "Bastardierung als Ursache der Apogamie im Pflanzenreiche." Jena.

Fagerlind, F. 1944. Die Samenbildung und die Zytologie bei agamospermischen und sexuellen Arten von *Elatostema* und einigen nahestehenden Gattungen nebst Beleuchtung einiger damit zusammenhängender Probleme. K. Svenska Vet.-Akad, Handl. III, **21**(4): 1–130.

Guérin, P. 1930. Le développement de l'oeuf et la polyembryonie chez l'*Erythronium dens canis* L. Compt. Rend. Acad. des Sci. Paris **191:** 1369–1372.

Guignard, L. 1922. La fécondation et la polyembryonie chez les *Vincetoxicum*. Mém. Acad. Sci. Inst. France II, **57:** 1–25.

Gustafsson, Å. 1946. Apomixis in higher plants. I. The mechanism of apomixis. Lunds Univ. Årsskr. N.F. Avd. II, **42**(3): 1–67.

Haberlandt, G. 1923. Zur Embryologie von *Allium odorum*. Ber. deutsch. bot. Gesell. **41:** 174–179.

———. 1925. Zur Embryologie und Cytologie von *Allium odorum*. Ber. deutsch. bot. Gesell. **43:** 559–564.

Hagerup, O. 1947. The spontaneous formation of haploid, polyploid, and aneuploid embryos in some orchids. K. Danske Vidensk. Selsk., Biol. Meddel. **20**(9): 1–22.

Håkansson, A. 1943. Die Entwicklung des Embryosackes und die Befruchtung bei *Poa alpina*. Hereditas **28:** 25–61.

Håkansson, A. 1944. Erganzende Beiträge zur Embryologie von *Poa alpina*. Bot. Notiser 1944, pp. 299–311.

Hall, J. G. 1902. An embryological study of *Limnocharis emarginata*. Bot. Gaz. **33:** 214–219.

Harland, S. C. 1936. Haploids in polyembryonic seeds of Sea Island cotton. Jour. Hered. **27:** 229–231.

Hegelmaier, F. 1897. Zur Kenntnis der Polyembryonie von *Allium odorum*. Bot. Ztg. **55:** 133–140.

Jeffrey, E. C. 1895. Polyembryony in *Erythronium americanum*. Ann. Bot. **9:** 537–541.

Johansen, D. A. 1931. Studies on the morphology of the Onagraceae. V. *Zauschneria latifolia*, typical of a genus characterized by irregular embryology. Ann. N. Y. Acad. Sci. **33:** 1–26.

Kappert, H. 1933. Erbliche Polyembryonie bei *Linum usitatissimum*. Biol. Zentbl. **53:** 276–307.

Kasparayan, A. S. 1938. Haploids and haplo-diploids among hybrid twin seedlings in wheat. Compt. Rend. (Dok.) Acad. des Sci. U.R.S.S. **20:** 53–56.

Kausik, S. B., and Subramanyam, K. 1946. A case of polyembryony in *Isotoma longiflora* Presl. Current Sci. [India] **15:** 257–258.

Kihara, H. 1936. A diplo-haploid twin plant in *Triticum durum*. Agri. and Hort. [Tokyo] **11:** 1425–1434.

Kostoff, D. 1939. Frequency of polyembryony and chlorophyll deficiency in rye. Compt. Rend. (Dok.) Acad. des Sci. U.R.S.S. **24:** 479–482.

Maheshwari, P. 1950. Polyembryony. Palaeobotanica, Sahni Memorial. Vol.

—— and Johri, B. M. 1941. The embryo sac of *Acalypha indica* L. Beihefte bot. Centbl. **61A:** 125–136.

—— and Srinivasan, A. R. 1944. A contribution to the embryology of *Rudbeckia bicolor* Nutt. New Phytol. **43:** 135–142.

Mathur, K. L., and Khan, R. 1941. The development of the embryo sac in *Vogelia indica* Lamk. Proc. Indian Acad. Sci. Sect. B. **13:** 360–368.

Mauritzon, J. 1933. "Studien über die Embryologie der Familien Crassulaceae und Saxifragaceae." Diss. Lund.

Modilewski, J. 1925. Zur Kenntnis der Polyembryonie von *Allium odorum* L. Bull. Jard. Bot. de Kieff **2:** 9–19.

——. 1928. Weitere Beiträge zur Embryologie und Cytologie von *Allium*-Arten. Bull. Jard. Bot. de Kieff **7/8:** 57–64.

——. 1930. Neue Beiträge zur Polyembryonie von *Allium odorum* L. Ber. deutsch. bot. Gesell. **48:** 285–295.

——. 1931. Die Embryobildung bei *Allium odorum* L. Bull. Jard. Bot. de Kieff **12/13:** 27–48.

Müntzing, A. 1937. Polyploidy from twin seedlings. Cytologia, Fujii Jubl. Vol., pp. 211–227.

——. 1943. Characteristics of two haploid twins in *Dactylis glomerata*. Hereditas **29:** 134–140.

Nielsen, E. L. 1946. The origin of multiple macrogametophytes in *Poa pratensis*. Bot. Gaz. **108:** 41–50.

Nissen, O. 1937. Spalteåpringenes størrelse has tvillingplanter med ulike kromo-somtall. Bot. Notiser 1937, pp. 28–34.

Ramiah, K., Parthasarthi, N., and Ramanujam, S. 1933. Haploid plant in rice (*Oryza sativa*). Current Sci. [India] **1**: 277–278.

——, ——, and ——. 1935. Polyembryony in rice (*Oryza sativa*). Indian Jour. Agr. Sci. **5**: 119–124.

Randall, T. E., and Rick, C. M. 1945. A cytogenetic study of polyembryony in *Asparagus officinalis* L. Amer. Jour. Bot. **32**: 560–569.

Randolph, L. F. 1936. Developmental morphology of the caryopsis in maize. Jour. Agr. Res. **53**: 881–916.

Samuelsson, G. 1913. Studien über die Entwicklungsgeschichte einiger Bicornes-Typen. Svensk. Bot. Tidskr. **7**: 97–188.

Schnarf, K. 1929. "Embryologie der Angiospermen." Berlin.

Shattuck, C. H. 1905. A morphological study of *Ulmus americana*. Bot. Gaz. **40**: 209–223.

Silow, R. A., and Stephens, S. G. 1944. "Twinning" in cotton. Jour. Hered. **35**: 76–78.

Skovsted, A. 1939. Cytological studies in twin plants. Compt. Rend. des Trav. Carlsberg Lab. Ser. Physiol. **22**: 427–446.

Stephens, E. L. 1909. The embryo sac and embryo of certain Penaeaceae. Ann. Bot. **23**: 363–378.

Swamy, B. G. L. 1943. Gametogenesis and embryogeny of *Eulophea epidendraea* Fischer. Proc. Natl. Inst. Sci. India **9**: 59–65.

——. 1948. Agamospermy in *Spiranthes cernua*. Lloydia **11**: 149–162.

Tinney, F. W. 1940. Cytology of parthenogenesis in *Poa pratensis*. Jour. Agr. Res. **60**: 351–360.

Tretjakow, S. 1895. Die Beteilung der Antipoden in Fällen der Polyembryonie bei *Allium odorum*. Ber. deutsch. bot. Gesell. **13**: 13–17.

Webber, J. M. 1938. Cytology of twin cotton plants. Jour. Agr. Res. **57**: 155–160.

——. 1940. Polyembryony. Bot. Rev. **6**: 575–598.

Woodworth, R. H. 1930. Cytological studies in the Betulaceae. III. Parthenogenesis and polyembryony in *Alnus rugosa*. Bot. Gaz. **89**: 402–409.

Yamamoto, Y. 1936. Über das Vorkommen von triploiden Pflanzen bei Mehrlingskeimlingen von *Triticum vulgare* Vill. Cytologia **7**: 431–436.

CHAPTER 11

EMBRYOLOGY IN RELATION TO TAXONOMY

Although the existing systems of classification of angiosperms are based mainly on the external characters of the flowers, fruits, and seeds, it is now generally accepted that cytology, anatomy, embryology, and genetics can contribute results of considerable significance in a number of doubtful cases where floral morphology alone has not proved adequate.

Many years ago Hofmeister and Strasburger indicated the possibility of using embryological characters in taxonomy, but until the invention of the microtome such investigations were confined to a few skilled workers, and even their observations were not always free from errors and misinterpretations. With the commencement of the twentieth century, much higher standards were set in descriptive embryology. A number of workers, particularly in Germany and Sweden, began to discuss the bearings of their data on the interrelationships of the families and genera which were being studied by them. Unfortunately the preparation of the material is a very time-consuming task, which requires a great deal of patience and skill. The embryology of several families is therefore quite unknown, and even with regard to others the existing data are often quite fragmentary and inadequate. Enough has been done, however, to indicate that the embryological method has great possibilities for the future (see especially Schnarf, 1933, 1937; Mauritzon, 1939; Maheshwari, 1945a,b; Just, 1946).

It is difficult to enumerate all the embryological features which are of taxonomic significance, for almost every structure has been shown to yield results of importance. The following characters are, however, considered to be of major value in delimiting the larger plant groups:

1. *Anther tapetum.* Whether it is of the glandular or the amoeboid type.

2. *Quadripartition of the microspore mother cells.* Whether it takes

place by furrowing or by the formation of cell plates, and whether the mode of division is successive or simultaneous.

3. *Development and organization of the pollen grain.* Number and position of the germ pores and furrows; adornments of the exine; place of formation of the generative cell; number and shape of the nuclei in the pollen grain at the time of its discharge from the anther.

4. *Development and structure of the ovule.* Number of integuments and the alterations in structure which they undergo during the formation of the seed; presence or absence of vascular bundles in the integuments; shape of the micropyle, whether it is formed by the inner integument, or the outer, or both; presence or absence of an obturator.

5. *Form and extent of the nucellus.* Whether it is broad and massive or thin and ephemeral; presence or absence of a hypostase; place of origin of the integument or integuments, whether close to the apex of the nucellus or near its base; persistence or gradual disappearance of the nucellus during seed formation.

6. *Origin and extent of the sporogenous tissue in the ovule.* Nature of archesporium, whether it is one-celled or many-celled; presence or absence of wall layers; presence or absence of periclinal divisions in the cells of the nucellar epidermis.

7. *Megasporogenesis and development of the embryo sac.* Arrangement of megaspores; position of functioning megaspore; whether the embryo sac is monosporic, bisporic, or tetrasporic; number of nuclear divisions intervening between the megaspore mother cell stage and the differentiation of the egg.

8. *Form and organization of the mature embryo sac.* Shape of the embryo sac and the number and distribution of its nuclei; persistence or early disappearance of the synergids and antipodal cells; increase in number of antipodal cells, if any; formation of embryo sac caeca or haustoria.

9. *Fertilization.* Path of entry of the pollen tube; interval between pollination and fertilization; any tendency toward a branching of the pollen tubes during their course to the ovule.

10. *Endosperm.* Whether it is of the Nuclear, Cellular, or Helobial type; orientation of the first wall in those cases in which it is Cellular; presence or absence of endosperm haustoria and the manner in which they formed if present; nature of food reserves in

endosperm cells; persistence or gradual disappearance of endosperm in the mature seed.

11. *Embryo.* Relation of the proembryonal cells to the body regions of the embryo; form and organization of the mature embryo; presence or absence of suspensor haustoria.

12. *Certain abnormalities of development.* Parthenogenesis; apogamy, adventive embryony, polyembryony etc.

An evaluation of the characters mentioned above has been of considerable service in the determination of the proper position of several difficult groups and subgroups, and sometimes it has given a new orientation to our ideas of their affinities. Without going into details, for which a reference may be made to the work of Mauritzon (1939), the following selection is offered as an illustration.

Empetraceae. Don (1827), who first erected the group "Empetreae," considered it to be so different from the Ericaceae that he rejected any possibility of a close alliance between them. He believed instead that the Empetreae was more closely related to the Euphorbiaceae and the Celastraceae. "The Euphorbiaceae and Empetreae agree in the imbricate aestivation of the calyx, in the stamens being opposite to the divisions of the calyx, and both of these being of an equal and definite number; in having bilocular anthers; in their superior ovarium; in the plurality of styles; in their divided stigmas; and lastly in the arrangement of the ovula, and the presence of a copious albumen." He went so far as to say that whether the Empetreae was to be considered as a section of the Euphorbiaceae or a separate family allied to the latter was a matter of individual taste.

Bentham and Hooker (1880) felt less sure about a relationship between the Euphorbiaceae and Empetraceae and assigned the latter to their *ordines anomali* under the Monochlamydeae. Shortly afterwards, Pax (1896) also denied that the Empetraceae showed any recognizable affinities with either the Ericaceae or the Euphorbiaceae. The floral structure and in particular the structure of the ovules left no doubt in his opinion that it was to be placed in the order Sapindales close to the Celastraceae[1] and Buxaceae.

However, Agardh (1858), Gray (1858), Baillon (1892), and Hallier (1912) considered the Empetraceae to be related to the Ericaceae,

---

[1] Among recent writers Hutchinson (1948) still thinks that the Empetraceae has its nearest relatives in the Celastrales.

regarding it as a reduced apetalous and polygamous or dioecious derivative of the latter.

That this last view is the correct one and that the Empetraceae is to be classed under the Ericales have now been definitely established on the basis of the embryological data brought forward by Samuelsson (1913). This order is characterized by the following

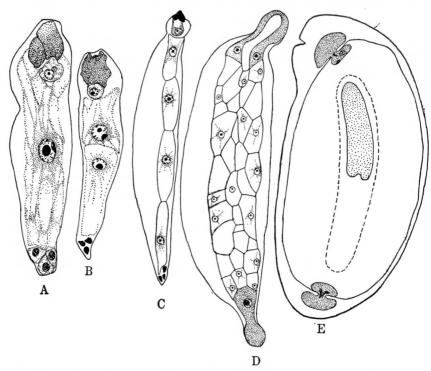

Fig. 198. Development of endosperm in *Empetrum nigrum*. *A*, embryo sac at time of fertilization. *B*, two-celled stage of endosperm. *C*, four-celled endosperm. *D*, more advanced stage, showing differentiation of micropylar and chalazal haustoria. *E*, l.s. nearly mature seed. (*After Samuelsson, 1913*.)

well-marked embryological features: (1) absence of a fibrous layer in the anthers; (2) anther tapetum of the glandular type with multinucleate cells; (3) microspores remaining together in tetrads (Fig. 97*J*); (4) pollen grains two-celled; (5) unitegmic ovules with a thin nucellus, which soon disappears so that the embryo sac comes in direct contact with the integumentary tapetum; (6) absence of parietal cells in the ovule; (7) embryo sac monosporic and eight-nucleate, broader at the micropylar end and narrower at the chalazal; (8) a fluted hollow style, which connects the lumen of the ovary with the outside and along which the pollen tubes make their way into the ovary; (9) endosperm cellular; the first two divisions transverse, giving rise to a row of four superposed cells (Fig. 198*A–C*); (10) formation of endosperm haustoria at both ends of the embryo sac, micropylar as well as chalazal (Fig. 198*D, E*); (11) a single-layered seed coat formed from the outermost layer of the integument, the remaining layers becoming absorbed during the growth of the endosperm and embryo; (12) seeds albuminous with fleshy endosperm and straight embryo.

All these are perfectly standard stages in Ericean embryology, and their combination is quite unknown in any other order. The Empetraceae show a close correspondence in all respects, while the Sapindales and Celastrales differ in so many ways that there is no doubt as to the correctness of Samuelsson's view.[1a]

Lennoaceae. On the basis of his morphological studies on the Lennoaceae, Solms-Laubach (1870) felt convinced that it belonged to the Ericales, and Hutchinson (1926) accepted this disposition of the group. But there were certain points in Solms-Laubach's own descriptions which seemed to militate against this view, and consequently Engler and Gilg (1924) removed the Lennoaceae to the order Tubiflorae and placed it in the neighborhood of the Boraginaceae. This received support from Süssenguth's (1927) anatomical and morphological study of *Lennoa*, and more recently Copeland (1935) has also expressed his agreement with it on the basis of his work on *Pholisma*. As remarked by Copeland, at the very outset the equality in number of their stamens and corolla lobes (contrasted with the obdiplostemony of the Ericales), alternate arrangement of the floral members, adnation of the filaments to the corolla, and dehiscence of the anthers by longitudinal slits, form weighty objections against an assignment of the Lennoaceae to the Ericales. Further, certain other characters possessed by the Lennoaceae, *viz.*, their short and solid style, normally developed endothecium, separate pollen grains, and multilayered seed coat, render its

[1a] See also Hagerup (1946) who has confirmed this opinion as the result of his morphological studies on the Empetraceae.

assignment to the Bicornes completely untenable and make it seem more probable that its correct place is under the Tubiflorae as a separate suborder occupying a primitive position.

Cactaceae. The members of this family present a motley assemblage with every variation from the leafy *Pereskia* to the tall ribbed columns of *Pachycereus*, the flat joints of *Opuntia*, the phylloclades of *Epiphyllum*, and the tubercled spheres of *Mammillaria*. There has been considerable divergence of opinion as to its relationships. Wettstein (1935) assigns it to the Centrospermae; Engler and Diels (1936) to a separate order Opuntiales near the Passifloraceae; Warming (1904) to the order Cactales following the Centrospermales; and Hutchinson (1926) to the same order but next to the Cucurbitales (Cucurbitaceae, Begoniaceae, Datiscaceae, and Caricaceae).

Practically no embryological work had been done on the Cactaceae until the publication of the papers of Mauritzon (1934) and Neumann (1935) on *Rhipsalis* and *Pereskia* respectively. Although additional data are desirable, Wettstein's views have received very definite support from the observations of these authors.[1b] The Cactaceae agree with the rest of the Centrospermae in possessing the following embryological characters: (1) anther tapetum glandular and its cells two- to four-nucleate; periplasmodium absent; (2) divisions of microspore mother cells simultaneous; (3) pollen grains trinucleate; (4) ovules campylotropous with strongly curved and massive nucelli; (5) micropyle formed by the swollen apex of the inner integument which protrude out and approach the funiculus; (6) a hypodermal archesporial cell which cuts off a wall cell; (7) formation of a nucellar cap arising from periclinal divisions of the cells of the nucellar epidermis (Fig. 199C); (8) functioning of the chalazal megaspore of the tetrad; (9) formation of a monosporic eight-nucleate embryo sac;[2] (10) functioning of the perisperm as the chief storage region.[3]

An additional point of considerable interest is the occurrence of a

---

[1b] See also Buxbaum (1944, 1948, 1949) who agrees that the Cactaceae are closely allied to the Aizoaceae and should be placed under the Centrospermales.

[2] Archibald (1939) reports an Allium type of embryo sac in *Opuntia aurantiaca*, but her figures are not convincing and it seems probable that the development is really of the Polygonum type as in the other Cactaceae.

[3] The only exception in this respect is the family Thelygonaceae, in which the endosperm forms the chief storage tissue (Woodcock, 1929).

minute air space between the two integuments in the chalazal region of the ovules of *Pereskia* (Fig. 199*A*) and *Opuntia* (Neumann, 1935; Archibald, 1939). This has also been noted since then in several members of the Centrospermae. A radial elongation of the terminal cells of the nucellar epidermis, followed by some periclinal divisions in later stages (Fig. 199*C*), is common to the Aizoaceae and Cactaceae. Further, some significant similarities of an anatomical nature have recently been recorded between the spiny or scaly

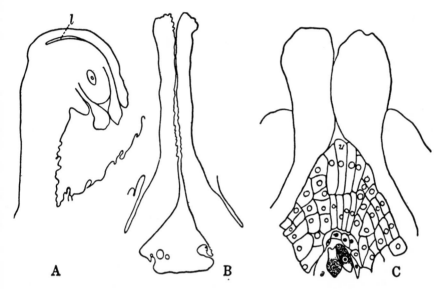

Fig. 199. Ovary and ovule of *Pereskia amapola*. *A*, l.s. young ovule, showing a prominent air space *l* between inner and outer integuments. *B*, l.s. pistil showing stylar canal. *C*, l.s. upper lart of ovule, showing nucellar cap and micropyle formed by inner integument. (*After Neumann, 1935.*)

emergences of *Pereskia* and *Rhipsalis* (Cactaceae) and *Anacampseros* (Portulacaceae).[4] Present evidence, therefore, seems to be entirely in favor of regarding the Cactaceae as a sort of bridge between the Aizoaceae and Portulacaceae. Among specific similarities between the Portulacaceae and Cactaceae, Neumann (1935) cites the following: (1) microspore mother cells forming one to two (only rarely more than two) rows in the anther loculus; (2) micropyle in close proximity to the funiculus; (3) T-shaped tetrad of

[4] For details, see Chorinsky (1931).

megaspores; (4) long synergids; and (5) embryo sac constricted in the middle portion. On the other hand, if we turn to the Passifloraceae, we find a number of striking differences, for here (1) the nucellar epidermis does not undergo any periclinal divisions; (2) it is usually the uppermost megaspore which functions, not the chalazal; (3) the ovule is completely anatropous with a perfectly symmetrical nucellus; and (4) the outer integument grows up to a higher level than the inner and takes part in the formation of the micropyle (see Schnarf, 1931).

Garryaceae. The systematic position of the Garryaceae has been disputed for a long time. Engler and Gilg (1924) placed it among the most primitive families of the dicotyledons, and the same course has been adopted by Engler and Diels (1936) in the latest edition of the "Syllabus der Pflanzenfamilien." Others, like Bentham and Hooker (1880) and Wangerin (1910), have taken a different view and assigned it to the highest of the Archichlamydeae placing it close to the Cornaceae.

Hallock's (1930) work on the morphology and embryology of *Garrya elliptica* necessitates a fresh appraisal of the situation. She reports as follows:

1. The staminate flower, although apparently monochlamydeous, invariably shows the primordia of the sepals in the earlier stages of its development.

2. The pistillate flower is not naked. The two whorls of alternately arranged "bractlets" or "folioles" seen on the top of the ovary represent the reduced perianth lobes (the members of the outer whorl are thick and green, and those of the inner are more delicate and petal-like). The presence of a vascular supply in these structures and the definite position which they occupy with respect to each other and to the pistil supports this view, and from this fact it further follows that the ovary is inferior and the flower parts epigynous and not hypogynous.

3. The integument, described as "complete or incomplete" (Engler and Gilg, 1924), is a thick and massive structure. It is only in later stages that it begins to be consumed by the embryo and therefore appears to be "incomplete."

4. The nucellus is thin and ephemeral, disappearing completely at the sides of the embryo sac.

5. There is a single archesporial cell which divides to form a wall cell and the megaspore mother cell.

6. The mature embryo sac is eight-nucleate and arises from the chalazal cell of a linear tetrad of megaspores.

7. The endosperm becomes cellular at a very early stage.

8. The fertilized egg forms a long, tubular, somewhat vermiform structure designed to penetrate rather deeply into the endosperm.

From a consideration of the sum total of these characters, Hallock concludes that the Garryaceae are not primitive but must be considered as the highest of the Umbelliflorae immediately preceding the Sympetalae. She further suggests that the dioeciousness of *Garrya* may also be a derived rather than a primitive feature.

One point which has not been satisfactorily settled by Hallock but which is nevertheless of considerable importance, is the nature of the rudimentary haustorial structures observed by her at both ends of the endosperm. She considers them to be derived from the synergids and the antipodal cells, but her illustrations do not seem to prove this interpretation. It is more likely that they really originate from the micropylar and chalazal cells of the endosperm. If this interpretation turns out to be correct, it would form one of the strongest arguments in favor of the advanced position of the Garryaceae.

Onagraceae. The family Onagraceae affords one of the best examples of the utility of embryological characters in taxonomic considerations. An unfailing characteristic of this family, ocurring in every genus and species so far investigaged, is the peculiar monosporic four-nucleate embryo sac, consisting of an egg apparatus and single polar nucleus. The only exception is the genus *Trapa*. This has been placed variously by different systematists: (1) under the Onagraceae; (2) as an appendix to the Onagraceae; (3) as an isolated member of the Halorrhagidaceae; (4) as the only genus of a separate family, Hydrocaryaceae or Trapaceae.

Embryological evidence strongly favors the last view. In addition to its eight-nucleate embryo sac, *Trapa* has a well-developed suspensor haustorium (Fig. 200), both these features being unknown in any member of the Onagraceae. Further, in the Onagraceae the ovary is inferior and tetralocular, with axile placentae bearing numerous ovules, and the fruit is generally a loculicidal capsule. In *Trapa*, on the other hand, the ovary is semi-inferior and bilocular, with only one ovule in each chamber, and the fruit is a large one-seeded[5] drupe whose fleshy layer soon disappears, leaving only the

[5] Of the two ovules in the ovary, one aborts at an early stage in its development.

stony endocarp with two to four upwardly directed prongs representing the persistent sepals.

Callitrichaceae.   The genus *Callitriche* comprises about 25 species, which are extremely reduced in both vegetative and floral structure.   The male flower consists of a single terminal stamen, and the

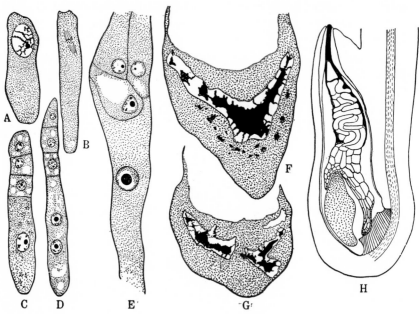

Fig. 200.   Development of embryo sac and embryo in *Trapa*.   *A*, megaspore mother cell in synizesis.   *B*, same, undergoing first meiotic division.   *C*, tetrad of megaspores.   *D*, two-nucleate embryo sac with three nonfunctioning megaspores. *E*, upper part of mature embryo sac.   *F,G*, two consecutive sections through lower part of embryo sac, showing hypertrophied and degenerating antipodal nuclei. (*After Ishikawa, 1918.*)   *H*, diagrammatic l.s. of young seed, showing two integuments, massive suspensor, and embryo.   (*After Tison, 1919.*)

female of a short-stalked bicarpellary ovary situated between a pair of delicate bracteoles.   Each cell of the ovary becomes divided by a false septum, and there is a single pendulous anatropous ovule in each of the four loculi.   There is a pair of long styles placed transversely like the carpels.

The exact position of *Callitriche* has always been considered doubtful.   According to Bentham and Hooker, R. Brown, De Candolle, and Hegelmaier and Hutchinson, it is related to the Halorrhagidaceae; Clarke (1865) recommended that it should be placed under the Caryophyllaceae; and Baillon (1858) included it under the Euphorbiaceae. Pax and Hoffman (1931) are in general agreement with Baillon's views but consider that the best course is to assign it to a separate family Callitrichaceae, placed close to the Euphorbiaceae.

The work of Jørgensen (1923, 1925) has, however, revealed a combination of embryological characters in *Callitriche* which make

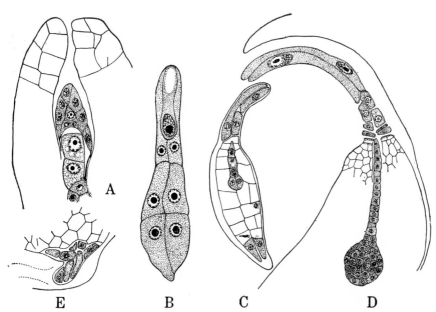

Fɪɢ. 201. Some stages in development of embryo sac and endosperm of *Callitriche*. *A*, l.s. young ovule, showing reduced nucellus, single integument, and row of three cells comprising two megaspores and binucleate dyad cell. *B*, twelve-celled stage of endosperm; only six cells seen in section. *C*, later stage, showing laying down of micropylar and chalazal haustoria. *D,E*, portions of embryo sacs, showing micropylar and chalazal haustoria. (*After Jørgensen, 1923.*)

all of these assignments seem very unlikely. The ovule is tenui-nucellate and has a single massive integument (Fig. 201*A*); the endosperm is cellular (Fig. 201*B*) and forms well-developed haus-toria (Fig. 201*C–E*). These features are so characteristic of the Tubiflorae that they suggest a closer relationship of the Callitrich-aceae with the Labiatae or Verbenaceae than with any of the families named in the preceding paragraph.[6] In the absence of adequate

[6] This view also receives support from the structure of the fruit and the gyno-basic style of *Callitriche*.

anatomical and cytological data, Jørgensen wisely refrains from committing himself further but concludes that in any case the present assignment of the Callitrichaceae to the Geraniales is open to serious objection.

Liliaceae-Allioideae. The extensive studies made on the family Liliaceae by Schnarf, Stenar, and other embryologists have given some new orientations to our ideas of the interrelationships between the subfamilies and tribes included under it. Considering the subfamily Allioideae, Krause (1930) has divided it into four tribes, viz., Agapantheae, Allieae, Gillesieae, and Miluleae. The embryology of the last two tribes is relatively unknown and they will therefore be left out of consideration, but Stenar's (1933) work on the Agapantheae and Allieae indicates a much closer relationship between them than was previously anticipated. Indeed, as Stenar says, *Agapanthus* and *Tulbaghia* are only South African Allieae with a rhizome instead of a bulb, and in *Tulbaghia* the resemblance extends even to the possession of the leek-like odor characteristic of *Allium*. Regarding the relative positions of these two genera, *Agapanthus* (ovule anatropous, parietal cells present, embryo sac of Polygonum type) is to be regarded as the more primitive, and *Tulbaghia* (ovule hemianatropous, parietal cells absent, embryo sac of Allium type) as relatively advanced. The latter connects with *Nothoscordum* which also has hemianatropous ovules devoid of parietal tissue. Here the development of the embryo sac may be of the Allium type (*N. fragrans*) or the Polygonum type (*N. striatum*).

Gagea, which was believed to have an embryo sac of the Adoxa type (Stenar, 1927), used to be considered as the most advanced member of the Allieae, but further work done on this genus revealed that the embryo sac is of the Fritillaria type (see Maheshwari, 1946). The question arises, therefore, as to whether it should be retained in the Allieae or transferred to the Lilioideae, where the Fritillaria type is of general occurrence. In support of the second alternative it may be added that even on other grounds Baillon (1894) considered *Gagea* to be closely allied to *Tulipa*, which is a member of the Lilioideae, and this assignment has been accepted by Hutchinson (1934, 1948).[7]

[7] See also Schnarf (1948).

Liliaceae-Asphodeloideae. According to Krause (1930) the sub-family Asphodeloideae comprises the following tribes: Asphodeleae, Hemerocallideae, Aloeae, Aphyllantheae, Johnsonieae, Dasypogo-neae, Lomandreae, and Calectasieae. The Asphodeleae is further subdivided into Asphodelinae, Anthericinae, Chlorogalinae, Odonto-stominae, Eriosperminae, Xeroneminae, and Dianellinae. To the Asphodelinae belong the genera *Asphodelus, Asphodeline, Paradisia, Diuranthera,* and *Eremurus;* and to the Anthericinae belong *Bul-binella, Bulbine, Bulbinopsis, Anemarrhena, Terauchia, Simethis, Debesia, Anthericum, Alectorurus, Chlorophytum, Verdickia, Eremo-crinum, Thysanotus, Dichopogon, Arthropodium,* and a few others. Although only a few genera under these two subtribes have so far been investigated, the information available at present may be summarized as shown in the accompanying table.

Asphodelinae	Anthericinae
Ovules orthotropus or hemitropous	Ovules typically anatropous
Aril present	Aril absent
Division of microspore mother cells simultaneous	Division of microspore mother cells successive
Embryo sac does not produce any haustorial outgrowth	Embryo sac produces a lateral haustorium

Now, *Paradisia* (Stenar, 1928a), which has been placed by Krause under the Asphodelinae, has no aril, the divisions of its microspore mother cells are of the successive type, and its embryo sac forms a haustorium similar to that of *Anthericum* (Schnarf, 1928). In *Bul-bine,* on the other hand, which has been placed under the Antheri-cinae, there is a clear and well-developed aril, the divisions of the microspore mother cells are of the simultaneous type, and there is no embryo sac haustorium. The case for an interchange of the posi-tions of these two genera is therefore quite evident, and in a revised classification of the Asphodeloideae, *Paradisia* should be placed under the Anthericinae and *Bulbine* under the Asphodelinae.

In a more recent paper Schnarf and Wunderlich (1939) go still further and emphasize that on embryological grounds the Asphodelinae and Antbericinae may not be placed even under a common tribe but ought each to be given the status of an independent tribe. In support of this view is cited the work of Bouvier (1915), who reports several anatomical differences also between the Asphodelinae and Antbericinae.

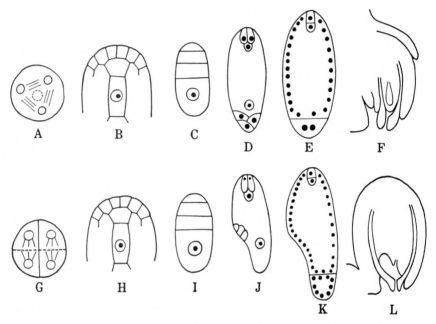

Fig. 202.   Diagram showing comparison of the more important embryological features of Asphodelinae and Aloineae (*A–F*) with those of Antbericinae (*G–L*). *A*, Asphodelinae-Aloineae; simultaneous division of microspore mother cell. *B*, nucellus, showing megaspore mother cell and parietal cell. *C*, tetrad of megaspores. *D*, mature embryo sac. *E*, embryo sac, showing Helobial endosperm. *F*, l.s. ovule, showing aril. *G*, Antbericinae; successive division of microspore mother cell. *H*, nucellus, showing megaspore mother cell and parietal cell. *I*, tetrad of megaspores. *J*, mature embryo sac, showing lateral haustorium. *K*, embryo sac, showing Helobial endosperm. *L*, l.s. ovule; note absence of aril. (*After Schnarf, 1944.*)

On the other hand, embryology indicates such a close alliance between the Asphodelinae (*Asphodelus, Asphodeline, Eremurus, Bulbinella, Bulbinella, Bulbinopsis,* and *Alectorurus*) and the Aloineae (*Haworthia, Gasteria, Aloe, Kniphofia, Apicra,* and *Lomatophyllum*) that both of them may well be united into the same subfamily or tribe (Schnarf, 1944). The following characters are common to both: (1) divisions of the microspore mother cells of the simultaneous type; (2) generative cell cut off exactly opposite to the furrow in the pollen grain; (3) ovule crassinucellate with two integuments and an aril; (4) megaspore mother cell separated from the nucellar epidermis by parietal cells; (5) embryo sac of Polygonum type; and (6) endosperm of the Helobial type (demonstrated in *Gasteria* and *Kniphofia* and inferred in *Aloe* from the position of the primary endosperm nucleus). The more important differences between the Asphodelinae-Aloinae and the Anthericinae are presented in Fig. 202.

Liliaceae-Lilioideae. Of the genera included under the subfamily Lilioideae (Krause, 1930), *Lilium, Fritillaria, Tulipa, Lloydia,* and *Erythronium* have been shown to have a tetrasporic embryo sac, usually of the Fritillaria type; *Nomocharis* is uninvestigated. Only *Calochortus* has been found to have an embryo sac of the monosporic eight-nucleate type (Cave, 1941). It is interesting to note that this genus also differs from the remaining members of the Lilioideae in some other respects. The fruit of *Calochortus* is a septicidal capsule, while that of the other genera is loculicidal. In *Calochortus* the chromosome numbers are 6, 7, 8, 9 and 10 (Newton, 1926; Beal, 1939; Owenby, 1940), while in the remaining genera the number is usually 12. On the basis of these and some other differences in the structure and germination of the seed, Buxbaum (1937a, b) proposed that *Calochortus* should be transferred to an independent subfamily under the Liliaceae. This opinion, which is strongly supported by the embryological data brought forward by Cave (1941), may now be accepted without reservation.[8]

Conclusion. There are several other notable examples of the aid which embryology has rendered in the solution of taxonomical problems, but it is unnecessary to cite all of them here. What has already been written is sufficient evidence of the value of embryological data in an elucidation of the interrelationships of families and genera. Although it is not claimed that these data will always prove important, they should form a part of any thorough taxonomic analysis. It is worth while, therefore, for every student of embryology to try to assess the bearing of his observations and those of his predecessors on the taxonomic position of the group of plants which he is studying. Many of his conclusions are bound to

[8] See also Schnarf (1948).

be of a tentative nature and will have to be stated with due caution, but every contribution, however small, will be one step nearer to the final goal, and occasionally there will emerge fresh ideas and new viewpoints which will more than compensate for the effort expended upon the work.

References

Agardh, J. G. 1858. "Theoria Systematis Plantarum." Lund.

Archibald, E. E. A. 1939. The development of the ovule and seed of jointed cactus (*Opuntia aurantiaca* Lindley). South African Jour. Sci. **36:** 195–211.

Baillon, H. 1858. Recherches sur l'organogénie du *Callitriche* et sur ses rapports naturels. Bul. Soc. Bot. de France **5:** 337.

——. 1892. "Histoire des plantes." Vol. 11. Paris.

——. 1894. "Histoire des plantes." Vol. 12. Paris.

Beal, J. M. 1939. Cytological studies in relation to the classification of the genus *Calochortus*. Bot. Gaz. **100:** 528–547.

Bentham, G., and Hooker, J. D. 1862–1883. "Genera plantarum." London.

Bouvier, W. 1915. Beiträge zur vergleichenden Anatomie der Asphodeloideae. Denkschr. Akad. der Wiss. Wien, Math.-Nat. Kl. **91:** 539–577.

Brown, R. 1814. "General Remarks on the Botany of Terra Australis." London.

Buxbaum, F. 1937*a.* Die Entwicklungslinien der Lilioideae. I. Die Wurmbaeaoideae. Bot. Arch. **38:** 213–293.

——. 1937*b.* Die Entwicklungslinien der Lilioideae. II. Die systematische Stellung der Gattung *Gagea*. Bot. Arch. **38:** 305–398.

——. 1944. Untersuchungen zur Morphologie der Kakteenblüte. I. Das Gynaecium. Bot. Arch. **45:** 190–247.

——. 1948. Zur Klärung der phylogenetischen Stellung der Aizoaceae und Cactaceae im Pflanzenreich. Jahrb. d. schweiz. kakt. Ges. **2:** 3–16.

——. 1949. Vorläufer des Kakteen-Habitus bei den Phytolaccaceen. Österr. bot. Ztschr. **96:** 5–14.

Cave, M. S. 1941. Megasporogenesis and embryo sac development in *Calochortus*. Amer. Jour. Bot. **28:** 390–394.

Chorinsky, F. 1931. Vergleichend-anatomische Untersuchung der Haargebilde bei Portulacaceen und Cactaceen. Österr. bot. Ztschr. **80:** 308–327.

Clarke, B. 1865. On the structure and affinities of Callitrichaceae. Jour. Bot. **3.**

Copeland, H. F. 1935. The structure of the flower of *Pholisma arenarium*. Amer. Jour. Bot. **22:** 366–383.

Don, D. 1827. On the affinities of the Empetreae, a natural group of plants. Edinburgh New Phil. Jour. **2:** 59–63.

Engler, A., and Diels, L. 1936. "Syllabus der Pflanzenfamilien." 11th ed. Berlin.

—— and Gilg, E. 1924. "Syllabus der Pflanzenfamilien." 9th and 10th eds. Berlin.

Gray, A. 1858. "Manual of the Botany of the Northern United States." New York.

Hagerup, O. 1946. Studies on the Empetraceae. K. Danske Vidensk. Selsk., Biol. Meddel. **20**(5): 1–49.

Hallier, H. 1912. L'origine et le système phylétique des Angiospermes exposés à l'aide de leur arbre généalogique. Arch. Néerland. III B. **1**

Hallock, F. A. 1930. The relationship of *Garrya*. The development of the flowers and seeds of *Garrya* and its bearing on the phylogenetic position of the genus. Ann. Bot. **44**: 771–812.

Hegelmaier, F. 1867. Zur systematik von *Callitriche*. Verhandl. Bot. Ver. f. der Brandenb. **9**: 1.

Hutchinson, J. 1926. "The Families of Flowering Plants. I. Dicotyledons." London.

————. 1934. "The Families of Flowering Plants. II. Monocotyledons." London.

————. 1948. "British Flowering Plants." London.

Ishikawa, M. 1918. Studies on the embryo sac and fertilisation in *Oenothera*. Ann. Bot. **32**: 279–317.

Jørgensen, C. A. 1923. Studies on Callitrichaceae. Bot. Tidskr. **38**: 81–126.

————. 1925. Zur Frage der systematischen Stellung der Callitrichaceen. Jahrb. f. wiss. Bot. **64**: 440–442.

Just, Th. 1946. The use of embryological formulas in plant taxonomy. Bul. Torrey Bot. Club **73**: 351–355.

Krause, K. 1930. Liliaceae (In Engler and Prantl's "Natürlichen Pflanzenfamilien, 2d ed. **15A**: 227–390).

Maheshwari, P. 1945*a*. The place of angiosperm embryology in research and teaching. Jour. Indian Bot. Soc. **24**: 25–41.

————. 1945*b*. Embryology of angiosperms as a field for research. Nature [London] **156**: 354–355.

————. 1946. The Fritillaria type of embryo sac: a critical review. Jour. Indian Bot. Soc. M. O. P. Iyengar Comm. Vol., pp. 101–119.

Mauritzon, J. 1934. Ein Beitrag zur Embryologie der Phytolaccaceen und Cactaceen. Bot. Notiser 1934, pp. 111–135.

————. 1939. Die Bedeutung der embryologischen Forschung für das natürliche System der Pflanzen. Lunds Univ. Årsskr. N.F. II, **35**(15): 1–70.

Neumann, M. 1935. Die Entwicklung des Pollens, der Samenanlage und des Embryosackes von *Pereskia amapola* var. *argentina*. Österr. bot. Ztschr. **84**: 1–30.

Newton, W. C. F. 1926. Chromosome studies in *Tulipa* and some related genera. Jour. Linn. Soc. London, Bot. **47**: 339–354.

Ownbey, M. 1940. A monograph of the genus *Calochortus*. Ann. Missouri Bot. Gard. **27**: 371–560.

Pax, F. 1896. Empetraceae (in Engler and Prantl's "Natürlichen Pflanzenfamilien," 1st ed.).

———— and Hoffman, C. 1931. Callitrichaceae (in Engler and Prantl's Natürlichen Pflanzenfamilien, 2d ed).

Samuelsson, G. 1913. Studien über die Entwicklungsgeschichte einiger Bicornes-Typen. Svensk Bot. Tidskr. **7**: 97–188.

Schnarf, K. 1928. Über das Embryosackhaustorium bei *Anthericum*. Österr. bot. Ztschr. **77:** 287–291.

——. 1931. "Vergleichende Embryologie der Angiospermen." Berlin.

——. 1933. Die Bedeutung der embryologischen Forschung für das natürliche System der Pflanzen. Biol. Gen. [Vienna] **9:** 271–288.

——. 1937. Ziele und Wege der vergleichenden Embryologie der Blütenpflanzen. Verhandl. zool.-bot. Gesell. Wien **86/87:** 140–147.

——. 1944. Ein Beitrag zur Kenntnis der Verbreitung des Aloïns und ihrer systematischen Bedeutung. Österr. bot. Ztschr. **93:** 113–122.

——. 1948. Der Umfang der Lilioideae im natürlichen System. Österr. bot. Ztschr. **95:** 257–269.

—— and Wunderlich, R. 1939. Zur vergleichende Embryologie der Liliaceae-Asphodeloideae. Flora **33:** 297–327.

Solms-Laubach, H. G. 1870. Die Familie der Lennoaceen. Abh. naturf. Gesell. Halle **11:** 119–178.

Stenar, H. 1927. Über die Entwicklung des siebenkernigen Embryosackes bei *Gagea lutea* Ker. Svensk Bot. Tidskr. **21:** 344–360.

——. 1928*a*. Zur Embryologie der Asphodeline-Gruppe. Ein Beitrag zur systematischen Stellung der Gattungen *Bulbine* und *Paradisia*. Svensk Bot. Tidskr. **22:** 145–159.

——. 1928*b*. Zur Embryologie der Veratrum- und Anthericum-Gruppe. Bot. Notiser 1928, pp. 357–378.

——. 1933. Zur Embryologie der Agapanthus-Gruppe. Bot. Notiser 1933, pp. 520–530.

Süssenguth, K. 1927. Über die Gattung *Lennoa*. Flora **122:** 264–305.

Tison, A. 1919. Sur le suspenseur du *Trapa natans* L. Rev. Gen. Bot. **31:** 219–228.

Wangerin, W. 1910. Cornaceae (In Engler, A. "Das Pflanzenreich." IV. **229:** 1–110.

Warming, E. 1904. "A Handbook of Systematic Botany." Engl. Transl. London.

Wettstein, R. 1935. "Handbuch der systematischen Botanik." Vienna.

Woodcock, E. 1929. Seed development in *Thelygonum cynocrambe* L. Papers Mich. Acad. Sci., Arts, and Letters **11:** 341–345.

CHAPTER 12

EXPERIMENTAL EMBRYOLOGY

As mentioned in the first chapter, modern embryology seems to comprise three main disciplines. The first, or descriptive embryology, is a study of the various developmental processes that take place in a plant from the initiation of the sex organs to the maturation of the embryo. The second, or phylogenetic embryology, attempts to evaluate these data in determining the interrelationships of the different orders and families with a view to improving the existing schemes of classification. The third, or experimental embryology, is concerned with an imitation and a modification of the course of nature, with a view to understanding the physics and chemistry of the various processes underlying the development and differentiation of the embryo, so as to bring them under human control to the furthest extent possible.

In attempting to summarize the present position of the subject of experimental embryology, it seems convenient to discuss it under the following topics: control of fertilization; embryo culture; induced parthenogenesis; production of adventive embryos; and induced parthenocarpy.

Control of Fertilization.[1]   Ever since the rediscovery of Mendel's laws in 1900, breeders have been increasingly active in crossing different varieties, species, and genera with a view to producing newer and more useful types. However, their attempts are often thwarted by one or more of the following difficulties: (1) disharmony in time of flowering of the two parents; (2) failure of pollen to germinate on the stigma; (3) slow growth of pollen tubes; (4) bursting or dying of pollen tubes in the style; and (5) inability of the sperms to effect fertilization.

Of these, the first is largely a physiological problem. A disharmony in the time of flowering of the two parents can be partially overcome by altering the environmental conditions, chiefly tempera-

[1] For further information on some aspects of this problem, see Blakeslee (1945) and Maheshwari (1950).

ture and photoperiod.   More effective, however, is the storage of pollen from one season to another, for this has the advantage of enabling the breeder to cross two varieties which are separated from each other not only in time but also in space.   With modern air transport, pollen may be sent from one part of the world to another in a very short time.

Important though the question of the storage and viability of pollen is, it has attracted proper attention only in recent years. Under natural conditions most pollens remain viable for only a few days or weeks, but this is not universal.   The range of variation in this respect may be illustrated by a few examples from common plants.[2]   In *Hordeum* (Anthony and Harlan, 1920) and *Oryza* (Nagao and Takano, 1938) fertilization cannot be secured with certainty unless the pollen is transferred directly from the anther to the stigma. In *Sorghum* (Stephens and Quinby, 1934) no seed could be obtained when pollen was used 5 hours or more after collection from the dehiscing anthers.   In some experiments at Coimbatore 65 per cent of the pollen grains of *Gossypium* were found to retain their viability up to the twenty-fourth hour after collection but none after twice this period (Banerji, 1929).   At New Delhi the pollen of *Solanum melongena* remains viable for only 1 day in summer and 2 to 3 days in winter (Pal and Singh, 1943).   At the other extreme, however, is the pollen of *Phoenix dactylifera*, which is said to retain its viability for a whole year[2a] and which used to be an important article of commerce in the past.

Most pollens fall between the two extremes mentioned above, but recent work shows that, whatever the viability might be under natural conditions, it can almost always be prolonged to an appreciable extent by storing the pollen under proper conditions.   Holman and Brubaker (1926), who have reviewed the older literature, mention the extension of longevity of *Cyclamen* pollen from 18 to 185 days and that of *Listera ovata* from 40 to 164 days.   Samples of *Typha* pollen which had been stored in a calcium chloride desiccator for 71, 94, 116, and 158 days, gave respectively 75, 70, 65, and 56 per cent germination, and 2 per cent of the pollen grains remained

---

[2] For further information on this topic see Maheshwari (1944).

[2a] Stout (1924) contradicts this and says that he found no evidence of survival of air-dry pollen for more than 77 days, but as pointed out by Holman and Brubaker (1926), it is possible that under favorable conditions the period may be much longer.

viable even after 336 days. Air-dry pollen of *Coffea* stored in the ordinary way loses its germination power within a week, but when kept in a desiccator it retains that power for more than a month (Ferwerda, 1937). Pfeiffer (1944), who made similar experiments with *Cinchona*, found that 5 to 19 per cent of the pollen retained its viability even after a year's storage in darkness at a temperature of 10°C. and a humidity of 35 to 50 per cent. Nebel (1939) has been able to preserve apple pollen for $4\frac{1}{2}$ years and sour cherry pollen for $5\frac{1}{2}$ years at a temperature of 2 to 8°C. and a humidity of 50 per cent. Even grass pollen, which is notoriously ephemeral, has been kept alive for 15 to 30 times its natural period of viability. To mention only two examples, the pollen of *Saccharum spontaneum* (a wild grass used in crosses with sugarcane), spread out on a watch glass in diffused light, remained viable for only about 6 hours; the same pollen stored in vials plugged with cotton and kept at room temperature, for 12 to 24 hours; and the same kept at 7°C., for more than a week (Sartoris, 1942). Similarly, the pollen of *Zea mays* stored in pollinating bags in direct sunlight at a maximum temperature of 46°C. remained viable for only 3 hours; that stored in shade at a maximum temperature of 30°C., for 30 hours; and the same kept in tassel at a temperature of 4.5°C. and a relative humidity of 90 per cent, for 8 to 9 days (Jones and Newell, 1948).

The data given above indicate that the most important factor in pollen storage is temperature and the next is relative humidity. We know very little about the effect of light; but strong light is undoubtedly harmful, and diffused light or even complete darkness seems to be more conducive to successful storage.

Equal in importance to the viability of pollen is the receptivity of the stigma, but this is less amenable to control. In many plants the stigma is receptive for only a short period, and if the pollen is not transferred to it at the right time, it fails to germinate, or the germination is so slow that the flower withers and falls off before the pollen tubes can reach the ovules. Attempts to prolong the receptivity of the stigma have usually been unsuccessful, or they are associated with secondary effects which make it difficult to derive much benefit from such prolongation. For instance, although a lowering of the temperature can lengthen the blooming period and also extend the period of receptivity of the stigma to a certain extent, it has an adverse effect on the rate of growth of the pollen tube, so that the net result is the same and fertilization still fails to take place.

However, the main difficulty is not so much in the initial germination of the pollen as in the subsequent growth of the pollen tube in a foreign style. This may be due either to the fact that the maximum length attainable by the pollen tubes of the male parent is inadequate for enabling them to reach the ovules, or that the unfavorable medium through which they have to make their way causes an excessive retardation of their growth.

When the failure of a cross is due to such causes, one obvious remedy is to try the reciprocal cross, but frequently even this is unsuccessful. An alternative method is to amputate the style and reduce it to a suitable length. In a cross between *Zea* and *Tripsacum*, Manglesdorf and Reeves (1931) shortened the style of the former to a length suitable for the pollen tubes of *Tripsacum* and thereby obtained intergeneric hybrids. However, since the cut end of the style is not always as suitable for pollen germination as the stigma, sometimes it is desirable to use a different method in which the middle portion of the style is removed and the upper and lower portions are then joined together and held in place (Buchholz, Doak, and Blakeslee, 1932).

The Buchholz method, based on experiments with flowers of *Datura*, may be briefly described as follows. On the plant which is to serve as the maternal parent, a nearly mature unopened bud is selected. One operator now makes a transverse cut through the bud at the point *k* (Fig. 203*A*, *B*), where the fluted inner surface of the corolla shows a marked constriction. A second operator places the style on a previously prepared gauge and makes a clean square cut at the desired distance from the stigma, discarding the lower part of the style. The newly cut end of the stigma-bearing portion of the style is now inserted in a closely fitting grass straw, which is lowered over the stump of the basal part of the style. The moment the two cut surfaces come in contact, further lowering of the straw gives an upward thrust to the part bearing the stigma. This enables the operator to know when contact is made and the process is complete. If the operation (Fig. 203*A–H*) is carried out carefully, the pollen tubes pass down the joint and are able to reach the ovules.

A Japanese worker, Yasuda (1931), has gone one step further and attempted an actual graft of the style upon the ovary in *Petunia violacea.* He cut off the style of one flower and glued it with gelatin to the ovary of another flower whose style had been previously cut away. In order to prevent the falling apart of the grafted style, he supported it against an iron wire, tying the support and the style with a spider's thread (Fig. 203*I*). When the operation was successful, the grafted style grew normally and attained its usual size.

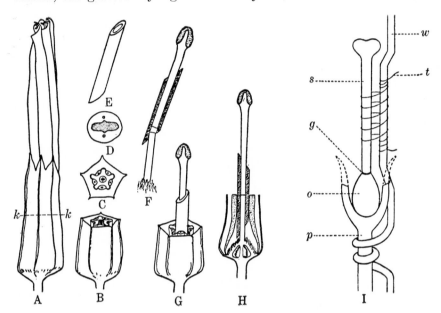

FIG. 203. Diagrams showing technique of splicing (*A–H*) and grafting (*I*) of styles. (*kk* = level at which transverse cut is made through flower bud; *s* = grafted style; *w* = wire support; *t* = spider's thread; *o* = ovary; *g* = gelatin joint between ovary and style; *p* = pedicel). (*A–H, after Buchholz, Doak and Blakeslee, 1932; I, after Yasuda, 1931.*)

On the other hand, if the tissues failed to unite, the style turned brown and shrank.

Yasuda's method requires a great deal of manipulative skill and has apparently never been tried by any other worker. Although it seems to be impracticable with plants having thin styles, it is possible that it can be used successfully when the styles are reasonably thick. A grafting of the style of the species used as the paternal parent on to the ovary of the maternal parent certainly seems to be a promising method of combating incompatibility factors between two species or varieties.

Yet another method of overcoming the difficulty caused by an extremely slow growth of the pollen tube would be a direct introduction of the pollen grains into the ovary. Somewhat reminiscent of the artificial insemination practiced in animals, this technique has not so far been perfected for plants. That it is entirely possible to do so, however, is indicated by some experiments of Dahlgren (1926), who succeeded in bringing about a fertilization of the ovules of *Codonopsis ovata* by this method. More recently, Bosio (1940) tried some intraovarial pollinations in *Helleborus* and *Paeonia*. He emasculated the flowers and either removed the stigmas or painted them with celloidin. Then an incision was made in the ovary and the pollen grains introduced into it artificially. In *Helleborus* the germination was inadequate to cause any fertilization, but in *Paeonia* several ovules were fertilized yielding viable seeds. In explanation of this difference in the behavior of the two genera, the author says that the pollen of the Ranunculaceae requires for its germination a sugary medium, with a pH close to neutral. Within the ovary of *Helleborus* there is no free liquid, and the pH of the cells lining it is about 4; in *Paeonia*, on the other hand, the cells at the base of the ovarian cavity secrete an abundant liquid, which has a suitable concentration of sugar and a pH of about 6. Germination of the pollen, therefore, fails in the former but is quite successful in the latter. In nature it occurs in both cases, since the stigma fulfils the required conditions.

In addition to these mechanical devices for bringing the pollen grains or pollen tubes in close proximity to the ovules, it seems possible that the same result may sometimes be achieved by the application of suitable chemical substances to either pollen grains or stigmas. From experiments in vitro, P. F. Smith (1942) has shown that 3-indoleacetic acid and 3-indolebutyric acid, in concentrations of one in a million, appreciably stimulate the germination of the pollen as well as the rate of elongation of the pollen tubes. More recently, Addicott (1943) has reported that several substances including vitamins, plant hormones, pyridines, and purines are able to bring about similar effects. He also states that germination of pollen and the subsequent growth of pollen tubes are not necessarily related phenomena and that one can be stimulated independently of the other. In his experiments, inositol increased the germination of *Milla* pollen up to 90 per cent over that of the controls without greatly affecting the length of the pollen tubes, while guanine increased the length of the tubes up to 157 per cent over that of the controls without significantly affecting the percentage of germination. Two other substances, paraaminobenzoic acid and acenaphthene, were found to affect both processes.

Eyster (1941) has recently reported that the self-incompatibility in *Petunia, Tagetes, Trifolium repens,* and *Brassica oleracea* can be counteracted by spraying the plants with a solution of α-naphthaleneacetamide. This chemical is said to "neutralize the effects of an ovarian secretion which diffuses into the style and inhibits or greatly retards the growth of pollen tubes." Lewis (1942), who used it with *Prunus avium,* found it ineffective in increasing or decreasing the rate of pollen tube growth, but it delayed the formation of an abscission layer at the base of the style and thereby allowed a longer time for the incompatible tubes to reach the ovary. In his opinion, therefore, the use of α-naphthaleneacetamide may not be confined to the counteraction of self-sterility but may also be used to combat interspecific sterility in certain plants.

That a change in chromosome number can also be of service in the inactivation of incompatibilities has been shown recently by the work of Stout and Chandler (1941) and Stout (1944). As the result of a series of controlled pollinations they found that the potentially fertile flowers of *Petunia axillaris* are entirely self-incompatible and produce no seeds or capsules on self-pollination. However, the self-pollinated flowers of tetraploid branches on the same plants (produced by colchicine treatment) produced large well-filled capsules. Flowers on the self-incompatible diploid branches also produced capsules when pollinated from flowers of tetraploid branches on the same plant, but tetraploid ♀ × diploid ♂ combinations on the same plant failed to yield any seeds.

Of interest in this connection are also some observations of Buchholz and Blakeslee (1929), Satina (1944), and Blakeslee (1945) on *Datura.* When pollen from a 2n plant is applied to the stigma of a 4n plant, fertilization takes place freely and some viable seeds are also produced; but in the reciprocal cross when pollen is applied from a 4n plant to a 2n stigma, seed formation is extremely rare. Histological studies have shown that the pollen tubes derived from the 4n male parent burst in the 2n styles and never reach the ovary. It was possible, however, to overcome this difficulty and change the $2n \times 4n$ cross from an incompatible to a compatible one in an ingenious way. Treatment with colchicine usually results in peri-clinical chimeras in *Datura*. Some of these have the doubled chromosome number in the epidermal layer but not in the underlying tissues. Since it is the epidermal layer which forms the transmitting tissue in the style in *Datura*, a periclinal chimera with a $4n$ epidermis should react exactly like a pure $4n$ parent so far as its relation to pollen tubes from a $4n$ male parent is concerned. This

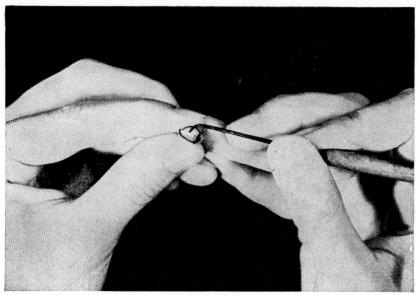

Fig. 204. Method of removing embryo from seed of *Iris* with help of sterile needle. (*After Randolph, 1945.*)

was actually found to be the case, and diploid pollen tubes from $4n$ males grew readily without bursting in styles of a periclinal chimera with a $4n$ epidermis.

Finally, there remains the difficulty that even after the pollen tubes have reached the ovary and ovules, fertilization may fail to occur for some obscure reason. To mention one example, when the flowers of *Ribes nigrum* are self-pollinated, the pollen tubes enter the ovules and "even lay themselves against the embryo-sac nucleus" but the male and female nuclei do not fuse and hence no seeds are formed (Ledeboer and Rietsema, 1940). Since there is no known method of overcoming this trouble, it is not necessary to discuss the point further.

Embryo Culture. In the preceding section we have considered the methods for overcoming some of the barriers to fertilization. It has frequently been observed, however, that even after gametic fusion has taken place something may arrest the growth of the embryo so that the resulting seeds are nonviable (see Sachet, 1948). Recent research has shown that in such cases it is frequently possible to excise the young embryos from the ovules and grow them in artificial media (Figs. 204–208)—a process not unlike the famous

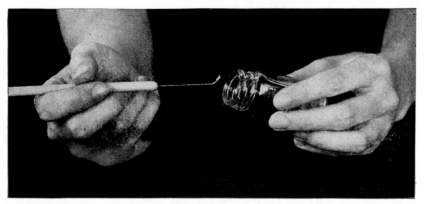

Fɪɢ. 205. Excised embryo being transferred to sterile culture bottle. (*After Randolph, 1945.*)

Caesarean section in which an immature animal embryo is removed from the body of the mother and grown in an incubator.

In tracing the development of this new technique of embryo culture, we find that Hannig (1904) was the first to make a successful attempt of this kind. Using certain crucifers (*e.g., Raphanus* and *Cochlearia*) as the objects of his study, he tested a variety of nutrient media containing sugars, mineral salts, plant decoctions, certain amino acids, and gelatin. Mature plants were reared from embryos that were only 1.2 mm. in length at the time of their excision, but presumably the radicle, plumule, and cotyledons had already been formed at this stage. Following Hannig, Stingl (1907) grew embryos of several cereals, but instead of placing them in culture media he transferred them to the endosperms of other genera

of the family.   Dietrich (1924), who experimented some years later
with a larger variety of plants, found that Knop's solution with 2.5
to 5 per cent cane sugar and 1.5 per cent agar enabled prompt and
regular growth of embryos removed from immature seeds of several
species.   He further observed that the cultured embryos tended to
skip the stages of development which had not been completed at the
time of excision and grew directly into seedlings.   His efforts to

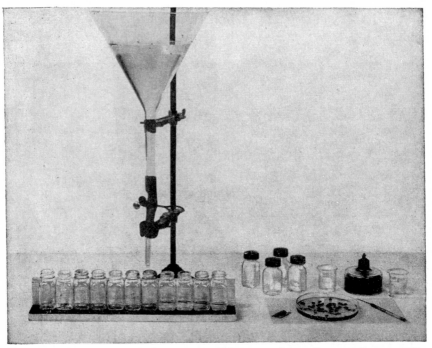

Fig. 206.   Apparatus and glassware used for preparing culture medium.   (*After
Randolph, 1945.*)

cultivate embryos less than one-third of their mature size were,
however, unsuccessful.

The work of Hannig, Stingl, and Dietrich, although of great
importance, seems to have been prompted more by curiosity than
any other reason, and it remained for Laibach (1925, 1929) to show
the possibilities of using this method to economic advantage.   While
making some interspecific crosses in the genus *Linum*, he found
that the cross *L. perenne* × *L. austriacum* yielded fruits of approximately normal size but that the seeds were greatly shrunken and

Fig. 207. Culture bottles, 6 to 10 days old. The first contains an undissected *Iris* seed lying in almost unchanged condition; the rest show seedlings which have arisen from excised embryos. (*After Randolph, 1945.*)

Fig. 208. Four-month-old seedlings of *Iris* grown from excised embryos (left); seedlings from undissected seeds sown at same time (right). (*After Randolph, 1945.*)

only about half as heavy as the normal ones. By dissecting out the embryos and placing them on damp blotting paper, he was able to induce their germination, and the resulting plants flowered and fruited abundantly. The reciprocal cross *L. austriacum* × *L. perenne* was more difficult, for here the fruits shed prematurely at a time when the seeds had only one-thirteenth of the weight of normal seeds and were incapable of germination. However, by excising the embryos when they were about a fortnight old and placing them on cotton wadding in little tubes containing 10 to 15 per cent sugar, he was able to promote their growth. A couple of weeks later they were removed from the sugar solution and placed on moist blotting paper, where they germinated within a few days and eventually yielded vigorous plants which flowered and fruited normally. Laibach, therefore, expressed the opinion that a similar method of "artificial premature birth" could perhaps be used to obtain offspring from various other crosses which had so far proved unfruitful. In conclusion he said: "In any case, I deem it advisable to be cautious in declaring combinations between higher plants to be unviable after fertilization has taken place and after they have begun to develop. Experiments to bring the aborted seed to development should always be undertaken, if it is desirable for theoretical or practical reasons. The experiments will not always be successful, but many a result might be obtained by studying the conditions of ripeness of the embryos and by finding out the right time for the preparing out of the seeds."

Laibach's brilliant exposition gave the lead for more intensive studies on the artificial culture of embryos, and during recent years a number of papers have appeared on the subject. In several crosses which were formerly unsuccessful, the hybrid embryos have been successfully reared to maturity.

In mentioning some specific cases where this technique has been employed with success, we may first refer to certain stone fruits, such as *Prunus avium* (sweet cherry), *P. domestica* (plum), and *P. persica* (peach). When crosses are made in which the early ripening varieties of these plants are used as female parents, the embryos abort and the seeds are not viable.[3] Tukey (1944) attempted arti-

---

[3] Histological studies showed that although fertilization takes place normally, the endosperm and embryo soon cease developing, followed also by a collapse of the nucellus and integument (Tukey, 1933).

ficial cultures of the embryos and succeeded in obtaining mature plants from them. The procedure adopted was to split the stony endocarp with a scalpel, cut carefully through the integuments, nucellus, and endosperm, and drop the embryos under aseptic conditions into bottles containing nutrient agar. The seedlings arising from them were first transplanted to sterile sand watered with a nutrient solution, then to soil, and finally grown in the field.

FIG. 209. Inflorescences of *Hordeum jubatum* (*A*), *Secale cereale* (*C*), and hybrid between them (*B*) raised by artificial culture of excised embryo. (*After Brink, Cooper, and Ausherman, 1944.*)

In time they developed into vigorous fruiting trees. A similar technique used for the embryos of *Iris* is illustrated in Figs. 204–208.

It has been observed that in crossing *Hordeum jubatum* and *Secale cereale* fertilization takes place within 4 hours after pollination but the hybrid seeds collapse and fail to germinate. Brink, Cooper, and Ausherman (1944) dissected out the hybrid embryos from 9- to 12-day-old seeds and reared them in artificial culture. The embryos attained considerable growth and one of the seedlings grew into a mature flowering specimen (Fig. 209). No seeds were set on this plant, but the fact that the hybrid was able to attain the flowering stage proves that the intergeneric combination is not lethal in itself and that causes of the death of the embryo have to be sought elsewhere.

Similar instances of the artificial culture of hybrid embryos have been recorded in various other plants. To mention a few examples, Jørgensen (1928) used this method to obtain hybrids between *Solanum nigrum* and *S. luteum*; Beasley (1940) between *Gossypium hirsutum* and *G. herbaceum*; Skirm (1942) between some species of *Prunus* and of *Lilium*; Smith (1944) between *Lycopersicum esculentum* and *L. peruvianum*; and Sanders (1948) between several species of *Datura*.

When the embryo is of a rather large size, it can often be dissected out with a needle while the seed is held between the fingers. With smaller embryos a dissecting microscope is necessary. The excised embryos are transferred into previously prepared culture bottles containing a nutrient medium. Since conditions favorable for the growth of the embryos are also favorable for the growth of various bacteria and fungi, even a slight carelessness may cause the cultures to become contaminated, resulting in death of the embryos. Suitable precautions must therefore be taken both at the time of dissection of the embryos and during their transfer to the culture medium. Various chemicals are available for sterilizing the seeds, and contamination of the culture room from air-borne spores may be reduced either by using air filters or by spraying the tables and walls with a 1 per cent solution of carbolic acid. The dissecting instruments are dipped in 70 per cent alcohol and flamed. The embryos, being delicate, are not treated with any solution but are dropped immediately after dissection into the sterile culture medium.

The composition of the medium is naturally a most important factor. Older embryos are largely autotrophic and usually present little difficulty. The present problem, however, is to try to rear embryos in younger stages of development. There are two objects in view. One is that hybrid embryos frequently abort at a very early stage before the differentiation of the cotyledons and, therefore, it is necessary to develop proper methods for taking care of them before degeneration has commenced; the other is the long-range question of understanding the nutritional physiology of embryo development, of which we have little or no knowledge up to this time.

All the work so far has been of an exploratory nature only, but some of the attempts made in this direction deserve special mention. In 1936 La Rue reported having grown embryos of *Taraxacum, Chrysanthemum, Lactuca, Coreopsis, Lycopersicum, Nicotiana, Bryophyllum, Zea,* and *Vallota* which were only 0.5 mm. in length. His experiments, as well as those of some of his predecessors, made it clear that inorganic media alone are not adequate for the culture of young embryos, since they also require sugar and other heat-stable factors present in such substances as yeast extract or fibrin digest. In some of his culture media, La Rue substituted indoleacetic acid for yeast extract.[4]

Since embryos are nourished inside the seed by the endosperm, Van Overbeek *et al.* (1942) thought of using coconut milk as one of the ingredients of the culture medium. By adding this they succeeded in growing embryos of *Datura stramonium* which were still in the heart-shaped stage and measured only 0.15 mm. in length (the mature embryo is approximately 6 mm. long). Further study revealed, however, that, in addition to the "embryo factor" necessary for the growth of the embryo, coconut milk also contains one deleterious substance which inhibits root growth and another which causes a callus-like growth but no differentiation.

Blakeslee and Satina (1944) found that powdered malt extract shows embryo factor activity if sterilized by filtration instead of by heat. At the same time Van Overbeek, Siu, and Haagen-Smit (1944) discovered that extracts of *Datura* ovules, yeast, wheat germ, and almond meal also possess this quality.[5] Finally, they claim to have obtained a purified embryo factor preparation which, on the basis of dry weight, showed an activity 170 times that of coconut milk.

Unfortunately neither coconut milk nor the purified "embryo factor" preparations have given any uniform results in the hands of other workers. Working with selfed and hybrid embryos involving four species of *Datura*, Sanders (1948, 1950) has explained that differences exist not only in the nutritive requirements of the different species and their hybrids but also in those of embryos of the

---

[4] La Rue was also able to culture small bits of embryonic tissues, only 0.5 mm. in length, and raise complete plants from them in *Lactuca canadensis, Taraxacum officinale, Chrysanthemum leucanthemum,* and *Lycopersicum esculentum.*

[5] Kent and Brink (1947) report the presence of "embryo factor" in casein hydrolysate and in water extracts of date, banana, and tomato.

same species at different stages of their development. The pH value of the culture medium is an additional factor that has to be kept in mind, a pH of about 6.0 having been found most favorable for *Datura*. Regarding the constituents of the medium, Sanders reports that in her experiments Seitz-filtered malt extract gave a definite increase in growth values, while the addition of diastase or auxins was of no advantage.

In conclusion it may be said that the artificial culture of embryos is important in several ways. It is the method par excellence for understanding the nutritive requirements of the developing embryo; it gives us an insight into the factors that influence embryonic differentiation; and it promises to be of great economic value as a means of achieving a much wider range of hybrid combinations than has been possible up to this time. Further, seeds which normally remain dormant for several weeks or months can now be made to germinate not only without giving the embryos a period of rest but even before they have become mature.[6] To give a single example, *Iris* seeds, which normally germinate only after two to several years, can now be made to yield seedlings in the same year, so that the breeder saves himself the uncertainty and delay which troubled him previously (Randolph, 1945).

There are two chief limitations in exploiting the embryo culture method to the fullest advantage. First, young embryos, especially of hybrids, often fail to grow in artificial media. Second, excised embryos tend to germinate immediately to produce miniature seedlings rather than to continue their usual growth and attain full differentiation. This premature germination results in curious growth patterns and weaker seedlings.[7] For a solution of these difficulties we require a better knowledge of the nutritive requirements of the embryos in terms of *known* chemical substances. Future research will no doubt help to clear some of the present obscurities in this connection and may well enable us not only to obtain an uninterrupted growth of embryos in artificial media but also to follow the entire process of fertilization and embryogeny in a petri dish.

---

[6] Since excised embryos are able to skip this "after-ripening" or "resting" period in culture, this method has recently been used to make quick tests of the germinability of peach seeds used by nurserymen (Tukey, 1944).

[7] See Kent and Brink (1947) for some suggestions for bringing about a continuation of the embryonic type of growth.

Induced Parthenogenesis. In normal fertilization the sperm imparts not only the activating stimulus but also a set of genes embodying the contribution of the male parent toward the make-up of the new individual. The prime interest in induced parthenogenesis lies in the fact that if the stimulus can be provided without the usually accompanying paternal genes, it would greatly facilitate the task of the geneticist in producing a homozygous true-breeding type, which otherwise requires a long and laborious process of self-fertilization (East, 1930).

Ever since the initial discovery of a *Datura* haploid (Blakeslee *et al.*, 1922) a variety of physical and chemical treatments have been tried to achieve this result. The chief of these are (1) exposure to very high or very low temperatures soon after pollination; (2) use of X-rayed pollen on stigma; (3) use of foreign pollen or of delayed pollination; and (4) chemical treatment.

To give an exhaustive survey of the successes and failures that have attended these efforts is beyond the scope of this book. A few examples are mentioned, however, to indicate the nature of the work that has been done.[8]

Concerning the effect of temperature, it is interesting to note that Müntzing (1937) obtained a haploid plant of *Secale cereale* by exposing the spikes to low temperatures (0.3°C.),[9] while Nordenskiöld (1939) achieved the same result by exposing them to high temperatures (41 to 42°C.).

Kihara and Katayama (1932) obtained three haploids of *Triticum monococcum* from spikes which had been exposed to X-rays at the time of meiosis. Later, Katayama (1934, 1935) pollinated the stigmas with X-rayed pollen, and out of 91 seedlings raised by him, 16 turned out to be haploids. In another strain, which normally produces about 0.5 per cent haploids, Kihara (1940) was able to increase the percentage to 13.66 by using the same method. However, other workers have been less successful, and Smith (1946) reports that he failed to obtain any increase in the number of haploids by X-ray treatment.

The use of foreign pollen for inducing haploidy was first brought

[8] For further information on this topic, see reviews by Ivanov (1938) and Kostoff (1941).

[9] Müntzing had really attempted to produce a doubling of chromosomes but obtained instead a semilethal haploid.

into prominence by Jørgensen (1928) whose observations on *Solanum nigrum* have already been referred to on page 314. Following interspecific or intergeneric crossings, similar results have been reported in *Brassica* (Noguchi, 1929), *Oenothera* (Gates and Goodwin, 1930), *Triticum* (Nakajima, 1935), and a few other plants.

Kihara (1940) found that in *Triticum monococcum* the frequency of haploids could also be made to increase by merely delaying the time of pollination. By applying pollen on the sixth day after emasculation, he obtained two haploids among 10 plants; on the seventh day, four haploids among 44 plants; on the eighth day, five haploids among 18 plants; and on the ninth day, three haploids among 8 plants.

Yasuda (1940) injected aqueous solutions of Belvitan into the ovaries of *Petunia violacea*. In ovules fixed and sectioned 3 days after treatment, he observed some striking changes. In some cases the nucellar cells[10] were found to have enlarged as the result of such stimulation; in others the egg had divided once or twice, forming a small proembryo; and in still others the antipodal cells had increased in volume. In explanation of the fact that division occurred only in the egg and the other cells merely enlarged, Yasuda says that in embryonic cells Belvitan promotes cell division, while in mature cells it causes only a growth of the cell wall.

Yasuda's observations, although interesting, are still in a preliminary stage, for it is not clear whether the embryos he obtained were haploid or diploid, nor does he mention if he succeeded in following them to later stages of development.

In conclusion, it might therefore be confessed that so far we have not succeeded in finding a suitable method for inducing parthenogenesis in higher plants. Although exposure to temperature extremes and other shocks and pollination with X-rayed or foreign pollen have apparently given some positive results in special cases, the number of parthenogenetic plants obtained by these methods is too small to warrant the deduction of a definite causal relationship between the treatment and results. What is really needed is an agent for producing haploid plants which will give positive results with approximately the same consistency as colchicine does in producing polyploidy. A logical method of approaching the problem

---

[10] These must really be the cells of the integumentary tapetum, for the nucellus disorganizes at an early stage in all members of the Solanaceae.

would be to know what changes take place inside the embryo sac in known cases of haploid parthenogenesis and then attempt to duplicate them artificially. From the very meager information that we possess in this regard it seems that although the egg can frequently be made to develop parthenogenetically, the real difficulty lies in an initiation of endosperm formation. Thus, Katayama (1932) found several-celled embryos in unpollinated ovaries of *Triticum* fixed on the ninth day after castration, but further development stopped owing to lack of endosperm. On the other hand, in those ovaries in which pollination is not unduly delayed, triple fusion is presumed to take place normally, resulting in endosperm formation which enables the maturation of the haploid embryos. Similarly, Kihara and Yamashita (1938), who used X-rayed pollen, believe that owing to the greatly reduced rate of growth of the pollen tubes arising from such pollen grains, the egg begins to divide parthenogenetically but the polar nuclei are eventually fertilized in the usual way.

These ideas need to be verified by making proper developmental studies, for the objection arises as to why, in cases of delayed pollination or the use of foreign pollen or X-rayed pollen, the egg should begin dividing first, when in most angiosperms the endosperm nucleus is the first to divide and the zygote undergoes its first division only after a few endosperm nuclei have been formed.

Production of Adventive Embryos. Since embryos arising asexually from the cells of the nucellus or the integument carry the full chromosome complement of the maternal parent, they are genetically identical with the latter. This phenomenon is of great importance in some of our cultivated plants, especially fruit trees. In *Citrus* it is used to yield large numbers of uniform rootstocks, since much of the variation in the size and productivity of the trees is due to the variability of the stocks. In *Mangifera*, those varieties which form adventive embryos can be as safely propagated by seeds as by budding or grafting. In others, with only a zygotic embryo, seed propagation does not give a type true to the mother and one must resort to vegetative propagation. Since seedlings can be raised much more cheaply, a method of inducing the formation of adventive embryos would obviously have a great advantage (see Leroy, 1947).

Recognizing the importance of adventive embryony in horticulture, many attempts have been made to produce it experimentally but without any marked success up to this time.

Haberlandt (1921, 1922) made the observation that in natural adventive embryony the proliferation of the embryo-initiating cells is invariably preceded by a degeneration of some of the adjoining cells. He was led by this to put forward the so-called "necrohormone theory," according to which the stimulus for cell division and proliferation is supplied by certain substances liberated from the adjacent degenerating cells. Proceeding on this basis, he tried to produce adventive embryos in *Oenothera* by pricking the ovules with a fine needle or by gently squeezing the ovary so as to damage the cells slightly. In one ovule he obtained two embryos, which he considers to be of nucellar origin (Fig. 210).

In repeating Haberlandt's technique, Hedemann (1931) obtained a two-celled embryo and a free nuclear endosperm in an unpollinated ovary of *Mirabilis uniflora* which had been pricked with a fine insect needle. No chromosome counts could be made, however, to ascertain whether the embryo was haploid or diploid, and the mode of its origin (whether from the egg or the nucellus) does not seem to have been conclusively established.

After Hedemann, no other worker has reported any success in the artificial production of adventive embryos by Haberlandt's methods, and Beth (1938), who made several unsuccessful attempts with *Oenothera* and other plants, denies the nucellar origin of the embryos even in Haberlandt's material.[11] He considers that in Haberlandt's experiments emasculation either was incomplete or had been performed too late, and that the embryos arose from an accidental fertilization of twin embryo sacs.[12]

Recently, Van Overbeek, Conklin, and Blakeslee (1941) injected several chemical substances into the ovary of *Datura stramonium* in the hope of inducing parthenogenetic development of the egg cell. This attempt was unsuccessful, but they obtained instead, on injection of a 0.1 per cent solution or emulsion of the ammonium salt of naphthaleneacetic acid or indolebutyric acid, several multicellular warty outgrowths which filled the embryo sacs (Fig. 211).

---

[11] See also criticism by Gustafsson (1947) who concludes that there is no evidence, experimental or morphological, to show that adventive embryony is induced by substances from dying cells.

[12] As mentioned on pp.96,97 twin embryo sacs frequently occur in the Onagraceae.

The shape and contents of the cells closely resembled those of the integumentary tapetum and they also showed the diploid number of chromosomes. It is concluded, therefore, that these structures were derived by a proliferation of the cells of the integumentary tapetum, as is the case with many adventive embryos. However,

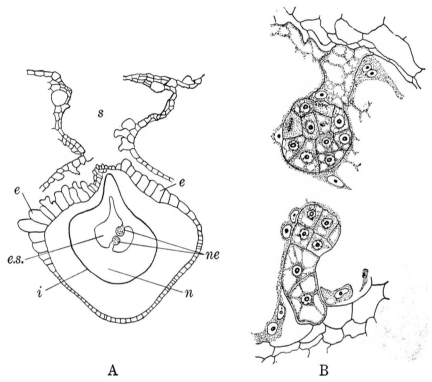

A   B

FIG. 210. Artificial production of adventive embryos in *Oenothera lamarckiana* (*s* = wound caused by pin-prick; *e* = ovular epidermis; *e.s.* = embryo sac; *i* = inner layer of inner integument; *n* = nucellus; *ne* = nucellar embryo). *A*, diagram of ovule punctured on upper side by fine needle; note two embryos inside embryo sac. *B*, enlarged view of two embryos. (*After Haberlandt, 1921.*)

in view of their undifferentiated nature and the obscurity regarding their final fate or potentialities, Van Overbeek *et al.* wisely refrain from calling them true embryos and designate them as "pseudoembryos."

Of considerable interest in this connection are also the recent observations made by Fagerlind (1946) on *Hosta.* Adventive em-

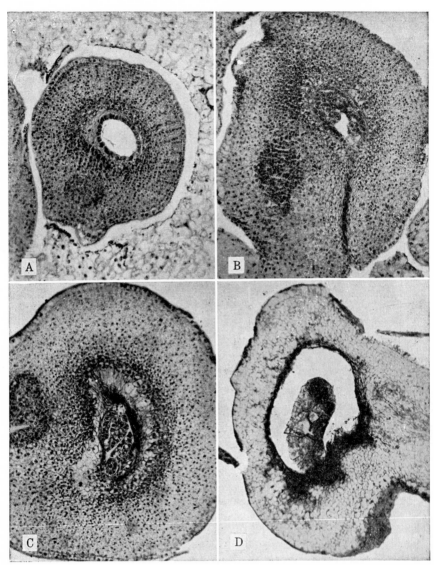

Fig. 211.   Sections of ovules of *4n Datura stramonium* from unpollinated ovaries injected with 0.1 per cent naphthaleneacetic acid.   *A*, l.s. ovule 10 days after treatment, note prominent integumentary tapetum.   *B*, l.s. ovule of same age, showing proliferation of cells of integumentary tapetum.   *C*, l.s. ovule 15 days after treatment; note groups of cells occupying cavity of embryo sac.   *D*, l.s. ovule 21 days after treatment, showing "pseudoembryo" in embryo sac surrounded by degenerating cells of integument.   (*After Van Overbeek, Conklin and Blakeslee, 1941.*)

bryony has been known in this genus for a long time, but fertilization is essential for the production of the embryos. Unpollinated flowers wither and fall away without forming seeds (Strasburger, 1878).

Fagerlind performed three sets of experiments. In the first he pollinated some of the pistils with a large quantity of pollen and others with a small quantity of it; in the second he used foreign pollen; and in the third the ovaries were treated only with growth hormones. Those pistils which had received an adequate quantity of pollen set seeds normally, the embryos being of nucellar origin. In others, where the amount of pollen was insufficient, some of the ovules increased in size but others remained small. On microscopic examination the former showed the remains of a pollen tube, a more or less well developed endosperm, and a number of adventive embryos which seemed to be fully capable of further development. On the other hand, those ovules which had failed to grow showed neither pollen tubes nor endosperm but only the earliest stages in adventive embryony, characterized by the appearance of a few richly protoplasmic nucellar cells. In older stages, such "unpollinated ovules" (*i.e.*, ovules not penetrated by a pollen tube) showed a progressive shrinkage and drying up of their tissues, accompanied by a degeneration of the embryo sac as well as the embryo initials.

In the second experiment, in which the pistils were treated with pollen from other genera, *viz.*, *Hemerocallis*, *Lilium*, *Galtonia*, and *Canna*, all of them withered and fell off exactly like unpollinated pistils.

In the third set of experiments, in which some of the pistils were treated with 1 per cent heteroauxin in lanolin and the controls with pure lanolin, the latter dried up within 4 or 5 days. The auxin-treated pistils, on the other hand, continued to remain attached to the plant and three weeks later they showed the presence of young adventive embryos. No endosperm was formed, however, and the embryos seemed to lack the capacity of developing further.

Although of a preliminary nature, Fagerlind's observations seem to indicate that in plants showing adventive embryony it is possible to prepare the ovule for the production of adventive embryos by the application of suitable growth hormones, but the real difficulty lies in bringing about endosperm formation. Unfortunately the nature of the stimulus which may lead to a division of the unfertilized secondary nucleus remains unknown. Until this is discovered, the only way of overcoming the difficulty would probably be to perfect a technique for excising the adventive embryos and growing them in artificial culture.

Finally, it may be added that although a method of inducing adventive embryony has undoubted possibilities, there is also a need sometimes for the elimination of adventive embryos. In *Citrus*, for example, where a number of nucellar embryos may mature simultaneously with the zygotic embryo, it is quite difficult to distinguish the two kinds of seedlings in early stages. Further, the zygotic embryo sometimes becomes crowded out by the nucellar embryos so that all the seedlings are asexual. It would be a distinct advantage to the breeder if he could exercise some control over the two processes, eliminating either zygotic or nucellar embryos according to his requirements at the moment.

Induced Parthenocarpy.[13] Some of the world's most important fruits are seedless or have only abortive seeds. As examples may be mentioned varieties of banana, cucumber, orange, pineapple, grape, grapefruit, persimmon, and breadfruit. A good many of these varieties are believed to have arisen by gene mutation, and some have been obtained by hybridization.

Recently attempts have been made to produce seedless fruits on seeded varieties by withholding pollination and applying certain chemical substances to the pistil. As early as 1849 Gaertner obtained seedless fruits in certain cucurbits whose stigmas had been "pollinated" with the spores of *Lycopodium*. Millardet (1901) induced fruit formation in certain varieties of the European grape by pollinating the stigmas with pollen of *Ampelopsis hederacea*, and a partial development of the ovary in certain cucurbits by treating the stigmas with *powdered* pollen. A year later Massart placed dead pollen upon the stigmas of an orchid and observed a slight increase in the size of the ovary. Subsequently, Fitting (1909) painted the stigmas with an *extract* of pollen and ascribed a hormonal action to the latter. Additional experiments of a similar nature made by later workers (see especially Laibach, 1932, 1933)

---

[13] For more detailed information on this topic, see Maheshwari (1940), Gustafson (1942), and Swarbrick (1947).

proved conclusively that pollen has a definite influence on the growth of the ovary which is independent of fertilization or maturation of seeds.

More extensive studies on the role of pollination in fruit growth —without the accompanying fertilization—were made by Yasuda (1930, 1933, 1934, 1939). Although all plants did not react favorably, he achieved an appreciable measure of success with certain members of the Solanaceae and Cucurbitaceae. His experiments and observations may be summarized as follows:

1. Castrated flowers were treated with pollen of the same species in different stages of maturity. As was to be expected, ovaries treated with mature and viable pollen developed into normal fruits; but immature or overmature pollen also, although incapable of causing fertilization, frequently stimulated fruit formation, with the difference that in this case the fruits were devoid of seeds.

2. In a second lot the same procedure was followed using foreign pollen, *i.e.*, pollen from another plant belonging to the same or a different family. When fruits were produced, these were either devoid of seeds or showed only abortive ones.

3. The styles of a number of flowers of *Solanum melongena* were cut off at their junction with the ovary at different intervals after pollination. When the operation was sufficiently delayed, the pollen tubes were able to reach the ovules, resulting in fruits with viable seeds. But if it was performed at a time when the pollen tubes were close to the base of the style but had not entered the ovary, the fruits were seedless. In control experiments, in which the styles were removed as before but the stigmas were left unpollinated, no fruits of any kind were produced.

4. In a fourth set of experiments, the styles were cut off as before but regrafted on the ovaries with an intervening layer of gelatin. The plants were then divided into two lots, one lot being self-pollinated and the other left unpollinated. The ovaries of the former occasionally developed into seedless fruits, but the unpollinated ovaries usually failed to grow further. When they did produce fruits on some very rare occasions, these were much smaller than those of the first lot.

5. Finally, pollination was entirely omitted and in its place aqueous extracts of pollen were injected into the ovary. *Solanum melongena* ovaries, injected with an extract of *Petunia* pollen, grew to

a size of 4.1 by 7.3 cm.   Also, out of 50 cucumber ovaries injected with extracts of cucumber pollen, three continued growth. Of these last, one attained a size of 4.3 by 20.3 cm., comparing favorably with a normal cucumber.

As a result of these experiments, supported by some microscopic studies, Yasuda arrived at the following conclusions: (1) pollen tubes secrete or carry some chemical substance which diffuses into the tissues of the ovary and thereby induces fruit formation; (2) if the pollen tubes are allowed to grow only up to the base of the style, so as to permit chemical diffusion but not fertilization, the resulting fruits are devoid of seeds; and (3) seedless fruits can also be obtained by pollinating the stigmas with immature, overmature, or incompatible pollen, or by using extracts of pollen.

The fact that extracts of pollen, like the pollen tubes themselves, could also induce parthenocarpic growth left no room for doubt that the stimulation is entirely chemical in nature.   In 1934 Thimann showed that many pollens contain considerable quantities of an auxin or growth substance, and this led some workers, notably Gustafson (1936, 1938a, b), to experiment with some synthetic hormones to see if they could bring about fruit formation.

Several substances were tried, chiefly indoleacetic, indolepropionic, indolebutyric, n-naphthaleneacetic, and phenylacetic acids. These were made up into a lanolin paste of about 0.5 to 1 per cent strength and smeared on the stigma.   In some cases it was found better to remove the style just above the ovary and apply the paste to the cut surface of the latter; this facilitated the diffusion of the chemical into the ovary.   The flowers were subjected to three different kinds of treatments.   Some were pollinated in the usual way, others were treated with the substances named above, and the rest were left untreated.   The first lot produced normal fruits, while the third withered and dropped without forming any fruits. As a result of the second treatment, some parthenocarpic fruits were formed in tomato, pepper (Fig. 212A), tobacco (Fig. 212B), eggplant, crookneck squash, *Petunia*, and *Salpiglossis*, although the average weight of these fruits was somewhat lower than that of normal fruits.

Gardner and Marth (1937) employed a different technique. They sprayed the ovaries with aqueous solutions of several substances, of which naphthaleneacetic acid was found to be the most effective. *Ilex opaca* was used for most of the experiments, partly because of its dioecious nature and partly because of its broad stigma, which tends to facilitate diffusion. Considerable success was achieved in obtaining seedless fruits in this plant. Some posi-

FIG. 212.   *A*, fruit production in *Capsicum;* left, from fertilized ovary; right, after treatment of pistil with indolebutyric acid.   *B*, fruits in *Nicotiana;* two on left, from fertilized ovary; two on right, after treatment of pistil with potassium salt of indoleacetic acid.   An unfertilized and untreated pistil is shown in the middle. *(Photographs supplied by Dr. F. G. Gustafson.)*

tive results were also obtained with strawberries but none with apples and pears.

Similar experiments were soon undertaken by other workers, and a few studies have also been made on the comparative histology and vitamin content of normal fruits (resulting from pollination) as well as parthenocarpic ones (resulting from hormone treatment).

As far as present evidence goes, there is no essential difference between the two except that in parthenocarpic fruits the ovules become shriveled and shrunken and no embryos are formed (Fig. 213). To explain why some plants are naturally parthenocarpic (*e.g.*, varieties of *Musa*, *Ananas*, *Vitis*, etc.) while others are not, Gustafson (1939*a*,*b*) studied the auxin content of the ovary in a

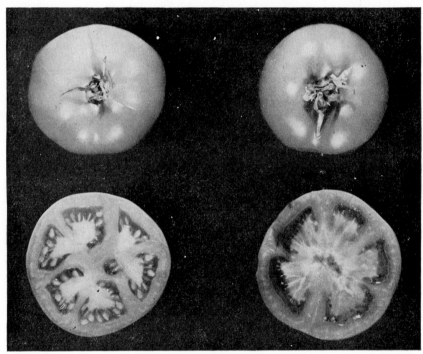

FIG. 213.   Fruit production in tomato; left, from fertilized ovary; right, induced by hormone treatment.   (*Photograph supplied by Dr. A. W. Hitchcock.*)

few forms of each kind.   In every instance he found it to be higher in the ovaries of the parthenocarpic varieties than in the ovaries of the nonparthenocarpic ones.   Obviously, then, the reason why some plants produce parthenocarpic fruits is that their ovaries contain enough auxin to promote growth without fertilization, while those of other plants do not possess it in sufficient quantity and it must therefore be augmented either by pollination and fertilization, or by pollination alone, or by an external application of the requisite growth-promoting substance.   In a detailed review of the subject, Gustafson (1942) says: "Some plants under some conditions produce enough growth hormone so that with or without pollination, as the case may be, they are able to prevent the absciss layer from being formed in the pedicel; and that under favorable nutritive conditions and with a minimum of competition, they are further able to transport the necessary food and bring about enlargement of the cells in the ovary to produce mature fruits without seeds, whereas other plants are unable to do this."

Although the hormonal method of producing seedless fruit is an invention of only the last 10 to 15 years' research, it has already begun to be applied on a commercial scale in some countries. In the United States there are several states where tomatoes are grown in greenhouses during the winter (January to March), but owing to the short days and low light intensity, the pollen is frequently defective, pollination inadequate, and pollen tube growth restricted. Many flowers, therefore, fall away without producing any fruits. Even the fruits that are set are frequently small in size or are not well filled with the gelatinous pulp characteristic of fruits of good quality. The economic losses resulting from these difficulties prompted the use of hormones in stimulating fruit growth.

As the chief objective in tomato culture is mainly to make up for the deficiency of good pollen, rather than to obtain fruits which are wholly seedless, castration is unnecessary. The procedure is merely to spray the chemical on the flowers in a suitable manner. Several substances have been tried, *viz.*, indolebutyric acid, indoleacetic acid, naphthaleneacetic acid, methylindolebutyrate, α-naphthylthioacetamide, potassium naphthaleneacetate, 2,4-dichlorophenoxyacetic acid, etc. Of all these, indolebutyric acid has been found to be one of the most effective, and the fruits resulting from its application are as large as those produced after natural pollination, if not larger (Fig. 213). The most marked improvement in size is seen during the period from January to February, when pollination is especially deficient and much of the pollen is nonviable. Indeed, the success achieved is so significant that treatment of greenhouse tomatoes with synthetic hormones bids fair to become a standard practice (Howlett, 1943, 1944; Mitchell and Marth, 1947).[14, 15]

[14] Some very spectacular results have also been achieved in pineapples (Van Overbeek, 1946). By using 2,4-dichlorophenoxyacetic acid and α-naphthalene-

The following problems need further study in this connection: (1) selection of the most effective chemical substance for inducing fruit set; (2) method and time of applying the substance; and (3) prevention of some undesirable secondary effects such as blossom-end rot and malformations in the fruit or the plant.

According to recent tests (Howlett, 1946) a combination of indolebutyric acid and β-naphthoxyacetic acid is superior to indolebutyric acid used alone, with regard to both fruit set and the filling of the loculi. It was also found that an aqueous solution of these chemicals is as effective as an emulsion.

Regarding the method of application, the usual procedure is to spray the inflorescences with an atomizer, but since this is laborious in large-scale projects some workers have suggested the so-called vapor method. The original procedure was to place the potted plants under bell jars and expose them for various lengths of time to vapors of the desired growth substances. Zimmerman and Hitchcock (1939) found this to be entirely successful with *Ilex opaca*. More recently another method has been tried, based on the aerosol principle used by entomologists for killing insects (see Zimmerman and Hitchcock, 1944; Hamner, Schomer, and Marth, 1944; Howlett, Freeman, and Marth, 1946). Briefly, the hormone is first dissolved in some liquid in which it is readily soluble and then added to a highly volatile liquefied gas; or, if the hormone is soluble in the liquefied gas itself, it is added directly to the latter. The mixture is then held under pressure in a container from which it can be released as a very fine mist. The gas soon volatilizes, leaving the hormone as a finely divided liquid or solid.

While the effectiveness of the aerosol method has been amply demonstrated and there is no doubt as to its rapidity and simplicity, the chief drawback is that it exposes not only the flowers

---

acetic acid, it has been possible to induce the flowering and fruiting of pineapples at any time of the year, even in varieties which are normally difficult to get into bearing. The procedure is simple. When the plants have produced sufficient leaves to support and mature a good-sized fruit, a few drops of an aqueous solution of one of the two chemicals are placed into the tip of each plant. One ounce of the dry chemical is sufficient for treating 113,000 plants.

[15] Stewart and Condit (1949) report that by spraying aqueous solutions of 2,4-dichlorophenoxyacetic acid and 2,4,5-trichlorophenoxyacetic acid they were able to obtain seedless figs of a size and sugar content comparable to that of caprified fruits.

but the whole plant to the chemical, resulting sometimes in malformations of the leaves. It is possible, however, that certain substances may have a less toxic effect than others and with further experience new formulae can be worked out which will induce a satisfactory fruit set without causing injury to the rest of the plant.[16]

Conclusion. Although experimental embryology is a new subject, it is already possible to recognize the fundamental problems which confront it. Their solution will be difficult and will no doubt demand many years of patient research, but this is precisely what makes the field so interesting and at the same time so promising. While descriptive and phylogenetic embryology will continue to stay, the future trend is clearly towards the experimental side. Here we have the frontier state within whose borders the geneticist, physiologist, cytologist, and embryologist all find a common ground.

References

Addicott, F. T. 1943. Pollen germination and pollen tube growth as influenced by pure growth substances. Plant Physiol. **18**: 270–279.

Anthony, S., and Harlan, H. V. 1920. Germination of barley pollen. Jour. Agr. Res. **18**: 525–536.

Banerji, I. 1929. Studies in cotton pollen. Agr. Jour. India **24**: 332–340.

Beasley, J. C. 1940. Hybridization of American 26-chromosome and Asiatic 13-chromosome species of *Gossypium*. Jour. Agr. Res. **60**: 175–182.

Beth, K. 1938. Untersuchungen über die Auslösung von Adventivembryonie durch Wundreiz. Planta **28**: 296–343.

Blakeslee, A. F. 1945. Removing some barriers to crossability in plants. Proc. Amer. Phil. Soc. **89**: 561–574.

———, Belling, J., Farnham, M. E., and Bergner, A. D. 1922. A haploid mutant in the Jimson weed, *Datura stramonium*. Science **55**: 646–647.

——— and Satina, S. 1944. New hybrids from incompatible crosses in *Datura* through culture of excised embryos on malt media. Science **99**: 331–334.

Bosio, M. G. 1940. Richerche sulla fecondazione intraovarica in *Helleborus* e *Paeonia*. Nuovo Gior. Bot. Ital. **47**: 591–598.

Brink, R. A., Cooper, D. C., and Ausherman, L. E. 1944. A hybrid between *Hordeum jubatum* and *Secale cereale* reared from an artificially cultivated embryo. Jour. Hered. **35**: 67–75.

---

[16] Howlett and Marth (1946) report that with greenhouse tomatoes a combination of β-naphthoxyacetic acid, indolebutyric acid, and 4-chlorophenoxyacetic acid is more satisfactory than other substances.

Buchholz, J. T., and Blakeslee, A. F. 1929. Pollen-tube growth in crosses between balanced chromosomal types of Datura stramonium. Genetics **14**: 538–568.

———, Doak, C. C., and Blakeslee, A. F. 1932. Control of gametophytic selection in Datura through shortening and splicing of styles. Bul. Torrey Bot. Club **59**: 109–118.

Dahlgren, K. V. O. 1926. Svensk Bot. Tidskr. **20**: 97.

Dietrich, K. 1924. Über Kultur von Embryonen ausserhalb das Samens. Flora **17**: 379–417.

East, E. M. 1930. The production of homozygotes through reduced parthenogenesis. Science **72**: 148–149.

Eyster, H. C. 1941. Pollen tube growth of a self-sterile strain of Petunia. Proc. S. Dak. Acad. Sci. **21**: 56–57.

Fagerlind, F. 1946. Hormonale Substanzen als Ursache der Frucht- und Embryobildung bei pseudogamen Hosta-biotypen. Svensk Bot. Tidskr. **40**: 230–234.

Ferwerda, F. P. 1937. Kiemkracht en Levensduur van Koffiestuifmeel. Arch. Koffiecult. Ned.-Ind. **11**: 135–150.

Fitting, H. 1909. Die Beeinflussung der Orchideenblüten durch die Bestäubung und durch andere Umstande. Ztschr. f. Bot. **1**: 1–86.

Gärtner, K. F. 1849. "Versuche und Beobachtungen über die Bastardzeugung im Pflanzenreich." Stuttgart.

Gardner, F. E., and Marth, P. C. 1937. Parthenocarpic fruits induced by spraying with growth promoting substances. Bot. Gaz. **99**: 184–195.

Gates, R. R., and Goodwin, K. M. 1930. A new haploid Oenothera, with some observations on haploidy in plants and animals. Jour. Genetics **23**: 123–153.

Gustafson, F. G. 1936. Inducement of fruit development by growth-promoting chemicals. Proc. Natl. Acad. Sci. [U.S.A.] **22**: 628–636.

———. 1937. Parthenocarpy induced by pollen extracts. Amer. Jour. Bot. **25**: 237–244.

———. 1938a. Induced parthenocarpy. Bot. Gaz. **99**: 840–844.

———. 1938b. Further studies on artificial parthenocarpy. Amer. Jour. Bot. **25**: 237–244.

———. 1939a. The cause of natural parthenocarpy. Amer. Jour. Bot. **26**: 135–138.

———. 1939b. Auxin distribution in fruits and its significance in fruit development. Amer. Jour. Bot. **26**: 189–194.

———. 1942. Parthenocarpy: natural and artificial. Bot. Rev. **8**: 599–654.

Gustafsson, Å. 1947. Apomixis in higher plants. II. The causal aspect of apomixis. Lunds Univ. Årsskr. N.F. Avd. II, **43**(2): 71–179.

Haberlandt, G. 1921. Über experimentelle Erzeugung von Adventivembryonen bei Oenothera lamarckiana. Sitzber. Preuss. Akad. der Wiss. [Berlin] **40**: 695–725.

———. 1922. Über Zellteilungshormone und ihre Beziehungen zur Wundheilung, Befruchtung, Parthenogenesis und Adventivembryonie. Biol. Zentbl. **42**: 145–172.

Hamner, C. L., Schomer, H. A., and Marth, P. C. 1944. Application of growth-regulating substance in aerosol form with special reference to fruit-set in tomato. Bot. Gaz. **106**: 108–123.

Hannig, E. 1904. Über die Kultur von Cruciferen Embryonen ausserhalb des Embryosacks. Bot. Ztg. **62**: 45–80.

Hedemann, E. 1931. Über experimentelle Erzeugung von Adventivembryonen bei *Mirabilis uniflora* und *Mirabilis fröebelii*. Biol. Zentbl. **51**: 647–652.

Holman, R. M., and Brubaker, F. 1926. On the longevity of pollen. Calif. Univ. Pub. Bot. **13**: 179–204.

Howlett, F. S. 1943. Growth promoting chemicals improve greenhouse tomato production. Ohio Agr. Expt. Sta. Bimo. Bul. **28**: 17–27.

———. 1944. Comparative value of growth regulating chemicals for greenhouse tomato production. Proc. Ohio Veg. & Potato Growers Assoc. 29th Ann. meeting **29**: 162–180.

———. 1946. Synthetic plant hormones in relation to greenhouse tomato production. Ohio Veg. and Potato Growers Rep. 1946, pp. 223–236.

———, Freeman, S., and Marth, P. C. 1946. Aerosol applications of growth regulating substances to greenhouse tomato. Proc. Amer. Soc. Hort. Sci. **48**: 485–474.

Ivanov, M. A. 1938. Experimental production of haploids in *Nicotiana rustica* L. Genetica **20**: 295–397.

Jones, M. D., and Newell, L. C. 1948. Longevity of pollen and stigmas of grasses: Buffalograss, *Buchloe dactyloides* (Nutt.)Engelm., and Corn, *Zea mays* L. Jour. Amer. Soc. Agron. **40**: 195–204.

Jørgensen, C. A. 1928. The experimental production of heteroploid plants in the genus *Solanum*. Jour. Genet. **19**: 133–211.

Katayama, Y. 1932. Crossing experiments in certain cereals with special reference to different compatibility between the reciprocal crosses. Mem. Col. Agr. Kyoto Univ. **27** (Genetic Ser. 2): 1–75.

———. 1934. Haploid formation by X-rays in *Triticum monococcum*. Cytologia **5**: 235–237.

———. 1935. Karyogenetic studies on X-rayed sex cells and their derivatives in *Triticum monococcum*. Agr. Col. Jour. Tokyo Imp. Univ. **13**: 333–362.

Kent, N., and Brink, R. A. 1947. Growth in vitro of immature *Hordeum* embryos. Science **106**: 547–548.

Kihara, H. 1940. [Formation of haploids by means of delayed pollination in *Triticum monococcum*.] Bot. Mag. [Tokyo] **54**: 178–185.

——— and Katayama, Y. 1932. [On the progeny of haploid plants of *Triticum monococcum*.] Kwagau **2**: 408–410.

——— and Yamashita, K. 1938. Künstliche Erzeugung haploides und triploides Einkornweizen durch Bestäubung mit röntgenbestrahlten Pollen. Comm. Papers, 30th Anniv. N. Akemine, pp. 9–20.

Kostoff, D. 1941. The problem of haploidy (cytogenetic studies on *Nicotiana* haploids and their bearings to some other cytogenetic problems). Bibl. Genetica **13**: 1–148.

Laibach, F. 1925. Das Taubwerden der Bastardsamen und die künstliche Aufzucht früh absterbender Bastardembryonen. Ztschr. f. Bot. **17**: 417–459.

Laibach, F.   1929.   Ectogenesis in plants: methods and genetic possibilities of propagating embryos otherwise dying in the seed.   Jour. Hered. **20**: 201–208.

———.   1932.   Pollenhormone und Wuchsstoff.   Ber. deutsch. bot. Gesell. **50**: 383–390.

———.   1933.   Versuche mit Wuchsstoffpaste.   Ber. deutsch. bot. Gesell. **51**: 386–392.

La Rue, C. D.   1936.   The growth of plant embryos in culture.   Bul. Torrey Bot. Club **63**: 365–382.

Ledeboer, M., and Rietsema, I.   1940.   Unfruitfulness in black currants.   Jour. Pomol. and Hort. Sci. **18**: 177–180.

Leroy, J. F.   1947.   La polyembryonie chez les *"Citrus."*   Son intérêt dans la culture et amélioration.   Rev. Bot. Appl. et Agr. Trop. **301/302**: 483–495.

Lewis, D.   1942.   Breakdown of self-incompatibility by α-naphthalene acetamide.   Nature [London] **149**: 610–611.

Maheshwari, P.   1940.   The role of growth hormones in the production of seedless fruits.   Sci. and Culture **6**: 85–89.

———.   1944.   On the longevity of pollen.   Indian Jour. Hort. **2**: 82–87.

———.   1950.   Contacts between embryology, physiology and genetics.   Proc. 37th Indian Sci. Cong., Bot. Sect., presidential address.

Mangelsdorf, P. C., and Reeves, R. G.   1931.   Hybridization of maize, *Tripsacum* and *Euchlaena*.   Jour. Hered. **22**: 329–343.

Massart, J.   1902.   Sur la pollination sans fécondation.   Bul. Jard. Bot. Brussels de P'État **1**: 85–95.

Millardet, A.   1901.   Rev. de Vitic. **16**: 677–680.

Mitchell, J. W., and Marth, P. C.   1947.   "Growth Regulators for Garden, Field and Orchard."   Chicago.

Müntzing, A.   1937.   Note on haploid rye plant.   Hereditas **23**: 401–404.

Nagao, S., and Takano, T.   1938.   Duration of the preservation of the fertilization possibility in pollen and stigma of rice plant.   Comm. Papers, 30th Anniv. N. Akemine, pp. 88–92.

Nakajima, G.   1935.   Occurrence of a haploid in *Triticum turgidum*.   Jap. Jour. Genet. **11**: 246–247.

Nebel, B. R.   1939.   Longevity of pollen in apple, pear, plum, peach, apricot, and sour cherry.   Proc. Amer. Soc. Hort. Sci. **37**: 130–132.

Noguchi, Y.   1929.   Zur Kenntnis der Befruchtung und Kornbildung bei den Reispflanzen.   Jap. Jour. Bot. **4**: 385–503.

Nordenskiöld, H.   1939.   Studies of a haploid rye plant.   Hereditas **25**: 204–210.

Pal, B. P., and Singh, H. B.   1943.   Floral characters and fruit formation in the egg plant.   Indian Jour. Genet. and Plant Breeding **3**: 45–58.

Pfeiffer, N.   1944.   Prolonging the life of *Cinchona* pollen by storage under controlled conditions of temperature and humidity.   Contrib. Boyce Thompson Inst. **13**: 281–294.

Randolph, L. R.   1945.   Embryo culture of *Iris* seed.   Bul. Amer. Iris Soc. **97**: 33–45.

Sachet, M.   1948.   Fertilization in six incompatible species crosses of *Datura*.   Amer. Jour. Bot. **35**: 302–309.

Sanders, M. E. 1948. Embryo development in four *Datura* species following self and hybrid pollinations. Amer. Jour. Bot. **35**: 525–532.

———. 1950. Development of self and hybrid embryos in artificial culture. Amer. Jour. Bot. **37**: 6–15.

Sartoris, G. B. 1942. Longevity of sugarcane and corn pollen—a method for long distance shipment of sugarcane pollen by airplane. Amer. Jour. Bot. **29**: 395–400.

Satina, S. 1944. Periclinal chimaeras in *Datura* in relation to development and structure, (A) of the style and stigma, (B) of calyx and corolla. Amer. Jour. Bot. **31**: 493–502.

Skirm, G. W. 1942. Embryo culturing as an aid to plant breeding. Jour. Hered. **33**: 210–215.

Smith, L. 1946. Haploidy in einkorn. Jour. Agr. Res. **73**: 291–301.

Smith, P. F. 1942. Studies of the growth of pollen with respect to temperature, auxins, colchicine and vitamin B_1. Amer. Jour. Bot. **29**: 56–66.

Smith, P. G. 1944. Embryo culture of a tomato species hybrid. Proc. Amer. Soc. Hort. Sci. **44**: 413–416.

Stephens, J. C., and Quinby, J. C. 1934. Anthesis, pollination and fertilization in *Sorghum*. Jour. Agr. Res. **49**: 123–136.

Stewart, W. S., and Condit, I. J. 1949. The effect of 2,4-dichlorophenoxyacetic acid and other plant growth regulators on the Calimyrna fig. Amer. Jour. Bot. **36**: 332–335.

Stingl, G. 1907. Experimentelle Studie über die Entstehung von pflanzlichen Embryonen. Flora **97**: 308–331.

Stout, A. B. 1924. The viability of date pollen. Jour. N. Y. Bot. Gard. **25**: 101–106.

———. 1944. Inactivation of incompatibilities in tetraploid progenies of *Petunia axillaris*. Torreya **44**: 45–51.

——— and Chandler, C. 1941. Change from self-incompatibility to self-compatibility accompanying change from diploidy to tetraploidy. Science **94**: 118.

Strasburger, E. 1878. Über Polyembryonie. Jena. Z. Naturw. **12**: 647–670.

Swarbrick, T. 1947. Growth regulating substances in horticulture. Jour. Roy. Hort. Soc. **72**: 313–327; 342–359.

Thimann, K. V. 1934. Studies on the growth hormones of plants. VI. The distribution of growth substance in plant tissues. Jour. Gen. Physiol. **18**: 23–34.

Tukey, H. B. 1933. Artificial culture of sweet cherry embryos. Jour. Hered. **24**: 7–12.

———. 1944. The excised–embryo method of testing the germinability of fruit seed with particular reference to peach seed. Proc. Amer. Soc. Hort. Sci. **45**: 211–219.

Van Overbeek, J. 1946. Control of flower formation and fruit size in the pineapple. Bot. Gaz. **108**: 64–73.

———, Conklin, M. E., and Blakeslee, A. F. 1941. Chemical stimulation of ovule development and its possible relation to parthenogenesis. Amer. Jour. Bot. **28**: 647–656.

Van Overbeek, J., Conklin, M. E., and Blakeslee, A. F. 1942. Cultivation in vitro of small *Datura* embryos. Amer. Jour. Bot. **29**: 472–477.

——, Siu, R., and Haagen-Smit, A. J. 1944. Factors affecting the growth of *Datura* embryos *in vitro*. Amer. Jour. Bot. **31**: 219–224.

Yasuda, S. 1930. Parthenocarpy caused by the stimulation of pollination in some plants of Solanaceae. Agr. and Hort. [Tokyo] **5**: 287–294.

——. 1931. An experiment to graft the style upon the ovary in *Petunia violacea*. Proc. Imp. Acad. Japan **7**: 72–75.

——. 1933. On the behaviour of pollen tubes in the production of seedless fruits, caused by interspecific pollination. Jap. Jour. Genet. **8**: 239–244.

——. 1934. Physiological research on self-incompatibility in *Petunia violacea*. Bul. Imp. Col. Agr. and Forestry, Japan **20**: 1–95.

——. 1939. Parthenocarpy induced by stimulation of pollination in some higher plants. Mem. Faculty Sci. and Agr. Taihoku Imp. Univ. **27**: 1–51.

——. 1940. A preliminary note on the artificial parthenogenesis induced by application of growth promoting substance. Bot. Mag. [Tokyo] **54**: 506–510.

Zimmerman, P. W., and Hitchcock, A. E. 1939. Experiments with vapors and solutions of growth substances. Contrib. Boyce Thompson Inst. **10**: 481–508.

—— and ——. 1944. Substances effective for increasing fruit set and inducing seedless tomatoes. Proc. Amer. Soc. Hort. Sci. **45**: 353–361.

CHAPTER 13

THEORETICAL CONCLUSIONS

The phylogeny and interrelationships of angiosperms present problems which have baffled botanists for many years. As shown in Chap. 11, embryology has been of appreciable help in reorienting our ideas on the interrelationships of several doubtful families and genera. In the present chapter we shall consider some problems of wider interest concerning the origin and homologies of the male and female gametophytes, endosperm, etc.

Male Gametophyte. In discussing the homologies of the male gametophyte of angiosperms, we must naturally turn to the condition in gymnosperms. The available evidence suggests that in the fossil gymnosperms the pollen grains were multicellular structures containing both prothallial and spermatogenous cells. Probably there were no pollen tubes and the sperms made their way directly to the archegonia. Swimming sperms are found even in some modern representatives of the group, *viz.*, the living cycads and *Ginkgo*, but in addition a pollen tube is also present. It is interesting to note that the tube originates from the upper end of the pollen grain and grows laterally into the nucellar tissues, acting as a haustorial and not a sperm-carrying structure. The basal end of the pollen grain hangs free in a cavity, which may be said to be composed partly of the pollen chamber and partly of the archegonial chamber. There are present, beside the two sperms, the prothallial cells (one in the Cycadales and two in the Ginkgoales), the stalk cell, and the tube nucleus. In *Microcycas* there are 16 to 22 sperms, which should probably be considered a primitive feature.

The Coniferales differ in two important respects: (1) the sperms do not possess any cilia, and (2) the pollen tube does not arise from the upper end of the pollen grain but from its lower end, penetrating through the nucellus and discharging its contents into the archegonium. The contents of the pollen grain and the tube vary in different genera. In *Araucaria*, *Podocarpus*, *Dacrydium*, and *Phyllocladus* there are several prothallial cells; in *Pinus* and

411

some other genera there are two prothallial cells; and in the Taxaceae, Cephalotaxaceae, and most genera of the Taxodiacea and Cupressaceae the prothallial tissue is completely eliminated. Another feature of considerable interest is the great disparity in the size of the two sperm cells in *Taxus*, *Torreya*, and *Cephalotaxus*, the smaller cell presumably being on the way to elimination. Some species of *Cupressus* are exceptional in having multiple male cells, all of which seem to be capable of functioning.

Coming to the Gnetales, *Ephedra* with its two prothallial cells, a stalk cell, a tube nucleus, and two male gametes shows considerable resemblance to *Ginkgo* and *Pinus*. The inner integument forms a long micropylar canal, but the pollen grains are drawn down into the pollen chamber formed by the disintegration of the nucellar cells. *Welwitschia* and *Gnetum* are only imperfectly known, but in both genera the pollen grains seem to have a prothallial cell, a generative cell, and a tube cell. The stalk cell is eliminated and the generative cell directly gives rise to the two male gametes.

Briefly then, although most gymnosperms possess a prothallial tissue, they show a tendency toward its elimination, and in several genera the male gametophyte is reduced to having a prothallial or a stalk cell, a tube nucleus, and two male gametes. Only the Cycadales and Ginkgoales have ciliated sperms. In the remaining members the cilia have been lost and it is the pollen tube which becomes the channel for the transportation of the male gametes. The male gametophyte of angiosperms may be assumed to have been derived from that of some gymnospermous ancestor by further simplification and elimination of the single prothallial or the stalk cell.[1]

Female Gametophyte. Schnarf (1936) put forward the view that the monosporic 8-nucleate embryo sac is the most primitive and that all the other types have been derived from it. This idea has also been favored by several other writers, the chief argument in its support being that this type is the most widely distributed in angiosperms and that the female gametophyte of the pteridophytes

---

[1] There have been occasional reports of the occurrence of a prothallial cell in some angiosperms like *Lilium*, *Eichhornia*, *Yucca*, *Sparganium*, *Atriplex*, and *Stellaria* (see Wulff and Maheshwari, 1938), but these are in the nature of freaks and abnormalities of little or no significance. Up to the present the occurrence of a prothallial cell is not known to be a regular feature in any angiosperm.

and gymnosperms is also monosporic. An additional argument in favor of the primitive nature of the monosporic 8-nucleate type is that all the other types can be easily derived from it while the reverse is almost impossible. The Oenothera type presents no difficulty; here only two divisions intervene between the functioning megaspore stage and the differentiation of the egg apparatus, and all the 4 nuclei are restricted to the micropylar part of the embryo sac. In the Allium type, wall formation does not occur after Meiosis II, and even if it does occur the cell plates soon dissolve, so that each dyad cell (or at least the functional one) contains 2 megaspore nuclei. Only two further divisions are now required to give rise to the 8-nucleate stage. In the tetrasporic types no permanent walls are laid down after any of the meiotic divisions. As a result all the 4 megaspore nuclei lie in a common cavity and may take up varying arrangements, one pair of nuclei lying at the micropylar end and the other at the chalazal (2+2), or one nucleus at the micropylar end and three nuclei at the chalazal (1+3), or one nucleus at each end and two at the sides (1+1+1+1). The megaspore nuclei may undergo two divisions or only one. The 2+2 position apparently leads to the Peperomia and Adoxa types; the 1+3 position to the Drusa, Fritillaria, and Plumbagella types; and the 1+1+1+1 position to the Penaea and Plumbago types.

Assuming then that the monosporic 8-nucleate embryo sac is the fundamental type, there are three principal theories as to its homologies:

1. The embryo sac of angiosperms is derived from a form like *Gnetum* in which all the nuclei of the embryo sac possess the same morphological value, and any of them can function as an egg and give rise to an embryo. First put forward by Hofmeister and Strasburger, this view may for convenience be called the Gnetalean theory.

2. The embryo sac of angiosperms is derived by reduction from the female gametophyte of some gymnosperm and consists of only two archegonia without any prothallial tissue (Fig. 214). According to this view the micropylar quartet represents one archegonium (the synergids are equivalent to neck cells and the polar nucleus to the ventral canal nucleus), and the chalazal quartet represents the second but nonfunctional archegonium (Porsch, 1907).

3. The micropylar quartet represents two archegonia and the

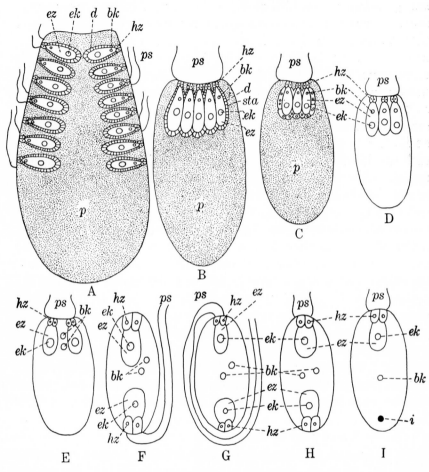

Fig. 214.   Diagrams illustrating derivation of angiosperm embryo sac from that of coniferous ancestor (bk = ventral canal nucleus; d = archegonial jacket; ek = egg nucleus; ez = egg cell; hz = neck cells; i = nonfunctional archegonium; p = prothallus; ps = pollen tube; sta = sterilized archegonia forming archegonia jacket). *A*, female gametophyte of hypothetical gymnosperm, essentially similar to modern *Sequoia*.   There are several laterally situated archegonia, each with its own jacket. As a rule each pollen tube fertilizes a single archegonium, but rarely one tube may fertilize two archegonia (left bottom).   *B*, female gametophyte of Cupressus type, showing fewer archegonia arranged in a compact group and enclosed in common jacket.   *C*, female gametophyte of *Ephedra*, showing further reduction in number of archegonia.   Jacket is supposed to have arisen by the sterilization of some archegonium initials.   *D*, hypothetical transitional stage, showing reduction in size of gametophyte and disappearance of archegonial jacket.   *E*, gametophyte

remaining four cells or nuclei are prothallial. According to this view one synergid and the egg constitute the first archegonium, the synergid being equivalent to the ventral canal cell; and the other synergid and the upper polar nucleus constitute the second archegonium. Neck cells are absent and both the archegonia are fertilized, one giving rise to the embryo and the other to the endosperm (Schürhoff, 1919, 1928).

The third view, which may be considered first for convenience, is based on the wholly erroneous assumption that one synergid is sister to the egg and the second to the upper polar nucleus, and that these two pairs of nuclei constitute two separate archegonia. Langlet (1927) produced evidence to show that the synergids are formed from one pair of sister nuclei and the egg and upper polar nucleus from another pair. During recent years this has received further confirmation and at present there is not a single authentic instance where the contrary has been definitely established. Schürhoff's theory may, therefore, be rejected without further discussion.

The second view, put forward by Porsch, has attracted considerable attention and is still favored by some embryologists (see especially Nilsson, 1941; Schnarf, 1942). In support of it have also been cited certain abnormal embryo sacs showing reversed polarity. It is suggested thereby that both the archegonia, micropylar as well as chalazal, were originally quite similar and that either of them was capable of functioning in the ancestral type of embryo sac (Swamy, 1946).

There are, however, some serious difficulties in accepting Porsch's view:

1. It assumes that the female gametophyte comprises only two archegonia, the prothallial tissue having disappeared completely. Even if this could happen, it is surprising that the archegonia

---

showing only two archegonia, each consisting of egg, ventral canal nucleus, and two neck cells corresponding to synergids. This is regarded as essentially similar to condition in *Balanophora*. *F*, as in *E*, but the two archegonia occupy opposite poles of embryo sac; pollen tube enters chalazal end of embryo sac. *G*, as in *F*, but pollen tube turns around embryo sac and enters it at micropylar end. *H*, embryo sac, showing pollen tube entering directly from above, as in majority of present-day angiosperms. *I*, embryo sac in which only upper archegonium is functional and lower soon degenerates. (*After Porsch, 1907.*)

themselves should have escaped all reduction, for they still maintain the same essential structures seen in the gymnosperms, being provided with neck cells as well as a ventral canal nucleus.[2]   Indeed, from this point of view, *Gnetum* and *Welwitschia* must be regarded as more advanced than the angiosperms, for they have no differentiated archegonia nor any other structures which can be interpreted as archegonia in terms of Porsch's hypothesis.

2. In all archegonia of the pteridophytes and gymnosperms the ventral canal nucleus is situated directly above the egg.   In angiosperms, on the contrary, the upper nucleus, which should have formed the ventral canal cell, is supposed to have given rise to the egg, while the lower, which should have organized into the egg, is said to represent the ventral canal nucleus!   The question also arises as to why the ventral canal nuclei belonging to two different archegonia, one micropylar and the other chalazal, should jointly fuse with a male gamete to give rise to the endosperm, while the egg cell (*i.e.*, the central antipodal cell) belonging to the chalazal archegonium ordinarily exercises no attraction whatsoever toward the second sperm.   Normally, the ventral canal nucleus is an inert structure, which is already disorganized at the time the egg is ready for fertilization, and even in those gymnosperms in which it is incidentally fertilized, the fusion nucleus does not undergo more than a very few abortive divisions.

3. In the angiosperms there are several known instances of embryos arising from synergids, either as the result of fertilization or even without it.   There is no recorded instance, however, where the neck cell of a true archegonium has behaved in a similar fashion.   Since the embryo sac of angiosperms is a more reduced structure than that of gymnosperms, it seems rather strange that the "neck cells" of the archegonium, which are headed toward extinction (they are already extinct in the embryo sacs of *Plumbago* and *Plumbagella*), should become egg-like and produce rival embryos.

4. In some species of *Peperomia* and in *Acalypha indica* the egg is associated with a single synergid.   Must we then suppose that here we have an archegonium in which one neck cell has disappeared, leaving the other to carry on the function of both?

5. A fifth objection is that the components of the chalazal quar-

[2] Even in the conifers there are some genera which do not have a ventral canal nucleus (Chamberlain, 1935).

tet, *i.e.*, the antipodal cells and lower polar nucleus, show a great variation in their behavior which is quite unknown for archegonia. Usually the antipodal cells are ephemeral and may disorganize even before any wall formation has taken place between the nuclei. In the Podostomaceae the primary chalazal nucleus remains undivided, and in the Oenotheraceae there is no nucleus at the chalazal end. These must be considered as instances of a tendency towards the reduction and final elimination of the chalazal archegonium. There are other plants, however, in which the antipodal cells persist and become very active. Sometimes they show nuclear divisions inside them, followed by fusions resulting in a high degree of polyploidy. In other cases, the divisions are accompanied by wall formation, resulting in a massive tissue which persists for a long time. Finally, in several plants, like *Drusa, Tanacetum,* and *Chrysanthemum*, even the initial number of antipodal cells exceeds three, and then the so-called archegonial plan cannot be recognized at all.

6. Some insuperable difficulties arise in applying Porsch's interpretation to the bisporic and tetrasporic embryo sacs. In the bisporic sacs the micropylar archegonium is derived from one megaspore nucleus and must correspond to one prothallus, while the chalazal archegonium is derived from another megaspore nucleus and must therefore correspond to a second prothallus, *i.e.*, the embryo sac is composed of two prothalli. Proceeding on the same analogies, in tetrasporic forms, like *Adoxa*, each archegonium must be supposed to represent two prothalli, for the synergids (*i.e.*, neck cells) are derived from one megaspore nucleus, and the egg and upper polar nucleus (*i.e.*, ventral canal nucleus) from a second megaspore nucleus. In the Fritillaria type, the micropylar archegonium represents one prothallus, but the chalazal will have to be considered as the equivalent of three prothalli which fuse at the megaspore stage. Strangest of all would be certain forms of *Tulipa*, belonging to the section Eriostemones, for here the micropylar archegonium, which consists of more than three cells, must be regarded as having originated from three megaspores.

That a single archegonium should correspond to one, two, and even three prothalli is incomprehensible, and it seems that the very simplicity of Porsch's theory, which led to its adoption in the past, must now be the ground for its final rejection (see also

Edman, 1931; Fagerlind, 1941). It seems impossible to interpret the female gametophyte of angiosperms, with all its varied modes of development (several of which were unknown at the time when Porsch enunciated his theory), in terms of archegonium formation. As is known from our knowledge of the prothalli of pteridophytes and gymnosperms, archegonia are initiated only in a cellular phase. In the angiosperms, on the other hand, we are taken back to the 2-nucleate stage of the embryo sac as the point of origin of the archegonium initials, which is pushing morphology into absurdity. It seems far more likely instead that the angiosperms have long passed the stage of archegonia or that they never had them at any time in their fossil history.

Coming finally to the Gnetalean theory, the name which has been given to it does not imply any direct derivation of the angiosperm embryo sac from that of the Gnetales. It assumes, however, that in the reduction of the prothallial tissue of the female gametophyte, the Gnetales and the angiosperms followed a more or less parallel course, leading to a complete loss of archegonia and a condition in which all the nuclei are to be considered as potential gametes. Because of the similar value attached to all the components of the embryo sac, it has also been called the *Gleichwertigkeitstheorie* or "theory of equivalence." No single botanist can be credited with its authorship, for it seems to have developed slowly as the result of certain opinions expressed from time to time by Hofmeister, Strasburger, and others. It has found support during recent years from further elucidations of the morphology and embryology of the Gnetales in general and of the genus *Gnetum* in particular (Thompson, 1916; Pearson and Thomson 1918; Fagerlind, 1941, 1946).

Before entering into a comparison of the embryo sac of *Gnetum* with that of the angiosperms, it may be well to recall the main facts in the development and organization of both.

Taking the angiosperms first:

1. The embryo sac may originate from 1, 2, or all 4 megaspore nuclei.

2. Only a few nuclear divisions occur after megasporogenesis, and there seems to be a tendency towards further reduction in this number.

3. The mature embryo sac may contain a maximum of 16 nuclei and a minimum of 4, the commonest being the 8-nucleate condition.

4. The functions of the sac seem to be adequately performed, whatever the number of nuclei entering into its composition and whether it is derived from one, two, or four megaspores.

5. The gametic characters are not confined to the egg cell alone; sometimes the synergids, and less often the antipodal cells also, may give rise to embryos.

6. The polar nuclei, although usually two, frequently exceed this number, and sometimes there is only one polar nucleus.

7. Endosperm formation is postponed until after fertilization and the primary endosperm nucleus shows varying degrees of polyploidy depending on the number of nuclei which have entered into its composition; one of the fusing nuclei is a male gamete.

Turning now to *Gnetum*:

1. As in the angiosperms, the gametophyte may be monosporic, bisporic, or tetrasporic.[3]

2. The number of divisions taking place after megasporogenesis is considerably less than in most other gymnosperms. At the conclusion of the divisions there are usually about 512 nuclei, but sometimes there are twice as many and rarely only half the number.

3. The nuclei become distributed at the periphery of the cell, leaving a large vacuole in the center. No compact tissue is formed except in the chalazal portion of the gametophyte.

4. Archegonia are absent and apparently every nucleus in the upper part of the gametophyte is a potential gamete. One or a few of the nuclei increase in volume and become surrounded by dense cytoplasm to form the eggs.

5. Fertilization may occur either in the free nuclear stage or after partial cell formation.

6. A certain amount of storage tissue (endosperm) is often present at the time of fertilization, but the bulk of it is formed only

---

[3] Lotsy (1899) states that in *G. gnemon* the mother cell divides into two cells, each of which may give rise to an embryo sac, *i.e.*, the development is bisporic; Thompson (1916) reports that the development is monosporic; and Fagerlind (1941) writes that in *G. gnemon* var. *ovalifolium* all four megaspore nuclei take part in the development, *i.e.*, the embryo sac is tetrasporic. The reports of Lotsy and Fagerlind of course need confirmation.

after the entry of the pollen tube. Its cells are multinucleate and nuclear fusions are common, but no male nucleus has been observed to take part.

If we now compare these two sets of observations, four points seem worthy of note:

1. In both cases there is a variation in the number of megaspore nuclei which take part in the development of the gametophyte. It may be stated parenthetically that no other genus among the gymnosperms resembles the angiosperms in this respect.

2. There is a tendency toward reduction in the number of nuclei of the embryo sac, but this is far more pronounced in the angiosperms.

3. Archegonia are completely suppressed in both cases.

4. There is a tendency toward a postponement in the formation of the storage tissue until after fertilization, and its development is preceded by nuclear fusions.

In inviting attention to these and to certain other similarities in the vegetative anatomy of the two groups, Thompson (1916) says: "In regard to the angiospermic relationship almost every structure described [in *Gnetum*]. . .shows some approach to the angiospermic condition and. . .some structures show conditions almost completely angiospermic.. . .   Such a body of evidence can scarcely be ignored or put aside as the result of parallel development.. . .   Accordingly the sum of the evidence from all sides seems to lead to the conclusion that angiosperms are phyletically related to Gnetales. This does not mean that any modern member of the Gnetales represents the type from which angiosperms were derived but that the ancestors of angiosperms were not far removed from the genus Gnetum."

Fagerlind (1941) also expresses himself in favor of "a more or less intimate genetical connection between the ancestral types of angiosperms and gymnosperms" and draws the following conclusions:

1. The polar nuclei of the angiosperms are the last remnants of the free nuclei seen in the female gametophyte of *Gnetum* and in the earlier stages of development of the gametophytes of other gymnosperms.

2. The central vacuole of the angiosperm embryo sac is homolo-

gous with the similar temporary or permanent vacuole seen in *Gnetum* and other gymnosperms.

3. The cells in the angiosperm embryo sac are homologous with the peripheral cells in the gametophyte of *Gnetum*; the egg is a fertile peripheral cell or an arrested archegonium, and the antipodal cells correspond to the lower nutritive part of the gametophyte of *Gnetum*.

4. The endosperm of angiosperms is arrested gametophytic tissue which is stimulated to further development through fusion with a male gamete.

Both these views, although interesting, leave one point unexplained. In the angiosperms the endosperm is formed only after the polar nuclei have fused with a male gamete. In *Gnetum*, on the other hand, there is no such fusion. A further difficulty, although less serious, is the presence of the synergids in one group and their absence in the other. They no doubt seem to be unessential elements, for embryo sacs without synergids (*Plumbagella* and *Plumbago*) seem to function just as satisfactorily as those with them; nevertheless the fact that they are the usual accompaniments of the angiosperm egg demands an explanation, which is not yet available.

If the embryo sac of angiosperms were to consist of only an egg and a variable number of free nuclei, irregularly placed at the periphery, we could probably assume its derivation from a condition like that in *Gnetum*. As it is, however, it seems best to conclude that while the angiosperms have probably passed through some such stages as are shown by *Gnetum*, we have no decisive evidence in favor of this view. Considered in this light, therefore, the Gnetalean view, although the most attractive of the three we have considered, can only be regarded as a working hypothesis, useful to stimulate further research, but entirely tentative for the present. Regarding the other two theories, proposed by Porsch and Schürhoff, there is now little to support them.

Fertilization. In gymnosperms the pollen grains land directly on the nucellus and the pollen tube has to grow only a short distance in order to reach the archegonium. In *Larix* and *Pseudotsuga* the apical portion of the integument becomes stigmatic, and in *Tsuga, Araucaria,* and *Agathis* pollen may germinate even on the ovuliferous scale.[4] In *Gnetum* germination frequently takes place in the micropylar canal at some distance from the apex of the nucellus.

The angiosperms differ from all known gymnosperms in having a closed carpel whose upper portion becomes differentiated into a style and stigma. Pollen grains never land directly on the nucellus but a considerable distance away from it on the tissues of the stigma, and the pollen tubes have to grow all the way down through the style before they can reach the ovules.

This difference, which is very significant, seems to be bridged to a certain extent by Johri's (1936) discovery of pollen grains in the stylar canal and ovary of *Butomopsis*. Here the style is a hollow structure which remains open at its upper end, so that the ovary is in direct communication with the exterior. As a rule the pollen grains germinate on the stigma as in other angiosperms and the pollen tubes travel down the walls of the hollow stylar canal to the ovary, but in one carpel a row of six pollen grains was found within the stylar canal, five of them having been seen in a single section (Fig. 215*A*,*B*). In another carpel eight pollen grains were seen (Fig. 215*C*) and in a third there was a pollen grain at the junction of the stigma and style (Fig. 215*D*). In a fourth there were two pollen grains in the stylar canal, the upper of which had germinated *in situ* (Fig. 215*E*). Finally one case was seen in which a pollen grain had germinated on the surface of an ovule (Fig. 215*F*,*G*).

Intracarpellary pollen grains have since been found in some other angiosperms, notably *Trillium*, *Ottelia*, *Fritillaria*, *Amianthium*, and *Erythronium*,[5] although it is not known if any of them germinate to form pollen tubes which take part in fertilization. In any case this is a remarkable phenomenon, which is comparable only to the condition in the Caytoniales, in which the carpel is closed at maturity but pollen grains are nevertheless found in the micropyles of many ovules (Harris, 1933, 1940). Presumably the carpel was open at its upper end at the time of pollination and the micropyles of the ovules were connected to the stigma by means of narrow canals through which the pollen grains were drawn in by some suction mechanism. In conclusion Harris says: "There is virtu-

---

[4] For further information, see Doyle (1945).

[5] Unpublished observations made by the author's pupils.

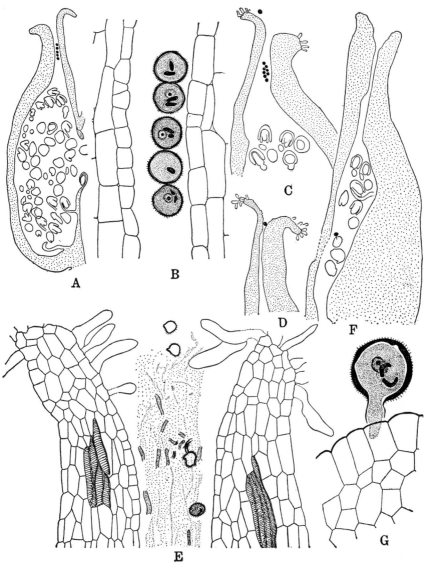

F<small>IG</small>. 215. Occurrence of pollen grains in stylar canal and ovary of *Butomopsis lanceolata*. *A*, l.s. carpel, showing a row of five pollen grains in the stylar canal. *B*, upper part of same, enlarged to show structure of pollen grains. *C*, upper part of carpel, showing eight pollen grains in stylar canal and one near stigma. *D*, one pollen grain near upper end of stylar canal. *E*, upper end of carpel, showing stylar canal with irregularly cut pollen tubes and two pollen grains. *F*, l.s. carpel showing pollen grain germinating directly on an ovule. *G*, pollen grain and part of ovule of *F*, enlarged to show nuclear details. (*After Johri, 1936.*)

ally no evidence to show what was the pollination mechanism of primitive angiosperms but it seems by no means unlikely that it may have been similar to what is postulated for *Caytonia*. Possibly the style was originally an open canal along which the pollen was conveyed to the ovules; a later stage would be the germination of the pollen grain before it reached the micropyle, at first no doubt at the bottom of the stylar canal, then at its middle and then at its top. The final change to occur—the closure of the stigma—makes it impossible for the pollen to pass down the stylar canal."[5a]

The condition in *Butomopsis* is exactly what Harris expects in his primitive angiospermous types and it seems likely that more comprehensive studies on other angiosperms with open styles may give some clue to a solution of the problem. Of considerable interest in this connection are also the carpels of the new Fijian genus *Degeneria* in which Bailey and Smith (1942) report that the carpel is a conduplicate structure whose margins are not coherent but tend to flare apart externally (see also Swamy, 1949). In most cases the cleft-like opening becomes more or less occluded, owing to the presence of numerous loosely interlocking papillae, but it is not impossible that sometimes the pollen may have direct access to the ovules.

Endosperm. There has been a great deal of discussion regarding the morphological nature of the endosperm of angiosperms, which is commonly neither haploid nor diploid but triploid.

Hofmeister (1858, 1859, 1861), in whose days neither syngamy nor triple fusion had yet been discovered, considered the endosperm of angiosperms to be a gametophytic structure whose growth and differentiation remained arrested until the entry of the pollen tube into the embryo sac.

Following Strasburger's (1884) discovery of syngamy in angiosperms, Le Monnier (1887) put forth the view that the fusion of the polar nuclei is also an act of fertilization, comparable to the fusion of the egg and the sperm nucleus. He therefore regarded the endosperm as a second embryo, modified to serve as food tissue for the zygotic embryo.

With Nawaschin's (1898) announcement of double fertilization, emphasis shifted from the fusion of the polar nuclei to the participation of the second male gamete in this event. Nawaschin re-

[5a] See Baum (1949).

garded triple fusion as an act of true fertilization, and this view was strongly supported by Sargant (1900). She compared it to a sexual union in that the fusion involved one normal male element (twin structure to the male gamete fertilizing the egg cell) and one normal female element (the upper polar nucleus, which is sister to the egg cell). However, there entered into the process a third nucleus from the chalazal end which "with its redundant chromosomes" upset the whole balance and brought about the degeneracy of the resulting tissue. The second embryo was thus "maimed" from the beginning and converted into a formless mass of tissue or "monster," enabling the survival of the first without a struggle.

Strasburger (1900) gave a different analysis and suggested that triple fusion is not true fertilization but only a growth stimulus. He emphasized the extremely reduced nature of the female gametophyte of angiosperms, with little or no reserves of food material. Triple fusion served as a stimulus toward its growth, he thought, and the endosperm was therefore to be regarded as belated gametophytic tissue. This postponement of endosperm formation was considered by him to be an advantage, for it avoided the waste of material which would occur if this massive tissue were lost by the plant with every unfertilized ovule.

The views presented above were based on the assumption that the endosperm is always a product of triple fusion. Detailed studies during the present century have revealed, however, that there is no such uniformity in its origin. In the entire family Onagraceae the embryo sacs are 4-nucleate, comprising only an egg apparatus and an upper polar nucleus. Here the primary endosperm nucleus arises from the fusion of the male gamete and single polar nucleus and is therefore diploid (Fig. 216*A*). The same is true of some reduced embryo sacs like those of *Butomopsis*, in which there is an egg apparatus, a single polar nucleus, and one degenerating antipodal nucleus (Fig. 216*B*), and of some members of the Balanophoraceae in which the upper polar nucleus alone is fertilized and the lower fuses with the 3 antipodal nuclei to form a degenerating structure which does not take part in further development. In *Ditepalanthus* (Fagerlind, 1938), on the other hand, the primary endosperm nucleus is tetraploid, being derived from a fusion of 3 polar nuclei and a male gamete. In *Fritillaria* and *Plumbagella*, it is formed from a fusion of the haploid upper polar nucleus. the triploid lower polar nucleus, and the haploid male gamete, and is therefore pentaploid (Fig. 216*D*,*E*). In *Penaea* and *Plumbago* there are 4 polar nuclei so that here also the endosperm is pentaploid (Fig. 216*F*,*G*). Still higher degrees of polyploidy are seen in *Acalypha indica* and *Peperomia* (Fig. 216*H*,*I*), and in one species *P. hispidula*, as many as 14 nuclei fuse to form a secondary nucleus which, after fusion with a male nucleus, gives rise to a 15*n* endosperm (Fig. 216*J*). In *Pandanus* even the nuclei of nucellar cells

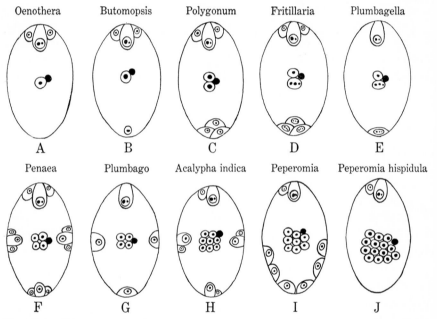

FIG. 216.   Diagrams of embryo sacs of various plants, showing variations in the number of nuclei fusing to form primary endosperm nucleus. In all cases, male nucleus entering into fusion is shown in solid black.

enter into the embryo sac and take part in the fusion, so that the endosperm shows varying degrees of polyploidy.

It is clear from the above that there is no uniformity in the origin of the endosperm, and that whatever the number of polar nuclei taking part in the fusion, the result is always a formless mass of cells without any semblance of a second embryo and designed solely to serve as a source of nutriment to the zygote.

The participation of a male gamete in the fusion is, however, a remarkably regular feature, which has been commented on by various authors. Long ago Thomas (quoted in Sargant, 1900) suggested that a tissue resulting from a nuclear fusion which includes a male element may perhaps be more suitable for the nourishment of an embryo arising from the same mixed stock than one derived from the maternal plant alone. A few years later Némec (1910) expressed a more or less similar opinion. He said that the fertilization of the polar nuclei has a double function: (1) the stimulation of endosperm development, and (2) the creation of a nutritive tissue which is physiologically compatible with the embryo.

According to Thomas and Némec, therefore, the hybridity of the endosperm is a method of adjusting its composition to the needs of the developing plant, for otherwise the hybrid embryo would be forced to depend upon the kind of food made available to it by the maternal parent alone.

Brink and Cooper (1940, 1947) have recently restated this view. They point out that in the gymnosperms the female gametophyte is packed with food materials which are readily available to the egg both at the time of fertilization and during the maturation of the embryo. In the angiosperms, on the other hand, the female gametophyte is a greatly reduced structure in comparison to the total mass of the ovule, and contains little reserve food at the time of fertilization. Further, there is a competition for food between the tissues within the embryo sac and those belonging to the nucellus and integument. In order that the reproductive process may be completed, it is necessary to have a mechanism which would tip the scale in favor of the endosperm and enable it to maintain a certain aggressiveness over the adjacent tissues of the ovule so that it can act as an efficient intermediary for the nutrition of the embryo. Brink and Cooper suggest that double fertilization is a means of conferring upon the endosperm the physiological advantage of hybridity so that it has "two chances instead of one (as in the gymnosperms) of receiving the genetic equipment necessary to perform its function."

This is an interesting hypothesis. Some previous writers have also expressed the view that the vigor of the endosperm and its parasitic relation to the nucellus might be attributed to its triploid chromosomal constitution. However, the question arises as to why the endosperm with its higher chromosome numbers should then succumb to the embryo, which also contains the diploid number like the nucellus and the integuments.

Embryo. The most difficult problem in the embryogeny of angiosperms is the derivation of the monocotyledonous state from the dicotyledonous. In the dicotyledons the two cotyledons are lateral structures and the stem tip is terminal, while in the monocotyledons the cotyledon occupies a terminal position and the stem tip is lateral. One view is that the single cotyledon arose by a fusion of two originally separate primordia; the other is that one of the cotyledons became suppressed at an early stage of development. Each of these views has been supported by a considerable mass of evidence, morphological as well as anatomical. The opinion has also been advanced that in certain plants the monocotyledonous state has arisen by a division of labor between the two cotyledons, one of which retained the cotyledonary position and function, while the other became modified to form the first plumular leaf.

It is natural to turn to a study of the development of the embryo as an aid in the solution of this problem. Ontogenetic studies should enable us to find the primordia of the two cotyledons and then to trace the development of one and the arrest of the other, or their fusion into a single member. Not enough work has yet been done to enable a final decision, but a few contributions bearing on this point are briefly referred to here.

Coulter and Land (1914) found a seedling of *Agapanthus umbellatus* (Liliaceae) with two well-developed cotyledons. A study of the embryogeny revealed that, as the proembryo increases in size, its basal or root end remains narrow and pointed while the shoot end widens and becomes broad and flat. Here the peripheral cells begin to divide more actively than the central cells and form a "cotyledonary zone" which assumes a tube-like form with two primordia growing at its tip. Meanwhile the apex of the proembryo is left in a depression. Subsequent to this stage, if both the primordia continue to develop equally, two cotyledons are formed. More frequently, however, the cells of one primordium lose their meristematic activity, resulting in a single cotyledon. In other words, both the primordia are present in the beginning, but later the whole growth may be diverted into a single primordium. Looking at the mature stage only, one naturally gets the impression that there is a single terminal cotyledon and a lateral stem tip.

In a slightly later publication, Coulter (1915) extended this view to include the embryo of grasses. He interpreted the scutellum as the functional cotyledon arising from the peripheral cotyledonary ring and the epiblast[6] as a second and greatly reduced cotyledon. From *Leersia* and *Zizania*, where the epiblast is a very conspicuous structure, he traces a gradation to the condition in *Zea*, in which this organ is practically nonexistent.

Turning now to the dicotyledons, we find that the seedlings of a number of genera and species show only a single cotyledon. The best known of these are: *Ranunculus ficaria*, *Corydalis cava*, *Abronia*, *Carum bulbocastanum*, *Blumium elegans*, *Erigenia bulbosa*, and several members of the Gesneriaceae. The embryogeny of these plants should be especially instructive in giving us an indication as to whether the monocotyledonous state is the more primitive or the dicotyledonous. Unfortunately most of the information available on them deals with the morphology and anatomy of the seedling rather than with the actual development of the embryo.

Mention may, however, be made of the work of Metcalfe (1936) on *Ranunculus ficaria*. The embryo is only a small club-shaped mass of cells embedded in the endosperm (Fig. 176). Further development takes place after the seeds are shed. It is interesting to note that during this process a small parenchymatous hump, supplied with a procambial strand, arises in the position in which the second cotyledon would be expected to originate if one were present. The position and mode of origin of this hump strongly suggest that it is the rudiment of the second cotyledon which fails to develop further.

In conclusion it might be said that, although embryology does not throw any light on the ancestry of the angiosperms, it indicates that the group is probably monophyletic in origin. There are no essential differences between the monocotyledons and dicotyledons as regards the development and organization of the male and female gametophytes and the endosperm, and the process of fertilization is the same in both the subgroups. Further, the differences in the organization of the embryo are not fundamental, for there are some dicotyledons in which only one cotyledon develops fully and the other becomes arrested, and some monocotyledons in which

[6] See p. 289.

both cotyledons develop equally. Regarding the relationship of the angiosperms with other groups, we are at present entirely in the dark. It is possible that a study of morphology and embryology of the Degeneriaceae, Winteraceae, Trochodendraceae, etc., may throw some light on the problem.

References

Bailey, I. W., and Smith, A. C. 1942. Degeneriaceae, a new family of flowering plants from Fiji. Jour. Arnold Arboretum **23**: 355–365.

Baum, H. 1949. Das Zustandekommen "offener" Angiospermengynözeen. Österr. bot. Ztschr. **96**: 285–288.

Brink, R. A., and Cooper, D. C. 1940. Double fertilization and development of the seed in angiosperms. Bot. Gaz. **102**: 1–25.

——— and ———. 1947. The endosperm in seed development. Bot. Rev. **13**: 423–541.

Chamberlain, C. J. 1935. "Gymnosperms, structure and evolution." Chicago.

Coulter, J. M. 1915. The origin of monocotyledony. II. Monocotyledony in grasses. Ann. Mo. Bot. Gard. **2**: 175–183.

——— and Land, W. J. G. 1914. The origin of monocotyledony. Bot. Gaz. **57**: 509–519.

Doyle, J. 1945. Developmental lines in pollination mechanisms in the Coniferales. Sci. Proc. Roy. Dublin Soc. **24**: 43–62.

Edman, G. 1931. Apomeiosis und Apomixis bei *Atraphaxis frutescens* C. Koch. Acta Horti Bergiani **11**: 13–66.

Fagerlind, F. 1938. *Ditepalanthus*, eine neue Balanophoraceen Gattung aus Madagaskar. Arkiv för Bot. **29A**(7): 1–15.

———. 1941. Bau und Entwicklung der *Gnetum*-Gametophyten. K. Svenska Vet.-Akad. Handl. **19**(8): 1–55.

———. 1946. Strobilus und Blüte von *Gnetum* und die Möglichkeit, aus ihrer Struktur den Blütenbau der Angiospermen zu deuten. Arkiv för Bot. **33A**(8): 1–57.

Harris, T. M. 1933. A new member of the Caytoniales. New Phytol. **23**: 97–114.

———. 1940. On *Caytonia thomas*. Ann. Bot. **4**: 713–734.

Hofmeister, W. 1858. Neuere Beobachtungen über Embryobildung der Phanerogamen. Jahrb. f. wiss. Bot. **1**: 82–186.

———. 1859. Neue Beiträge zur Kenntnis der Embryobildung der Phanerogamen. I. Dikotyledonen mit ursprünglich einzelligem, nur durch Zelltheilung wachsendem Endosperm. Abh. Königl. Sächs. Gesell. Wiss. 1859, pp. 535–672.

———. 1861. Neue Beiträge zur Kenntnis der Embryobildung der Phanerogamen. II. Monokotyledonen. Abh. Königl. Sächs. Gesell. Wiss. **7**: 629–760.

Johri, B. M. 1936. The life history of *Butomopsis lanceolata* Kunth. Proc. Indian Acad. Sci. Sect. B. **4**: 139–162.

Langlet, O. 1927. Über die Entwicklung des Eiapparates im Embryosack der Angiospermen. Svensk Bot. Tidskr. **21**: 478–485.

Le Monnier, G. 1887. Sur la valeur morphologique de l'albumen chez les angiospermes. Jour. de Bot. [Paris] **1**: 140–142.

Lotsy, J. P. 1899. Contributions to the life history of the genus *Gnetum*. Ann. Jard. Bot. Buitenzorg II, **1**: 46–114.

Metcalfe, C. R. 1936. An interpretation of the morphology of the single cotyledon of *Ranunculus ficaria* based on embryology and seedling anatomy. Ann. Bot. **50**: 103–120.

Nawaschin, S. G. 1898. Resultate einer Revision der Befruchtungsvorgänge bei *Lilium martagon* und *Fritillaria tenella*. Bul. Acad. Imp. des Sci. St. Petersburg **9**: 377–382.

Némec, B. 1910. "Das Problem der Befruchtungsvorgänge und andere zytologische Fragen." Berlin.

Nilsson, H. 1941. Die Homologie des angiospermen Embryosackes. Bot. Notiser 1941, pp. 50–58.

Pearson, H. H. W., and Thomson, M. R. H. 1918. On some stages in the life history of *Gnetum*. Trans. Roy. Soc. So. Africa, Cape Town **6**: 231–267.

Porsch, O. 1907. "Versuch einer phylogenetischen Erklärung des Embryosackes und der doppelten Befruchtung der Angiospermen." Jena.

Sargant, E. 1900. Recent work on the results of fertilization in angiosperms. Ann. Bot. **14**: 689–712.

Schnarf, K. 1936. Contemporary understanding of embryo sac development among angiosperms. Bot. Rev. **2**: 565–585.

———. 1942. Archegonium und Archegontheorie. Biol. Gen. Vienna **16**: 198–224.

Schürhoff, P. N. 1919. Zur Phylogenie des Angiospermen-Embryosackes. Ber. deutsch. bot. Gesell. **37**: 160–168.

———. 1928. Über die Entwicklung des Eiapparates der Angiospermen. Ber. deutsch. bot. Gesell. **46**: 560–572.

Strasburger, E. 1884. "Neue Untersuchungen über den Befruchtungsvorgang bei den Phanerogamen als Grundlage für eine Theorie der Zeugung." Jena.

———. 1900. Einige Bemerkungen zur Frage nach der doppelten Befruchtung bei Angiospermen. Bot. Ztg. II, **58**: 293–316.

Swamy, B. G. L. 1946. Inverted polarity of the embryo sac of angiosperms and its relation to the archegonium theory. Ann. Bot. **9**: 171–183.

———. 1949. Further contributions to the morphology of the Degeneriaceae. Jour. Arnold Arboretum **30**: 10–38.

Thompson, W. P. 1916. The morphology and affinities of *Gnetum*. Amer. Jour. Bot. **3**: 135–184.

Wulff, H. D., and Maheshwari, P. 1938. The male gametophyte of angiosperms (a critical review). Jour. Indian Bot. Soc. **17**: 117–140.

NAME INDEX

A

Addicott, 380
Afzelius, 71, 73, 76, 77, 87, 89, 135, 230, 335–337
Agardh, 359
Åkerberg, 348
Albrecht, 141
Alcala, 30, 46, 169, 222, 225
Aldama, 31, 191, 256
Alexandrov, 257
Alexandrova, 257
Amici, 3–6, 8
Anantaswamy Rau, 227
Anderson, 168, 193, 208
Anthony, 376
Arber, 256, 290
Archibald, 54, 56, 57, 337, 362, 363
Aristotle, 1
Arnoldi, 18, 19, 110
Artschwager, 143, 181, 188, 203, 211, 281
Asplund, 229, 230
Atwood, 193
Ausherman, 387
Avery, 290

B

Bacchi, 226, 348
Bailey, 424
Baillon, 359, 366–368
Bambacioni, 118, 119, 122
Bambacioni-Mezzetti, 77, 122
Bamford, 351
Banerji, 74, 159, 165, 166, 376
Baranow, 73
Barber, 157
Batchelor, 335, 337
Battaglia, 46, 333, 334
Baum, 424
Beal, 371
Beasley, 388

Beatty, 165–167
Beer, 43
Benetskaia, 159, 167
Benson, 68, 190
Bentham, 359, 364, 366
Berg, 58
Bergman, 124, 125, 325, 326, 329
Bernard, 304, 305
Berridge, 68
Beth, 394
Bhaduri, 71, 73, 260, 261, 277, 302
Bhargava, 57
Bianchi, 288
Billings, 39, 45, 161, 222, 334
Blackman, 195
Blakeslee, 192, 211, 314, 375, 378, 379, 381, 389, 391, 394, 396
Boehm, 32, 46, 67
Böös, 329
Bonnet, 33
Borthwick, 302
Borwein, 144, 269
Bosio, 380
Botschanzeva, 201
Boursnell, 58
Bouvier, 370
Bowers, 43
Boyes, 120
Brubaker, 376
Braun, 15
Brenchley, 257
Breslavetz, 201, 202
Brink, 141, 221, 269, 387, 389, 390, 427
Brongniart, 4
Brough, 31, 39, 139, 188
Brown, C. A., 68
Brown, R., 4, 366
Brown, S. W., 34
Brown, W. H., 87, 90
Brumfield, 155, 156
Buchholz, 192, 378, 379, 381
Buchner, 144
Buell, 67, 261
Buxbaum, 362, 371

SUBJECT AND PLANT INDEX

A

441